Formal Linguistics and the Teaching of Latin

Formal Linguistics and the Teaching of Latin: Theoretical and Applied Perspectives in Comparative Grammar

Edited by

Renato Oniga, Rossella Iovino and Giuliana Giusti

CAMBRIDGE
SCHOLARS

P U B L I S H I N G

Formal Linguistics and the Teaching of Latin:
Theoretical and Applied Perspectives in Comparative Grammar,
Edited by Renato Oniga, Rossella Iovino and Giuliana Giusti

This book first published 2011

Cambridge Scholars Publishing

12 Back Chapman Street, Newcastle upon Tyne, NE6 2XX, UK

British Library Cataloguing in Publication Data
A catalogue record for this book is available from the British Library

ISBN (10): 1-4438-2988-9, ISBN (13): 978-1-4438-2988-5

TABLE OF CONTENTS

Section II. Semantics and Pragmatics

Section III. History and Theory of Teaching

ACKNOWLEDGEMENTS

We wish to sincerely thank all the persons and institutions that have supported our enterprise: Dr. Carmela Palumbo and Dr. Daniela Beltrame, directors of the Regional School Offices for Veneto and Friuli - Venezia Giulia; Prof. Stefano Quaglia for the coordination between the two offices; Prof. Rainer Weissengruber, president of the Centrum Latinitatis Europae; Prof. William Short for his availability in reading a previous version of some papers; Carol Koulikourdi and Amanda Millar from CSP for their punctual and precious work.

This volume is published with the contribution of the MIUR, Project PRIN 2008 "Language didactics and formal linguistics: comparative grammar applications and perspectives", Research Unit at the Dipartimento di Studi Umanistici, University of Udine, Italy.

FOREWORD

The international conference *Formal Linguistics and the Teaching of Latin* was held in Venice on November 18-20, 2010. It was jointly organized by the Dipartimento di Glottologia e Filologia Classica of the University of Udine and the Dipartimento di Scienze del Linguaggio of the University Ca' Foscari of Venice. The conference was the first stage of a research project, supported by the Italian Ministry of Education (MIUR), which aims to contribute an improvement of language teaching in high schools and universities.

The debate over the role of grammatical reflection in language learning is nowadays more lively than ever. Our working hypothesis is that the achievements of formal linguistics, which compares different languages and tries to represent the way in which grammar rules are codified in the mind, may be useful to promote a new approach to the study of Latin.

The main theme of the conference, which brought together many researchers from all over Europe and the United States, was the comparison of certain linguistic phenomena in different languages (not only classical languages, but also modern languages), and their interpretation by means of the most updated theoretical tools of contemporary linguistics. The comparison leads us to highlight the similarities as well as the differences among languages: this results in a great advantage for the learners, who must be made aware of the limited area of linguistic variation.

A new comparative method, not only limited to the traditional Indo-European historical perspective, will allow students to approach Latin in a more motivating way: they will no longer learn by heart the inexplicable rules of school grammar, but will discover how human languages function and change, focalizing on what they already know of the language they are learning, before discovering the points of divergence from their mother tongue. In this perspective, the study of an explicit and scientific grammar loses any passive character, to become an activity which enhances linguistic awareness, meta-linguistic competence, and critical thought.

This volume is divided into three sections, reflecting the main subject areas that have been investigated by the conference participants, from the various methodological frameworks of contemporary Latin linguistics. The first section shows how formal accounts can revive the traditional fields of syntax and morphology. Particular attention is paid to some crucial problems of Latin grammar, such as word order, phrase and clause structure, prefixation and composition. The second section is devoted to two other fields that have increasingly stimulated new research in recent years, semantics and pragmatics, and addresses issues such as the mental representation of lexical items and idioms, discourse structure and the cognitive activity involved in translation. The last section is more specifically concerned with teaching: it contains perspectives on new methodological patterns and historical overviews on the tradition of Latin teaching in some European countries.

—Renato Oniga, Rossella Iovino, Giuliana Giusti
April 2011

INTRODUCTION

WHY FORMAL LINGUISTICS FOR THE TEACHING OF LATIN?

GIULIANA GIUSTI AND RENATO ONIGA

1. An interdisciplinary approach

The aim of this paper and of the whole book is to propose a new approach to the teaching of modern and classical languages that is solidly grounded in recent developments in formal linguistic theory. The approach we propose is *per se* not at all obvious in contemporary teaching methods and practices in high schools and universities, but is based on our independent experiences as scholars and teachers of respectively English Linguistics and Classical Latin, at different levels and in different programs.[1]

Contrary to the usual recommendations of general language pedagogy, which encourages a multidisciplinary perspective, current methods of teaching modern and classical languages have very little in common. The former focus on the use of language through interactive task-based activities and limit grammatical reflections to a minimum, while the latter are based on the prescriptive rules of "traditional" grammar, unrelated to the properties of natural languages and devoid of explicative power.

Paradoxically, the only real difference between classical and modern languages, namely the fact that there are no longer living L1-speakers of the former, is often dismissed by those who propose to go back to a "spoken Latin". But the most elementary historical considerations suggest that the revival of a dead language produces a new variety of that language, as was the case with Medieval and Humanistic Latin and, more recently, Hebrew.

The creation of a New Latin, going through the stage of a *pidgin* to become something inevitably different from the original, has already been censored by traditional Latinists, who have never ceased to deprecate the "barbarism" of a Modern Latin that would certainly have sounded ridiculous to ancient Romans (Waquet 1998; Janson 2004; Stroh 2008). Learning a "barbarized" Latin would perhaps be easier and require a shorter time, but it would not help us learn Classical Latin. Likewise, a Common Latin would be of little use as a *lingua franca* of the globalized World.

All in all, there is little reason to deny that Latin can only be studied through a corpus of written language, and the competences to be acquired are reading, understanding and translating. In this book, we suggest another way to make the learning of Latin easier and faster. We believe that "metalinguistic awareness", namely the conscious knowledge of how our unconscious language faculty works, provides a useful support to all language competences, and serves, moreover, as an indispensable part of the students' cultural education.

We will introduce the discussion by bringing together some observations made in the last decades in different fields, such as educational psychology, neurolinguistics and studies in second language acquisition. Our proposal, corroborated by experiments conducted in independent fields, is that learners can benefit in the process of acquiring/learning a foreign language from explicit reflections not only on the languages they are learning, but also on their native language, on other languages or dialects they know and, very importantly, on the general properties of the language faculty itself, which underlie all these instances of the same human capacity. In other words, our hypothesis here is that explicit knowledge of the fundamentals of Universal Grammar and the parametric variation that differentiates languages supports and enhances adult learners' knowledge of language, otherwise unconsciously activated by sufficient exposure to raw data during childhood.

A corollary of this hypothesis is that learning/acquiring more than one language (modern or extinct) not only does not hinder but can support the learning/acquisition process. Therefore, the curriculum must include adequate instruction in general and comparative linguistics, taking into crucial consideration the linguistics of the students' mother tongue.

Our paper is structured as follows. In section 2, we report on two different fields of research which empirically support the idea that explicit instruction on how the cognitive system works can enhance acquisition and improve performance. In section 3, we present the basic notion of structural dependency, which forms the basis of phrase grammar, in a minimal version suitable for adoption in the classroom. In section 4, we consider the three major areas of clause structure: the structure of the predicate and the special role of the subject as external to the Verb Phrase (VP), the structural position for temporal reference (T), which is separate and hierarchically higher than the VP and hosts the subject in its specifier to form a Tense Phrase (TP), and finally, the area of clause typing (CP), which hosts elements displaced by discourse features and is responsible for the apparent freedom of Latin word order.

2. The role of Universal Grammar in language learning

Many cognitive studies support the thesis of generative grammar that languages do not vary indefinitely and that, whatever language we speak, that language operates according to certain universal principles at the neural and conceptual levels (e.g. Jackendoff 1993: 28). In particular, some recent studies in neurolinguistics (cf. Musso et al. 2003, Moro 2008) have shown that explicit instruction about rules of a "possible language" can activate Broca's area, namely that part of the brain which is normally involved in the acquisition of language and results in learning and/or production disorders when damaged. Crucially, these experiments have demonstrated that logically plausible but linguistically "impossible" rules (for example, rules which make reference to linear order of words and not to structural notions), do not activate Broca's area (even if subjects perform the task successfully).

These experiments show that Broca's area can be activated by explicit rules, only if they conform to the abstract principles of mental grammar. On the basis of these results, we propose two hypotheses:

i. A grammar formulated in terms of deep properties of language (but not one based on acritical prescription, exceptions, and curiosities), can activate the area of the brain which is thought to be most properly involved in language acquisition.

ii. Such a grammar, by virtue of affecting a part of our cognitive system naturally related to linguistic competence, will enhance easier, faster and longer-lasting acquisition of that language.

Our hypotheses are corroborated by the independent observation by Cornoldi (1995) that, if learners (of any subjects) are made aware of how their cognitive system is activated with respect to a given task, they can control the task to a higher degree and, as a consequence of this, obtain better performances.

Consequently, we propose a "new comparative grammar" (Haegeman 1997), which aims at presenting the general properties of the human language faculty and how they are manifested in the given languages learned by the students. In our view, generative grammar is a good candidate for this goal, for the very reason that it has recently been adopted in many different areas of applied linguistics (e.g. L1- and L2-acquisition, language pathology and rehabilitation, language attrition and contact), as well as in traditional areas of linguistic scholarship (e.g. language change, typology, language description and reference grammars). One of the primary advantages of a formal approach to grammar is its empirical and explanatory adequacy. Such an approach aims to eliminate long lists of exceptions, special cases, and imprecise notions, by uncovering those mental mechanisms that are at the base of general rules, thus facilitating their memorization and application (cf. Cardinaletti 2007; 2008; Oniga 2008). The notions of grammar we need to give in class must be simple, intuitive, and easy to apply. They must utilize a terminology common to all studied languages, including the mother tongue of the learner and the modern languages taught in the curriculum.

Unfortunately, up to now the application of a generative approach to language teaching has been hampered by its conceptual and terminological complexity, which has made generative grammar a discipline only open to a restricted circle of specialists. In our view, it is possible to do away with the most technical and controversial aspects of generative grammar, while preserving its basic insights in order to articulate a framework that is simple enough to be disseminated but still precise and empirically valid. This has already been successfully attempted by reference grammars of different languages such as Italian (Renzi et. al. 1988-2001), Catalan (Solà et. al. 2002), Dutch (Broekhuis et al. 1994-2003), and Old Italian (Salvi and Renzi 2010).

3. The formal properties of syntactic structures

Language is a flux of sounds, produced and perceived one after the other, in a linear order. But these sounds phonologically realize a number of higher-level discrete elements (morphemes and words), which combine hierarchically in larger and larger configurations, such as phrases, clauses, and sentences. The network of relations between the two members of each pair of these elements is called "structural dependency", and is imposed by universal principles of grammar.

The universal principle of structural dependency is defined as follows. In (1a), X selects Y, and the resulting node X' (X-bar) is a projection of X. In (1b), X' is modified by Z, and the resulting node XP ends the projection possibilities of X (building what is defined as X-Phrase):

(1)   a.   X + Y $\rightarrow$ $[_{X'}$ X [Y]]
       b.   Z + X' $\rightarrow$ $[_{XP}$ Z $[_{X'}$ X [Y]]]

The order of the elements is determined by the type of language, but the hierarchical relation between two elements in the same pair is universal. In (1a) X selects Y, and we say that Y is the (structural) complement of X. In (1b) Z modifies X', and we say that Z is the (structural) specifier of X. The relation between two members of a pair must be asymmetric. This is a crucial property of Universal Grammar. While the selecting element X is a zero level category, complements (like Y) and specifiers (like Z) must be phrases (maximal level categories). This means that they contain a head which may select a complement and/or be modified by a specifier. Structure (1b) should therefore be reformulated as in (2a), whose tree diagram is given in (2b):

(2) a. $[_{XP}$ ZP $[_{X'}$ X [YP]]]

b.

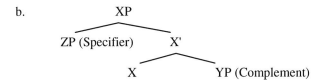

We can illustrate the abstract structure above through the analysis of Latin nominal expressions given by Giusti and Oniga (2007). Let us take a nominal expression such as that in (3a). The head N_i takes a complement (the object genitive NP_k) and a modifier (the subject genitive NP_j). Both NP_j and NP_k are phrases, even if NP_j is made of a single word, because the quantifier *omnis* "all" implies a non-overt head referring to human beings. The complement NP_k is in turn a complex nominal expression in the form of a gerundive construction:[2]

(3) a.

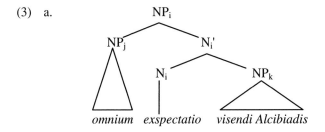

"everybody's expectation to see Alcibiades" (Nep. *Alc.* 6,1)

The structure in (3a) straightforwardly derives the unmarked order SubjGen - N - ObjGen, as independently argued for Classical Latin by Giusti and Oniga (2007) and Gianollo (2007).

Obviously, a nominal expression may be much larger: for example, it can include an adjective, as in (3b). The adjective is also merged as a specifier of N. This triggers sharing of gender, number and case features (all bundled in a single morpheme). Following Giusti (2010), we propose that N_i is moved or, better said, remerged, so that it can have two specifiers (or more if needed).[3] For this reason, we suggest that there are two occurrences of N_i in (3b): the one occurring in the lower position of the hierarchy is spelled out, the one in the upper position is non-overt and indicated in ~~strikethrough~~:

(3) b.

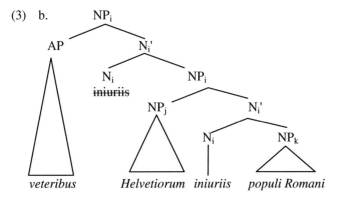

"the old offences by the Helvetii to the Roman people" (Caes. *Gall.* 1,30,2)

The merger of an upper copy of N_i in (3b) may look like a useless complication, and should not be adopted unless independently necessary. This is in fact the case of (4), where this operation derives the position of N to the left of a single adjective in the above cited *populi Romani* "the Roman people" (4a), or of an adjective and a genitive in *admiratio magna vulgi* (Cic. *fam.* 7,1,3) "the great admiration of the people" (4b):

(4) a. [NPi [Ni *populi*] [NPi [AP *Romani*] [Ni' [Ni ~~populi~~]]]]

b. [NPi [Ni *admiratio*][NPi [AP *magna* [Ni' [Ni ~~admiratio~~] [NPi [NPk *vulgi*]
            [N' [Ni ~~admiratio~~]]]]]]]

Comparing (3b) with (4b), we observe that the subject genitive is more strictly related to the head N than the descriptive adjective, in that the former is merged earlier in a bottom-up fashion. And in the same fashion, we can observe that the object genitive is more strictly related to N than the subject genitive. Hierarchy of merging is another crucial property of the language faculty that is generally ignored by traditional grammars. Remerge of a head allows for a straightforward representation of the relation between the head and its specifiers, at the same time representing the hierarchies among modifiers and arguments. For this reason, remerge (namely, syntactic movement) is a fundamental property of Universal Grammar, which can account for the great variation in word order typical of Latin.

Not only heads but also complements or specifiers can be remerged, as is illustrated in (5) for the phrases *caeli caerula templa* (Enn. *ann.* 48 Sk.) "the blue spaces of the sky" and *prima illa mea oratio* (Cic. *leg. agr.* 2,6) "that well-known my first speech":

(5)   a. $[_{TOP} [_{NPj} \text{caeli}] \text{TOP} [_{NPi} [_{AP} \text{caerula}] [_{NPi} [_{NPj} \text{caeli}] [_{Ni} \text{templa}]]]]$
     b. $[_{TOP} [_{AP} \text{prima}] \text{TOP} [_{NPi} [_{DemP} \text{illa}] [_{NPi} [_{PossP} \text{mea}] [_{NPi} [_{AP} \text{prima}]$
                                              $[_{N'} [_{Ni} \text{oratio}]]]]$

At this point, it is not important to discuss the nature of the category which hosts such phrasal movements. We only call it TOP hinting at its relevance to discourse features such as [Topic] or [Contrast] (Cf. Giusti 2006). We will briefly go back to this possibility in section 4 while discussing clause structure.

To sum up, our discussion so far has highlighted some important properties of structural dependency:

i.   Merge proceeds in pairs, in a bottom-up fashion.

ii.   The two elements of each pair are necessarily asymmetric (a head only merges with a maximal projection, a specifier of a head merges with a one-bar projection of that head)

iii.   The elements in the structure are arranged hierarchically: subjects are structurally higher than objects, demonstratives are higher than adjectives, features are bundled in a hierarchy (gender > number > case).

iv.   Merge (and remerge) either involves a zero level element (X) or a phrase (XP).

v.   An element (X or XP) can remerge and therefore have relations in more than one position.

   vi.   Only one copy of a remerged element is realized (for a general principle of economy), the other copies are silent.
   vii.   All relations must be recoverable.
   viii.   Inflectional morphology makes these relations explicit.
   ix.   For this reason, languages with rich inflection have more freedom of word order.

These notions are general and hold for all languages. We are convinced it is possible to present them in class in a fashion appropriate to the age and the level of the students/pupils (cf. Ghegin 2007). After all, notions of history, biology, astronomy and even genetics are introduced as early as second or third grade, establishing a foundation for later, more precise instruction.

The idea that all children speak a native language and that this language is a property of their minds; that 2000 years ago, the Latin language spread across Europe and was influenced by local languages, eventually giving rise to the Romance languages; that as regards the language faculty, the minds of ancient children were not different from the minds of those of the third millennium — these ideas are quite easy to articulate to students and may inspire them new motivation, new interest, and new affection for the discipline. In the following section, we give a sketch of how the structure of the sentence can be presented at a beginner's level.

4. The structure of the sentence

This section is divided into three parts. We start with a discussion of the traditional subject-predicate dichotomy, and observe that it is basically correct, provided the two elements are conceived as constituents (Noun Phrase and Verb Phrase), and not as words.

We go on observing that subject and predicate are not merged in a symmetric way, and that the clause hinges on a head T (tense) realizing semantic temporal reference in syntax. The complement of T is the predicate and its specifier is the subject.

The third point to be discussed is that the clausal structure further expands with a higher head C (complementizer), with its own phrase (CP). The CP area covers many different functions, one of which is to signal the type of the clause (embedded/main, declarative/interrogative, etc.); another is to host displaced elements remerged for discourse organization (topic, focus, etc.). The complete structure of the sentence, from VP to TP and further up to CP, is therefore given in (6):

(6)

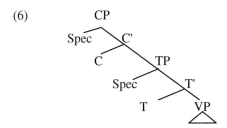

As above, we illustrate this abstract structure with concrete examples, in a bottom-up fashion: so, we start examining the structure of the VP.

Let us first consider how contemporary grammars define the "predicate". We may cite two very influential scientific works, but the same concepts are found in the generality of other grammars:

> Das Praedikat ist entweder ein Verbum (Verbalsatz, meist erzählend und feststellend, z. B. *Themistocles luxuriose vixit*; *sol lucet*) oder ein Nomen (Hofmann and Szantyr 1965: 411).

> Examples of predicate constituents are *laudat* and *simile est* in sentences *pater filium laudat* and *ovum ovo simile est* (Pinkster 1990: 1).

First of all, we notice that these current definitions reflect a very crucial ambiguity going back to the Greek and Medieval tradition. As was pointed out by Graffi (1986: 100), Aristotle uses the term *rhema* in the more general sense of "predicate" in *De interpretatione* (10, 19^b 12), but in the more restricted sense of "verb" in *Poetica* (20, 57^a 14). In the Middle Ages, Boethius introduces the Aristotelic ontological pair *to hypokeimenon* (*subiectum*) and *to kategoroumenon* (*praedicatum*) in the grammatical tradition. But, as is the case of the Aristotelian *rhema*, Boethius's *praedicatum* also remains ambiguous between the more general sense of "predicate" (including verbal and nominal predicate) and the strict sense of "noun" or "verb":

> Nomen subiectum est, oratio praedicatum (Boeth. *diff. top.* 1, p. 1175^b).
> "The noun is the subject, the discourse is the predicate".

> "Homo animal est": "homo" subiectum est, "animal" praedicatum (Boeth. *syll. hyp.* 1, p. 832^b).
> "'The man is a living being': 'the man' is the subject, 'a living being' is the predicate".

Ergo, ut arbitror, plene monstratum est, non semper subiectum nomen esse, semper autem praedicatum in solo verbo consistere (Boeth. *in herm. comm. sec.* 2, 5, p. 100, 25).
"Then, in my opinion, it has been fully demonstrated that not always the subject is a noun, but the predicate always consists in the single verb".

In our opinion, two mistakes emerge out of this tradition, and are still present in modern grammars. The first is defining the predicate as a single word (a verb or a noun/adjective), rather than a phrase. The second is that, despite seeing the verb/predicate as the pivot of the sentence, grammars claim that the minimal clause is made up of subject and verb, the object viewed as somehow less obligatory, less strictly related to the verb than the subject.

To sum up, the traditional analysis could be represented as in (7a). On the contrary, we argue that the correct structure of the clause is the one given in (7b):

(7)   a. [[SV] O]
      b. [S [VO]]

The reasons to prefer (7b) to (7a) are the following. The structure in (7a) may describe the sentences in (8)-(10), in which the object is apparently optional, but it is clearly wrong for the sentences in (11)-(13), in which the bare verb is not a possible predicate:

(8)   a. Mary eats
      b. Mary eats a doughnut

(9)   a. Maria mangia
      b. Maria mangia una focaccia

(10) a. [Nos] cenamus (Plaut. *Capt.* 481)
          "We have a meal"
      b. Nos cenamus avis, conchylia, piscis (Hor. *serm.* 2,8,27)
          "We are eating fowl, sea-shell and fish"

(11) a. *Mary devours
      b. Mary devours a doughnut

(12) a. *Maria divora
      b. Maria divora una focaccia

(13) a. *Ballaena voravit
      b. Ballaena meum voravit vidulum (Plaut. *Rud.* 545)
          "A whale devoured my bag"

The crucial observation is that, in (11)-(13), the object is obligatory, and is not only "the second argument of the predicate" (*contra* Panhuis 2006: 100). What is predicated of the subject is the complete predicate (verb plus object), and not just the verb. The intransitive verbs (8a)-(10a) mean something different from their transitive counterparts in (8b)-(10b). This is regularly observed in dictionaries: intransitive "eat", for example, means "have a meal" in the three languages observed. Latin provides many other examples. It is well-known that transitive *consulo* means "consult", "ask for advice", while intransitive *consulo* means "act", "take decisions", as appears in (14):

(14) a. Cumaeam consuluistis anum (Ov. *Fast.* 4,158).
          "You consulted the old Cumaean"
      b. Vultis crudeliter consulere in deditos victosque? (Liv. 8,13,15)
          "Do you want to act cruelly against those who surrendered and are defeated?"

It is important to make the learner aware that the clauses in (14) do not have the same predicate *consulere*. In (14a) the predicate is *consulere anum Cumaean*, while in (14b) the predicate is *consulere in deditos victosque*.

This method is not only more correct from the mental point of view, but it also encourages the student to search for the semantic value of the verb, looking up in the dictionary not just the possible meanings of the single word in isolation, but the interpretation of different structures, traditionally called "constructions", in which such a word may appear. This structural notion is not only relevant for direct objects, but for any kind of internal argument of the verb, such as a PP in (14b), or an indirect argument in (15), or a secondary predicate in (16), or a manner adverbial in (17):

(15) a. Pompeius awarded him *(citizenship)
      b. Pompeo lo insignì *(della cittadinanza)
      c. Eum Pompeius *(civitate) donavit (Cic. *Balb.* 7)

(16) a. Everybody considers you *(intelligent)
      b. Tutti ti considerano *(intelligente)
      c. Omnes te *(sapientem) existimant (Cic. *Lael.* 6)

(17) a. I feel *(good)
     b. Mi sento *(bene)
     c. *(Bene) est mihi (Plin. *epist.* 5,18,1)

We conclude that the verb and all its arguments (except the subject) form a constituent, which is the predicate of the sentence. This constituent has the verb as its pivotal element and is labelled Verb Phrase (VP).[4]

The structure of the VP is very important, not only to analyse the sentence correctly, but also to understand the mechanism of case assignment in a simple, intuitive fashion. Let us observe that, while hierarchical order of verb and object is the same in the four languages exemplified in (18), because the V always dominates the object NP, the linear order is verb-object in English and Italian (18a-b), but is object-verb in Latin (Cic. *Verr.* II 1,66) and German (subordinate clause), as in (18c-d):

(18) a. $[_{NP}$ Rubrius] $[_{VP} [_{V'}$ invites $[_{NP}$ his friends]]
     b. $[_{NP}$ Rubrio] $[_{VP} [_{V'}$ invita $[_{NP}$ gli amici di lui]]
     c. $[_{NP}$ Rubrius] $[_{VP} [_{V'} [_{NP}$ istius comites] invitat]
     d.   weil $[_{NP}$ Rubrius] $[_{VP} [_{V'} [_{NP}$ Freunde von dem] einladet]

This fact leads us to argue that the structural dependency of the object on the verb is what accounts for Accusative case assignment, not only in Latin or German, but also in English and Italian, as is clear with the personal pronouns in (19):

(19) a. Mary invites him/*he and her/*she
     b. Maria invita lui/*egli e lei/*ella

Notice that Accusative assignment does not imply a specific semantic relation of the nominal expression with the verb, but a given structural configuration. Precisely, Accusative is assigned by V to its complement.

In the following, we consider how Nominative case is assigned in the structure. First of all, let us observe that Nominative is assigned to the subject of a finite verb, as in (20a), but it is not assigned to the subject of an infinitival clause, as in (20b):

(20) a. Tu/*te ad me venies (Cic. *fam.* 5,19,2)
         "You will come to me"
     b. Scribis te/*tu ad me venturam (Cic. *fam.* 14,3,5)
         "You write that you will come to me"

So, Nominative assignment is clearly a property of finite T, while the subject of a non-finite T can be assigned case from an external head (as in the Accusativus cum Infinitivo), or can be a null element of a different kind.[5]

We must conclude that the subject NP and the predicate VP, which we claimed to be two separate constituents, do not combine in a symmetric configuration like (21a), which is not allowed by universal principles, but merge in an asymmetric configuration like (21b):

(21) a.

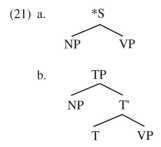

A theory that requires an asymmetric relation between the subject and the predicate does not really complicate the picture. On the contrary, it can describe and explain a number of properties of clauses in natural languages, including the differences in case assignment noticed above between finite and non-finite clauses.

More specifically, modern linguistic advances have established that "subject" is a structural notion and is combined with a predicate by the mediating role of Tense (cf. Lepschy 2000: 84). A finite clause like (18) does not only refer to a given inviting situation involving two arguments (Rubrius and the friends), but also locates it at a given time (the present). So the sentence is true if and only if a given individual (Rubrius) is doing something (inviting the friends) at a time contemporary to speech time, and it is not true otherwise. If the interpretive component is fed by the syntactic component, the structure of the clause must contain (overtly or covertly) the semantic features that locate this situation in the given TIME. Such a feature is a good candidate to be the pivot of the clause, and we call it Tense (T).[6]

Let us now inquire how T is realized in English, Italian and Latin. To express future time, as in (22), in Italian we have a single word realizing V and future Tense (*inviterà*), but in English we clearly see that the two categories are realized by independent words (*will invite*). To express a time in the past, previous to a past point of reference, we use the past perfect Tense as in (23), and we have two words in both languages. The adverbial inserted in SpecVP marks the VP-boundary overtly:[7]

(22) a. [$_{TP}$ [$_{NP}$ Mary] will   [$_{VP}$ soon [$_{V'}$ invite her friends]]
    b. [$_{TP}$ [$_{NP}$ Maria] inviterà   [$_{VP}$ presto [$_{V'}$ ~~inviterà~~ i suoi amici]]

(23) a. [$_{TP}$ [$_{NP}$ Mary] had   [$_{VP}$ just   [$_{V'}$ invited her friends]]
    b. [$_{TP}$ [$_{NP}$ Maria] aveva   [$_{VP}$ appena [$_{V'}$ invitato i suoi amici]]

In (22b), we propose that in Italian the verb remerges from its base position in VP to the position of T, in order to incorporate Tense morphology. This does not occur in English, for the obvious reason that future tense morphology is not an affix but a free morpheme. Notice that in (22) the English order adverb-verb is reversed in Italian, while in (23) the order auxiliary-adverb-verb is the same in the two languages. The difference in (22) and the similarity in (23) fall naturally from the remerge proposal.

In this perspective, *will invite*, *had invited* and *ha invitato* cannot be analysed simply as "(complex) verbs". The verb is the head of the predicate, while the auxiliary is the head of the clause. Furthermore, despite being a single word, *inviterà* is not just a verb but a structurally complex element, which is at the same time the head of the predicate (VP) and the head of the clause (TP).

The independent nature of auxiliary and verb is witnessed by the fact that it is possible to insert more elements between them (e.g. two hierarchically ordered adverbials and a floating quantifier), as in (24), and that the auxiliary can remerge in a higher position (to be defined below) in certain constructions leaving the verb unaffected, as in (25):

(24) [$_{TP}$ The children have repeatedly all kindly [$_{VP}$ invited their friends]]

(25) Has [$_{TP}$ Mary ~~has~~ just [$_{VP}$ invited her friends]]?

What happens in Latin? More than in Italian, the Tense inflection is an affix on the verb, in the sense that in Latin auxiliaries are less present in the verbal paradigm. But this richness of inflection does not make it necessary for the verb to move to T. This is witnessed by the fact that, contrary to Italian, "time and place adverbials are well attested in preverbal position" (Devine and Stephens 2006: 69), as in (26):

(26) a. Sed hoc mox videro (Cic. *Tusc.* 2,26)
      But this soon see.1stP. Fut.Perf.
      "But I will soon see that"
   b. Ad quae mox revertar (Cic. *div.* 1,47)
      To which soon come1stP.Fut.
      "To which I will soon come back"

We conclude that in Latin the verb is usually realized in its base position within the VP, but it can be realized also in T, as in Italian.

In order to better understand this and many other aspects of syntax in all languages, but especially in Latin, we must remember that TP is not the final layer of the clause, which has a third portion of structure. This part of clause structure is called CP, because in subordinate clauses its head is occupied by complementizers (subordinating conjunctions).

The CP area includes not only subordinators, but also discourse markers and displaced constituents. Since the seminal works by Cinque (1990) and Rizzi (1997), this area is defined as the "left periphery" of the clause. For example, the head of the CP is occupied by the auxiliary in (25) above, repeated here in (27a), whereas in (27b) we see a parallel case in Latin, from Cic. *off.* 3,59 *invitat Canius postridie familiares suos* "the next day Canius invites his friends":

(27) a. [$_{CP}$ Has [$_{TP}$ Mary ~~has~~ just [$_{VP}$ invited her friends]]]?
   b. [$_{CP}$ Invitat [$_{TP}$ Canius ~~invitat~~ postridie [$_{VP}$ familiares suos ~~invitat~~]]]

In (27b) we propose that the verb first merges in VP, then remerges in T (where the specifications for tense and subject agreement are contained), and finally remerges in C, due to the topicalization of the verb itself. Notice that the analysis in (27b) presupposes the intermediate step of V in T, which is independently observed in sentences like Sen. *epist.* 14,8 *gubernator contempsit Austri minas* "the pilot despised the menaces of the South-Wind", whose structure is given in (28):

(28) [$_{TP}$ gubernator [$_{T'}$ contempsit [$_{VP}$ Austri minas ~~contempsit~~]]]

Freedom in word order is naturally related to richness in morphology, but a motivated analysis goes much further than this. We observe that richness in verbal inflection allows for the verb in Latin to freely remain in its base position within the VP, as well as to remerge in T or even in C.

For the same reason, richness in case morphology allows for arguments to appear in displaced positions, because overt case morphology allows for reconstruction of the structural configuration in which the argument receives case. For example, as we know from (4a) in section 3, a NP like *suas copias* may also appear in the form *copias suas*, and now we can understand why this NP appears in its base position in (29a) from Caes. *Gall*. 1,22,3, but may also appear displaced in first position as in (29b), from Caes. *Gall*. 1,24,1:

(29) a. [$_{TP}$ Caesar suas copias in proximum collem subducit]
     b. [$_{CP}$ copias suas [$_{TP}$ Caesar ~~copias suas~~ in proximum collem subd.]]
        "Caesar withdraws his troops to the nearest hill"

Following this line of argument, we claim that it is uninteresting to classify languages as configurational or non-configurational. What is interesting, in our opinion, is to observe how universal properties of sentence structure allow for a restricted number of options and how these options interact in a given language to produce different word orders. These different arrangements arise out of precise structural relations. For this reason, despite the apparent freedom of word order in Latin, it is never in fact indifferent (in Marouzeau's terms), and conveys different discourse values (Salvi 2004; Devine and Stephens 2006).

Conclusion

In this brief overview of syntactic structures, we have argued that it is possible to express in a unified way the partial similarity and the partial differences characterizing simple sentences in Latin, English and Italian. We have seen that these languages, and probably all languages, make use of the same universal principles of phrase structure, even if some parameters are set differently in each language.

In general, we suggest that the concepts of "phrase" and "remerge" (namely, syntactic movement) are highly useful tools of contemporary formal linguistics: they are intuitive to native speakers of every language, they are appropriate for a scientifically advanced theoretical model, and they can be easily applied to language pedagogy.

Our main point has been that there are compelling reasons to formulate a new methodology of language teaching that emphasizes linguistic awareness more than traditional approaches. This methodology newly conceptualizes grammar as a science of the mind that both contributes to the students' overall education and facilitates learning modern and classical languages.

Notes

*We thank William Short, Anna Thornton, and Rossella Iovino for insightful comments on a previous version of this paper. We are also grateful to the audience of the FLTL-conference for constructive criticism and support. All remaining errors are ours.

[1] Our professional profiles are typical of many Italian academics of our generation: after obtaining a PhD, we held tenure positions as high school teachers before receiving university appointments. Our every-day experience of the old time as well as of today never fails to support our strong belief that an explicit instruction characterized by descriptive and explanatory adequacy can enhance the cognitive process of a learner of any language. Cf. our handbooks on English (Giusti 2003) and Latin (Oniga 2007) to be used in university courses.

[2] Complex structures not spelled out in detail are indicated as triangles. Notice that NP_j and AP are also represented as triangles. Despite being a single word, they have the status of specifiers, which can be complex structures. For this reason, we assume they are always phrases.

[3] "Remerge" of an element (or merge of a copy) refers to what is generally called "movement" in the principles-and-parameters framework. The minimalist program (Chomsky 1995; 2005) reduces all operations to merge and we believe this innovation provides a more intuitive representation of the idea that a given element can have a structural relation to more than one element at the same time. Other contributions in this volume (notably Salvi's and Iovino's) keep the notation of "movement" with no real difference in descriptive power.

[4] For reasons of space, we cannot enter into the issue of how the different orders within the VP are derived. There are two possibilities, the first is to assume that OV languages like Latin directly merge the head to the right of the complement. A competing theory claims that all languages are VO and that the OV order is derived by remerge of O to the left of V. A disseminating theory of grammar applied to Latin has to consider these two options seriously since Latin may have both orders. Other important factors to consider are frequency, markedness, and discourse structure. But these are beyond the scope of this paper. Cf. Salvi (this volume) for further details.

[5] Cf. Cecchetto and Oniga (2002; 2004); Szilágyi (this volume).

[6] Notice that TIME is a semantic feature, while Tense is its morpho-syntactic counterpart.

[7] In a finer analysis, the subject is first merged as the Specifier of the VP where it receives the thematic role as external argument of the verb, and then remerged in an external position (cf. Sportiche 1988, Larson 1988 for a seminal presentation of this fruitful hypothesis). This makes it parallel to the subject genitive that we claimed was merged in the specifier of the lower NP (sect. 2). In this brief sketch of how to teach linguistic advances in a Latin grammar, we do not pursue this apparent complication. However, we believe that it is worth presenting in a more complete description of the language, because it can derive "quantifier float", the only case in which the two modern languages considered here display a

discontinuous nominal expression, e.g. *The children have all eaten a cookie, I ragazzi hanno tutti mangiato un biscotto.*

References

Broeckhuis, H., den Dikken, M., Keize, E., van Riemsdijk, H. and R. Vos (eds) (1994-2003) *A Modern Grammar of Dutch,* I-IV, Tilburg, Tilburg University.

Cardinaletti, A. (2007) "L'approccio comparativo in linguistica e in didattica" *Quaderni Patavini di Linguistica* 23: 3-18.

—. (2008) "Le ragioni del comparare per insegnare le lingue", in U. Cardinale (ed.) *Nuove chiavi per insegnare il classico*, Novara, De Agostini Scuola, 267-289.

Cecchetto, C. and R. Oniga (2002) "Consequences of the Analysis of Latin Infinitival Clauses for the Theory of Case and Control" *Lingue e Linguaggio* 1: 151-189.

Cecchetto, C. and R. Oniga (2004) "A Challenge to Null Case Theory" *Linguistic Inquiry* 35: 141-149.

Chomsky, N. (1995) *The Minimalist Program*, Cambridge (Mass.), MIT Press.

—. (2005) "Three Factors in Language Design" *Linguistic Inquiry* 36: 1-22.

Cinque, G. (1990) *Types of A-bar Dependencies*, Cambridge (Mass.), MIT Press.

Cornoldi, C. (1995) *Metacognizione e apprendimento*, Bologna, il Mulino.

Devine, A.M. and L.D. Stephens (2006) *Latin Word Order. Structured meaning and information*, Oxford-New York, Oxford University Press.

Ghegin, F. (2007) "Didattica del sintagma nominale e dei suoi costituenti: morfologia e sintassi in prima media" *Quaderni Patavini di Linguistica* 23: 85-100.

Gianollo (2007) "The Internal Syntax of the Nominal Phrase in Latin. A Diachronic Study", in G. Purnelle and J. Denooz (eds) *Ordre et cohérence en Latin*, Communications présentées au 13e Colloque international de Linguistique latine (Bruxelles-Liège, 4-9 avril 2005), Genève, Droz, 65-80.

Giusti, G. (2003) *Strumenti di analisi per la lingua inglese,* Torino, UTET Libreria (2009^2).

—. (2006) "Parallels in Clausal and Nominal Periphery", in M. Frascarelli (ed.) *Phases of Interpretation*, Berlin, De Gruyter, 163-184.

—. (2010) "On feature sharing and feature transfer" *University of Venice Working Papers in Linguistics* 19: 157-174.

Giusti, G. and R. Oniga (2007) "Core and Periphery in the Latin Noun Phrase", in G. Purnelle and J. Denooz (eds) *Ordre et cohérence en Latin*, Communications présentées au 13e Colloque international de Linguistique latine (Bruxelles-Liège, 4-9 avril 2005), Genève, Droz, 81-95.

Graffi, G. (1986) "Una nota sui concetti di *rhema* e *logos* in Aristotele" *Athenaeum* 64: 91-101.

Haegeman, L. (ed.) (1997) *The New Comparative Syntax*, London, Longman.

Hofmann, J.B. and A. Szantyr (1965) *Lateinische Syntax und Stilistik*, München, Beck.

Iovino, R. (this volume) "Word Order in Latin Nominal Expressions: The Syntax of Demonstratives", 51-63.

Jackendoff, R. (1993) *Patterns in the Mind. Language and Human Nature*, Harvester Wheatsheaf, Hemel Hempstead.

Janson, T. (2004) *A Natural History of Latin*, Oxford-New York, Oxford University Press.

Larson, R. (1988) "On the Double Object Construction" *Linguistic Inquiry* 19: 335-391.

Lepschy, G.C. (2000) *La linguistica del Novecento*, Bologna, il Mulino.

Marouzeau, J. (1922) *L'ordre de mots dans la phrase latine. I: Les groupes nominaux*, Paris, Champion.

Moro, A. (2008) *The Boundaries of Babel. The Brain and the Enigma of Impossible Languages*, Cambridge (Mass.), MIT Press.

Musso, M., Moro, A., Glauche, V., Rijntjes, M., Reichenbach, J., Buechel, C. and C. Weiller (2003) "Broca's area and the language instinct." *Nature Neuroscience* 6: 774-781.

Oniga, R. (2007) *Il latino. Breve introduzione linguistica*, 2^a ed., Milano, Franco Angeli.

—. (2008) "La manualistica universitaria sulla lingua latina tra ricerca e didattica", in S. Rocca (ed.) *Latina Didaxis XXIII* (Atti del Congresso di Genova-Bogliasco, 11-12 aprile 2008), Genova, Compagnia dei Librai, 119-150.

Panhuis, D. (2006) *Latin Grammar*, Ann Arbor, University of Michigan Press.

Pinkster, H. (1990) *Latin Syntax and Semantics*, London, Routledge.

Renzi, L., Salvi, G. and A. Cardinaletti (eds) (1988-2001), *Grande grammatica italiana di consultazione*, I-III, Bologna, il Mulino.

Rizzi L. (1997) "The Fine Structure of the Left Periphery", in L. Haegeman (ed.) *Elements of Grammar. Handbook in Generative Syntax*, Dordrecht, Kluwer, 281-337.

Salvi, G. (2004) *La formazione della struttura di frase romanza. Ordine delle parole e clitici dal latino alle lingue romanze antiche*, Tübingen, Niemeyer.

—. (this volume) "A Formal Approach to Latin Word Order", 23-50.

Salvi, G. and L. Renzi (eds) (2010), *Grammatica dell'italiano antico*, Bologna, il Mulino.

Sportiche, D. (1988) "A Theory of Floating Quantifiers and its Corollaries for Constituent Structure" *Linguistic Inquiry* 19: 425-449.

Solà, J., Lloret, M.-R., Mascaró, J., Pérez Saldanya, M. and G. Rigau i Oliver (eds) (2002) *Gramàtica del català contemporani*, Barcelona, Empúries.

Stroh, W. (2008) *Latein ist tot, es lebe Latein! Kleine Geschichte einer grossen Sprache*, Berlin, List.

Szilágyi, I. (this volume) "Control and AcI in Classical Latin: Structural Interpretation Problems and Innovative Tendencies", 85-100.

Waquet, F. (1998) *Le latin ou l'empire d'un signe. XVIe-XXe siècle*, Paris, Albin Michel.

SECTION I.

SYNTAX AND MORPHOLOGY

A FORMAL APPROACH
TO LATIN WORD ORDER

GIAMPAOLO SALVI

Le sujet s'accorde toujours avec le verbe,
sauf les occasions où le sujet ne s'accorde pas.
(G. Flaubert, *Bouvard et Pécuchet*, ch. V)

Introduction

The aim of this study is to investigate the possibility of a formal approach to Latin word order and to establish its limitations. Which principles underlie the formulation of a model capable of explaining the extreme variety of Latin word order? That such principles must exist has long been recognized by traditional scholarship, which supplies rules for "normal" usage (e.g. Kühner and Stegmann 1955: §§ 245-249; or Hofmann and Szantyr 1965: §§ 397-410). Such rules are not stated formally, and admit exceptions that allow for some freedom on the part of given speakers/writers ("style"). The admission of (uncontrolled) exceptions may appear to lend credence to the idea that Latin word order is substantially free, but a careful examination of the data shows that this is the wrong way to interpret them: as Harm Pinkster puts it (1988: 280), examples such as *valui poenam fortis in ipse meam* (Ov. *am.* 1,7,26)[1] 'myself have been strong to my own hurt', in which the poet seems deliberately to pair each word with a wrong mate, do not represent normal Latin usage in any sense; they are a stylistic device that contravenes the normal rules of the language for expressive effect. We can see the same process at work in modern languages where we have clearer intuitions about the grammaticality of sentences: an Italian sentence like the following one, from a XVIII c. poet: *Come (…) soffrirai (…) / del calzar polveroso in sui tapeti / le impresse orme indecenti?* (Parini, *Mattino*, 143-149)[2] 'How can you endure the dusty shoes' indecent footprints impressed on the carpets?', is not only no part of modern Italian speakers' competence, but surely never was.

The first serious attempt at a (partial) formal description of Latin word order in generative terms is the dissertation of David Ostafin (1986), based on two principles, which we will adopt in the following sections:

i. Since not all word orders (not all permutations of words) are possible, we must admit that Latin word order is governed by rules; but these rules are so liberal and permit so many permutations, that one may have the general impression that word order is as good as free.

ii. If, however, we limit our investigation to prose and exclude poetry (for the reasons briefly hinted at above), the limits on possible permutations appear more clearly, and general rules can be formulated.

In both our own work on this topic (Salvi 2004: ch. 2), and in the important book by Andrew Devine and Laurence Stephens (2006), which constitutes the widest-ranging description of Latin word order in (quasi-) formal terms to date,[3] other phenomena besides possible permutations are taken into account, in order to establish regularities. In section 1 we will illustrate these cues with reference to a modern language, Italian, and then apply them to Latin in 2-3. Sections 4-6 provide a (simplified) examination of Latin sentence structure (essentially on the basis of Salvi 2004: ch. 2), while section 7 attempts to apply these principles to the structure of phrases (building on the work of Devine and Stephens 2006). By these tentative analyses we hope to show that a formal grammar of Latin word order is indeed feasible in general terms, although certain specific examples may resist analysis for extrinsic reasons.

1. Permutations, intonation, pragmatic functions, grammatical tools

Let's take the possible *permutations* of three elements *Piero* 'Peter', *mangia* 'eats/is eating' and *la mela* 'the apple' in Italian (1): of the six permutations, five are grammatical and one is not[4] (notice that if we had taken the elements to be four, with *la* 'the' and *mela* 'apple' as two independent elements, of the twenty-four possible permutations the eighteen in which *la* does not immediately precede *mela* would have been ungrammatical, which proves that in Italian there is a rule which puts the article before the noun it modifies):

(1) a. Piero mangia la mela
     b. La mela mangia Piero
     c. Mangia Piero la mela
     d. Mangia la mela Piero
     e. Piero la mela mangia
     f. *La mela Piero mangia

Notice that without further specification, only ex. (1a) sounds "normal" to an Italian reader, but if we add an *intonational contour* to the examples, their grammatical status cannot be questioned (we adopt underlining in order to mark the pitch accent at the end of an intonational segment, commas to mark an intonational break, and capitals to mark a strong accent):

(1') a. Piero mangia *la mela*
      b. LA MELA mangia, Piero
      c. Mangia *Piero*, la mela
      d. Mangia *la mela*, Piero
      e. Piero, LA MELA mangia

Differences in word order and in intonation correlate with differences in meaning, in particular with those aspects of meaning that depend on the information structure of the sentence, that we will call *pragmatic functions*: the element with the pitch accent at the end of an intonational segment is the *focus/rheme* of the sentence, which may extend to the elements that immediately precede the stressed one: so in (1'a) the focus can be *la mela*, *mangia la mela* or *Piero mangia la mela* (but not *Piero... la mela*), in (1'c) the focus is *Piero*, in (1'd) *la mela* or *mangia la mela*; preverbal elements with a strong accent are contrastive focuses, as in (1'b,e); elements set out by an intonational break are topics if they are at the beginning of the sentence, as *Piero* in (1'e), or part of the background (non-rhematic) information if they are at the end of the sentence, as in (1'b-d).

   A single permutation can have different intonations: e.g. (1a) can have the intonations listed in (2):

(2) a. Piero mangia *la mela*
     b. Piero, mangia *la mela*
     c. PIERO mangia la mela
     d. Piero, MANGIA, la mela

But there are restrictions on the possible positions of focus and topic: so a contrastive focus must immediately precede the verb, as shown by the contrast between (3a) and (3b), the order *focus-topic* is ungrammatical (3c), and there can only be one preverbal contrastive focus (3d):

(3) a. Piero, LA MELA mangia
     b. *LA MELA Piero mangia
     c. *LA MELA, Piero, mangia
     d. *PIERO LA MELA mangia

There are also restrictions on what elements can appear as topics in a preverbal position: direct objects cannot do so:

(4) a. *La mela, Piero *mangia*
     b. *La mela, PIERO mangia
     c. *La mela, mangia *Piero*
        etc.

In the light of these restrictions, (1'b) and (1'e) are the only possible intonations and pragmatic interpretations of (1b) and (1e), respectively, and (1f) cannot be assigned an acceptable intonation/interpretation (since *la mela* can be neither topic nor focus).

So, the apparent permissiveness of Italian word order as exemplified in (1) is more restrictive, since the possible word orders are strictly tied to precise intonational contours and precise distributions of pragmatic functions.

The possibilities can be slightly widened if we use some *grammatical tools*, like the object resumptive pronoun *la* in (5), which signals that the direct object is not rhematic (therefore (5e) cannot be grammatical), and permits it to appear in preverbal position (5a-b):

(5) a. La mela, Piero *la mangia*
     b. Piero, la mela, *la mangia*
     c. La mangia *Piero*, la mela
     d. *La mangia*, la mela, Piero
     e. *La mangia *la mela*, Piero

The conclusions we have reached for Italian seem to be generally valid for other languages, too: 1) not all permutations of words are possible; 2) different permutations generally have a different intonation and/or a different pragmatic interpretation; 3) grammatical tools may be used to signal different pragmatic functions; 4) by examining the different pairings of permutations, intonations and pragmatic functions and the use of special grammatical tools, we can deduce the rules that govern the word order in a given language (as with the restrictions we have formulated above in relation to Italian) and eventually build a formal model that explains it.

In the case of Latin (and other ancient languages), the situation is somewhat more complicated: to start with, we have no direct information about intonation, which completely deprives us of one of the four sources listed above; in addition, the number of possible permutations is very high. This, as is well known, is due to the presence of a case system that allows one to recover the grammatical function of an element irrespective of its position (in contrast with the limitations on the movement of the direct object in Italian above). So we are left with the pragmatic functions and the grammatical tools, which we will briefly examine in the next two sections, before applying them to a sample analysis of sentence structure in sections 4-6. In section 7, we will turn our attention to the analysis of phrases, where we will see that in Latin, too, permutations can supply important cues when it comes to detecting the rules that govern word order.

2. Grammatical tools in Latin

Latin uses different tools to signal topics (2.1) and focuses (2.2). Certain other constructions can signal that a given element occupies a marked position in the sentence structure without specifying its pragmatic function (2.3).

2.1. Indicators of topic

Among the indicators of topic, we have the use of *de* 'as for, in the matter of' (6) and the construction of *nominativus pendens*, in which the topic of the sentence is expressed by a nominative noun phrase regardless of its grammatical function in the sentence structure, as in (7), where the required case would be a genitive (*(decumam partem) familiae*):

(6) *De Aufidiano nomine* nihil te hortor (Cic. *fam.* 16,19)
     "*In the matter of Aufidius's debt*, I put no pressure upon you"

(7) *familia* vero, babae babae, non mehercules puto decumam partem
     esse quae dominum suum noverit (Petron. 37,9)
     "*as for slaves* oh, oh! I don't believe, by Hercules, there's a tenth of
     them who know their own master"

2.2. Indicators of focus

The focus function of an element can directly depend on the semantic class
of the element focused: so interrogative (8a) and negative/restrictive (8b)[5]
words are normally focuses; or the function can be signalled by a particle,
such as the enclitic interrogative *-ne*, which marks the focalization of the
verb in (9):

(8) a. *Quid* proxima, *quid* superiore nocte egeris, *ubi* fueris, *quos*
         convocaveris, *quid* consilii ceperis, *quem* nostrum ignorare
         arbitraris? (Cic. *Catil.* 1,1)
         "*What* is there that you did last night, *what* the night before—
         where is it that you were—*who* was there that you summoned to
         meet you—*what* design was there which was adopted by you,
         with which you think that any one of us is unacquainted?"
     b. *non* sententiis suis *solum*, sed etiam studiis comprobavit (Cic.
         Mil. 12)
         "approved it *not only* by its votes but also by its expressions of
         sympathy"

(9) Est*ne* haec patera qua donatu's illi? (Plaut. *Amph.* 780)
     "*Is this or is it not* the bowl that was given you there?"

2.3. Non-specific indicators of marked word order

When the elements which make up a syntactic constituent are split and
occupy two different positions in the linear order (*hyperbaton*), we may
assume that this serves to mark a special function: in particular, that part of
the split constituent which has a special pragmatic function will occupy a
prominent position in the linear order, as in the start (10) or at the end of
the sentence (11); the function may be focus, as in the case of *magna(m)* in
(10a)/(11b) and *proprios* in (11a), topic, as in the case of the initial *partes*
in (10b), or non-rhematic background information, as in the case of the
final *controversia* in (11b):[6]

(10) a. *Magnam* haec res Caesari *difficultatem* ad consilium capiendum adferebat (Caes. *Gall.* 7,10)
"This action of Vercingetorix caused Caesar *great difficulty* in forming his plan of campaign"
b. *partes* mihi Caesar *has* imposuit (Cic. *Att.* 10,10,2)
"Caesar has assigned me *the following role*"

(11) a. Neque quisquam agri modum certum aut *fines* habet *proprios* (Caes. *Gall.* 6,22)
"No man has a definite quantity of land or *estate of his own*"
b. *magna* inter eos exsistit *controversia* (Caes. *Gall.* 5,28)
"and *a great dispute* arose among them"

Another class of markers which can serve to pick out a constituent with a marked pragmatic function at the start of a sentence are weak elements (pronouns and forms of the verb *sum*): these occupy the core sentence second position (a version of Wackernagel's Law),[7] so they can serve to single out sentence initial focused elements (12), especially when they split an otherwise unitary constituent (12b). But notice that the constituent that precedes the weak element can have other pragmatic functions, too, e.g. that of theme, as in (13) (and in (10b) above):

(12) a. ita *se* cum multis conligavit (Cic. *fam.* 9,17,2)
"so inextricably has he tied himself up with his multitude of counselors"
b. Isdem *igitur te* rebus etiam atque etiam hortor quibus superioribus litteris hortatus sum ut… (Cic. *fam.* 4,9,1)
"Repeating, therefore, the arguments I used in my former letter of exhortation, I exhort you again and again to…"

(13) Caninius noster *me* tuis verbis admonuit ut… (Cic. *fam.* 9,6,1)
"Our friend Caninius gave me your message, reminding me to…"

3. Pragmatic functions

In the absence of syntactic markers, the arguments one can advance in the study of Latin sentence structure are mainly based on the possible pairings of permutations and pragmatic values: we may assume that marked pragmatic values are paired with marked word orders and, if we observe the systematic recurrence of a given word order with a given pragmatic value, we may suppose that the observed word order makes use of a special structural position. But this kind of evidence is not without its problems.

Identifying the pragmatic values expressed in a sentence implies the perfect reconstruction of the author's communicative intentions, a task which is not always easy. Even if we assume that the principles which organize discourse are universally the same, there are always cases where two or more different ways of arranging what we want to say are equally suitable for our communicative needs. We can see this if we examine different translations of the same text: in the sentence reported in (14), the constituent *aedes* has been interpreted as a marked topic by Italian translator (a) and as part of the rheme by translator (b):

(14) *aedes* non somniatur (Petron. 74,14)
      "he doesn't aspire *to the mansion*"
      a. *i palazzi* non se li sogna nemmeno (A. Aragosti)
      b. non si sogna certo *un palazzo* (G. Reverdito)

Both solutions are defensible on pragmatic grounds, but neither has syntactic evidence that can support it. The missing information about the intonation would be decisive here.

To this, we may add that the great majority of Classical Latin texts are highly elaborated literary works in which figures of speech may replace expected word order: so in (15) the two noun phrases in italics have a parallel structure and a parallel information content, which we might expect to be reflected in a parallel word order, but for the sake of *variatio*, the parallelistic structure is substituted by a chiastic one:[8]

(15) ut vehementius *odio libidinis tuae* quam *legationis metu* moverentur
      (Cic. *Verr.* II 1,81)
      "that they were more deeply moved by *hatred for your immorality*
      than *fear of your authority*"

4. Sentence structure: the position of the verb

It is normally assumed that the basic position of the verb in Latin is sentence final. However, one may question the truth of this assumption because there are plenty of examples in which the verb occupies a different position in the linear order. But when one examines these apparent exceptions more closely, it turns out that the exceptions are subject to rules.

From the point of view of the possible permutations, it may be noticed that, if not absolutely final, the verb is normally nearly final (that is, followed by only one constituent, see 4.1), initial, or nearly initial (that is, preceded by only one constituent, see 4.2). The position of the verb is not random: it does not occur in the middle of a sentence, or, to be more precise, those cases in which it apparently occurs in the middle of a sentence can be reduced to one of the cases listed above (nearly final or nearly initial).[9] In the following sections we will show that when the verb is not final, there is always a specific reason for this deviation; that is, the deviation is governed by rules.

4.1. Verb in nearly final position

When the verb is followed by a constituent, this constituent is normally "heavy", that is, linearly long or structurally complex, in general consisting of or containing a subordinate clause, as in (16), or represents non-rhematic background information, as in (11b) above, or acts as the focus of the sentence, as in (17) and in (11a) above; the finite verb can also be followed by the non-finite part of a complex verb expression, as in (18):

(16) citiusque amore tui fratrem tuum odisse desinam *quam illius odium quicquam de nostra benevolentia detraham* (Cic. *fam.* 5,2,10)
"and I shall sooner cease to resent your brother's conduct because I love you, *than because of that resentment permit our mutual goodwill to be in the slightest degree impaired*"

(17) quin tibi ingenio praestiterit *nemo* (Cic. *rep.* 1,37)
"that *no one* has excelled you in natural capacity"

(18) si haec mala fixa sunt, ego vero te quam primum, mea vita, *cupio videre* (Cic. *fam.* 14,4,1)
"if [...] these ills can never be removed, I assure you, my dearest, that my desire is to see you as soon as possible"

The number of elements that follow the verb can also be more than one, provided that they belong to these types, as in (19), where we have a focus (*Brundisi*) and a heavy constituent (*si esset licitum per nautas*):

(19) Quas ego expectassem *Brundisi si esset licitum per nautas* (Cic. *fam.*
     14,4,5)
     "I should have awaited them *at Brundisium, had the sailors
     permitted*"

We will not attempt here to provide an explanation of how and why the
postverbal constituents come to occupy this position,[10] suffice it to have
shown in outline that this phenomenon can be accounted for by precise
rules.

4.2. Verb in initial and nearly initial position

The verb appears in sentence initial position when it signals a special
function of the sentence: interrogative (20), jussive (21), concessive (22),
adversative (23), asseverative (24) (asserting that an event really occurred
or occurs), presentative (25) (introducing a new subject in the universe of
discourse), and eventive (26) (introducing an event as the temporal or
causal consequence of a previous one). In all these cases the marked word
order must surely have been accompanied by a specific intonation that
served to disambiguate which of the listed functions the sentence actually
had, and this function could be signalled by specific words or grammatical
tools, too (as imperative mood in (21), *sed* in the following clause in (22),
tamen in (23), etc.):

(20) *solent* tibi umquam oculi duri fieri? (Plaut. *Men.* 923)
     "are your eyes ever in the habit of becoming hard?"

(21) si intelligis non me dicto Metelli, ut scribis, sed consilio eius
     animoque in me inimicissimo esse commotum, | *cognosce* nunc
     humanitatem meam (Cic. *fam.* 5,2,9)
     "if you are satisfied that it was not the "mere phrase", as you describe
     it, of Metellus, but his whole policy and the extreme bitterness of his
     animosity towards myself that distressed me, I would have you now
     at last recognize my kindness"

(22) *Erat* multo inferior numero navium Brutus, sed electos ex omnibus
     legionibus fortissimos viros, antesignanos, centuriones, Caesar ei
     classi attribuerat... (Caes. *civ.* 1,57,1)
     "Brutus was much inferior to the enemy in number of ships; but
     Caesar had manned them with his best soldiers, chosen out of all the
     legions, and headed by centurions of distinguished bravery"

(23) ...quae ille obtectus armis militum vitavit; *vulnerantur* tamen complures, in his Cornelius Balbus, M. Plotius, L. Tiburtius, centuriones militesque nonnulli (Caes. *civ.* 3,19,7)
"Vatinius escaped the danger, by means of the soldiers, who protected him with their shields; but Cornelius Balbus, M. Plotius, L. Tiburtus, centurions, and some private men, were wounded"

(24) Ego tua gratulatione commotus, quod ad me pridem scripseras velle te bene evenire quod de Crasso domum emissem, | *emi* eam ipsam domum HS XXXV aliquanto post tuam gratulationem (Cic. *fam.* 5,6,2)
"Roused by your congratulations — for you wrote to me some time ago, wishing me luck on having bought a house from Crassus — I have now bought that very house for three thousand five hundred sestertia, a considerable time after you congratulated me on having done so"

(25) *Relinquebatur* una per Sequanos via, qua... (Caes. *Gall.* 1,9,1)
"There remained one other route, through the borders of the Sequani, by which..."

(26) Trans Rhenum ad Germanos pervenit fama diripi Eburones atque ultro omnes ad praedam evocari. *Cogunt* equitum duo milia Sugambri, qui... (Caes. *Gall.* 6,35,4)
"Across the Rhine the report reached the Germans that the Eburones were being pillaged; nay, more — that all were invited to come and plunder. Two thousand horsemen were collected by the Sugambri, who..."

The verb in initial position can be preceded by elements describing the frame of the event, as in (21) and in (24).

In section 6 we will try to outline a formal model to explain this phenomenon.

5. Sentence structure: focalization

Using the grammatical tools described in section 2 allows us to identify a position designed to accommodate focused elements at the beginning of the sentence: in (27) *quid* and *nihil* are identified as focuses by their meaning (interrogative and negative), in (28) *adeo* and *telis* by being accompanied by focusing particles (-*n* and *potius*); in (29) *multae* by being separated from the noun it modifies (*insidiae*) by hyperbaton, and in all the examples the identified elements are immediately followed by a weak pronoun (*me*, *te*, etc.):

(27) a. *quid me* ista res consolatur in tantis tenebris et quasi parietinis rei publicae? (Cic. *fam.* 4,3,2)
         "*What* consolation is that to me, amid this oppressive gloom, and what I may call the crumbling walls of the Republic?"
    b. *nihil te* omnino fefellit (Cic. *fam.* 9,2,2)
        "*nothing* whatever escaped your notice"

(28) a. adeo*n me* ignavom putas? (Ter. *Andr.* 277)
        "Do you deem me so cowardly?"
    b. ut *potius* telis *tibi* Gallorum quam periuriis intereundum esset (Cic. *Font.* 49)
        "that it would have been *better* to be destroyed by the weapons of the Gauls than by their perjuries"

(29) *multae mihi* a Verre *insidiae* terra marique factae sint (Cic. *Verr.* I 3)
     "*many stealthy attacks* have been made against me on land and sea by Verres"

In the next section, we will outline a formal model for the initial part of the sentence in which the facts presented in 4.2 and 5 will find their place.

6. A (partial) formal model of Latin sentence structure

The generalizations reviewed in the preceding sections can be explained by a simple formal model, which we formulate here using the theoretical framework of Generative Grammar.

The following phrase structure tree[11] offers a model of some of the generalizations we have proposed above: the sentence is constituted by a kernel (TP) which contains all the constituents; of these, the verb occupies the final position, while the other constituents are represented in the order *subject - indirect object - direct object - other complements*, possibly the unmarked word order, but certainly not the only possible one.[12] The beginning of the sentence provides two more sorts of positions, to which those elements having a specific pragmatic function can be moved: one of them is reserved for constituents with the function of topic or frame (TopP) and the other for constituents with the function of focus and for the preposed verb (FocP). Their relative position reflects the fact that topics/frames precede focused elements (as in (6) above, where *de Aufidiano nomine* is topic and *nihil* is focus) and the preposed verb (as shown in (21) and (24) above). We place focused elements and the preposed verb in the same sort of position because these are in complementary distribution: in the same sentence we can have sentence initial focusing or verb preposing, but not both.

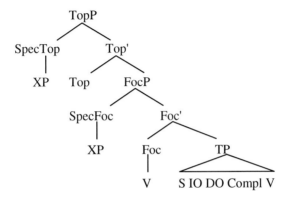

Of the two positions available under TopP and under FocP, one hosts phrases (SpecTop and SpecFoc), while the other hosts heads, that is, word level categories (Top and Foc). In the specific case of FocP, the SpecFoc position can be occupied by the focused phrase (which may be constituted by a sole word, too) and the Foc position by the preposed verb. The assumption of these two different positions allows us to draw an important distinction: while a focused element moves into the SpecFoc position "for its own benefit" (in order to function as the focus of the sentence), moving the verb has the aim of signalling that the whole sentence has a certain function (interrogative, jussive, etc.). We may represent this by positing that in the latter case, the sentence contains an abstract operator which expresses the semantic type of the sentence and occupies the SpecFoc position: being abstract, this operator is not visible, but it becomes indirectly "visible" through the presence of the verb adjacent to it in Foc, so the sentence meaning can be correctly identified.

Here we give a sample analysis of two of the previous examples on the basis of this sentence structure:

(10a)   [Magnam]$_{Foc}$ [haec res]$_S$ [Caesari]$_{IO}$ [difficultatem]$_{DO}$ [ad consilium capiendum]$_{COMPL}$ [adferebat]$_V$

(24)   [Ego]$_{TOP}$ [tua gratulatione commotus...]$_{TOP}$ [(Operator$_{asseverative}$) emi]$_{FOC}$ [eam ipsam domum]$_{DO}$ [HS XXXV]$_{COMPL}$ [aliquanto post tuam gratulationem]$_{COMPL}$

We will not deal with the final part of the sentence here (see 4.1), but notice that a potential problem with such an analysis is the fact that focused elements appear not only in the dedicated focus position at the beginning of the sentence (section 5), but also in postverbal position (section 4.1). In Italian, too, we have two possibilities for focalization: in postverbal position, as in (1'a,c,d), etc. and in preverbal position, as in (1'b,e), etc. but these cases are distinct semantically: in preverbal position we only have contrastive focus, in postverbal position mainly information focus (see É. Kiss 1998 for this difference), whereas no such distinction seems valid for Latin. The possible semantic difference between the two focus positions of this language must still be studied in depth.

7. The structure of phrases

In this section, we will approach some problems relative to the structure of phrases, mainly drawing on the work of Ostafin (1986) and Devine and Stephens (2006).[13] Our aim here will be to show that, although Latin has a very permissive word order, there are gaps in the possible range of permutations which must be explained; in other terms, rules governing word order are necessary.

7.1. N-genitive / genitive-N

Let us begin with a simple case: the relative order of a noun and its genitive argument in the noun phrase (NP). The unmarked order, according to Devine and Stephens (2006: 4.1), is *N-genitive*, both with an objective (30a) and with a subjective genitive (30b);[14] in these examples both the noun and the genitive are equally rhematic: the string *N-genitive* appears in series of NPs composed mainly of simple nouns, so we can conclude that neither the noun nor the genitive is especially highlighted; instead, it is the noun phrase as a whole that is presented as distinct from the other elements in the series:

(30) a.   in his rebus pro mea parte versor quarum ille princeps fuit, aequitate, industria, temperantia, *defensione miserorum, odio improborum* (Cic. *Verr.* II 4,81)
"I practise, to the utmost of my power, those virtues in which he was preeminent,—equity, industry, temperance, *the protection of the unhappy*, and *hatred of the dishonest*"

   b.   qui scelus fraudemque nocentis possit dicendo subicere *odio civium* supplicioque constringere (Cic. *de orat.* 1,202)
"who, likewise, is able, by means of his eloquence, to expose guilt and deceit to *the hatred of his countrymen*, and to restrain them by penalties"

If the genitive is focused, it normally precedes the noun, as we can see in (31), where *condicionis* is contrasted with *victoriae*:

(31)   magis ad *condicionis spem* quam *victoriae* (Cic. *Att.* 11,12,3)
"giving *hope* more *for a negotiated settlement* than *for victory*"

But a focused genitive can apparently appear after the noun too, as in (32), with focus on *mei/severitatis/dignitatis/rei publicae*:

(32)   Nihil enim contra me fecit *odio mei*, sed *odio severitatis*, *odio dignitatis*, *odio rei publicae* (Cic. *har. resp.* 5)
"he did nothing out of *hatred of me personally*, but out of *hatred for authority*, *for high position* and *for the republic*"

Similarly, if the focus is on the noun, we find both *N-genitive* (33a) (*calamitate/metu c.*) and *genitive-N* (33b) (*calamitate/c. formidine*):

(33) a.   non modo a *calamitate* sed etiam a *metu calamitatis* (Cic. *Manil.* 14)
"not only from *disaster* but also from *fear of disaster*"

   b.   non solum… *calamitate* sed etiam *calamitatis formidine* liberatos (Cic. *Manil.* 16)
"preserved not only from *disaster* but also from *fear of disaster*"

In addition, according to the analysis by Devine and Stephens (2006: 336-337), when the NP contains a prenominal modifier, the order *genitive-N* is a free variant of the unmarked *N-genitive* order, not determined by pragmatic considerations:

(34) Deinde hoc ita fit ut viri fortes, etiam si ferro inter se comminus
     decertarint, tamen *illud contentionis odium* simul cum ipsa pugna
     armisque deponant (Cic. *Pis.* 32)
     "But this is a common state of things, that brave men, even after they
     have fought together in close combat sword in hand, still lay aside
     the hostility engendered by the contest at the same time that they
     cease from the battle itself, and lay down their arms"

Finally, as already noted in relation to (15), stylistic considerations may
introduce free variation, as in the case of the chiasmus in (35):

(35) ex *luctu civium* et ex *Caepionis odio* (Cic. *de orat.* 2,124)
     "from the *grief of the citizens* and *hatred for Caepio*"

The results of this brief survey are not entirely satisfying, even so. Each
possible pairing of word order and pragmatic functions is attested: the *N-
genitive* order can be either unmarked (30), or entail focus on N (33a) or
on the genitive (32), and similarly the *genitive-N* order can be either
unmarked (34), or entail focus on N (33b) or on the genitive (31).
Seemingly, therefore, no overarching rule can be formulated. This is
probably due to the fact that the structure is too simple, being composed of
only two elements. So we will have to look for more complex cases.

7.2. Permutations governed by rules

In the following sections, we will examine cases of permutations of three
elements: we will start by presenting the well-studied case of the
prepositional phrase (Ostafin 1986: ch. 4; Devine and Stephens 2006: 568-
575), and then move to some cases of nominal modification.

7.2.1. Prepositional phrases

In the case of a set of three elements, the possible permutations are six. If
we take a prepositional phrase (PP) that contains a NP composed of two
elements and for the time being we exclude the two non-attested
permutations in which the preposition would be final (see below), there
remain four possible word orders. Of these, in Classical Latin prose only
three are attested. Let us begin with a preposition that, as its complement,
has a noun modified by a genitive: [P [N genitive]]. Since the order in the
NP can be *N-genitive* and *genitive-N*, we expect to find the orders: *P-N-
genitive* and *P-genitive-N*, as in fact we do:

(36) a. De numero eorum (Caes. *Gall.* 2,4,4)
          "respecting their number"
      b. in hostium numero (Caes. *Gall.* 1,28,1)
          "in the light of enemies"

The genitive can also appear before the preposition (37a), but the noun cannot (37b):[15]

(37) a. deorum in numero (Cic. *nat. deor.* 1,118)
          "numbered among the gods"
      b. *numero in deorum

The same is true of a noun modified by an adjective (38)-(39) or by a numeral (40)-(41):

(38) a. cum reliquis civitatibus (Caes. *Gall.* 5,11,9)
          "with the other states"
      b. in locis reliquis (Caes. *Gall.* 8,43,2)
          "in other places"

(39) a. reliquis in locis (Caes. *Gall.* 6,25,5)
          "in other parts"
      b. *locis in reliquis[16]

(40) a. in tres partes (Caes. *Gall.* 6,32,1)
          "into three parts"
      b. in partes tres (Caes. *Gall.*1,1,1)
          "into three parts"

(41) a. tres in partes (Cic. *fin.* 4,4)
          "into three parts"
      b. *partes in tres

From these limited permutations, we may conclude that in Latin it was possible to extract a part of the NP complement of a preposition and to move it to the left of the PP, but the element extracted could not be the head noun of the NP. The only possible structure was therefore: [X [P [...N...]]] (with X an argument or modifier of N).

As for the other two non-attested permutations, those with the preposition in final position, there must be a rule which says that one cannot shift all the parts of the complement: something must remain after the preposition.[17] This may be clearly seen in the following example, discussed in Devine and Stephens (2006: 571-572): in the question the quantifier (*quot* 'how many') precedes the preposition, but in the answer *tres* 'three' has to follow it because otherwise nothing would appear after the preposition (**tres in*):

(42) *Quot in partes* distribuenda est omnis doctrina dicendi? *In tres* (Cic. *part.* 3)
"*Into how many parts* should the subject of rhetoric be divided? *Into three*"

7.2.2. Quantifiers and other modifiers in the noun phrase

In their discussion of adjectival phrases (AP) headed by *expers* 'lacking', Devine and Stephens (2006: 393-396 and 566) also treat structures in which *expers* has a complement consisting of a genitive NP composed of a noun modified by a quantifier: [A [Q N]]. Among the many examples cited we find only four possible permutations:

a) the complement can follow the adjective with the order *Q-N* (43a) or *N-Q* (43b) - notice that both these orders are independently attested in the construction of a noun modified by a quantifier (44), the order *Q-N* being the unmarked one:[18]

(43) a. si nullus defunctis sensus superest, evasit omnia frater meus vita incommoda et in eum restitutus est locum, in quo fuerat antequam nasceretur, et *expers omnis mali* nihil timet, nihil cupit, nihil patitur (Sen. *dial.* 11,9,2)
"if the dead retain no feeling whatever, my brother has escaped from all the ills of life, and has been restored to that state in which he had been before he was born, and, *exempt from every ill*, he fears nothing, desires nothing, suffers nothing"
b. nonne *expertes* sunt *religionum omnium*? (Cic. *nat. deor.* 1,119)
"Aren't they *devoid of all religions*?"

(44) a. Subito Labienus duabus portis *omnem equitatum* emittit (Caes. *Gall.* 5,58,4)
"Labienus unexpectedly sends out *all the cavalry* by two gates"

b. his rebus impulsus *equitatum omnem* prima nocte ad castra hostium mittit ad flumen Bagradam (Caes. *civ.* 2,38,3)
"Urged by these considerations, early the night, he sent *all his cavalry* towards the enemy's camp, by the river Bagradas"

b) the complement can also precede the adjectival head - in this case the order of the elements in the NP is Q-N:[19]

(45) M. autem Antonium omnino *omnis eruditionis expertem* atque ignarum fuisse (Cic. *de orat.* 2,1)
"Marcus Antonius was entirely destitute and *devoid of all learning* whatsoever"

c) finally, the quantifier can precede the adjectival head, while the noun follows it:

(46) ego contra hoc quoque laboris praemium petam, ut me a conspectu malorum quae nostra tot per annos vidit aetas, tantisper certe dum prisca [tota] illa mente repeto, avertam, *omnis expers curae* quae scribentis animum, etsi non flectere a vero, sollicitum tamen efficere posset (Liv. 1 *praef.* 5)
"I myself, on the contrary, shall seek in this an additional reward for my toil, that I may avert my gaze from the troubles which our age has been witnessing for so many years, so long at least as I am absorbed in the recollection of the brave days of old, *free from every care* which, even if it could not divert the historian's mind from the truth, might nevertheless cause it anxiety"

We refrain here from drawing too precise conclusions from these facts because we are not sure if the examples cited exhaust all the possibilities, but the following generalizations seem to emerge. A quantifier can be moved to phrase initial position in two ways: either the whole quantified NP is preposed (in this case the quantifier comes first) or only the quantifier is preposed. In other words, in Latin there is a rule that moves a quantifier to the beginning of a wider phrase: the quantifier can move on its own, or it can drag the whole NP with it.

In order to check this suggestion, we have examined NPs which contain a comparative adjective quantified by *multo* 'much',[20] with the structure: [N [Q A]]. The results are parallel to those just reviewed: the AP can follow the head noun with the order *Q-A* (47a) or, more rarely, *A-Q* (47b) (by the way, both these orders are independently attested (48)); the

AP can also precede the head noun with the quantifier preceding the adjective (49a), but not the other way round (49b);[21] finally, the sole quantifier can precede the noun (50a), but this is not possible for the adjective alone (50b):

(47) a. *sociis multo fidelioribus* utimur quam quisquam usus est (Cic. *Att.* 5,18,2)
         "I find *the allies much more loyal* than anyone has ever done"
     b. Et ne hoc in causis, in iudiciis, in amicorum periculis, in concursu hominum, in civitate, in foro accidere miremur, cum agitur non solum ingeni nostri existimatio (...) sed *alia* sunt *maiora multo*, fides, officium, diligentia, quibus rebus adducti, etiam cum alienissimos defendimus, tamen eos alienos, si ipsi viri boni volumus haberi, existimare non possumus (Cic. *de orat.* 2,192)
         "That we may not be surprised, too, that this happens in causes, in criminal trials, when our friends are in danger, and before a multitude in the city and in the forum, where not only our reputation for ability is at stake (...), but where *other things of* [*much*] *greater importance* are concerned: fidelity, duty to our clients, and earnestness in discharging that duty; we are so moved by such considerations, that even when we defend total strangers we cannot regard them as strangers, if we wish ourselves to be thought of as honest men"

(48) a. quod *multo carius* est (Cic. *ad Brut.* 1,11,1)
         "what is *much more valuable*"
     b. haec mihi *ampliora multo* sunt quam illa ipsa, propter quae haec laborantur (Cic. *fam.* 3,13,1)
         "All this is a *much greater* honour to me than the thing itself for which the trouble is being taken"

(49) a. quae res municipibus Anagninis *multo maiori dolori* fuit (Cic. *dom.* 81)
         "this was *a far greater source of distress* to the townsfolk of Anagnia"
     b. *maiori multo dolori

(50) a. *multo arte maiore* praeditus (Cic. *Tusc.* 5,104)
         "endowed with *a far greater art*"
     b. *maiore arte multo

At this point we may try to formulate a model capable of generating the possible permutations: as a starting point, we assume the structure in (i), where the complex AP modifier follows the head noun, and the quantifier precedes the adjective it modifies;[22] parallel to what we have seen in the clause, the NP also has a position dedicated to focus elements (see section 6). Example (47a) reflects this structure without the focus position. Due to its meaning, the quantifier *multo* is subject to focalization: it can focalize alone, as in (ii) and ex. (50a), or it can drag the entire AP along, as in (iii) and in example (49a). In the NP, too, focalization may involve final position (47b), as in the sentence structure (see 4.1 above): we can assume that in these cases the focalization of the quantifier is followed by the anteposition of the NP voided of the quantifier, which leaves the quantifier in final position (iv):[23]

(i) $( )_{Foc} [_{NP}N [_{AP}Q A]]$

(ii) $( )_{Foc} [_{NP}N [_{AP}Q A]] \rightarrow (Q)_{Foc} [_{NP}N [_{AP}- A]]$

(iii) $( )_{Foc} [_{NP}N [_{AP}Q A]] \rightarrow ([_{AP}Q A])_{Foc} [_{NP}N -]$

(iv) $( )_{Foc} [_{NP}N [_{AP}Q A]] \rightarrow (Q)_{Foc} [_{NP}N [_{AP}- A]] \rightarrow [_{NP}N [_{AP}- A]] (Q)_{Foc}$

The generalizations we have identified in the construction in which *multo* modifies a comparative adjective cannot, however, be directly applied to all types of quantifiers: if we observe, e.g., the permutations possible in an AP which contains an adjectival head modified by a NP formed by a noun and a numeral: [A [Num N]], we see that all the permutations are attested: *A-Num-N* (51a) as well as *A-N-Num* (51b), *Num-N-A* (52a) as well as *N-Num-A* (52b), *Num-A-N* (53) as well as *N-A-Num* (54):

(51) a. latas iiii pedes (Caes. *civ.* 2,9,5)
         "to the depth of four feet"
     b. latas pedes II S (Vitr. 5,1,6)
         "two and one half feet broad"

(52) a. quindecim pedes latas (Caes. *Gall.* 7,72,3)
         "fifteen feet broad"
     b. pedes lx longum (Caes. *civ.* 2,10,1)
         "sixty feet long"

(53) ferrum autem *tres longum* habebat *pedes* (Liv. 21,8,11)
     "it had an iron head *three feet in length*"

(54) a. pedes latas quaternos (Cato, *agr.* 151,3)
         "four feet wide"
     b. annos natus circiter viginti (Sall. *Iug.* 64,4)
         "was about twenty years old"

In the light of the analysis above, permutations *N-Num-A* and *N-A-Num* are not expected.[24]
The case is different in structures where a noun is accompanied by two modifiers, e.g. a universal quantifier and a demonstrative, with the structure [Q [Dem N]] (as in English [*all* [*these examples*]]). Devine and Stephens (2006: 515-520) have only found four of the six possible permutations: *Q-Dem-N* (55a), *Dem-Q-N* (55b), *Dem-N-Q* (55c) and *N-Dem-Q* (55d), and they give no examples for the orders with the demonstrative in final position (but see below, ex. (58)). Notice that both *Q-N* alternates with *N-Q* (56) and *Dem-N* alternates with *N-Dem* (57):

(55) a. Deinde illa exponunt duo, quae quasi contineant *omnem hanc quaestionem* (Cic. *ac.* 2,40)
         "Then they set out the two propositions that 'hold together' *the whole of this investigation*"
     b. nos autem *hanc omnem quaestionem* de finibus bonorum et malorum fere a nobis explicatam esse his litteris arbitramur (Cic. *fin.* 1,12)
         "But we now think that *this whole question* about the ends of good and evil is, I may almost say, thoroughly explained in this treatise"
     c. nec sequor magos Persarum quibus auctoribus Xerses inflammasse templa Graeciae dicitur, quod parietibus includerent deos, quibus omnia deberent esse patentia ac libera, quorumque *hic mundus omnis* templum esset et domus (Cic. *leg.* 2,26)
         "I do not agree with the doctrine of the Persian Magi, by whose advice they say Xerxes set fire to the temples of the Greeks, because they enclosed between walls the gods, to whom all things are free and open, and whose proper temple and dwelling place is *the boundless universe*"
     d. At quanta conantur! *Mundum hunc omnem* oppidum esse nostrum! Incendi igitur eos, qui audiunt, vides. Quantam rem agas, ut Circeis qui habitet *totum hunc mundum* suum municipium esse existimet? (Cic. *fin.* 4,7)

"But what great attempts they make! They say that *this universal world* is our town; accordingly, this excites those who hear such a statement. You see, now, how great a business you are undertaking; to make a man who lives at Circeii believe that *this universal world* is merely a town for himself to live in"

(56) a. omnis Gallia (Caes. *Gall.* 4,20)
"all Gaul"
     b. Gallia omnis (Caes. *Gall.* 5,29)
"all Gaul"

(57) a. hac oratione (Caes. *Gall.* 1,3)
"by this speech"
     b. *legem hanc* mihi, iudices, statuo (Cic. *Verr.* II 3,5)
"*This law*, judges, I establish against myself"

In order to formulate a model capable of generating the possible permutations, we assume as a starting point the structure in (i), in which the quantifier, which has scope over the whole phrase, modifies the NP constituted by the demonstrative and the noun in this order (the unmarked one, as stated by Devine and Stephens 2006: 511-515); given its meaning, the quantifier may move into the position dedicated to focus elements. This structure is reflected in ex. (55a). The demonstrative can adjoin to the quantifier to form a complex determiner, which may focalize, as represented in (ii) - see ex. (55b).[25] The final position of the quantifier or of the complex determiner is obtained, as above, by the focalization of these elements followed by the anteposition of the NP voided of them, as in (iii)/(55c) and (iv)/(55d), respectively:

(i) $( )_{Foc} [_{NP}Q [_{NP}Dem N]]$
        $(Q)_{Foc} [_{NP}- [_{NP}Dem N]]$

(ii) $( )_{Foc} [_{NP}Q [_{NP}Dem N]] \rightarrow ( )_{Foc} [_{NP}Dem-Q [_{NP}- N]]$
        $(Dem-Q)_{Foc} [_{NP}- [_{NP}- N]]$

(iii) $( )_{Foc} [_{NP}Q [_{NP}Dem N]] \rightarrow (Q)_{Foc} [_{NP}- [_{NP}Dem N]] \rightarrow$
        $[_{NP}- [_{NP}Dem N]] (Q)_{Foc}$

(iv) $( )_{Foc} [_{NP}Q [_{NP}Dem N]] \rightarrow ( )_{Foc} [_{NP}Dem-Q [_{NP}- N]] \rightarrow$
        $(Dem-Q)_{Foc} [_{NP}- [_{NP}- N]] \rightarrow [_{NP}- [_{NP}- N]] (Dem-Q)_{Foc}$

The focalization of the demonstrative is much rarer in this construction, but nevertheless possible. See the following example, brought to my attention by Renato Oniga:

(58) qui si permanet incorruptus suique similis, necesse est ita feratur, ut
     penetret et dividat *omne caelum hoc*, in quo nubes, imbres, ventique
     coguntur, quod et umidum et caliginosum est propter exhalationes
     terrae (Cic. *Tusc.* 1,43)
     "which, should it remain uncorrupt and without alteration, must
     necessarily be carried on with such velocity as to penetrate and
     divide *all this atmosphere*, where clouds, and rain, and winds are
     formed, which, in consequence of the exhalations from the earth, is
     moist and dark"

In this case the derivation entails the focalization of the demonstrative
followed by the anteposition of the NP voided of it, as in (v):

(v)   ( )$_{Foc}$ [$_{NP}$Q [$_{NP}$Dem N]] → (Dem)$_{Foc}$ [$_{NP}$Q [$_{NP}$- N]] →
        [$_{NP}$Q [$_{NP}$- N]] (Dem)$_{Foc}$

The examples reviewed in this section show that from the joint use of
limited permutations and semantic information we can gain some idea of
the rules that govern word order in Latin phrases. Although the formal
models proposed here are only tentative, they show how this task might be
accomplished.

Conclusion

The data available for the study of Latin word order are severley limited:

a) We have no negative evidence: in the case of a living language, we
    have at our disposal both positive and negative data: what one can or
    could say, and what one cannot say; in the case of a dead language or
    of a past stage of any language, we only have what has been written,[26]
    and we cannot directly check which possibilities were ungrammatical –
    we can at best formulate hypotheses about non-attested possibilities: is
    their absence systematic (due to their ungrammaticality), or casual?
    (not to mention attested examples which could be ungrammatical
    owing to errors in transmission or to the causes discussed in the
    introduction).
b) We have no information about intonation, which could be an essential
    cue in the interpretation of word order, owing to the systematic pairing
    we may suppose to have existed between intonation and pragmatic

functions, on the view that it is mainly pragmatic functions that shape Latin word order.

c) We can make no direct check on the precise meaning of an utterance – in the case of living languages this check is based on speakers' intuitions, which may be very subtle; while in the case of past stages, it may be very rough.

Such limitations as these may hinder our comprehension of single examples, and in many cases we will have to give up on supplying a complete analysis of a structure, for lack of relevant information.

Nevertheless, the main lines of the system of Latin word order take shape quite clearly even on the basis of this limited evidence. The formal approach, of which we have sketched out some of the principal guidelines, may contribute to a deeper understanding of this complex system.

Notes

* I am very grateful to Renato Oniga, who has read a previous version of this study and provided me with some insightful suggestions and some crucial examples. My thanks to Eric Southworth and to Judit Tapazdi for their help with the English text.

[1] Instead of the plainer: *ipse fortis in meam poenam valui.*

[2] Instead of the normal: *...le orme indecenti del calzar polveroso impresse in sui tapeti.* See Roggia (2003) for these stylistic reorderings in Italian poetry.

[3] See also Oniga (2007: 199-206).

[4] These grammatical judgements reflect my own usage. For other speakers all six permutations might be grammatical (see e.g. Cinque 1997), but that does not change the essence of my point. For a general view of Italian word order, see Salvi and Vanelli (2004: 297-313).

[5] Cf. also *nihil* in (6).

[6] Note the colloquial Italian translation: *Ne è nata tra loro una grande, di controversia*, with a similar splitting and the same distribution of information.

[7] For the problems related to the identification and treatment of weak elements in Latin and to their position in the sentence structure, see Salvi (2004: ch. 4); cf. also Devine and Stephens (2006: 3.3).

[8] Cf. also Devine and Stephens (2006: 330).

[9] Devine and Stephens (2006: 2.2) also speak of verbs in second position: in our analysis, their examples are cases of a nearly final verb followed by a focused constituent.

[10] For an explanation, see Salvi (2004: II.2.2) and Devine and Stephens (2006: 1.7 and 2.2).

[11] In the following discussion we neglect certain pieces of formalism not relevant to our point; these are explained in the general reference works on Generative Grammar and, in a simplified way, also in Salvi (2004: 3-10) and in Giusti and Oniga (this volume).

[12] The basic ordering of indirect object and direct object is controversial since Latin can quite freely vary the order of the elements in the kernel of the sentence (a phenomenon called *scrambling* in the generative literature). Mainly for theoretical reasons (see Kayne 2005: 5.2.6), here I adopt the position of Elerick (1990). But for discussion see Salvi (2004: fn. 44) and, for an alternative point of view, see Devine and Stephens (2006: 1.2), Oniga (2007: 177).

[13] Most of the examples used stem from these works, but have been augmented, where necessary, by examples from our own research.

[14] Giusti and Oniga (2006) convincingly argue that subjective genitive and objective genitive occupy different positions in the (deep) structure of the Latin noun phrase. In our own discussion we treat only problems relative to the pairing of word order and pragmatic functions on surface structure, and so omit reference to this difference here.

[15] This order is possible in poetry: *sanguine cum soceri* (Ov. *met.* 14,799) 'with the blood of the father-in-law'.

[16] This order is possible in poetry: *sedibus in patriis* (Ov. *trist.* 1,1,34) 'in my homeland', and in prose it is used by Livy: *aciemque per mediam* (Liv. 9,43,15) 'and through the middle of the line'.

[17] József Herman used to say that this was the only rule of Latin word order - a rather defeatist position, as I hope I have shown in this study.

[18] We cite also examples in which the elements are not contiguous, as (43b) and others below, because the hyperbaton does not modify the structural relations between the words: if *X... YZ* was possible, *XYZ* was possible, too. See Devine and Stephens (2006: ch. 6) for discussion.

[19] But *N-Q* is attested, too: *illa sensus omnis expertia* (Curt. 6,3,7) 'those things which lack any sensitivity'.

[20] Our search has taken in all the relevant classical prose works, but unfortunately we have not been able to extend it to other quantifiers with the same function, such as *paulo* 'a little', *quanto* 'how much' and *tanto* 'so much'. See also Devine and Stephens (2006: 578-583).

[21] Renato Oniga has brought to my attention the following examples from Livy with *A-Q-N* order: *Lucretius cum ingenti praeda,* maiore multo gloria *rediit* (Liv. 3,10,1) 'Lucretius returned with vast spoils and *far greater glory*', *Camillus* meliore multo laude *quam cum triumphantem albi per urbem vexerant equi insignis, iustitia fideque hostibus victis cum in urbem redisset, taciti eius verecundiam non tulit senatus quin sine mora voti liberaretur* (Liv. 5,28,1) 'Camillus, having returned to the City distinguished *by a far better kind of glory* than when he had entered it in triumph drawn by white horses —for he had conquered his enemies by justice and fair-dealing —uttered no reproaches, but the senators were ill-at-ease till they should free him, without delay, from the obligation of his vow'. I am inclined to ascribe this permutation to Livy's "poetic" style (see also fn. 16 above), but other solutions are possible (e.g. a parenthetical interpretation for *multo*). A more detailed inquiry is required on this topic.

[22] In a more elaborated model of NP structure, N could have reached its initial position by movement from a position after the modifier. We omit discussion of

this possibility here for the sake of simplicity, but see Giusti and Oniga (2006) for a discussion.
[23] This derivation can be applied to (48b), too, and is assumed to be the way sentence final focus is derived in Romance languages (Zubizarreta 1998: ch. 3).
[24] It might be assumed that these permutations are variants of *Num-N-A* and *A-N-Num*, respectively, with N preposed into a position for topics, a position assumed by Devine and Stephens (2006: 4.2-3) to be present in the structure of phrases, too. The relevant APs would be interpreted as 'measured in feet, its length is sixty' (52b), 'measured in feet, their width is four' (54a), 'as for his age, he was about twenty' (54b). But we will not examine this question further here.
[25] Devine and Stephens (2006: 517-518) assume that *Q-Dem* and *Dem-Q* correspond to two different positions for the quantifier and, consequently, to two different types of quantification (strong and weak). It is not clear to us how the distinction between strong and weak quantification, possible in the case of quantifiers such as *multi* 'many' (498-499), may be applied to a universal quantifier (see the discussion in Heim 1987: 21-24); furthermore the interpretation of the relevant examples does not seem to support such a distinction.
[26] Where the choice of the written code by itself severly limits the range of possible utterance types.

References

Cinque, G. (1997) "L'italiano (Mesa redonda: L'ordre des mots dans les langues romanes)", in R. Lorenzo (ed.) *Actas do XIX Congreso Internacional de Lingüística e Filoloxía Románicas. Universidade de Santiago de Compostela, 1989*, vol. I, A Coruña, Fundación Barrié, 1107-1114.

Devine, A.M. and L.D. Stephens (2006) *Latin Word Order. Structured meaning and information*, Oxford-New York, Oxford University Press.

Elerick, C. (1990) "Latin as an SDOV Language: The Evidence from Cicero", in G. Calboli (ed.) *Papers on Grammar III*, Bologna, CLUEB, 1-17.

É. Kiss, K. (1998) "Identificational focus versus information focus" *Language* 74: 245-273.

Giusti, G. and R. Oniga (2006) "La struttura del sintagma nominale latino", in R. Oniga and L. Zennaro (eds) *Atti della Giornata di Linguistica Latina. Venezia, 7 maggio 2004*, Venezia, Cafoscarina, 71-100.

Giusti, G. and R. Oniga (this volume) "Why Formal Linguistics for the Teaching of Latin?", 1-20.

Heim, I. (1987) "Where Does the Definiteness Restriction Apply? Evidence from the Definiteness of Variables", in E.J. Reuland and

A.G.B. ter Meulen (eds) *The Representation of (In)definiteness*, Cambridge, Mass., MIT Press, 21-42.

Hofmann, J.B. and A. Szantyr (1965) *Lateinische Syntax und Stilistik*, München, Beck.

Kayne, R.S. (2005) *Movement and Silence*, Oxford-New York, Oxford University Press.

Kühner, R. and C. Stegmann (1955) *Ausführliche Grammatik der lateinischen Sprache*, II: *Satzlehre*, 1. Teil, 3. Auflage, Leverkusen, Gottschalk.

Oniga, R. (2007) *Il latino. Breve introduzione linguistica*, 2ª ed., Milano, Franco Angeli.

Ostafin, D.M. (1986) *Studies in Latin Word Order: A Transformational Approach*, doctoral dissertation, University of Connecticut, Storrs.

Pinkster, H. (1988) *Lateinische Syntax und Semantik*, Tübingen, Francke.

Roggia, C.E. (2003) "Sintassi dell'*ordo verborum artificialis*. Preliminari ad una indagine sulla poesia del Settecento" *Studi Linguistici Italiani* 29: 161-182.

Salvi, G. (2004) *La formazione della struttura di frase romanza. Ordine delle parole e clitici dal latino alle lingue romanze antiche*, Tübingen, Niemeyer.

Salvi, G. and L. Vanelli (2004) *Nuova grammatica italiana*, Bologna, il Mulino.

Zubizarreta, M.L. (1998) *Prosody, Focus, and Word Order*, Cambridge, Mass., MIT Press.

WORD ORDER IN LATIN NOMINAL EXPRESSIONS: THE SYNTAX OF DEMONSTRATIVES

ROSSELLA IOVINO

Introduction and aims

In this paper I analyse the syntax of Latin demonstratives (DEMs) *hic*, *ille*, *iste*, within the framework of generative grammar.[1] The data show that DEMs display many similarities but also some substantial differences among each other.

I argue that the freedom in the arrangement of the elements in Latin nominal expressions (NEs) is only apparent and due to a non-systematic analysis of the data, which does not take into account the distinction between basic and marked orders, the latter being derived by syntactic movement. In particular, following Giusti (1993; 1997) and Oniga (2007), I show that DEMs are always in the highest specifier of the NE, namely, in SpecDP. In addition, I demonstrate that *ille* but not the other demonstratives can introduce an adjective in complex appositive structures.

Beyond the theoretical contribution, I will also suggest at various points in the paper how linguistic theory can be useful in updating Latin grammars for classroom activities.

1. The corpus

To consider the syntax of Latin DEMs in a diachronic perspective, I will refer to a corpus of data selected from the literary production of authors active from the end of the 3rd century BC to the beginning of the 4th century AD.

I consider simple nominal expressions (SNEs) and complex nominal expressions (CNEs) separately. The former consist of just a DEM and a N (such as *homo hic* or *ille vir*), whereas the latter include at least one other element, such as a possessive, a numeral and/or one (or more) adjectives (*haec magna diligentia*; *illa iudicia senatoria*). We will observe how this separation is useful to make certain properties emerge from the quantitative analysis. In particular, I give a quantitative analysis of SNEs gathered in selected texts of Plautus, Cicero, Livy, Seneca, Tacitus, Gellius, Ammianus Marcellinus and St. Augustine. As for CNEs, which are numerically less frequent in Latin, I extend the comparative survey to the larger corpus collected by the *B(ibliotheca) T(eubneriana) L(atina)*.

2. The data

2.1. Word order in SNEs

Hic is attested with roughly the same frequency as *ille* (namely 131 times for the former and 125 times for the latter) in the texts belonging to the archaic and classical-imperial period (3rd BC-2nd AD). *Iste* on the other hand, presents a lower number of occurrences (only 21 cases). This is illustrated in Table 1:

Hic, haec, hoc 131 (47%)		Ille, illa, illud 125 (46%)		Iste, ista, istud 21 (7%)	
Hic > N (94%) 123	N > *hic* 8 (6%)	*Ille* > N 101 (81%)	N > *ille* 24 (19%)	*Iste* > N 16 (76%)	N > *iste* 5 (24%)
Total 277					
44,5%	2,8%	36,5%	8,6%	5,8%	1,8%

Table 1 (3rd BC-2nd AD)

As for their position, *hic*, *ille* and *iste* precede the noun in very high percentages (respectively 94%, 81% and 76%). This suggests that the prenominal position for DEM constitutes a 'rule', which could (and maybe should) find space in Latin reference grammars. In particular, I suggest a new definition of 'rule' as a generalization which can be formulated not only from observable data, but also interpreting the mental processes that produce them in Universal Grammar. In this sense, the rule is not an *ipse dixit* to accept without criticism. There are however cases in which DEM can be postnominal, e.g. (1):

(1)   a.   *actor **hic** /ratio **haec** /verbum **hoc***
        b.   *moderator **ille**/res publica **illa**/nomen **illud***
        c.   *liber **iste**/laus **ista**/iudicium **istum***

From a purely statistical point of view, Table 1 shows that *hic* (8/131; 6%; 2,8% of the total) and *iste* (5/21; 24%; 1,8% of the total) are postnominal in a very small number of cases, while *ille* can follow the noun more frequently (24/125; 19%; 8,6% of the total). In all cases, the postnominal position is statistically marked with respect to the prenominal one.

The late imperial period (3rd-4th AD) shows a rise of postnominal positions:

Hic, haec, hoc		Ille, illa, illud		Iste, ista, istud	
137 (48%)		87 (31%)		59 (21%)	
Hic > N	N > *hic*	*Ille* > N	N > *ille*	*Iste* > N	N > *Iste*
118 (87%)	19 (13%)	48 (55%)	39 (45%)	39 (66%)	20 (34%)
Total 283					
41,7%	6,7%	17%	13,8%	13,8%	7%

Table 2 (3rd – 4th AD)

The postnominal occurrences of both *hic* and *ille* are, in fact, doubled (6% → 13%; 19% → 45%). This process also involves *iste* which follows the noun in 34% of the occurrences, compared with 24% of the archaic and classical-imperial period.

2.2. Word order in CNEs

A DEM can occupy different positions in CNEs. At first glance, this phenomenon may contribute to reinforce the idea that Latin word order is totally free. Nevertheless, this hypothesis will be rejected, confirming Marouzeau's (1922:1) observation that "l'ordre des mots en latin est libre, il n'est pas indifférent". I will argue instead that, starting from a basic unmarked order, the different surface orders are obtained by syntactic movement or remerge (cf. Giusti and Oniga (this volume) fn. 3) of an item from a lower base position into a higher derived one.

The data collected below represent a corpus consisting of 262 CNEs. In this sample, DEM precedes a possessive in 6% of the occurrences (16/262), as in (2):

(2) a. **Hunc suum** *dolorem* (Cic. *Sext.* 32)   DEM>POSS>N
     b. **Illam meam** *cladem* (Cic. *Sext.* 31)
     c. **Ista sua** *sponte* (Cic. *fin.* 1.25)

It precedes a numeral in 12% of the occurrences (30/262), as in (3):

(3) a. **Huic uni** *crimini* (Cic. *Cluent.* 48)   DEM>NUM>N
     b. **Illum primum** *motum* (Cic. *Lael.* 29)
     c. **Isti duo** *adulescentes* (Naev. *fr.* 83)

It precedes descriptive adjectives in 37,5% of the occurrences (97/262), independent of the semantic class to which the adjective belongs (Cinque 1994, 2010; Scott 2002), as in (4):

(4) a. **His tantis**$_{[quantity]}$ *sceleribus* (Cic. *Cluent.* 29)   DEM>ADJ>N
     b. **His novis**$_{[age]}$ *civibus* (Liv. 6,4,4)
     c. **Hoc insaestimabile**$_{[evaluation]}$ *bonum* (Sen. *nat.* 1,4)
     d. **Illum dentatum**$_{[physic property]}$ *virum* (Plaut. *Pseud.* 1040)
     e. **Ista divina**$_{[classifier]}$ *studia* (Cic. *sen.* 24)
     f. **Istum magnum**$_{[dimension]}$ *hominem* (Cic. *Deiot.* 23)

DEM can also immediately precede the noun (55/262; 20%), in turn followed by an adjective, a cardinal or ordinal numeral, or a possessive, as in (5), (6), (7):

(5) a. **Hanc virginem** *adultam*$_{[age]}$ (Liv. 3,44,4)   DEM>N>ADJ
     b. **Haec urbs** *praeclara*$_{[evaluation]}$ (Cic. *Mil.* 93)
     c. **Illum adulescentem** *Oppianicum*$_{[origin]}$ (Cic. *Cluent.* 21)
     d. **Illa iudicia** *senatoria*$_{[classifier]}$ (Cic. *Cluent.* 60)
     e. **In isto artificio** *accusatorio*$_{[purpose]}$ (Cic. *S.Rosc.* 49)

(6) a. **Hic pagus** *unus* (Caes. *Gall.* 1,12,5)   DEM>N>NUM
     b. **Hoc crimen** *primum* (Cic. *Mil.* 50)

(7) a. **Huius iudicis** *nostri* (Cic. *Mil.* 16)   DEM>N>POSS
     b. **Ille amicus** *noster* (Gell. 5,21,9)

In the CNEs presented so far, which make 75,5% of the occurrences, DEM occupies the first position. However, it is also possible to find it in second position, following an adjective (35/262, 13,5%), as in (8), following a possessive (8/262; 3%), as in (9) and following a numeral (6/262; 2%), as in (10):

(8) a. **Maximam**$_{[dimension]}$ **hanc** *rem* (Liv. 6,41,8)   ADJ>DEM>N
     b. **Equestria**$_{[classifier]}$ **haec** *spolia* (Liv. 8,7,13)
     c. **Ex vetere**$_{[age]}$ **illa** *disciplina* (Cic. *Cluent.* 76)
     d. **Miserum**$_{[evaluation]}$ **istum** *puerum* (Apul. *apol.* 85)

(9) a. ***Noster hic*** *populus* (Cic. *rep.* 3,24)   POSS>DEM>N
    b. ***Meum illum*** *casum* (Cic. *Sext.* 53)
    c. ***Tuus iste*** *Stoicus sapiens* (Cic. *ac.* 119)

(10) a. ***Una haec*** *pugna* (Liv. 8,30,7)   NUM>DEM>N
     b. ***Tres illi*** *fratres* (Apul. *met.* 9,35)
     c. ***Duo isti*** *Graeci versiculi* (Gell. 19,11,1)

Notice that in all combinations of DEM with another modifier of the noun, the highest number of cases have DEM preceding the other modifier.

From these data, the placement of DEM appears to demonstrate considerable freedom even if this freedom is limited to prenominal position. But, it is possible to find some NEs in which DEM occurs postnominally. However, the data show that only *ille* can appear after the noun in the CNEs (15/262; 6%), as in (11)-(12):

(11) a. ***Cato ille*** *noster* (Cic. *Att.* 2,5,1)
     b. ***Medicum illum*** *suum* (Cic. *Cluent.* 40)

(12) a. ***Terram illam*** *beatam* (Cic. *Mil.* 105)
     b. ***Bello illo*** *maximo* (Cic. *rep.* 1,25)

Furthermore, in all the above cases, *ille* is followed by a possessive or a descriptive adjective, and never by a numeral or a quantifier.

3. A unified syntactic theory of Latin DEMs

In this section, I deal with the entire phenomenology of the data observed so far, both in SNEs and in CNEs, within a unified theory.

3.1. The categorial *status* of DEMs

Following Giusti (1993, 1997), I assume that DEM is a maximal projection which occupies the specifier of a functional projection. Giusti (1993, 1997) observes that in some languages DEM can co-occur with an article (ART), as in (13):

(13) a. **autòs o** anèr (this the man) Dem > Art > N   (Modern Greek)
     b. **ez a** ház (this the house) Dem > Art > N   (Hungarian)
     c. **toj** covek-**ot** (this man-the) Dem >N > Art   (Macedonian)
     d. om**ul acesta** (man-the this) N > Art > Dem   (Romanian)

For this reason, Giusti (1997, 2002) proposes that DEM and ART do not realize the same syntactic features and are merged in different structural positions. In particular, studying data from Romanian, Giusti (1993, 1997) proposes that the article is inserted in the head D, while DEM is inserted into the specifier of a functional projection (FP) adjacent to NP. DEM can be realized either in the lower position or in the higher position, being moved to SpecDP:

(14) a. **Băiatul acesta** (frumos) $[_{DP} [_{D°}$ N-art $[_{FP}$ **Dem** $[_{NP}$ N̶]]]
         boy-the this nice
         "this nice boy"
     b. **Acest** (frumos) **băiat** (frumos) $[_{DP}$ **Dem** $[_{FP}$ D̶e̶m̶ $[_{NP}$ N]]]
         this (nice) boy (nice)
         "this nice boy"

In (14a) the noun appears in D because it incorporates the enclitic article, while DEM remains *in situ*; on the contrary, in (14b) DEM raises to SpecDP. As concerns Latin, Oniga (2007: 95) suggests that also in this language DEMs are modifiers of the noun.

Furthermore, Brugè (1996) notes that not only in Romanian but also in Spanish, DEM can be both prenominal and postnominal (*este libro/el libro este*). In this perspective Brugè (1996) proposes that also in Spanish DEM can either remain *in situ* or move into SpecDP, to check the referentiality of the NE:[2]

(15) a. $[_{SpecDP}$ Ø ... $[_{D°}$ *el* $[_{AgrP} [_{Agr°}$ *libro* $[_{FP}$ **este** ... $[_{NP} [_{N'} [_{N°}$ *l̶i̶b̶r̶o̶*]]]]]]]]
     b. $[_{SpecDP}$ **este** ... $[_{AgrP} [_{Agr°}$ *libro* $[_{FP}$ e̶s̶t̶e̶ ... $[_{NP} [_{N'} [_{N°}$ *l̶i̶b̶r̶o̶*]]]]]]]

In (15a) DEM remains in its merge position and the presence of an article in D is obligatory, on the contrary, in (15b) DEM moves into SpecDP, so the article remains overt. Notice that the low position of DEM in Spanish must be lower than in Romanian, since it allows for the noun to move across it, even if Spanish N does not move to D (because the article is not an affix).

3.2. The absence of the article and the syntax of DEMs

The Romanian and Spanish data demonstrate that the presence of an article has important consequences for the syntax of the demonstrative. In the absence of an article, the Latin data presented above, in which DEM occurs prenominally in the great majority of cases, can be taken to show that in Latin DEM is always in SpecDP, as expressed in (16):[3]

(16) a. [$_{SpecDP}$ *hic* [$_{NP}$ *homo*]]
   b. [$_{SpecDP}$ *ille* [$_{NP}$ *vir*]]
   c. [$_{SpecDP}$ *iste* [$_{NP}$ *liber*]]

The case of SNEs, in which DEM follows the noun (see Table 1), have a marked interpretation as already noted by Marouzeau (1922) and recently stressed by Devine and Stephens (2006). They observe, in fact, that "the main trigger for the postnominal demonstrative in [...] deictic and anaphoric examples [...] is the semantics of the demonstrative. While the noun is occasionally pragmatically marked, in most cases it is not" (pg. 514). This suggests that SNEs showing a postnominal demonstrative should be derived assuming that the noun moves to the left of DEM, namely to the periphery of the nominal expression (cf. Giusti 1996, Giusti and Oniga 2007, Salvi this volume), as in (17):

(17) a. [$_{TopP}$ *Actor* [$_{SpecDP}$ *hic* [$_{AgrP}$ ... [$_{NP}$ ~~*actor*~~]]]]
   b. [$_{TopP}$ *Moderator* [$_{SpecDP}$ *ille* [$_{AgrP}$ ...[$_{NP}$ ~~*moderator*~~]]]]
   c. [$_{TopP}$ *Liber* [$_{SpecDP}$ *iste* [$_{AgrP}$ ...[$_{NP}$ ~~*liber*~~]]]]

The crucial point is that in the absence of an article, Latin *requires* that the DEM be inserted in SpecDP. In this perspective, DEM shows the same semantic properties both when it precedes the noun and when it follows it. The further movement of N to the left periphery is due to the dislocation to the left of an item, for reasons of information structure and may account for the 'mise en relief'. In this way the 'rule' previously identified on an the quantitative empirical basis (§ 2.1) can now be explained from the theoretical point of view.

3.3. The syntax of *hic* (and *iste*) in CNEs

In this section, I argue that DEM occurs in SpecDP, also in CNEs. In (18) I give all the possible orders for *hic*. For reason of space, I do not give the corresponding data for *iste* (which are attested, however). In CNEs, DEM occurs in first (18a-f) or second position (18g-i), but always precedes N:

(18) a. ***Hunc** suum dolorem* (Cic. *Sext.* 32)   **DEM** > POSS > N
   b. ***Huic** uni crimini* (Cic. *Cluent.* 48)   **DEM** > NUM > N
   c. ***Haec** magna diligentia* (Plaut. *Rud.* 820)   **DEM** > ADJ > N

    d. ***Hanc*** *virginem adultam* (Liv. 3,44,4)   **DEM** > N > ADJ
    e. ***Hic*** *pagus unus* (Caes. *Gall.* 1,12,5)   **DEM** > N > NUM
    f. ***Huius*** *iudicis nostri* (Cic. *Mil.* 16)   **DEM** > N > POSS
    g. *Maximam* ***hanc*** *rem* (Liv. 6,41,8)   **ADJ** > DEM > N
    h. *Noster* ***hic*** *populus* (Cic. *rep.* 3,24)   **POSS** > DEM > N
    i. *Una* ***haec*** *pugna* (Liv. 8,30,7)   **NUM** > DEM > N

The syntactic structures for each possible order are given in (19). As for
the cases in which DEM occurs in second position (19g-i), I propose the
activation of the left periphery of the NE, as suggested for SNEs above.

(19) a. [$_{SpecDP}$ ***hunc*** [$_{AgrP}$ *suum* [$_{AgrP}$ *dolorem* …]]]
    b. [$_{SpecDP}$ ***huic*** [$_{NumP}$ *uni* [$_{AgrP}$ *crimini* …]]]
    c. [$_{SpecDP}$ ***haec*** [$_{AP}$ *magna* [$_{AgrP}$ *diligentia* …]]]
    d. [$_{SpecDP}$ ***hanc*** [$_{AgrP}$ *virginem* [$_{AP}$ *adultam* …]]]
    e. [$_{SpecDP}$ ***hic*** [$_{AgrP}$ *pagus* [$_{NumP}$ *unus* …]]]^4
    f. [$_{SpecDP}$ ***huius*** [$_{AgrP}$ *iudicis* [$_{ZP}$ *nostri* …]]]
    g. [$_{TopP}$ *maximam* [$_{SpecDP}$ ***hanc*** [$_{AgrP}$ *rem* …]]]
    h. [$_{TopP}$ *noster* [$_{SpecDP}$ ***hic*** [$_{AgrP}$ *populus* …]]]
    i. [$_{TopP}$ *una* [$_{SpecDP}$ ***haec*** [$_{AgrP}$ *pugna* …]]]

Interestingly, and quite surprisingly, the corpus does not show instances of
CNEs in which either *hic* or *iste* is postnominal. A larger corpus is needed
to make sure that this gap is not accidental. But we tentatively take it as
being significant and calling for an explanation. This will be done in the
next section. Up to now our hypothesis that in Latin DEM is always in
SpecDP has been confirmed by marked and unmarked cases.^{5}

3.4. The syntax of *ille* in CNEs

The orders presented in (18) and analysed in (19) are shared by the three
DEM (*hic*; *iste*; *ille*), as noted in §2.2 from a purely empirical perspective.
Ille occurs in an additional syntactic position: it is, in fact, the only DEM
which can follow the noun in CNEs, as it can be seen in (20):

(20) a. ***Medicum illum*** *suum* (Cic. *Cluent.* 40)   N > **DEM** >POSS
    b. ***Causam illam*** *integram* (Cic. *Sext.* 70)   N > **DEM** >ADJ
    c. ***Vim illam*** *nefariam* (Cic. *Sext.* 76)   N > **DEM** >ADJ
    d. ***Lectum illum*** *genialem* (Cic. *Cluent.* 14)   N > **DEM** >ADJ
    e. ***Terram illam*** *beatam* (Cic. *Mil.* 105)   N > **DEM** >ADJ
    f. ***Bello illo*** *maximo* (Cic. *rep.* 1,25)   N > **DEM** >ADJ

g. *Piraeus ille* magnificus (Cic. *rep*. 3,44)   N > **DEM** >ADJ
h. *Stillicidia illa* infinita (Sen. *nat*. 1,3,6)   N > **DEM** >ADJ
i. *Aetas illa* simplicior (Sen. *nat*. 1,17,5)   N > **DEM** >ADJ
l. *Sonus ille* celestis (Sen. *nat*. 2,27,3)   N > **DEM** >ADJ
m. *Chilo ille* sapiens (Gell. 1,3,17)   N > **DEM** >ADJ
n. *Librum illum* divinum (Gell. 2,18,2)   N > **DEM** >ADJ
o. *Vitam illam* tranquillam (Cic. *Cluent*. 153)   N > **DEM** >ADJ

Notice that in postnominal position *ille* can only be followed by an adjective that could also be found as a predicate (after a copula).[6] Despite the limited number of examples, I take this as not just chance, and propose an account in comparative perspective. In fact, similar structures are found in other Indo-European languages.

It is also relevant to compare these instances of *ille* with the Romance definite article, which has developed from the weakening of DEM (cf. Renzi (1976) and for an analysis in the generative framework Giusti (2001)) and the special adjectival article *cel/cea* which can be found in Romanian (Cornilescu 1992, Giusti 1993, Coene 1999).

In describing Old High German, Ramat (1984) argues that DEMs and postnominal relative pronouns (which in SOV languages refer to a known referent) share the same origin, so it is possible to assume a basic construction of the type N DET ADJ. Ramat (1984) adds that the determiner can be both a DEM or a REL, depending on the context. Obviously, it can also be an ART. This hypothesis sheds light on Latin NEs of the type N-*ille*-ADJ, that seem to coincide perfectly with the basic construction proposed by Ramat (1984). A Latin NE such as *Chilo ille sapiens* refers, in fact, to a known referent and can be (not surprisingly) paraphrased in Italian with a DEM (21a) or with a relative (21b) or with an article (21c), as shown below:

(21) *Chilo ille sapiens*
      a. Chilone, quello sapiente (Chilon, the sapient one)
      b. Chilone, che è sapiente (Chilon, who is sapient)
      c. Chilone il sapiente (Chilon the sapient)

This Latin structure has been preserved in Romanian. Coene (1999) has observed that in this peripheral Romance language, a noun can be joined to 'bare adjectives' (22a), but it can also be preceded by the so-called 'DEM-article' *cel* (22b):

(22) a. *Profesoar-ă bătrână*
         Teacher-the old
         "the old teacher"
     b. *Profesoar-ă **cea** bătrână*
         Teacher-the the old
         "the old teacher"

It is interesting to observe that the restriction in the use of *cel* is the same as the one found in Latin for the postnominal use of *ille*. In fact, Cornilescu (1992) and Giusti (1993) point out that in Romanian *cel* can only introduce predicative adjectives. This can be seen in the contrast between the grammaticality of *cel* in (23a) and its ungrammaticality in (23b). In the latter, the presence of *cel* is inhibited by the presence of a following classifier adjective, which cannot be used with a predicative value:

(23) a. *Demnitarul cel înalt*   Cornilescu (1992: 222)
         official the tall/*high
         "the tall official"
     b. *omul (*cel) biet*
         man-the (the) pitiable
         "the poor man"

Coene (1999) proposes that in the Romanian structures N+*cel*+ADJ, the noun, being known, moves to the left periphery of the NE. This can also be assumed for the Latin structure N+*ille*+ADJ. Furthermore, exactly like *cel*, also *ille* is a morphologically rich determiner, which, together with the adjective, gives rise to an appositive DP, which modifies the noun. This is represented in the following structure:

(24) [$_{DP/TopP}$ NP [$_{AgrP}$ [$_{DP}$ *ille* ADJ Nø] [$_{NP}$ N̶P̶]

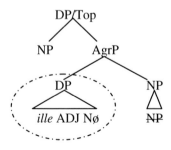

This proposal maintains the categorial *status* of DEM as a specifier of a functional projection, its general position in SpecDP, and at the same time, distinguishes structures like N+*ille*+ADJ, in which DEM introduces an 'appositive DP' from structures in which a 'simple DEM' is present. In this analysis, 'appositive DEM' and 'simple DEM' occur in different syntactic positions, inserted at different levels of the syntactic tree.

Conclusion

In this paper, I have shown how the tools of modern linguistics in general, and of generative grammar in particular, can be useful to the study of classical languages. In particular, referring to a few theoretical points can be of great help in approaching the *vexata quaestio* of word order within Latin NEs. Such an approach focuses on grammar, conceived as the science of language and not as a set of rules to learn by heart. Studying Latin in this perspective allows us to observe that all the syntactic elements are inserted in precise positions of a coherent syntactic structure, which the generative grammar has showed to be universal, and is similar to modern languages, some of which may be also known by the student. It would be desirable that not only specialists, but also school teachers could use such a formal approach.

This research obviously leaves some questions open. First of all, it is not clear why NP-topicalization can take place across a DEM in SNEs (17), but not in CNEs (18)-(19). Second, it is not clear whether noun movement across a simple ADJ or across a complex modifier such as [*ille*+(predicative) ADJ] is movement of the same kind or not. At the present I do not have answers for these questions, which I leave for future research.

Notes

* I thank Renato Oniga and Giuliana Giusti for their support and advice, without which none of this would have been possible.

[1] Among the works that apply the theory of generative grammar approach to the study of Latin, cf. e.g. Cecchetto and Oniga (2002); Oniga (2007); Polo (2005); Salvi (2004; 2005); Zennaro (2006); and Giusti and Oniga (2004; 2007).

[2] In the framework of Cinque (1994), Brugè (1996) suggests that in both structures in (16) the nominal heads move from its merge position (N°) into the head of a functional projection, which verifies the agreement with the other elements of the phrase.

[3] In Cinque (2010)'s terms, the syntactic movement of the noun is understood as specifier movement and not as a head movement.
[4] As for the order Dem > Num, Devine and Stephens (2006: 497) observe that "in the neutral order the demonstrative c-commands the number phrase as in English".
[5] It can also be observed that the position of the Latin DEM is similar but not identical to that of the article in Romance languages. The article, in fact, was 'born' after a process of weakening of *ille* (Giusti 1998).
[6] According to Cinque (2010), the predicative adjective can be defined as an 'indirect modification adjective', used as the predicate of a reduced relative clause.

References

Brugè, L. (1996) "Demonstratives movement in Spanish: A comparative approach" *University of Venice Working Papers in Linguistics* 6.1: 1-53.

Cecchetto, C. and R. Oniga (2002) "Consequences of the Analysis of Latin infinitival Clauses for the Theory of Case and Control" *Lingue e Linguaggio* 1: 151-189.

Cinque, G. (1994) "On the Evidence for Partial N-Movement in the Romance DP", in G. Cinque, J. Koster, J.-Y. Pollock, L. Rizzi and R. Zanuttini (eds) *Paths Towards Universal Grammar. Studies in Honor of Richard Kayne* Washington, Georgetown University Press, 85-110.

—. (2010) *The Syntax of Adjectives. A Comparative Study*, Cambridge (Mass.), MIT Press.

Coene, M. (1999) *Definite Null Nominals in Romanian and Spanish*, PhD diss., ms. Univesiteit Antwerpen.

Cornilescu, A. (1992) "Remarks on the determiner system of Rumanian: the DEM *al* and *cel*" *Probus* 4: 189-260.

Devine, A.M. and L.D. Stephens (2006) *Latin Word Order. Structured meaning and information*, Oxford-New York, Oxford University Press.

Giusti, G. (1993) *La sintassi dei determinanti*, Padova, Unipress.

—. (1996) "Is there a FocusP and a TopicP in the Noun Phrase structure?" *University of Venice Working Papers in Linguistics* 6.2: 105-128.

—. (1997) "The Categorial Status of Determiners", in L. Haegeman (ed.) *The New Comparative Syntax*, London, Longman, 95-123.

—. (2001) "The birth of a functional category: from Latin ILLE to the Romance article and personal pronoun" in Cinque G. and G. Salvi (eds) *Current Studies in Italian Syntax: Essays offered to Lorenzo Renzi*, Amsterdam, North-Holland, 157-171.

Giusti, G. and R. Oniga (2006) "La struttura del sintagma nominale latino", in R. Oniga and L. Zennaro (eds) *Atti della "Giornata di*

Linguistica Latina", *Venezia, 7 maggio 2004*, Venezia, Cafoscarina, 71-100.
—. (2007) "Core and Periphery in the Latin Noun Phrase", in G. Purnelle and J. Denooz (eds) *Ordre et cohérence en Latin,* Communications présentées au 13ᵉ Colloque international de Linguistique latine (Bruxelles-Liège, 4-9 avril 2005), Genève, Droz, 81-95.
—. (this volume) "Why Formal Linguistics for the Teaching of Latin?", 1-20.
Harris, M. (1980) "The marking of definiteness in Romance" in J. Fisiak (ed.) *Historical Morphology*, Berlin, Mouton de Gruyter, 141-156.
Marouzeau, J. (1922) *L'ordre de mots dans la phrase latine. I: Les groupes nominaux*, Paris, Champion.
Oniga, R. (2007) *Il latino. Breve introduzione linguistica*, 2ᵃ ed., Milano, Franco Angeli.
Panhuis, D. (1982) *The Communicative Perspective in the Sentence: A Study of Latin Word Order*, Amsterdam, Benjamins.
Polo, C. (2005) "Latin word order in generative perspective: An explanatory proposal within the sentence domain", in K. É. Kiss (ed.) *Universal Grammar in the Reconstruction of Ancient Languages*, Berlin, Mouton de Gruyter.
Ramat, P. (1984) "La nascita di nuove categorie morfologiche: il caso dell'articolo e del pronome relativo nelle lingue germaniche", in *Linguistica tipologica*, Bologna, il Mulino, 117-135.
—. (1986) *Introduzione alla linguistica germanica*, Bologna, il Mulino.
Renzi, L. (1976) "Grammatica e storia dell'articolo italiano" *Studi di grammatica italiana* 5: 5-42.
Salvi, G. (2004) *La formazione della struttura di frase romanza. Ordine delle parole e clitici dal latino alle lingue romanze antiche*, Tübingen, Niemeyer.
—. (2005) "Some firm points on Latin word order: The left periphery", in K. É Kiss (ed.) *Universal Grammar in the Reconstruction of Ancient Languages*, Berlin, Mouton de Gruyter.
Scott, J. G. (2002) "The Stacked Adjectival Modification and the Structure of Nominal Phrases", in G. Cinque (ed.) *Functional Structure in DP and IP*, Oxford, Oxford University Press, 91-115.
Zennaro, L. (2006) *La sintassi dei verbi a ristrutturazione in latino*, PhD diss., ms. University Ca' Foscari of Venice, available online at http://lear.unive.it/bitstream/10278/261/1/Atti-3-10s-Zennaro.pdf.

THEORETICAL AND APPLIED PERSPECTIVES IN THE TEACHING OF LATIN SYNTAX: ON THE PARTICULAR QUESTION OF WORD ORDER

CONCEPCIÓN CABRILLANA

Introduction and structure

This paper is intended to present an approach to word order in the area of knowledge studied by the academic subject Latin Syntax.

The configuration of this issue, i.e. the way we deem it should be put forward, was partly developed during the preparation of a recently published handbook on Latin Syntax.[1] The material disclosed herein[2] has undergone certain modifications affecting, mainly, the structure of the contents and it has been organised as follows: after explaining the concept of word order (§ 1) and the main perspectives of analysis (§ 2), this question will be further developed taking as a starting point the data from the multifarious types of texts in different stages (§ 3) so as to take the diachronic approach as a basis, and provide an account of the eventually interrelated factors that explain, distinctly, the different phenomena concerning word order (§ 4). It is here that the innovating character of this type of presentation lies, for it combines the advantages of theoretical research and the results of the analysis of the written material.

1. The starting point: the concept of word order

The starting point must be, logically enough, the definition of the concept of word order itself, which could be briefly outlined as: a non-arbitrary sequence – given the linear character of the linguistic sign – of lexical units, more or less strictly regulated, in order to enable communication.

Two aspects that, generally speaking, converge systematically in every language all over the world[3] are the syntactic and the informative or pragmatic aspect. Yet, the relevance and the pre-eminence of each of these aspects does not have to be the same in all languages; in inflective languages, such as Latin, word order is less relevant (and, hence, more variable) from the syntactic point of view than in modern languages such as English or Spanish, where the relative order of constituents is in itself a feature of syntactic characterisation.

Broadly speaking, it may be said that syntactic order is modified or influenced by pragmatic and textual reasons; although, since the latter depend on the communicative interactions of speakers in each specific moment, they cannot be reduced to mere statistic data. Hence, it is difficult to establish (strict) norms regarding word order in a textual, literary language such as Latin and this explains the controversies this matter has raised and keeps raising among scholars.

Thus, in order to facilitate a well-grounded comprehension of this complex question, it is useful to list the most relevant analyses carried out over the last few years. In this regard, it seemed more advantageous to structure the presentation of the status quo of this topic following the main approaches developed[4] so far before undertaking the analysis of the more and less essential constituents subject to different arrangements. Then, the paper goes through the main points that must be referred to when alluding to the basic postulates established or adopted by the major theoretical-methodological approaches.

2. Major perspectives of analysis

2.1. Descriptive and structural studies

At this point, it is necessary to mention Linde's work (1923) on the verb-final position, a position that, in general, tends to appear less often as more diachronic samples[5] are provided by the author. Yet, it has been mainly Marouzeau's work that has determined, to a great extent, the approach to word order in Latin during the first half of the 20th century and even some time later on; from among his abundant contributions, his idea that word order in Latin is free yet not indifferent might be the reference that has been identified with his work more frequently. Besides, Marouzeau starts, *a priori,* from the existence of a marked order versus an unmarked one and then places the question of word order as a matter halfway between syntax and stylistics, consigning the communicative intention of the speaker to exceptional cases of "mise en relief".

From a formally structuralist perspective, Rubio (1982) agrees with Marouzeau in considering a marked / unmarked word ordering, but he thinks that 'no question is more properly syntactic' than the question of word order in Latin (1982: 191). The 'general rules' governing it (1982: 199-200) could be summarised[6] as follows:

> "1. The predicative syntagm. -Usually, the subject appears in sentence-initial position and the predicate closes the sentence.
> 2. Determinative syntagm. -Determinants usually precede the determined element. This norm applies to the different variants of the determinative syntagm: be it an adverb-verb syntagm, an adjective-noun syntagm or a syntagm consisting of a noun depending on a verb or on another noun.
> 3. Prepositions precede the noun they govern; conjunctions precede the elements they link."

Still, things are neither so simple nor so clear as they appear to be; and this is proved by the long list of exceptions to the *ordo rectus* pointed out by Rubio (1982: 203-217). As we shall prove, neither can word order in Latin be reduced to such simple "rules", nor can we consign many of the "transgressions" of those previously-established norms to stylistic reasons.

2.2. Typological approach

Greenberg's work (1963) marked a clear point of inflection in the typological approach. His formulation of implicative universals, based upon the study of 30 different languages, establishes the correspondence between the arrangement of the elements that are considered essential in a sentence (S, O, V) and a series of syntactic features such as the existence of Prepositions (Prep.) or Postpositions (Post.), the order of Adjectives (A) or Relatives (Rel) with regards to Nouns (N), the expression of comparison, etc.

Latin was not one of the languages studied by Greenberg; and Tovar (1979) tried to establish a relationship between the afore-mentioned universals and the word order rules put forward by Rubio, as shown in Table 1:[7]

Table 1. Inclusion of Latin in Greenberg's typological table

	SOV	SVO	VSO
Post. + A-N	6	1	-
Post. + N-A	5	2	-
Prep. + A-N	**1 (Latin)**	4	-
Prep. + N-A	-	6	6

As can be seen in the table, if Rubio's norms are accepted, Latin would not correspond, from a typological point of view, to any of the 30 languages analysed by Greenberg; hence – according to Tovar – it would be necessary to modify some of its regularities.

Considering these and other discrepancies, the implicative character of Greenberg's "universals" has been reformulated and clarified in different studies on linguistic typology where the lack of agreement[8] comes as no surprise. The reason for these discrepancies lies, to a great extent, in the differences between the data and text types offered by the different Latin authors and, mainly, in the analysis and interpretation of those data.

2.3. Functional approach

The studies carried out from a functional perspective are intended to show the parallelism between (grammatical) word order and the order of ideas; and they insist on the relevance of pragmatic and textual conditioning in word order.

In order to differentiate, on the one hand, the basic notion of known, presupposed or shared information – by the interlocutors – and, on the other hand, that of new or informationally relevant contents, it seems more adequate to resort to the concepts of Topic and Focus – formerly Theme and Rheme – because, on top of these two basic pragmatic functions, which are syntactically integrated in the predication, two more syntactically extra-clausal functions (which are, notwithstanding, linked to the said predication from a semantic and pragmatic point of view) can be distinguished in certain cases: the Theme (which presents a universe of discourse with regards to which whatever the predication states is relevant) and the Tail (which presents information intended to clarify or modify some of the constituents in the predication, as an "additional afterthought"). These functions are roughly illustrated by the examples in (1):

(1)   a.   *de Tadiana re,*$_{\text{Theme}}$ mecum *Tadius*$_{\text{Topic}}$ locutus est te ita scripsisse,
          nihil esse iam quod laboraretur$_{\text{Focus}}$ (Cic. *Att.* 1,5,6)
          "in that matter about Tadius' property, he tells me you have
          written him that there is no necessity for him to trouble any more
          about it"

      b.   ibi pauca extare circa *uestigia*$_{\text{Term specified by the Tail}}$ habitati quondam
          soli, *uinearum palmetorumque reliquias*$_{\text{Tail}}$ (Plin. *nat.* 5,13)
          "and there are to be seen the certain tokens of a soil formerly
          inhabited, the vestiges of vineyards and date-tree groves"

There are at least two essential facts that, generally speaking, must be taken into account when considering word order from a pragmatic perspective: (i) both in the linguistic discourse and in the subsequent information processing procedure, any given element limits the one preceding it at an informational level, which explains why the usual informational arrangement is a Topic-Focus one; (ii) the structural (syntactic) order and the informative (pragmatic) order do not need to coincide. In general, the informative distribution prevails over the syntactic one.

Especially in an inflective language as Latin, pragmatic and discursive conditionings could be judged to play an essential role in word order: let us consider (among others, with regards to sentence-initial position) the role of relative pronouns, phrase connectors[9] or adverbs and anaphoric pronouns. Moreover, Theme constituents appear, due to their pragmatic function (they create the frame in which a predication is interpreted), in sentence-initial position: prepositional phrases with *de* + abl. (2a), *quod* + ind. sentences (2a), infinitive constructions (2b), the *nominatiuus pendens* (2c), or the so-called anacoluthon or "left-dislocations" (2d) are not ungrammatical phenomena, as they are sometimes believed to be, but pragmatic arrangements that appear in many languages:

(2)   a.   *quod ad me scribis de sorore tua*, testis erit tibi ipsa, quantae mihi curae fuerit… (Cic. *Att.* 1,5,4)
"as to your sister, now that you mention her, she herself will tell you the pains I have taken…"
   b.   *cur amem me castigare*, id ponito ad compendium (Plaut. *Cas.* 517)
"as for lecturing me for being in love, cut that short"
   c.   *plebes* incredibile memoratu est quam *ea* intenta fuerit (Sall. *Iug.* 40,3)
"but as to the people, it's incredible what eagerness they displayed"
   d.   uerum *meam uxorem*, Libane, nescis qualis sit? (Plaut. *Asin.* 60)
"but my wife, Libanus, don't you know how she is?"

3. Data analysis

Taking into account the incoherencies observed between the explanatory theories and the linguistic data, it seems necessary to devote a section to the description and analysis of those very data, both at sentence level (§ 3.1) and at the level of the noun phrase (§ 3.2).

3.1. Sentence level: basic elements

In this section, we will only focus on the analysis of the elements considered essential at sentence level;[10] a summary of several individual studies is offered in table 2:

Table 2. Relative position of S(ubject), O(bject) and V(erb)[11]

	OV	VO	SOV	SV	VSO	OSV	VOS	OVS	
S.C. Bacc.	100/100	-/-	100/100	-	-	-	-	-	Álvarez-P. 1988
Leges II BC	96.2 / 96	3.8 / 4	93.5 / 96	3.8	-	2.5/4	-	-	Álvarez-P. 1988
Terence	67	33							Moreno 1989
Caes. *Gall.* 1	73/90	26/9							Panchón 1986
Cic. *Mil.*	54/71	45/28							Panchón 1986
Cic. *Att.* 1	81	19	53.6	5.5	1.4	27.7	0.5	1.4	Cabrillana 1993b
Celsus	86.7	13.3	61.5	4.8	-	7.2	8.4	18.1	Pinkster 1992
Pompeian Inscrip.	64.2	35.8	56.8	33.6	1.1	2.1	1.1	5.3	Ramat 1984
Petronius *Cena Trim.*	57.6/82 69	42.4/18 31	47.6	19	6.5	15.2	5.6	6.1	Hinojo 1985
Vulg. Joel	(+)	+							G. Fuente 1983
Vetus, Rut	9.8	90.2							Talavera 1981
Per. Aeth.	38.5	61.5	19.8	40	17.6	6.4	13.3	2.9	Hinojo 1986
Chiron.	79.5	20.5							Cabrillana 1999
Anon.Vale. 2- 6th c.	41.2	58,8							Adams 1976b
Braulius 8th c.	76.5 68.2/79.5	23.5 31.8/20.5	46.5	17.7	3.8	20.1	1.7	10.2	G.Sanchidrián 1994
Libellus 10th c.	61.9/67.6	38.1/32.4	53.6	23.8	1.6	11.1	1.6	8.4	Carrera 1983

In an initial approach to these data, the features of each of the texts analysed can be briefly commented on, focusing, mainly, on the basic OV / VO ordering, in order to trace the diachronic evolution of Latin.

Thus, the data show quite clearly that Archaic Latin is almost exclusively reduced to the OV type; some attempts to explain this rigidity[12] appeal to the fact that these are archaic inscriptions and that they belong to a genre – the legal genre – that is archaic by default and prone to more or less fixed arrangements and commonplaces.

A similar parallelism can be drawn for classical Latin (observance of a basic SOV ordering, although with less rigidity). This reflection is relevant because authors such as Adams (1976a) state that in Plautus' language, taken as a reflection of colloquial Latin, a typological change SOV > SVO had already taken place, which means that Classical Latin would maintain an "artificial", archaic, conservative ordering (namely, SOV), utterly unrelated to spoken Latin (Adams, 1976a: 93). This hypothesis seems hardly plausible: on the one hand, in Plautus the most frequent order is OV;[13] on the other hand, it is difficult to explain the VO/OV alternation in Plautus by defining it as a constant change in register (colloquial/literary). The main reason, though, is that this type of processes tends to be gradual.[14] Besides, the fact that the VO order is relatively frequent in Plautus can partly be explained by resorting to pragmatic, textual reasons, rather than to syntactic or typological ones: as opposed to mostly narrative texts in classical prose, where textual cohesion and the maintenance of one single perspective are essential features, the language of comedy, due to its dialogue-based nature, is more prone to frequent changes between Topic and Focus, which accounts for many a phenomenon concerning word order. Furthermore, in the language of comedy, there is greater variety of phrasal modality and a higher frequency, for instance, of impressive or interrogative phrases, in which the verb shows a different order.[15] In the case of classical Latin, the comparison between Caesar's data (*Gall.* 1), those taken from the speeches (*Mil.*) and correspondence (*Att.* 1) of Cicero or from Celsus's technical work also prove up to which extent the different text types affect word order.

As to Vulgar and Late Latin, we must make a difference between the data from prototypically vulgar[16] works and word order in biblical texts. Thus, for instance, in the episode of Trimalchio's feast, considered closer to spoken language, a higher frequency of the VO order could be expected; yet, statistics shows that the percentages resemble those in the rest of the work, which makes Hinojo (1985: 249) conclude that Petronius's language still belongs to an OV type, although this word order is not so predominant as in other Latin authors from different periods. Nevertheless, the *Satiricon* does not only differ from Caesar or Tacitus, but also from late works such as the *Peregrinatio* or the *Anonymus Valesianus II*; therefore, Petronius' language would be "halfway between classical and literary authors and late and vulgar authors";[17] and it seems to be a good example of the gradual nature of the change in syntactic order in Latin (OV > VO). The contrast between these texts and the instances of technical prose is also significant: in two texts from the same period (*Peregr.* and *Chiron.*), the percentages show opposite trends, which could be a new proof of the "conservative" tendency of more technical language and, hence, of the influence of the different text types.

Finally, in Medieval Latin, a natural extension of Late Latin (3rd to 6th century A.D.), word order change to VO would have been completed, as can be seen in romance languages. Notwithstanding, this turns to be a simplistic formulation if we analyse, for instance, two medieval Spanish texts: S. Braulius *Epistles*, 8th century, and the *Libellus a Regula Sancti Benedicti subtractus*, a monastic rule from the 10th century built upon elements taken from different types of Latin. In both cases, in spite of the fact that these are religious texts, it is not the word order of biblical LatinVO, but that of classical literary Latin OV that the authors intend to observe.

3.2. Noun Phrase level: A(djective), N(oun) and G(enitive)

Table 3 displays data from a corpus including relevant texts from the point of view of word order in the NP.[18] The interpretation of these data will be divided into two sections: the clarifications that can be pointed out regarding the generic group A(djective)-N(oun) (§ 3.2.1) and those affecting the G(enitive)-N(oun) group (§ 3.2.2).

3.2.1. Adjective and Noun

As to the position of A, in general, a tendency to pre-position (AN) can be observed, and it appears even in late medieval texts whose intention is to preserve the order of literary Latin. In fact, leaving aside those biblical texts (*Vulg. Joel, Vetus Ruth*) in which the order of the original Hebrew version is literally translated (either directly or indirectly), only a few vulgar texts show a gradual process towards an NA arrangement.

Still, the global data are explained when the different categories of adnominal modifiers that have proved relevant in typological studies[19] about word order in noun phrase are specified. This is so because the type of features denoted by demonstratives or quantifiers are very different from those of adjectives, properly called, although the label "adjective" comprises sometimes any element establishing a concordance relationship with the nucleus of the noun phrase.

Table 3. Relative position of A(djective), N(oun) and G(enitive)

	A-N	N-A	qualif.	dem.	pos.	quant.	G-N	N-G	
S.C. Bacc.	+	(+)	5/7	3/-	2/-	7/-	41.7	58.3	Álvarez-P. 1988
Leges, II B.C.	+	(+)	18/84	335/1	5/6	51/25	54.2	45.8	Álvarez-P. 1988
Terence	+	(+)	+/ (+)	+ / (-)	(-) / +		+	(+)	Moreno 1989
Caes. *Gall.* 1	78	21		+ / (-)	+ / (-)	+ /(+)	48.5	51.5	Panchón 1986
Cic. *Mil.*	73	26		+ / (-)	+ / (-)	+ /(+)	50.6	49.4	Panchón 1986
Sall. *Catil.*	59.3	40.6					42.5	57.4	Gutiérrez 1994
Cic. *Att.* 1	67.1	32.9	24.8/ 15.4	19.8/ 3.4	12.6/ 11.8	1.4/ 0.3	42.5	57.5	Cabrillana 1993c
Cic. *de orat.*	+	(+)	60.2/ 39.8	88.5/ 11.5	45.7/ 54.3	83/17	40.2	59.8	Lisón 2001
Liv. 26-28	+	(+)	60.2/ 39.8	92.9/ 7.1	22.7/ 77.3	86.2/ 13.8	47.7	52.3	Lisón 2001
Sen. *epist.* 1-5	+	(+)	73.2/ 26.8	91.5/ 8.5	45.6/ 54.4	92/8			Lisón 2001
Petronius *Cena Trim.*	62.5 45.2	37.5 54.8					46.2 42	53.8 58	Hinojo 1985
Per. Aeth.	32	68					7.5	92.5	Hinojo 1986
Vulg. Joel	38.5	61.5	39/61	-/4	-/72	-/1	-	100	G. Fuente 1983
Braulius, 8th c.	58.9	41.1					45.8	54.2	G. Sanchid. 1994
Medieval Latin							48	52	Hinojo 2000

According to the data in Table 3, most of the authors do not make a distinction or do not specify whether the label "adjective" involves both categories. Yet, this distinction is relevant because, apart from expressing different semantic contents and of presenting different distributional features, its position in the noun phrase is not the same.

Thus, generally speaking, it must be said that the first adnominal category (quantifiers and pronouns) usually precedes the N (on occasions the difference is minimum), with the sole exception of possessives.[20] Yet, as far as adjectives properly called are concerned, the situation is not so clear and both pre-position[21] and postposition are advocated in their case, unless pragmatic[22] factors converge. Still, both statements may be further explained. Perhaps, instead of considering whether A comes before N or not, it might be more suitable to consider that one adjective acquires, at least in some cases, a different value depending on whether it precedes or follows the noun (*res publica / publica res*).

In this regard, there are data[23] that prove that the more subjective an adjective is (for instance, when it expresses a gradable or comparable feature), the more frequently it precedes the noun and vice versa,[24] and, hence, the sequence NA would be the unmarked order.[25]

Of course, the disjunction or distance between A and N is, on many occasions, relevant, and may be determined by contextual and semantic reasons; thus, it is relatively normal for adjectives with a special semantic/intensive content (*summus*, *magnus*, etc.), usually subjective, to come first. The example in (3) is a good sample of the relevance of this type of pragmatic conditioning: the adjective *uno*, which, due to its very meaning brings the noun it determines to the focus, acquires a greater communicative dynamism as it is dissociated from its nucleus and it appears in anastrophe:

(3)   Nam nos ex omnibus molestiis et laboribus *uno illo in loco* conquiescimus (Cic. *Att.* 1,5,7)
      "it is the only place I find restful after a hard day's work"

3.2.2. Genitive and Noun

With regards to the Genitive, the data in Table 3 clearly show that, except in late vulgar texts (*Peregrinatio*), the two possible dispositions (GN or NG) are equally frequent;[26] this might explain why this is one of the less studied aspects of word order in Latin.[27]

Just as in the case of adjectives, it is hardly operative to talk about an unmarked or habitual order considering these global data. Still, in Latin, as in Greek,[28] the semantic differences might be relevant, just as in the case of adjectives. In fact, descriptive studies already pointed out certain distribution criteria. Thus, Marouzeau (1922), for instance, explains that the GN order is not found in the case of partitive genitives, possessives and gerunds. In this regard, the recent study by Devine and Stephens (2006: 352-356) refers to the presupposed usual order in certain terms in the genitive that, like cases of unalienable possessions, designate kinship (*filius*), while other terms (*uxor*, *auunculus*, *patruus*) tend to appear after the element they complement. Yet, more statistical data would be required with regards to this issue, as well as a study focusing not only on the work of a single author.

4. Main factors determining word order

4.1. Previous clarifications

Considering both the more and less general data that can be provided for word order analysis, it is useful to present a non-exhaustive review of the factors that influence word order to a greater or to a lesser extent. Hence, a sort of 'abstraction' of some of the data offered so far is included next.

But before going further into this matter, it must be pointed out that the lack of agreement between scholars about the main motivation of the different phenomena concerning word order lies, mostly,[29] in the fact that an emphasis has been exclusively made on a specific approach,[30] whereas only the joint consideration of the different levels involved will make it possible to pose an "integrated theory" on word order in Latin.[31]

Besides, word order goes beyond sentence level taken as a syntactic unit, which is the usual context of analysis, and many of its features can be explained at the wider level of text and textual cohesion.[32] Still, leaving aside these generalizations, the relevance of text type, the importance of the pragmatic conditionings of each specific context or of the different stylistic elements, it is possible to single out some of the main factors that should be taken into account when analysing word order in a given Latin text.

4.2. Relative and absolute positions: S position

What has been said about S position is a good example of the simplification that has been present in certain studies so far. Considering that in continuous texts S is not usually explicitly stated, we must clarify statements that defend that Subject "appears in sentence-initial position" (cf. § 1.1). Since in many texts there is no explicit S, another sentence constituent appears in sentence initial position. But, even if the Subject is made explicit, it does not necessarily have to be constantly placed in sentence-initial position. As a matter of fact, sentence-initial position is basically influenced by textual and pragmatic reasons: S will appear in sentence-initial position depending on the specific pragmatic function it is assigned (Topic or contrastive Focus) and not on the mere fact of being the Subject. The position of S is also influenced by its semantic nature (anaphoric pronouns behave differently from proper nouns).

Considering these two facts, it should be said that S does not occupy an absolute (initial) position in the sentence; instead, when it appears explicitly, it usually precedes the Object, which in turn precedes the Verb, except when a different order is prompted by either pragmatic or semantic reasons.

The relative character of word order is also exemplified by the fact that the presence of a term in the predication can influence the relative order of the other ones. Thus, for instance, it has been proved[33] that the presence of O increases the tendency of S to appear before V, but not the other way round.

4.3. Pragmatic and semantic factors: V position

As far as V position is concerned and leaving aside the question of subordinate sentences with finite verbs (which in fact seem to present a clear tendency to sentence-final V position), in main sentences it is not possible to turn Rubio's statement affirming that "predicates close the sentence" into a rule. Linde's (1923) established data, which basically coincide with more recent studies,[34] are significant enough and reveal substantial differences between authors, genres and text types.

But these global data must be clarified: sentence modality (assertive, interrogative, and impressive) is a sheer corrective factor.[35] In fact, as has also been proved for Latin,[36] it is rather habitual in different languages for V in imperative sentences (commands, wishes, concessions, etc.), versus declarative ones, and also, though less often, in interrogative ones to appear in sentence-initial position due to pragmatic reasons, to a great extent, since it presents the most relevant information.

Considering declarative sentences only, the less frequent word orders are mostly prompted by pragmatic factors; thus, V sentence-initial position may be associated with the pragmatic function of the contrastive Focus (4a-b) or it may also serve to mark a narrative discontinuity when the author wants to call our attention on a new event (5):

(4)   a.   *est*, *est* illa uis profecto (Cic. *Mil.* 84)
           "there is, there is indeed, such a heavenly power"
      b.   *uidi enim*, *uidi* penitusque *perspexi* in meis variis temporibus et
           sollicitudines et laetitias tuas (Cic. *Att.* 1,17,6)
           "for I have seen – I have seen and attested on many an occasion
           in my life – both your sorrow and your joy in my changing
           fortunes"

(5)   *Intercedit* M. Antonius, Q. Cassius, tribuni plebis (Caes. *civ.* 1,2,1)
      "M. Antonius and Q. Cassius, tribunes of the people, opposed their
      negative to this decree"

Indeed, verb initial word order does not always involve its focalisation. This is the case of the so-called presentative sentences, in which a new entity, which is bound to become the Topic,[37] is introduced in the discourse by using verbs that express existence, such as *esse, apparere, relinquere, manere*, etc. Given this context, VS word order becomes the normal one, as proved by examples in (6), and it is not the verb (V) but the subject (S) that is focalized and then referred to as a Topic in the following relative clause:

(6)   a.   *Est* in carcere *locus*, *quod* Tullianum appellatur, *ubi…*(Sall. *Catil.* 55,3)
         "there is a place in the prison, which is called the Tullian dungeon, and which…"
      b.   *relinquebatur una* per Sequanos *uia, qua…* (Caes. *Gall.* 1,9,1)
         "there was left one way, [namely] through the Sequani, by which…"

Apart from pragmatic reasons, the semantic and syntactic nature of verbs is also relevant. The copulative, intransitive or passive nature of verbs has to do, in a way, with their position in the sentence or with the relative order of the rest of the constituents. Thus, although in many cases specific research with sufficiently significant data corpora is required, it can be generally said that it is in fact in sentences without O (intransitive sentences, copulative sentences or sentences with monovalent predicates) where a greater tendency for V to appear in sentence-initial position[38] can be observed; as is the case in most existential-locative sentences.[39]

4.4. Constituent type, complexity and hierarchical level

There is a fact that usually remains unconsidered, namely, the heterogeneous nature and the syntactic complexity of the constituents. Thus, for instance, when establishing the O/V order, if the O function is expressed through an accusative, OV is certainly the usual word order; but the contrary happens if the said function is fulfilled by a subordinate clause with *ut* + subj.[40] Thus, it seems clear that in such cases, apart from the categorial difference (noun [or prepositional] phrase versus the subordinate clause), the syntactic complexity of the element, whatever it may be, influences its relative position in the sentence.[41] Evidently enough, in sentences such as (7a) and (7b), the different position of *mitto* is prompted by the complexity of the final complement:

(7)   a. his pontibus pabulatum *mittebat* (Caes. *civ.* 1,40,1)
          "over these bridges he kept sending supplies"
      b. nuntios *mittit* ut sibi subsidio uenirent (Caes. *civ.* 3,80,3)
          "[Caesar] sends messengers [to Scipio and Pompeius] asking
          them to come to his aid"

It is also very important to take the syntactic level in which the satellites
are inserted into account in order to justify their relative position in the
sentence. As is well known, certain satellites (Adjuncts) complement the
predicate as a whole (V + arguments + other satellites) placing, for
instance, a given status quo against the background of certain specific
coordinates –either temporal or spatial, etc. This is the case of *interim* and
Romae in (8a). It is not by chance (and no stylistic reasons should be seen
in this) that in similar noun phrases such as *eo die, illo tempore,* etc.
ablative absolute (8b) and "*cum*" clauses, or subordinate clauses with *dum*
+ ind. (8c) appear frequently in sentence-initial position, thus influencing
the relative order of the terms of the sentence they are complementing:

(8)   a. *interim Romae* C. Manilius Limetanus tribunus plebis rogationem
          ad populum promulgat (Sall. *Iug.* 40,1)
          "meanwhile, at Rome, Gaius Mamilius Limetanus, tribune of the
          commons, proposed to the people a bill"
      b. *Anco regnante,* Lucumo… Romam commigrauit (Liv. 1,34,1)
          "during the reign of Ancus… Lucumo removed to Rome"
      c. *dum haec in conloquio geruntur,* Caesari nuntiatum est… (Caes.
          Gall. 1,46,1)
          "while these things are being transacted in the conference it was
          announced to Caesar that…"

Similarly, other types of satellites (Disjuncts) provide information about
the attitude of the speaker regarding the content (veracity) of a whole
sentence, about the way that content is expressed, about the structure and
expositive order of the text, about the dimension and the scope of a given
statement, and so on. Thus, it is usual for these disjuncts to appear in
sentence-initial position or, if anything, before or after the whole sentence
about which they are providing the information; this is the case of
examples in (9):

(9) a. *sine dubio*, iudices, in hac causa ea res in discrimen adducitur (Cic. *Verr.* II 1,6)
         "and, indeed, beyond all question, o judges, that matter depends on your decision in this cause"
     b. *secundum te* nihil est mihi amicius solitudine (Cic. *Att.* 12,15)
         "according to you I have not a greater friend than solitude"

From this perspective, some interesting tendencies are observed in Latin; thus, Ros (2005) points out that satellites, particularly when they are expressed by means of adverbial subordinate clauses, tend to appear in a more external position, preceding – in general – the whole predication.

This broad principle is influenced, in turn, by the iconicity principle: the position of the subordinate clause is an attempt to reflect its semantic nature iconically. Hence, prototypical conditional, concessive and temporal clauses (that is to say, those that play the role of adjunct satellites) precede the main clause from a logical and chronological point of view; and, as a result, they also precede the main clause from the point of view of word order. The opposite happens in the case of consecutive or final clauses.

Therefore, the semantic nature (iconicity principle), the level of syntactic integration (adjuncts vs. disjuncts) and the more or less marked communicative dynamism and cohesive capacity (Topic vs. Focus) are interrelated factors that contribute to the explanation of the position of an adverbial subordinate clause in a given textual situation.

Conclusion

To conclude, it can be said that an orderly exposition based upon the real situation, that is, upon the data provided by the analysis of the texts, and combining different perspectives and levels of analysis (syntactic, semantic, pragmatic, (con)textual, etc.) proves to be particularly clarifying, useful and adjusted to reality in order to explain word order in Latin.

Notes

[1] Baños (2009). On many cases, the different topics were developed in further detail thanks to the suggestions made by the students they were intended for, who had already been reading and working with previous online versions in the Liceus Web Portal (http://www.liceus.com/cgi-bin/aco/areas.asp?id_area=4).

[2] Taken, basically, from Baños and Cabrillana (2009).

[3] Moreno Cabrera (2000: 715).

[4] Cf. Cabrillana (1993a), Lisón (2001).

[5] From Cato to the *Peregrinatio*.

[6] My translation.

[7] Each figure in the table refers to the number of languages combining certain features.

[8] Cf. Cabrillana (1993a: 236-240). Apart from those who consider Latin an SOV language (Tovar, 1979; Hawkins, 1983), some (Adams, 1976a) defend - at least during the classical period – that in colloquial Latin the habitual word order was SVO, and some others (Panhuis, 1982) define Classical Latin as an ambivalent language.

[9] Cf. Pinkster (1995: 327-328).

[10] I will not go into other stricter arrangements (adverb-verb, preposition-governed element or conjunction-predicate) that present a high degree of regularity and where the deviations observed are duly explained by stylistic and informative factors.

[11] The corpus analysed by the aforementioned studies comprises texts that range from the *Lex XII Tabularum* (ca. 450 B.C.) to a text from the late Middle Ages, the *Libellus a Regula Sancti Benedicti subtractus* (10th century A.D.). Since the studies from which these data have been taken (last column on the right) follow very different criteria, it is necessary to make certain clarifications regarding constituent order in nominal syntagms that are also valid for Table 3:
(i) some authors do not provide any figures or percentages for some of the dispositions observed in the table, yet, they do provide indications in this regard; in such cases "+" marks the most frequent disposition, "(+)" a documented, significantly frequent disposition (more than 20%) and "(-)" or "-" a scarcely significant or nonexistent one;
(ii) when two figures are listed in the same box (57,5/82,0), they refer to the main and to the subordinate sentence, respectively; when only one figure appears, it means that this distinction has not been made;
(iii) the nature of the data compared is not always the same: some authors focus on main declarative clauses (Moreno, 1989), while most of them do not point out sentence modality; some others concentrate on the relative position of the V and the O, and there are some (Panchón, 1986) who focus on the absolute position of the verb in the sentence (final / non-final) regardless of its transitive or non-transitive nature;
(iv) when referring to arrangements such as SOV, SVO and so on, certain authors make an abstraction of the presence or absence of an explicit Subject, while some others (Hinojo, 1985; 1986) gather data from sentences with an explicit Subject only.

[12] Cf. Adams (1976a).

[13] Cf. Porzio (1986).

[14] As is proved by the fact that, for instance, the inscriptions in Pompey do not show a predominant SVO order – in spite of their proximity to the spoken registers – or by the fact that the data from Trimalchio's feast resemble those observed in Petronius work as a whole. Cf. Moreno (1989: 528).

[15] Cf. Pinkster (1995: 217).

[16] As Petronius *Satiricon*, the *Peregrinatio Egeriae* or the *Mulomedicina Chironis*.

[17] Hinojo (1985: 250); my translation.

[18] When two figures appear in the table (5/7) these may refer both to the absolute number of examples and to the percentages; the first figure refers to examples of preceding arrangements and the second one to examples of postponed dispositions. The rest of the indications coincide with those contemplated for these same cases in table 2.

[19] Cf. Rijkhoff (1997).

[20] Cf. Lisón (2001: 107-155).

[21] Cf. Rubio (1982: 199-200).

[22] Pinkster (1995: 239-240).

[23] Lisón (2001: 59-106).

[24] For an adjective referring to objective features the NA order is preferred (Lisón, 2001: 64).

[25] As Pinkster (1995: 240) points out.

[26] As opposed to Rubio (1972), who defended that GN was the unmarked position, or to Adams (1976a), who advocated for an NG order for Latin.

[27] Cf. Lisón (2001: 157).

[28] Where possessive or pertinentive genitives precede the noun (GN), while ablative or partitive genitives come after it (NG).

[29] Cf. Cabrillana (1993a: 250).

[30] Stylistic (Marouzeau), syntactic (Rubio), typological (Adams) or pragmatic (Panhuis).

[31] Cf. Molinelli (1986: 495). In spite of the fact that, at present, the idea that word order analysis must be "multifunctional" (Cabrillana 1996) is progressively becoming more widespread, the problem lies in defining the different factors, their scope and relevance in a given text which presents, in itself, features that are specific to the genre it belongs to; and it is also necessary to consider figures of speech or stylistic devices (chiasm, parallelism, prolepsis, anastrophe, alliteration, etc.) which, with more or less intensity and depending on each author's specific style, "distort" the regularity of a given position. All in all, the *variatio* principle is, to a lesser or greater extent, consubstantial to Latin literary texts.

[32] Cf. Pinkster (1995: 211-243).

[33] Cf. Cabrillana (1993b), at least for Cic. *Att.* 1.

[34] Cf. Panchón (1986: 215-217).

[35] Cf. Cabrillana (1999: 321-322).

[36] Cf. Pinkster (1995: 217).

[37] Cf. Spevak (2005).

[38] Cf. Bolkestein (1995).

[39] Cf. Devine and Stephens (2006: 150-151; 209; 213).

[40] Similarly, a final satellite such as *honoris causa/gratia* usually precedes the finite verb, whereas conjunctional subordinate clauses follow it.

[41] Cf. Pinkster (1995: 215). Even in the same subordinate clauses, the different formal types are associated to different positions (cf. Bolkestein, 1989a).

References

Adams, J.N. (1976a) "A Typological Approach to Latin Word Order" *Indogermanische Forschungen* 81: 70-99.

—. (1976b) *The Text and Language of a Vulgar Latin Chronicle (Anonymus Valesianus II)*, London, University.

Álvarez-Pedrosa, J.A. (1988) "Estudio comparado del orden de palabras en inscripciones jurídicas arcaicas griegas y latinas" *RSEL* 18(1): 109-128.

Baños, J.M. (ed.) (2009) *Sintaxis del latín clásico*, Madrid, Liceus.

Baños, J.M. and C. Cabrillana (2009) "Orden de palabras", in J.M. Baños (ed.) *Sintaxis del latín clásico*, Madrid, Liceus, 679-707.

Cabrillana, C. (1993a) "Panorama de los estudios sobre el orden de palabras en latín" *Minerva* 7: 223-254.

—. (1993b) "Posiciones relativas a la ordenación de constituyentes (I). Estudios de la posición de Sujeto, Objeto y Verbo en latín", *Habis* 24: 249-266.

—. (1993c) "Ordenación de constituyentes en la determinación adjetiva en latín" *Verba* 20: 399-412.

—. (1994) "Posiciones relativas en la ordenación de constituyentes (II). Estudio de la posición de Sujeto, Predicado Nominal y Verbo en latín" *Habis* 25: 451-460.

—. (1996a) "Multifunctional analysis of word order", in H. Rosén (ed.) *Aspects of Latin,* Innsbruck, Innsbruker Beiträge zur Sprachwissenschaft, 377-388.

—. (1999) "Type of Text, Pragmatic Function and Constituent Order: a Comparative Study between the *Mulomedicina Chironis* and the *Peregrinatio Egeriae*" in H. Petersmann and R. Kettemann (eds) *Latin vulgaire-latin tardif V*, Heidelberg, Winter, 319-330.

Carrera, M. (1983) "Orden de palabras en un texto latino alto-medieval" *RSEL* 13: 63-89.

Devine, A.M. and L.D. Stephens (2006) *Latin Word Order. Structured meaning and information*, Oxford-New York, Oxford University Press.

García de la Fuente, O. (1983) "Orden de palabras en hebreo, griego, latín y romanceamiento castellano medieval de Joel" *Emerita* 51: 41-61; 185-213.

García Sanchidrián, M.L. (1994) "El orden de palabras en las cartas de San Braulio" *Actas del VIII Congreso Español de Estudios Clásicos*, I, Madrid, Ediciones Clásicas, 549-553.

Greenberg, J.H. (1963) "Some Universals of Grammar with particular Reference to the Order of the Meaningful Elements" in J.H. Greenberg (ed.) *Universals of Language*, Cambridge (Mass.), MIT Press, 71-113.

Gutiérrez Galindo, M.A. (1994) "Latin word order and chiastic arrangements", *TEMA* 1: 163-195.

Hawkins, J.A. (1983) *Word Order Universals*, San Diego: Academic Press.

Hinojo, G. (1985) "Del orden de palabras en el *Satiricón*", in J.L. Melena, (ed.) *Symbolae Ludovico Mitxelena Septuagenario Oblatae*, Vitoria, UPV, 245-254.

—. (1986) "El orden de palabras en la *Peregrinatio Aetheriae*", *StudZam* 7: 81-87.

—. (2000) "El orden de palabras en el latín medieval", in M. Pérez González (ed.) *Actas del III Congreso Hispánico de Latín Medieval*, II, León: Universidad de León, 627-635.

Linde, P. (1923) "Die Stellung des Verbs in der lateinischen Prosa" *Glotta* 12: 153-178.

Lisón, N. (2001) *El orden de palabras en los grupos nominales en latín*, Zaragoza, Monografías de la Universidad de Zaragoza.

Marouzeau, J. (1922-1949) *L'ordre des mots dans la phrase latine*. I: *Les groupes nominaux*, Paris, Champion, 1922; II: *Le verbe*, Paris, Champion, 1938; III: *Les articulations de l'énoncé*, Paris Champion, 1949.

Molinelli, P. (1986) "L'ordine delle parole in latino: studi recenti" *Lingua e Stile* 21.2: 485-489.

Moreno, A. (1989) "Tipología lingüística y orden de palabras en el latín de Terencio", *Actas VII Congreso Español de Estudios Clásicos* I, Madrid, Ediciones Clásicas, 523-528.

Moreno Cabrera, J.C. (2000) *Curso Universitario de Lingüística General. Tomo I: Teoría de la gramática y sintaxis general* Madrid, Síntesis.

Panchón, F. (1986), "Orden de palabras en latín (Cesar, *BG*; Cic. *Pro Milone*)", *StudZam* 7: 213-29.

Panhuis, D. (1982) *The Communicative Perspective in the Sentence. A Study of Latin Word Order*, Amsterdam, Benjamins.

Pinkster, H. (1992) "Notes on the Syntax of Celsus" *Mnemosyne* 45.2: 513-524.

—. (1995) *Sintaxis y Semántica del latín*, Madrid, Ediciones Clásicas.

Porzio, M.L. (1986) "Latin Declension: A Theoretical and Methodological Approach" *Papers on Grammar* II: 1-18.

Ramat, P. (1984) "Per una tipologia del latino pompeiano" *Linguistica Tipologica*, Bologna, il Mulino, 137-142.

Rijkhoff, J. (1997) "Order in the Noun Phrase", in A. Siewierska (ed.) *Constituent Order in the Languages of Europe*, Berlin/New York, Mouton de Gruyter, 321-382.

Ros, H. (2005) "The position of satellites in Latin word order", in G. Calboli (ed.) *Papers on Grammar IX. Latina lingua!*, Roma, Herder, 681-694.

Rubio, L. (1982) *Introducción a la sintaxis estructural del latín*, Barcelona, Ariel.

Spevak, O. (2005), "A propos de '*uerbum primo loco*': essai de synthèse", in G. Calboli (ed.) *Papers on Grammar IX. Latina lingua!*, Roma, Herder, 731-740.

Talavera, F.J. (1981) "Aspectos vulgares de la Vetus Latina. Análisis especial del orden de palabras en el libro de Rut" *Analecta Malacitana* 4: 211-227.

Tovar, A. (1979) "Orden de las palabras y tipología: una nota sobre el latín" *Euphrosyne*, n. s. 9: 161-171.

CONTROL AND ACI IN CLASSICAL LATIN: STRUCTURAL INTERPRETATION PROBLEMS AND INNOVATIVE TENDENCIES

IMRE SZILÁGYI

Introduction

The aim of this study is to describe the interaction of the two basic infinitive constructions of classical Latin: the *accusativus cum infinitivo* (AcI) and the control structure, and to explore some of the reasons why the latter structure spread at the cost of the former in the Romance languages.

The control structure is one of the most important infinitive constructions of many modern languages. It can be illustrated with an Italian sentence, such as *Il ragazzo dice di aver letto il libro* 'The boy says (that) he has read the book'. According to studies dealing with this topic (see Graffi 1994: 7.4., Manzini, M. R. 1991, Radford 1988: 6.6., Salvi and Vanelli 2004: III.3.1.), in a sentence like this the interpretation of the unexpressed subject of the infinitive *aver letto* (also called PRO) is determined, or rather controlled, by one of the constituents of the main clause, in this case by the subject *il ragazzo*.

The Latin translation of the above example is *Puer dicit se librum legisse,* which shows the AcI, the most frequent infinitive structure in Latin. This three-part construction consists of 1) a main/governing verb (or *verbum regens*, here *dicit*), 2) an infinitive (*legisse*), and 3) an element in the accusative case (*se*) expressing the subject of the infinitive.

Since AcI is widely discussed in even the most elementary grammars dealing with Latin syntax, in the present study we will not go into further details regarding the background of this structure (see e.g. the detailed description in Menge 2000: 674-693). Notice only that, contrary to control, the subject of the infinitive is overt in the AcI even when it is coreferential with the subject of the superordinate clause (as is shown by the element *se* in our Latin example), but (also contrary to control) it allows for the expressibility of the subject of the infinitive in the case in which it is different from the subject of the governing verb.

1. Control structures in classical Latin

Although it is obvious that the AcI plays the leading role in classical Latin, we can also observe the phenomenon of control, as is shown in the examples below:

(1)   ... rem unam ex duabus facere *conamini* (Cic. *fin.* 2,20)

(2)   ... in colloquium venire [...] *gravaretur* (Caes. *Gall.* 1,35,2)

(3)   Darius [...] Scythis bellum inferre *decrevit* (Nep. *Milt.* 3,1)

(4)   (Albinus) commeatum stipendium [...] *maturat* in Africam portare (Sall. *Iug.* 36,1)

(5)   ... ingrati esse *vitemus* (Sen. *epist.* 81,22)

(6)   *Desii* iam de te esse sollicitus (Sen. *epist.* 82,1)

Apart from the verbs in italics in (1)-(6): *conor* 'try', *gravor* 'have difficulty doing sth.', *decerno* 'decide', *maturo* 'hurry', *vito* 'avoid' and *desino* 'finish', there are several other verbs which can be used in a control structure where the controller is the subject of the main verb, such as *audeo* 'dare', *contendo* 'strive', *instituo* 'start, take up', *disco* 'learn', *nitor* 'endeavor'. The control analysis is further confirmed in (5) and (6) by *ingrati* and *sollicitus*, the predicate complements in the nominative case (cf. the argumentation of Cecchetto and Oniga (2004), claiming that PRO inherits the case of the controller). In addition to this, we can also observe that all the above examples contain a present infinitive.

In a theoretical presentation of Latin control structures, Cecchetto and Oniga (2002) call the phenomenon of control a "problem of incompatibility". Briefly, they mean that in Latin the infinitive possesses the morphological feature [+T(ense)]; that is, it has three different tense forms and, according to the hypothesis of the authors, this [+T] feature is incompatible with PRO, which characterizes the control structure. This is why Latin prefers AcI and avoids control (cf. section 3), the latter being restricted exclusively to cases with a present infinitive.

The dominance of control observed in languages like Italian or English is due to the fact that the infinitive system of these modern languages can only have [-T]. This is supported by the total lack of future infinitive forms and the use of a periphrastic structure containing an auxiliary (e.g. Italian *aver amato*, English *have loved*) instead of the Latin synthetic perfect infinitive.

In Szilágyi (in press) we showed that the Latin verbs which govern a (subject) control structure form a well-defined group: they express the subject's wish, intention or ability with reference to an action which can only be carried out referring to the same subject (following our terminology, the subject of the main verb and the infinitive must be coreferential).

As for the time relation expressed by the infinitive, it means either simultaneity / immediate future realization, as is shown in all the examples above, or an atemporal value, as in (8a). The obligatory use of the present infinitive in control structures can be construed as an unmarked form used to express this restricted time-spectrum.

2. Alternation between control and AcI

In Bolkestein (1976) (serving as a starting point for, e.g. Pinkster 1990: 7.4.2., Menge 2000: 676, Cecchetto and Oniga 2002: 174), using several syntactic and semantic tests, the author shows that despite superficial structural similarity, a sentence like *dico te scribere* 'I say that you are writing' is an AcI structure, while a sentence such as *hortor te scribere* 'I encourage you to write' is a control structure. According to Bolkestein, in the former sentence the elements *dico* and *te* are not in an inherent syntactic-semantic relation, or rather the element *te* is not the object of the verb *dico*; in the latter sentence the same element is the object argument of the verb *hortor*.

In this section, we will examine cases in which the same verb, depending on the syntactic-semantic configuration, may appear both in AcI and in a control structure, and we will relate these alternations to what we have said about control structures in section 1, in order to establish more accurate differentiating criteria for these structures. Let us examine the two pairs of sentences below:

(7)   a.   si esse vis felix ... (Sen. *epist.* 31,2)
      b.   Ego Catilinam perire volui (Cic. *Phil.* 8,15)

(8)   a.   Nemo ergo scit praeter sapientem referre gratiam? (Sen. *epist.* 81,11)
      b.   Scio plerosque ita scripsisse ... (Nep. *Them.* 9,1)

While in sentences (7a) and (8a), which represent examples of control structures, one can observe all the characteristic features of the control construction established in section 1, the AcI structures in (7b) and (8b) do not share the same characteristics. Sentences (8) show clearly that the main verb *scio* has different semantic values: while in (8a) it expresses ability or aptitude to do something, as observed in section 1, in (8b) it means 'I know, as far as I know'. This strongly correlates with the fact that (8a) contains the present infinitive *referre*, giving the sentence an atemporal value, while the perfect infinitive *scripsisse* in (8b) expresses antecedence in relation to the event expressed by the main verb.

Furthermore, both in (7a) and (8a), the subject of the main verb is coreferential with the unexpressed subject of the infinitive; on the other hand, in (7b) and (8b), as cases of AcI, the subject of the infinitive is expressed separately in relation to the subject of the main verb, using an element in the accusative (*Catilinam* and *plerosque*). Finally, we can also observe that, parallel to (5) and (6), the predicate complement *felix* of (7a), which is a sentence with subject control, is in the nominative case as well.

3. Anti-control

In classical Latin, the predominance of AcI in relation to the control structure becomes evident even if we take into account that ancient authors often avoid the latter construction and use AcI instead, even when all the necessary conditions for its use are met. In Szilágyi (in press) we called this phenomenon 'anti-control'. Anti-control is established using the passive infinitive. Its most obvious cases contain the verb *volo/velle* 'want' (and its variants: *nolo* 'don't want' or *malo* 'prefer'). To illustrate this phenomenon, let us examine the following example:

(9) Quicquid est tale, non est ira, sed quasi ira, sicut puerorum, qui si ceciderunt, terram verberari volunt (Sen. *dial.* 3,2,5)

What is relevant to us in the above example is the part (*pueri*) *terram verberari volunt* 'the children want to beat the ground' (viz. as they are angry when they fall over). According to sections 1 and 2, in such examples we could fully expect to find active infinitives instead of passive ones (that is to say in (9) the form *verberare* instead of *verberari*), since from a logico-semantic point the subject of the main verb and the infinitive are obviously coreferential and in similar cases, as shown in (7a) in relation to the verb *volo/velle* itself, Latin can also use a control structure. However, the use of the passive infinitive *verberari* results in an AcI instead of a control structure, and its literal meaning 'the children want the ground to be beaten' corresponds to that of the control structure (as the syntactic subject of the conjugated verb *volunt* may imply 'by them'). The following two examples also illustrate anti-control (with the AcI structures highlighted):

(10) (Caesar) munitioni castrorum *tempus relinqui volebat* (Caes. *Gall.* 5,9,7)

(11) Id agamus, ut meliorem vitam sequamur quam volgus, non ut contrariam: alioquin *quos emendari volumus*, fugamus a nobis et avertimus (Sen. *epist.* 5,3)

In other examples the above mentioned main verbs are followed by active infinitives instead of passive ones; therefore they participate in a control structure, not in an AcI, as is shown in the examples below (with the relevant part of the control structure highlighted):

(12) Cum Artaxerxes Aegyptio regi *bellum inferre voluit* ...(Nep. *Iph.* 2,4)

(13) "Desilite" inquit, "milites, nisi *vultis aquilam* hostibus *prodere*" (Caes. *Gall.* 4,25,3)

(14) Eo deliciarum pervenimus, ut nisi *gemmas calcare nolimus* (Sen. *epist.* 86,7)

Comparing examples (9)-(11) with (12)-(14), we may conclude that in classical Latin, in relation to *volo/velle* (and its variants), the use of AcI or control structure is unpredictable. Notice that it is this unpredictability and the fact that the author (or the Latin native speaker) could freely choose which structure to use that distinguishes this phenomenon from the one discussed above in the previous section, where we could also observe the alternation between control and AcI, but where the choice of the structure is determined by grammatical rules, so one can predict which construction will be used. The example in (15) can also prove the unpredictability shown in this section, as in its first part we can find a control structure (cf. the active infinitive *violare* 'hurt'), while in the second part there is an AcI governed by the same main verb (cf. the passive infinitive *minui* 'decrease'):

(15) (Satrapes) *violare clementiam* quam regis *opes minui maluit* (Nep. *Alc.* 10,3)

Finally, we can state that other verbs can also show the phenomenon of anti-control. One of these verbs is *cupio* 'wish', which has all the characteristic features established in section 1 for control verbs, but it can participate in two different structures, illustrated by the examples below:

(16) Ego vero *te* quam primum, mea vita, *cupio videre* (Cic. *fam.* 14,4,1)

(17) ... qui *eum admoneri cupiebat* (Nep. *Paus.* 5,1)

While (16) contains an active construction (see the active infinitive *videre*) and a control structure with the verb under discussion, in (17) we find an AcI with the passive infinitive *admoneri*.

4. Some phenomena which might have contributed to the spreading of control

In the history from Latin to the Romance languages, the AcI almost entirely disappeared in favor of control structures. In this section, we will argue that even classical Latin had some inherent structural phenomena which were leading in this direction and which may have resulted in this evolution. As a starting point, we have to state that there is a strong interaction between synchrony and diachrony, and that on the basis of the synchronic state of a language one can draw conclusions both about some of its past processes and its future tendencies.

4.1. Impersonal constructions

After some impersonal verbs and impersonal constructions, such as *licet* 'it is permitted', *oportet/necesse est* 'it is necessary', Latin often uses AcI with a passive infinitive (highlighted by us), as seen below:

(18) Ad mortem te, Catilina, *duci* iussu consulis iam pridem oportebat (Cic. *Catil.* 1,1)

(19) ... declararent, utrum proelium *committi* ex usu esset necne (Caes. *Gall.* 1,50,4)

(20) Certiorem facit Datamen, tempus esse maiores res *parari* et bellum cum ipso rege *suscipi* (Nep. *Dat.* 11,1)

(21) Cum vero illa, quae officia esse dixi, proficiscantur ab initiis naturae, necesse est ea ad haec *referri* (Cic. *fin.* 3,22)

With impersonal verbs and constructions, however, we can often find an active infinitive instead of a passive one, as is shown in the examples below:

(22) ... quamquam haec quidem "praeposita" recte et "reiecta" *dicere* licebit (Cic. *fin.* 3,15)

(23) Quid enim necesse est […] voluptatem in virtutum concilium *adducere*? (Cic. *fin.* 2,12)

(24) Facinus est *vincire* civem Romanum (Cic. *Verr.* 5,170)

In our opinion, contrary to what we have seen in (18)-(21), examples (22)-(24) may have two structural interpretations: one can construe them as an AcI structure in which the subject of the infinitive is not expressed (cf. 4.3. (47)-(49)), or they are analysed as control structures with so-called arbitrary control (see the references listed in the Introduction). Impersonal constructions imply some unpredictability similar to that observed in the previous section with regard to verbs like *volo/velle*; however, there is a difference: here in the case of one of the variants even the structural interpretation is ambiguous.

Following a logical reasoning similar to (15) in the previous section, the example below shows that in just one sentence, one and the same impersonal verb (*attinet* 'serve') may involve both a passive (*dari*) and an active (*fingere*) construction, thus substantiating the above mentioned unpredictability:

(25) Quid attinet luxuriosis ullam exceptionem *dari* aut *fingere* aliquos, qui ... (Cic. *fin.* 2,21)

The constructions under discussion may contain an element in the dative case (or rather an indirect object), which can be construed as a controlling element. In Latin, control phenomena with indirect objects can be found apart from the above analysed structures, as is shown in the example below:

(26) Permitte mihi hoc loco referre versum tuum (Sen. *epist.* 24,19)

In this example, the element *mihi* can be interpreted as the controller of the unexpressed subject of the infinitive *referre*. Turning back to the impersonal constructions, in all the examples below the verb *licet* is accompanied by an element in the dative case (highlighted in italics), which can be construed as the controller of the subject of the infinitive:

(27) Licet enim legibus eorum *cuivis ephoro* hoc facere regi (Nep. *Paus.* 3,5)

(28) *Paucis* deponere felicitatem molliter licuit (Sen. *epist.* 74,18)

(29) Si enim *Zenoni* licuit, cum rem aliquam invenisset inusitatam, inauditum quoque ei rei nomen imponere, cur non liceat *Catoni*? (Cic. *fin.* 3,15)

The hypothesis about indirect object control is further confirmed by the infinitives *facere, deponere,* and *imponere* in (27)-(29): if with an impersonal verb there is an element which can be interpreted as an indirect object controller, as a general rule, the infinitive is active, and not passive. Furthermore, if we accept Cecchetto and Oniga's (2004) hypothesis stating that PRO inherits the case of the controller, the so-called *dativus cum infinitivo* structure, in which with an impersonal verb even the predicate complement is in the dative case, can be considered as another piece of evidence in favour of the indirect object control theory. The dative and infinitive (*dativus cum infinitivo*) is illustrated by the following example with the predicate complements in the dative case highlighted:

(30) Illis *timidis* et *ignavis* esse licet [...] vobis necesse est *fortibus viris* esse (Liv. 21,44,8)

Finally, in the constructions under discussion it is possible for the active perfect infinitive to appear (in italics), either with an element in the dative case (also in italics), acting as a controlling element according to our analysis, as in (31)-(33), or without it, as in (34)-(35):

(31) Atque ego, tametsi *viro* flagitiosissumum existumo impune iniuriam *accepisse* ... (Sall. *Iug.* 31,21)

(32) *Artifici* iucundius pingere est quam *pinxisse* (Sen. *epist.* 9,7)

(33) Laudi ducitur *adolescentulis* quam plurimos *habuisse* amatores (Nep. *praef.* 4)

(34) Quid deinde prodest *secessisse*? (Sen. *epist.* 82,4)

(35) … maius dedecus est parta amittere quam omnino non *paravisse* (Sall. *Iug.* 31,17)

In our opinion, in comparison to the starting stage, in which the control structures always required a present infinitive (cf. section 1), the use of the perfect infinitive in these constructions could become more widespread through the interaction of the two phenomena presented in this section: the indirect object which can be interpreted as a controlling element and the impersonal constructions.

Finally, the following examples show that one can find perfect infinitives in sentences which can be construed as control structures not only in impersonal constructions ((36) has to be interpreted deontically, not epistemically!), cf. what we have stated in 4.3. about the ellipsis of the element in the accusative, expressing the subject of the infinitive:

(36) Non discere *debemus* ista, sed *didicisse* (Sen. *epist.* 88,2)

(37) Addebat Messala Valerius renovandum per annos sacramentum in nomen Tiberii; interrogatusque a Tiberio, num se mandante eam sententiam prompsisset, *sponte dixisse respondit* (Tac. *ann.* 1,8,4)

4.2. Deponent verbs

Some ancient authors' works and some special structures (e.g. participial constructions) can also feature active forms of (many) deponent verbs. Taking this into consideration, in a given syntactic structure one might doubt whether the meaning of the passive forms of these verbs is active or passive. However, if, following the grammatical tradition, we regard these verbs as having a passive form with an active meaning, the strategy of passivization, presented above in sections 3 and 4.1, intended to create an unambiguous AcI and to avoid control or an ambiguous structure, no longer exists. We wish to clarify this train of thought with the help of the following examples, all of which contain a deponent verb that, according to Neue (1897), can be unambiguously related to a non-deponent (active) equivalent:

(38) Ubi […] intellexit […] diem instare, quo die frumentum militibus
     metiri oporteret (Caes. *Gall.* 1,16,5)

(39) ... neque esse quidquam negotii […] hanc (legionem) sub sarcinis
     adoriri (Caes. *Gall.* 2,17,2)

(40) Illud quoque efficimus, ut nihil *imitari* velint nostri (Sen. *epist.* 5,3)

(41) ... Lacedaemonios bello *persequi* iusserit (Nep. *Con.* 4,1)

Our analysis can begin by examining *frumentum metiri oporteret*, the
relevant part of (38). Since in this impersonal sentence one can find the
deponent verb *metior*, in harmony with our argumentation in this section
and with what we have seen in 4.1, we cannot be certain whether for a
Latin native speaker an example like this represented the case shown in
(18)-(21), where the infinitive has a passive form with a passive construal
('it was necessary for the grain to be weighed') and thus realizes an AcI,
or belongs to the type shown in (22)-(24) due to the active meaning of
metior, which entails that it can (also) be construed as a control structure
with the meaning 'it was necessary to weigh the grain'. However, if the
speaker takes the latter interpretation of the verb *metior* and of the
sentence under discussion, we cannot resort to the strategy of passivization
and thus to the forming of an unambiguous AcI, which is an option in the
case of non-deponent verbs, as we have seen in the previous section with
regard to impersonal constructions.
    The above argumentation can be also applied to (39), which represents
an impersonal construction with the deponent verb *adorior* 'attack'.
    In (40) we find the polyvalent verb *volo/velle* (which has been given a
detailed analysis in section 3), together with the deponent verb *imitor*. In
accordance with what has been outlined so far, one might ask: should we
construe the relevant part of the example as an anti-control AcI structure
presented in (9)-(11) with the literal interpretation 'so that they want
nothing of us to be imitated' (cf. the analysis of (9)) or as 'so that they
don't want to imitate anything of us', in accordance with the examples of
control in (12)-(14)?
    Finally, let us examine (41) with the verb *iubeo* 'order', meaning 'he
ordered that the people of Sparta should be pursued in a war'. As we can
see, the person who receives the order is not expressed in the sentence. In
such cases Latin almost always uses AcI with a passive infinitive, as in the
examples below:

(42) a. Equum empturus *solvi* iubes stratum (Sen. *epist.* 80,9)
     b. ... pontem [...] iubet *rescindi* (Caes. *Gall.* 1,7,2)

Nevertheless, (41) contains the deponent verb *persequor*, so we need to ask the same question as before: does it have a passive construal, as is expected in such structures, or an active one, which can (also) permit a control structure interpretation (arbitrary control, cf. the impersonal constructions in 4.1. and one of the possible interpretations of (38) and (39))? The following example shows that we can rarely find an active infinitive also with the verb *iubeo* even if the person who is given the order is not expressed:

(43) (Haruspices) iusserunt simulacrum Iovis facere maius et in excelso conlocare (Cic. *Catil.* 3,20)

Thus, in (43), as in (42a-b) and (41), the person who receives the order is not expressed, but while the examples in (42) contain a passive infinitive, and so an unambiguous AcI, as is required by classical Latin, in (43) we can find the active *facere* and *conlocare* instead of their passive equivalents *fieri* and *conlocari*, which means that (43) cannot receive an unambiguous structural interpretation, as it may also be construed as a control structure. This is the point of view from which it is similar to (41) with the deponent verb *persequor*.

4.3. Elliptical phenomena

In classical Latin, it is quite common for one or more elements to be omitted in a sentence, as is illustrated in the following three examples:

(44) Nostri acriter in eos impetu facto reppulerunt [*eos*] (Caes. *Gall.* 5,17,3)

(45) ... sperans [...] sese casum victoriae inventurum [*esse*] (Sall. *Iug.* 25,9)

(46) Hunc vos beatum [*esse dicitis*] (Cic. *fin.* 2,65)

In (44) the object of the verb *reppulerunt* is unexpressed, presumably due to the fact that it can be deduced from the phrase *in eos*, mentioned previously. In (45) one cannot find the element *esse* of the complex active infinitive expressing posteriority in an AcI, which is a quite common phenomenon. Finally, in (46) two elements are omitted: both the governing verb (*dicitis*) and the infinitive (*esse*) of a sentence which can be construed as an AcI.

The sentences containing an AcI with the subject of the infinitive unexpressed form an important group in our discussion. To illustrate this, let us examine the examples below:

(47) Renuntiatum est facilem esse [*ascensum*] (Caes. *Gall.* 1,21,2)

(48) Addidisti ad extremum etiam indoctum fuisse [*Epicurum*] (Cic. *fin.* 1,26)

(49) Quod facere te moneo, scio certe fecisse [*te*] (Sen. *epist.* 24,16)

In (47) and (48), it is the wider context that helps us to identify the elliptical subjects of the infinitives as the common noun *ascensus* and the Greek philosopher *Epicurus*. As for (49), in its first part, beginning with *quod* we can observe the element *te*, which is not repeated in the second half of the sentence, so this case is similar to (44).

In the three examples above the elliptical subject of the infinitive is not coreferential with the subject of the main verb (*renuntiatum est, addidisti* and *scio*). However, there are also cases in which the two subjects under discussion are coreferential (and the subject of the infinitive is not expressed), which entails that we can re-evaluate such examples as control structures (instead of AcI structures). This phenomenon can be divided into several subgroups. The first subgroup is illustrated in the following two examples:

(50) ... intellegebam ex eo loco, si te haberem, posse *me* Brundisium referre (Cic. *Att.* 3,2)

(51) Trinovantes [...] legatos ad Caesarem mittunt pollicenturque *sese* ei dedituros (Caes. *Gall.* 5,20,1)

(50) and (51) show that when an element in the accusative case (*me* and *sese* in the two examples) can be matched with two different syntactic roles in one and the same sentence, it is expressed only once. The elements in question should in fact have two different functions in our examples: from the one hand, they should be the subjects of the infinitives (*posse*) *referre* and *dedituros* (*esse*) in the AcI depending from the governing verbs *intellegebam* and *pollicentur*; on the other hand, they should express

the reflexive argument of the verbs *refero* and *dedo*. In our analysis, the elements *me* and *sese* are construed as the reflexive arguments of the above mentioned verbs and not as the subjects of the infinitives, which can be explained, on the one hand, by the fact that the omission of the subject of the infinitive can also be found in other examples, just as it has been accounted for throughout this section; on the other hand, if the reflexive argument were omitted, the syntactico-semantic construal of the sentences would suffer a loss.

We may draw a parallel between the examples (50)-(51) and (52), which does not have an AcI:

(52) Malo te legas, quam epistulam meam (Sen. *epist.* 24,21)

In this sentence, the element *te* is the reflexive argument of the verb *lego*. We may presume that the author uses a conjugated verbal structure (instead of an AcI) for similar reason as (50) and (51) contain the element *me* and *sese* only once, as reconstructing (52) as a (hypothetical) AcI, the element *te* would appear twice: *Malo te legere te/Malo te legi a te* 'I would rather you read yourself.'

In another group of examples, in which the subject of the infinitive also remains unexpressed if the subject of the main verb and the infinitive (the latter two highlighted in italics) are coreferential, we can either find a future infinitive (53) or a present infinitive which may express simultaneity or posteriority ((54)-(57)). In some of the examples, as in (53) and (54), the elliptical subject of the infinitive appears in the wider context (see the element *se*), so a parallel may be drawn with (44) and (49):

(53) (Caesar) negat *se* more et exemplo populi Romani posse iter ulli per provinciam dare et, si vim facere conentur, *prohibiturum ostendit* (Caes. *Gall.* 1,8,3)

(54) Caesar questus, quod, quum ultro in continentem legatis missis pacem ab *se* petissent, bellum sine causa intulissent, *ignoscere* imprudentiae *dixit* (Caes. *Gall.* 4,27,5)

(55) ... namque *aperuisse* videbatur, omnia in sua potestate esse *velle* (Nep. *Dion* 6,4)

(56) Non ego cum Danais Troianam *exscindere* gentem Aulide *iuravi* (Verg. *Aen.* 4,425)

(57) ... legati veniunt, qui *polliceantur* obsides *dare* atque imperio populi
     Romani *obtemperare* (Caes. *Gall.* 4,21,5)

As for the timeline expressed by the infinitive in examples (53)-(57),
notice that this mainly corresponds to what we have stated in section 1
about the future or sometimes atemporal value of the infinitive in
connection with the control structure. It is perhaps not accidental,
therefore, that the ellipsis of the subject of the infinitive is relatively more
frequent in examples of this type, which also permits a control structure
interpretation for the sentence.

Finally, let us examine the last group of examples:

(58) *Uxor* invicti Iovis esse nescis (Hor. *carm.* 3,27,73)

(59) ... summos illi promitterent honores *habituri* mihi (Apul. *met.* 7,14)

(60) Sensit medios *delapsus* in hostes (Verg. *Aen.* 2,377)

(61) Phaselus ille, quem videtis, hospites / ait fuisse navium *celerrimus*
     (Catull. 4,1-2)

In these examples, one may observe that in addition to the fact that the
subject of the infinitive is not expressed, the predicative complement ((58),
(61)) and the nominal part of the infinitive ((59), (60)), highlighted in
italics, is not in the accusative case, as is typical of AcI, but in the
nominative case, typical of the control structure (cf. (5), (6), (7a)), thus
possessing two characteristic features of the control structure.

Taking into consideration that the examples above have a poetic nature
as well, we cannot rule out a possible Greek influence. In any case, from
the syntactic point of view, these examples are just like the control
structures in modern languages. This is also supported by the fact that the
infinitive may express not only simultaneity (58) or posteriority (59), but
also antecedence, as in (60) and (61) (cf. (36), (37)).

Conclusion

In the present work, after describing the control structure available in
classical Latin, and stating that the verbs governing this structure form a
well-defined group (section 1), we examined the control structure in
comparison with AcI, the most productive infinitive structure in classical
Latin.

In section 2, we showed that it is possible to distinguish the two structures using syntactic-semantic parameters.

In section 3, we described a phenomenon called anti-control, which derives from the hegemony of AcI in classical Latin. Anti-control means that, through the passivization of the infinitive, Latin can use AcI with certain verbs even if all the conditions for using a control structure are met. There, we noticed a pattern that may be related to the spreading of control structures at a later period: since anti-control is by no means obligatory, as was shown e.g. with regard to the verb *volo/velle*, observing ancient authors, Latin native speakers could choose which of these two structures to use in the case of certain verbs. In other words they could choose control instead of AcI.

In section 4, we continued our analysis of the factors which may have contributed to the more frequent use of the control structure. In 4.1. we showed how the use of the perfect infinitive could increase through the interaction of the impersonal verbs and the indirect object control. In 4.2. we focused on deponent verbs and stated that if we give these verbs an active construal in spite of their passive form, in certain structures we cannot use an unambiguous AcI, then these structures may (also) be construed as control structures. Finally, in 4.3. we showed that there were many elliptical phenomena in classical Latin, which – in connection with the other control-increasing processes – may have resulted in the increased omission of the subject of the infinitive, which implies the possibility of re-analysis of the construction as a control structure (instead of an AcI) if the subject of the main verb is coreferential with the subject of the infinitive.

References

Bolkestein, A.M. (1976) "A.c.i.- and ut-clauses with verba dicendi in Latin" *Glotta* 54: 263-291.

Cecchetto, C. and R. Oniga (2002) "Consequences of the analysis of Latin infinitival clauses for the theory of Case and Control" *Lingue e Linguaggio* 1: 151-189.

Cecchetto, C. and R. Oniga (2004) "A Challenge to Null Case Theory" *Linguistic Inquiry* 35: 141-149.

Graffi, G. (1994) *Sintassi*, Bologna, il Mulino.

Manzini, M.R. (1991) "Il soggetto delle frasi argomentali all'infinito", in L. Renzi and G. Salvi (eds) *Grande grammatica italiana di consultazione* II, Bologna, il Mulino, 485-497.

Menge, H. (2000) *Lehrbuch der lateinischen Syntax und Semantik* (completely re-elaborated by T. Burkard and M. Schauer), Darmstadt, Wissenschaftliche Buchgesellschaft.

Neue, F. (1897) *Formenlehre der lateinischen Sprache*, III. *Das Verbum*, Berlin, S. Calvary&Co.

Oniga, R. (2007) *Il latino. Breve introduzione linguistica*, 2ª ed., Milano, Franco Angeli.

Pinkster, H. (1990) *Latin Syntax and Semantics*, London, Routledge.

Radford, A. (1988) *Transformational Grammar*, Cambridge, University Press.

Salvi, G. and L. Vanelli (2004), *Nuova grammatica italiana*, Bologna, il Mulino.

Szilágyi, I. (in press) "AcI e controllo in latino classico con considerazione dei fenomeni paralleli dell'italiano moderno", *Rivista Italiana di Linguistica e Dialettologia*.

IUBEO AND CAUSATIVE STRUCTURE

FRANCESCO COSTANTINI

1. Introduction

In this article I would like to address the question whether Latin *verba iubendi*, in addition to being used as lexical verbs, may also be used as causative verbs – that is, functional verbs introducing an additional argument (see Zubizarreta 1985, Reinhardt and Siloni 2005, Pylkkänen 2008), as earlier suggested in some traditional grammars (Kühner and Stegmann 1966, Traina and Bertotti 1965).[1]

I restrict my analysis to the verb *iubeo* ('order', 'demand', 'tell (someone to do something)', 'bid')[2] although other verbs, like *curo* (see Iovino in press), may share very similar properties. It is a well-established observation (see Kühner and Stegmann 1966) that *iubeo* can select for both *Accusativus cum infinitivo* (AcI) and object control infinitives, depending on the voice of the infinitive verb. This syntactic pattern is striking because these two structures differ in all relevant respects (see Bolkestein 1976, Szilágyi this volume).

To account for this, I claim that *iubeo* can be used as a causative verb and that all its syntactic peculiarities can be derived assuming its status of causative verb.

The article is organized as follows: in section 2, I provide a preliminary discussion concerning the syntax of *iubeo*. In section 3, I discuss the properties of object control infinitives and AcI. In section 4, I show that the syntax of *iubeo* shares some properties with object control predicates and some others with AcI-selecting predicates. In section 5, I propose that this peculiar syntactic behavior is compatible with the nature of *iubeo* as a causative verb, and I discuss evidence in favor of this hypothesis. In section 6, I present further syntactic evidence in favor of the hypothesis proposed here. In particular, I show that sentences having *iubeo* as their main predicate appear to be monoclausal. In section 7, I present some conclusive remark on *iubeo* as a causative verb from a diachronic viewpoint.

2. Preliminary remarks

It has been noted in the literature that *iubeo* appears to exhibit a particular syntactic pattern in that it can select for two types of infinitival arguments: an AcI clause if the infinitive verb is passive, an object control infinitival clause if the infinitive is active (see Kühner and Stegmann 1966: 715-716; Szilágyi this volume).

I will show in section 4 that this generalization does not appear to be completely accurate. For the moment, however, I would like to draw attention to another point.

Starting from the seminal work by Bolkestein (1976) (see also Schoof 2001, Cecchetto and Oniga 2002), AcI and object control infinitives have been taken to be quite different structures. In AcI, the accusative noun phrase is an argument of the infinitival verb, whereas in object control the accusative noun phrase is an argument of the main verb.

(1)   a. AcI

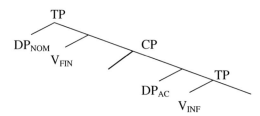

     b.   A+I/Control

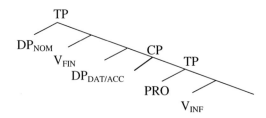

Thus, while AcI-selecting verbs are biargumental, object control verbs are triargumental: their thematic grid is different.

If this is correct, since *iubeo* apparently allows for both AcI and object control, it should be associated with two thematic grids. That is to say that there should be two lexical entries for *iubeo*.

This is an unwelcome result, however, even if such cases are not unheard of. Bolkestein (1976) discusses the case of *admoneo*, which also triggers both the AcI structure and the object control structure and may in fact have two lexical entries. Yet, the two lexical entries of *admoneo* are clearly associated with two different meanings: (i) 'inform of a possible unpleasant situation', a *verbum dicendi* (AcI-selecting), and (ii) 'give a cautionary advice' (object control verb). Nothing of this holds for *iubeo*, whose semantics (excluding its institutional meaning, see note 2) appears to be essentially the same in the AcI and in the control construction.

The puzzle may be rephrased in these words: if *iubeo* has only one lexical entry, why does it take two different syntactic constructions? If it has two lexical entries, why does it show a uniform meaning whatever the embedded clause may be?

In the next section, I consider in greater detail the specific properties of AcI and object control to better understand why *iubeo* appears to display this peculiar syntax.

3. AcI vs. object control

Bolkestein (1976:263) claims that AcI structures and object control structures differ with respect to a series of syntactic and semantic properties:[3]

A) Optionality of a dative argument: A dative argument can be adjoined to verbs selecting for AcI, but not to object control verbs:

(2)   a.   Ei dicunt me venire.
          "They say I am coming"
      b.   *Ei/Eum hortantur me venire.

B) Voice variability: While in real AcI the voice of the infinitive can vary, in control infinitives the active voice only is available:

(3)   a.   Dicunt me mitti
          "They say I am being sent"
      b.   *Hortantur me mitti

C) Semantic restrictions: Control verbs impose semantic restrictions on the accusative noun phrase, whereas verbs selecting for AcI do not:

(4)   a. Dicunt portam patere
           "The say the door is open"
       b. *Hortantur portam patere

D) Impersonal passivization: Impersonal passivization is available with
AcI-selecting verbs, but not with control verbs:[4]

(5)   a. Me venire dicitur
           "It is said that I am coming"
       b. *Me venire hortatur

Building on these contrasts, Bolkestein proposes that the accusative and
the infinitive are part of the same clause in AcI, whereas they are not in
control structures (as illustrated in (1)). She observes that if the accusative
noun phrase were the subject of the infinitival clause in both sentences,
one would not expect the contrasts in sentences (2)-(5). If instead one
assumes that the accusative noun phrase is part of the infinitival clause in
AcI and of the main clause in object control, then the data above can be
accounted for straightforwardly.

A) While in sentence (2a) *me* is the subject of the infinitival clause, in
(2b) it is the "addressee" of the main verb, not the embedded subject. The
dative argument satisfies the grammatical function of addressee. Thus, it is
compatible with sentence (2a) only.

B) Bolkestein observes that "apparently one cannot tell a person to
undergo some activity as a patient" (Bolkestein 1976: 277).[5] Accordingly,
a verb like *hortor* is incompatible with an infinitive that assigns the patient
theta-role to its subject, like a passive infinitive (as in (3b). Such a
restriction does not hold for AcI (see (3a)).

C) Since PRO must satisfy the agent theta-role, the controller must
have the semantic feature [+human]. This explains the contrast between
(4a) and (4b).

D) Impersonal passives absorb the external argument of a verb, do not
assign accusative Case, and assign Nominative case to the internal
argument. Since the accusative noun phrase and the infinitive verb form
the internal argument of *dicere* in (5a), the sentence is grammatical. The
string *me venire* in (5b), on the other hand, is not a constituent and cannot
be raised as a whole to the subject position.

4. The syntax of *Iubeo*

The syntactic pattern of *iubeo* does not conform to that of AcI-selecting verbs or to that of object control predicates:

A) Like control verbs, *iubeo* does not allow the adjunction of an addressee.[6]

(6)   a.   *Iubeo ei/eum te venire
      b.   *Iubeo ei/eum pontem fieri

B) Like AcI predicates, however, *iubeo* allows for voice variability.[7]

(7)   a.   Vocari iussi te (Plaut. *Cas.* 280)
           "I asked to have you called".
      b.   Balineum calfieri iubebo (Cic. *Att.* 2,3)
           "I will order the bath to be heated"
      c.   eisque colonis agros dari iubet (Cic. *leg. agr.* 2,75)
           "He ordered lands to be given to those colonists"

C) Like AcI predicates, *iubeo* does not impose semantic restrictions on the accusative noun. This can be seen in the previous examples, in which the infinitival verb is passive. Although rare, some examples can be found where the accusative noun phrase is [-human] and the infinitival verb is the copula or a non-agentive active verb, and not a passive verb. The following sentences involve the copula *esse*.

(8)   a.   Sirempse legem iussit esse Iuppiter (Plaut. *Amph.* 73)
           "Jupiter doth decree that the selfsame law obtain"
      b.   Secretumque iubes grandius esse tibi (Mart. 11,45,4)
           "You require that greater secrecy should be provided for you"
      c.   Tu desiderium dominae mihi mitius urbis esse iubes (Mart. 12,21,9)
           "You bid my longing for the Queen City be allayed"

The absence of semantic restrictions imposed on the noun phrase is also attested by the following sentences, where *iubeo* is passivized, and where the infinitive verb is transitive:

(9)   Autumnum sterilis ferre iubetur hiems (Mart. 8,68,10)
      "Barren winter is bidden to bear autumn's fruits"

As *hiems* is [-human], it cannot serve as a controller. Hence, it appears rather to be the external argument of the infinitival clause. The infinitival structure is then an AcI.

The following examples, moreover, show that the infinitival verb embedded under *iubeo* can be non-agentive. *Verba affectuum*, for instance, can be found in some examples having *iubeo* as the main predicate.

(10) a. Ipsa quam sexus iubet maerere (Sen. *Her.* 1686)
         "She herself, whose sex impels to mourning"
     b. Nunc nata iubet maerere neposque? (Lucan. 9,1048)
         "Do your daughter and her child at last bid you grieve"

Vapulare 'to get beaten' also does not assign agent role to its subject, but it can be embedded under *iubeo*.

(11) Vapulare ego te vehementer iubeo (Plaut. *Curc.* 568)
     "A good sound hiding is what I recommend for you"

In all these examples the accusative noun phrase appears to be the argument of a non-agentive predicate. These examples may then be considered as instance of AcI and not of object control.

I underline that in examples (9)-(11), AcI occurs regardless of the active voice of the infinitival verb. These examples suggest that the divide between AcI structures and object control structures does not lie on the diathesis of the infinitival verb, as suggested by Kühner and Stegmann (1966), but on the argument structure of the embedded verb. Apparently, AcI is possible when the infinitival verb is non-agentive, whereas object control is the unmarked pattern when the infinitival verb is agentive.

D) Finally, like AcI verbs, *iubeo* is permissible in the impersonal passive construction.

(12) Etiam postridie Idus rebus divinis supersederi iussum (Liv. 6,1,12)
     "Religious rites were omitted also on the day after the several Ides".

Moreover, like object control verbs, *iubeo* does not allow for variability of the tense of the infinitival verb.[8]

(13) *Iubeo te venisse/venturum esse

All in all, *iubeo* shares some properties (B, C, D) with AcI predicates and some others (A, unavailability of tenses other than the present) with control predicates. In some examples, the accusative noun phrase appears to be an argument of *iubeo*. In others, it is apparently an argument of the infinitive verb, not of *iubeo*.

The question is, then: What kind of verb is *iubeo*? Is it a (triargumental) control verb? Or is it a (biargumental) AcI-selecting verb? In the next section I claim that *iubeo* is neither an object control verb nor an AcI-selecting verb. I propose that it is a causative verb and show that this status accounts for its syntactic paradigm.

5. Hypothesis: *Iubeo* as a causative verb

Here I explore the hypothesis that, at least in some cases, *iubeo* is a causative verb; that is, a functional predicate, semantically related to volition, which modifies the valency of a lexical verb, adding an argument to those required by the verb in the infinitive and 'internalizing' the external argument of a transitive verb (see Zubizarreta 1985).

Under this hypothesis, *iubeo* heads a maximal projection within the functional domain of the clause, as suggested by Cinque (1998), and forms a unique verbal complex with the infinitive – so that it belongs to the same clausal domain as the infinitive. In the active construal, the nominative (the causer) and the accusative DP (the causee) are also part of the same clausal domain.

(14)

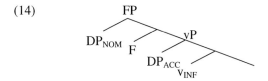

This idea is at odds with the claim that *iubeo* takes AcI or object control clausal arguments, because both AcI-selecting verbs and object control predicates are not included in the same clausal domain as the infinitive verb. Moreover, the accusative DP does not belong to the same clausal domain of the nominative DP (in AcI) or of the infinitive verb (in object control).

Let us now consider how the properties (A) to (D) above can be derived from the hypothesis discussed here.

Property (A) derives from the fact that the nominative DP and the accusative DP satisfy the argument structure of the causative construction. Thus, no additional argument is admitted.

Property (B) derives from the fact that the causative functional head is merged higher than the voice functional head.[9] This recalls the causative structure in Germanic languages rather than in Romance. In Germanic languages, a causative verb can embed a passive infinitive, whereas in Romance languages this leads to ungrammaticality.

(15) a. He will let his son be arrested by the police. (Kayne 1975)
     b. *Farò essere arrestato Mario.
        "I will make to-be arrested Mario".

Property (C) derives from the fact that causative verbs do not constrain the thematic properties of the full verb (see Folli and Harley 2007). Thus, the accusative DP need not satisfy the agentive theta-role.

Property (D) derives from the fact that the accusative DP and the infinitive are in fact part of the same constituent, that is, the causativized vP.

Finally, tense invariability derives from the fact that the causative functional head occurs below tense heads (see Cinque 1998).

A series of clues suggests the hypothesis is feasible. First, in his commentary on the works of Terence, Donatus translates the text in (16a) as in (16b). That is, he translates *comprendi iube* with the imperative *comprehende*.

(16) a. Comprendi iube (Ter. *Eun.* 836)
        "Have him arrested".
     b. IVBE COMPREHENDI […] pro 'comprehende' (Don. *Ter. Eun.* 836)
        "'Have him arrested' instead of 'arrest him'"

This suggests that *iubeo* might have had the status of a sort of imperative auxiliary, that is, a functional verb, in Donatus' time (though not necessarily in Terence's time, but nothing prevents us from surmising that this status also belonged to an older period of the language, as the next hints suggest).[10]

Second, *iubeo* occurs in greetings and salutation formulas, where it appears to be semantically impoverished, as it expresses a wish, not an order.[11]

(17) a. Salvere iubeo spectatores optumos (Plaut. *Cas.* 1)
        "Greetings, ye worthiest of spectators"
     b. quam ob rem valde iubeo gaudere te (Cic. *fam.* 7,2,3)
        "So I bid you rejoice right heartily"

c. illum salutavi, post etiam iussi valere (Cic. *Att.* 5,2,2)
    "He was busy about something there, when I greeted him"

Fruyt and Orlandini (2008) label this use of *iubeo* as 'weak causative' as opposed to the 'strong causative' use of *iubeo* expressing a real order. This also suggest that *iubeo* might not have always used as a full verb.

Finally, grammarians of late antiquity sometimes annotate *iubeo* simply as *volo* 'I want' – that is, as a volitional verb rather than as a verb expressing a real command.

(18) a. 'iubeo' […] id est volo, ut Vergilius 'reddique viro promissa iubebant (Eugraph. *Ter. Andr.* 533)
         "I order […] that is I want, as Vergil (*Aen.* 5,386) 'they wanted to give him the promised prize'"
     b. IUBES vis […]: nam aliter hoc verbum Aeneae persona non recipit (Serv. *Aen.* 2,3)
         "*Iubes, vis* […]: since Aeneas does not accept this word otherwise"
     c. IUBENT volunt, ut infandum regina iubes renovare dolorem (Serv. *Aen.* 2,261)
         "*Iubent volunt*, as 'Beyond all words, O queen, is the grief thou bidst me revive'"

Here, again, the semantics of *iubeo* appears to be someway weakened and not incompatible with a causative verb.

6. *Iubeo*, causativity and monoclausality

In this section, I present some syntactic diagnostics to test the hypothesis described above. As I have mentioned earlier, if used as a causative verb, *iubeo* should be part of the same clause as the infinitive. Thus, in sentences where *iubeo* is a causative verb, monoclausality tests should hold.

According to Zennaro (2006a,b), in Latin there are at least two tests of monoclausality. These tests were originally applied to the analysis of modal verbs and later to other categories of verbs hypothesized to have the status of functional/restructuring verbs, that is, *verba voluntatis* (Zennaro 2006b, Costantini and Zennaro, in press) and aspectual verbs (Zennaro 2006b, Iovino in press).

The first test concerns the relative word order of functional verbs and infinitives. The argument builds on Salvi's (2004) observation that the

unmarked order SOXV can change into SOVX if the two constituents V
and X form a 'relatively strict unit'. In Salvi's view, the sequence of
infinitive plus matrix verb can be such. Thus, as for modal, volitional, and
aspectual predicates, while the order SOIV (where I stands for 'infinitive')
is the most frequent, the order SOVI can occur as well.

There is no consensus on whether the two structures, SOIV and SOVI,
are syntactically equivalent. Salvi (2004) claims they are not. In his view,
the former involves an infinitive complement clause followed by a main
verb, whereas the latter involves a verbal complex. Zennaro (2006b), on
the other hand, proposes that both structures involve a verbal complex.
Whether the two structures are equivalent is however immaterial here.
What matters – and this is uncontroversial – is that the order SOVI is to be
taken as involving a verbal complex. This suggests that SOVI structures
are monoclausal.

As to *iubeo*, the unmarked clause structure has the infinitive that
precedes *iubeo*.

(19) a [Popillius] omnium primum id legere iubet (Liv. 45,12,4)
        "Popilius bade him read this first of all"
     b. Cn. Octauium classem in Siciliam ductam Cn. Cornelio consuli
        tradere iussit (Liv. 30,44,13)
        "He ordered Gnaeus Octavius to take the fleet to Sicily and turn it
        over to Gnaeus Cornelius, the consul"
     c. [Fabius] sensim suos signa inferre iussit (Liv. 10,29,8)
        "Fabius commanded his own men to push forward by degrees"

However, the VI order is well attested too:

(20) a. Pontem qui erat ad Genāvam *iubet rescindi* (Caes. *Gall.* 1,7,1)
        "He ordered the bridge at Genava to be broken down"
     b. ad eum locum scalas *iussit ferre* (Liv. 24,46,2)
        "He ordered them to carry ladders to that place"
     c. id decemviros *iubet vendere* (Cic. *leg. agr.* 2,38)
        "He orders the decemvirs to sell it"
     d. harum ipsarum civitatum militibus navibus nauarchis Syracusanus
        Cleomenes *iussus est imperare* (Cic. *Verr.* II 5,84)
        "Cleomenes of Syracuse was put in command of the men and
        ships and captains of these same communities"

Thus, *iubeo* and the infinitive may form a verbal complex.

The second test of monoclausality concerns the position of pronouns within a clause. Pronouns can be grouped into three classes (see Cardinaletti and Starke 1999): strong pronouns, weak pronouns, and clitic pronouns. This distinction holds even for languages having only one morphological class of pronouns. In German, for instance, pronouns display a clear distinction between a strong and a weak use from a syntactic viewpoint (Cardinaletti and Starke 1996).

Salvi (2004) proposes an analysis along the same lines with respect to Latin pronouns. He argues that Latin pronouns may be used as strong or weak pronouns, depending on the syntactic context in which they appear and on their interpretation. Particularly, he proposes that they have a 'strong' use when they appear in a syntactic position where any other nominal phrase can occur. They have a 'weak' use when they are interpreted as discourse anaphors and occupy the syntactic position following the first constituent of a sentence (excluding linkers like *enim*, *vero*, *autem*, etc.); that is, the "Wackernagel" position.

Zennaro (2006a,b) points out that in some examples involving modal and aspectual verbs, pronominal arguments of an infinitive verb occur in such position. In other words, they behave as if there were one clausal domain only including the inflected verb and the infinitive. He argues that this can be taken as a proof of the monoclausal status of the sentence.

Turning again to *iubeo*, we see that in some instances pronominal arguments of the embedded verb can occur in Wackernagel position:

(21) a. alterum *illi* iubet praetorium tendi (Caes. *civ.* 3,82)
         "He ordered that a second [pavilion] should be erected for him"
    b. Nunc *istanc* tantisper iube petere atque orare mecum (Plaut. *Asin.* 686)
         "Meanwhile now tell her to ask [me for it] and tease with me"
    c. Ego *tibi* argentum iubebo iam intus ecferri foras (Plaut. *Bacch.* 93)
         "I'll tell them to bring you out some money at once"

These examples are compatible with a monoclausal analysis. Thus, *iubeo* is consistent with the status of causative verb.

Conclusion

To conclude, the above data appear to provide reasonable evidence in favor of the claim that that *iubeo*, *at least in some cases,* is a causative verb, that is, a functional verb, and not a full verb.

If this is correct, from a diachronic viewpoint, *iubeo* is likely to have undergone the 'auxiliary cline', the pattern of linguistic change whereby a full verb becomes a functional verb a (causative, in the case of *iubeo*) and eventually a functional morpheme (this phase may perhaps have been represented by the use of *iubeo* as an imperative auxiliary – see Donatus' comment on Terence in (16b)).

These considerations might be tentatively connected to the fact that *iubeo* has disappeared from Romance languages. If *iubeo* was a causative verb, it must have competed with the *facere*+infinitive construction, which, although disfavored in the classical prose, becomes more and more common in later ages and is rather frequent in the Vulgate (see Muller 1912: 24). Thus, conjecturally, *facio* may have replaced *iubeo* as a causative verb, which may explain why *facio*, unlike *iubeo*, is present in most Romance languages.

Notes

[1] Notice that *iubeo* derives from PIE *Hioudh-eie-o 'to cause to move' (de Vaan, 2008), i.e. a causative verb. However, this does not guarantee that *iubeo* is a causative verb (cf. *moneo*).

[2] In the specific lexicon of Roman institutions, *iubeo* also means 'decree, enact', as in the fixed formula *velitis iubeatis*, used to introducing a *rogatio*, or *senatus creverit populus ve iusserit* 'the senate dictated and the people decreed' (Cic. *leg.* 3,9). In the present article, I will only consider the syntactic properties of *iubeo* in its generic meaning.

[3] I omit one of the contrasts mentioned by Bolkestein, as it is not relevant to the present discussion. Bolkestein observes that while in real AcI the tense of the infinitive can vary, in control infinitives the present tense only is available:

    (i)   a.   Dicunt me venisse/venturum esse.
             "They say I have come/I will come".
        b.   *Hortantur me venisse/venturum esse.

[4] Note that the personal passive is possible even with control verbs (examples quoted in Bolkestein 1976).

    (i)   Nostri admonentur stationes disponere. (Caes. *Gall.* 8,12)
        "Our men are admonished to put out guards".
This is expected if the accusative noun phrase is an argument of the main verb.

[5] This intuition has been formalized by Farkas (1988), who claims that the controller must refer to an individual who brings about the situation referred to by the infinitival clause and participates such situation as an intentional agent. This explains the contrast between the following sentences:

    (i)   a.   John ordered Mary [PRO to leave].
        b.   #John ordered Mary [PRO to be allowed to leave].
        c.   #John ordered Mary to receive a letter.
        d.   #John ordered Mary to wonder at such bravery.

In sentence (ia), the implicit subject of the infinitival (PRO) is an intentional agent. In sentences (ib,c,d), PRO is not an agent - the infinitive verb is passive (in (ib)), the embedded subject is assigned a goal or benefactive theta-role (in (ic)), or an experiencer theta-role (as in (id)).

[6] Few examples where a dative addressee is followed by the AcI are in fact attested in late texts. For instance:

(i)   iussit […] centurioni custodiri eum Paulum
      "He ordered the centurion to take into custody Paul".

In this specific case, however, in most of the codices *custodiri* is in the active form *custodire*, which would make the structure much akin to (apparent) object control structures.

[7] The translations are adapted from the Loeb editions.

[8] See note 3.

[9] As Zennaro (2006a,b) points out, in Latin there might be a higher voice head, because restructuring verbs may be passive if the full verb is too.

(i)   Si qua potestur investigari via. (Pacuv. *Trag.* fr. 100 R.³)
      "If some way can be found".

This holds for *iubeo* as well:

(ii) Iussast dari puella. (Ter. *Phorm.* 416)
      "They ordered to give the girl".

[10] The construal *iubeo* in the imperative followed by an infinitive is in fact attested in Cicero, too.

(i)   Dionysium iube salvere. (Cic. *Att.* 4,14,2)
      "Give my regards to Dionysius".

Here *iubeo* expresses a wish rather than a command.

[11] In general, *iubeo* has a weaker meaning than *cogo* or *impero*, as a verse of Terence clearly shows:

(i)   Iubam? Cogo atque impero. (Ter. Eun. 389)
      "Bidding? No, it's my enforcement and royal order".

This is not a sufficient proof that *iubeo* is a functional verb, however.

References

Bolkestein, A.M. (1976) "A.c.i.- and ut-Clauses with verba dicendi in Latin" *Glotta* 54: 263-291.

Cardinaletti, A. and M. Starke (1996) "Deficient pronouns: a View from Germanic", in H. Thráinsson, S.D. Epstein and S. Peter (eds) *Studies in Comparative Germanic Syntax*, II, Dordrecht, Foris, 21-65.

—. (1999) "The Typology of Structural Deficiency: On the Three Grammatical Classes", in H. van Riemsdijk (ed.) *Clitics in the Languages of Europe*, Berlin, Mouton de Gruyter, 145-233.

Cecchetto, C. and R. Oniga (2002), "Consequences of the analysis of Latin infinitival clauses for the theory of Case and Control" *Lingue e Linguaggio* 1: 151-189.

Cinque, G. (1998) "The interaction of passive, causative and restructuring in Romance" *University of Venice Working Papers in Linguistics* 8: 29-51.

Costantini, F. and L. Zennaro (in press), "Some aspects of the syntax and semantics of the *verba voluntatis*", in M. Lenoble, D. Longrée and C. Bodelot (eds) *De linguae latinae usu, Actes du 13e Colloque international de Linguistique latine, Bruxelles et Liège, 4-9 avril 2005*, Leuven, Peeters.

Folli, R. and H. Harley (2007) "Causation, obligation, and argument structure: On the nature of little v" *Linguistic Inquiry* 38:197-238.

Fruyt, M. and A. Orlandini (2008) "Some cases of linguistic evolution and grammaticalisation in the Latin verb", in Roger Wright (cd.) *Latin vulgaire-latin tardif VIII: actes du VIIIe Colloque international sur le latin vulgaire et tardif, Oxford, 6-9 septembre 2006*, Hildesheim-New York, Olms-Weidmann, 230-237.

Iovino, R. (in press) "Restructuring structures with modal and aspectual verbs in archaic and classical Latin", paper presented at 24th Scandinavian Conference of Linguistics, Joensuu, August 25-27, 2010, to be published in the Proceedings.

Kühner, R. and C. Stegmann (1966) *Ausführliche Grammatik der lateinischen Sprache*, II: *Satzlehre*, 1. Teil, 4. Auflage, Hannover, Hahn.

Muller, H.F. (1912), *Origine et histoire de la préposition "à" dans le locutions du type "Faire faire quelque chose à quelqu'un"*, Poitiers, Masson.

Pylkkänen, L. (2008) *Introducing Arguments*, Cambridge (Mass.), MIT Press.

Reinhart, T. and T. Siloni (2005) "The Lexicon-Syntax Parameter: Reflexivization and Other Arity Operations" *Linguistic Inquiry* 36: 389-436.

Salvi, G. (2004) *La formazione della struttura di frase romanza. Ordine delle parole e clitici dal latino alle lingue romanze antiche*, Tübingen, Niemeyer.

Schoof, S. (2003) "Impersonal and personal passivization of Latin infinitive constructions: A scrutiny of the structures called AcI", in K. Jong-Bok and S. Wechsler (eds) *Proceedings of the ninth international conference on Head-Driven Phrase Structure Grammar*, Stanford, CA, CSLI Publications, 293-312.

Szilágyi, I. (this volume), "Control and AcI in classical Latin: Structural interpretation, Problems and Innovative tendencies", 85-100.

Traina, A. and T. Bertotti (1965) *Sintassi normativa della lingua Latina*, Firenze, Cappelli.

de Vaan, M. (2008) *Etymological Dictionary of Latin and other Italic Languages*, Leiden-Boston, Brill.

Zennaro, L. (2006a) "La sintassi di *possum* e *debeo* e la ristrutturazione", in R. Oniga, L. Zennaro (eds) *Atti della Giornata di Linguistica Latina. Venezia, 7 maggio 2004*, Venezia, Cafoscarina, 237-251.

—. (2006b) *La sintassi dei verbi a ristrutturazione in latino*, PhD diss. University Ca' Foscari of Venice.

Zubizarreta, M.L. (1985) "The relation between morphophonology and morphosyntax: The case of Romance causatives" *Linguistic Inquiry* 16: 247-289.

RELATIVE CLAUSES OF THE "THIRD TYPE" IN LATIN?

ANNA POMPEI

1. Introduction

This paper aims at analysing the semantics of Latin relative clauses (henceforth RCs). After featuring a possible classification of Latin RCs from a crosslinguistic perspective (§2), the difference between restrictiveness and non-restrictiveness (§3) and its applicability to Latin (§4) are examined. The concept of maximalization is then introduced (§5) and applied to correlatives, circumnominals, and free RCs of Latin (§6).

2. Typology of Latin RCs

In Latin, a RC can be defined as a subordinate clause introduced by a relative pronoun or a relative adverb.[1] However, from a crosslinguistic point of view, the formation of RCs through relative pronouns is a marked strategy of relativization: typological definitions of RCs do not make any reference to the presence of relative pronouns. On the other hand, the existence of a link between the RC and (a constituent of) the matrix clause is highlighted. Lehmann (1986: 664), for instance, remarks that when we speak about a RC, we need to refer to a nominal head; therefore, he prefers to use the term *relative construction*.[2] More recently, de Vries (2002: 14) lists as defining properties of RCs their subordination and the fact that they are connected to surrounding material by a *pivot* constituent. In his definition, the pivot is an element semantically shared by the matrix clause and the RC, i.e. it coindexes them. In both the matrix and the RC, the pivot may be realized as a full noun (*lexical head*) or represented by a pronoun, or may even be phonetically null.[3] If the pivot is realized as a lexical head outside the RC we speak of an *external head*, which RCs might precede (1) or follow (2). According to Lehmann (1984: 48-49), these are *prenominals* and *postnominals* respectively:

(1) *Cavarinum cum equitatu Senonum secum proficisci iubet, ne quis aut*
     ex huius iracundia aut ex eo, quod *meruerat,* odio *civitatis motus*
     existat (Caes. *Gall.* 6,5,2)
     "He orders Cavarinus to march with him with the cavalry of the
     Senones, so that no commotion should arise either from his hot
     temper, or from the hatred of the state which he had earned".

(2) [...] *Haedui questum quod* Harudes, qui *nuper in Galliam trans-*
     portati essent, fines eorum popularentur (Caes. *Gall.* 1,37,2)
     "[ambassadors came] from the Aedui to complain that the Harudes,
     who had lately been brought over into Gaul, were ravaging their
     territories"

     When the pivot is found as a full noun within the RC it is an *internal*
head. Internally-headed RCs can be *circumnominal* (3) or *preposed* (4):

(3) [*tənay   ʔəwa: ʔəwu:w]   -pu   -Ly   ʔciyawx*
     yesterday house I-saw   DEF   LOC   I'll-sing
     "I'll sing in the house I saw yesterday"
     (Diegueño; Comrie 1981: 202)

(4) quae pars *civitatis Helvetiae insignem calamitatem populo Romano*
     intulerat, ea *princeps poenas persolvit* (Caes. *Gall.* 1,12,6)
     "that part of the Helvetian state which had brought a signal calamity
     upon the Roman people was the first to pay the penalty"

     Circumnominal RCs are embedded in the matrix clause, whereas
preposed RCs are extra-sentential, as the possible resumption by an
anaphora – such as *ea* – in the matrix clause clearly shows. Preposed RCs
are part of correlative structures. Crosslinguistically they always feature
both the realization of the lexical head and the relative pronoun. The same
happens in Latin circumnominal RCs, in contrast to what happens in other
languages (3):

(5) *Caesar necessariis rebus imperatis ad cohortandos milites,* quam in
     partem *fors obtulit, decucurrit* (Caes. *Gall.* 2,21,1)
     "Caesar, having given the necessary orders, ran down in a chance
     direction into whatever quarter fortune carried him, to encourage the
     troops"

When a lexical head is lacking, the pivot in the matrix clause can either be represented by a pronoun (6) or be missing (7); in the former case we speak of *semi-free* RCs, in the latter of *free* RCs:[4]

(6)   *virosque bonos* eos qui *habentur, numeremus, Paulos, Catones, Galos, Scipiones, Philos* (Cic. *Lael.* 21)
       "we would number on the list of good men those who are commonly so regarded, the Pauli, the Catos, the Gali, the Scipios, the Phili"

(7)   *ieiunus siet* qui *dabit* (Cato *agr.* 70,2)
       "He who administers the remedy must be fasting"

3. Restrictive RCs vs. Appositive RCs

The distinction between *restrictive* and *non-restrictive/appositive* RCs goes back to Port Royal.[5] Restrictive RCs help to fix the reference of the head noun they modify (8). In this case there is an intersection between two sets (Partee 1973), the former made by the entities with the same extension of the head, the latter containing what is codified by the RC (Figure 1):

(8)   *The students that study English will go on a trip to England*

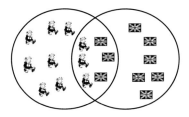

Figure 1 – Restrictive RCs as intersection

On the other hand, the non-restrictive RC modifies an already identified referent, not making any contribution to the reference building. Its function is rather to provide "a secondary comment (predication) on the head that it modifies, in addition to the main predication" (Croft, 1991: 52). For instance, if a headmaster talks to students' parents, he can say:

(9)   *The students, who study English, will go on a trip to England*

In this case, it is clear that the students are those attending the school; two predications are made about them, the former secondary, the latter main. Non-restrictive RCs are linked to the head noun through an anaphoric relationship at discourse level (Sells 1985).

From a crosslinguistic perspective, the distinction between restrictive and non-restrictive RCs can be marked by suprasegmental features, such as intonation contours, or even by morpho-syntactic constraints: for example English *that* cannot occur in non-restrictive RCs, just as Italian *il quale* cannot occur in the subject or object position of restrictive RCs.[6] A semantic criterion to establish the non-restrictiveness of a RC is when it modifies an already identified head noun, as usually happens with proper nouns. On the other hand, both restrictive and appositive RCs have the possibility of stacking, namely to recursively modify the same head.[7] Restrictive RCs can stack (10) because various other sets might intersect the one formed by the entities with the extension of the head (Figure 2):

(10) *The students that study English that had good marks will go on a trip to England*

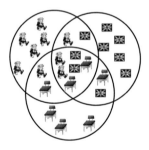

Figure 2 – Stacking in restrictive RCs

Appositive RCs can stack because various RCs may have an anaphoric link to the same head:

(11) *The students, who study English, who had good marks, will go on a trip to England.*

4. Restrictive and Appositive RCs in Latin

In Latin there are neither suprasegmental nor morpho-syntactic correlates for restrictiveness. However, many scholars (Touratier 1980: 239-386; Lehmann, 1984: 261-267; Lavency, 1998: 30-31; Pinkster, 1990: 80-81;

Vester, 1977) think that the opposition between restrictive and appositive RCs is relevant for Latin, too. Also in this language, this distinction can be tentatively determined by a careful examination of the context and information structure, making it possible to understand if a RC is necessary or not to fix the reference of an entity. Of course, the clause is normally non-restrictive if it modifies a noun or a pronoun which usually identify a single referent, as proper nouns (2) and personal pronouns mostly do. On the other hand, the cooccurrence of a cataphoric such as *is* with an external lexical head (1) usually requires a restrictive reading.[8] Also in Latin, both restrictive (12) and appositive (13) RCs can stack:

(12) *Nihil mihi nunc scito tam deesse quam* hominem eum quocum *omnia quae me cura aliqua adficiunt una communicem*, qui *me amet,* qui *sapiat,* quicum *ego cum loquar nihil fingam, nihil dissimulem, nihil obtegam* (Cic. *Att.* 1,18,1)
"Believe me, there is nothing at this moment of which I stand so much in need as a man with whom to share all that causes me anxiety: a man to love me; a man of sense to whom I can speak without affectation, reserve, or concealment"

(13) *cohortes V in* Eburones quorum *pars maxima est inter Mosam ac Rhenum,* qui *sub imperio Ambiorigis et Catuvolci erant, misit* (Caes. *Gall.* 5,24,4)
"He sent five cohorts among the Eburones, the greatest portion of whom lie between the Meuse and the Rhine, [and] who were under the government of Ambiorix and Cativolcus"

5. "Third Type" RCs: Maximalization

In the second half of the last century, a 'third type' of RC semantics was proposed. It was introduced by Carlson (1977) and Heim (1987) regarding so-called *degree relatives*[9]. It was later extended by Grosu and Landman (1998) to all RCs whose semantics is wholly internal, which they call *maximalizing* RCs. The latter cannot be considered restrictive or appositive, but are part of a continuum which shows an increasing contribution to the semantics of the whole relative construction by the RC: it begins at one extreme where the semantics of a simple noun phrase receives no contribution from a RC (which in this case does not exist) and extend to the other extreme, where the RC, as a bare CP, does not allow any contribution of external material (which cannot be present[10]):

←——→

Simplex XPs   Appositives Restrictives Maximalizers   Simplex CPs
Figure 3 – RC semantic continuum

Restrictive RCs are positioned in the middle of this continuum, as they contribute in the same way as the head noun to the relative construction, intersection being a symmetric operation (§2). Appositive RCs are placed on their left, where the RC-external material mainly contributes to the semantics of the relative construction, since their link with the head is indirect and mediated by an interclausal anaphora. On the other hand, maximalizing RCs stay on the right, where the RC-external material is reduced to a minimum and its semantic contribution to the relative construction has to be traced back to a RC-internal interpretation or to an interpretation which is, however, predictable from the RC. This means that the whole semantic content of the relative construction lies within the RC. For these reasons maximalizing RCs are considered *sortal-internal* whereas both restrictive and appositive are *sortal-external*.[11] This point dramatically distinguishes maximalizing RCs from restrictives, with which they are often confused. According to Grosu and Landman (1998: 126), maximalizing semantics concerns the RCs that they call *internally headed*, such as (3) or (14), as well as correlatives (15) – which likewise have an internal head – and free RCs (16), being without lexical head by definition:

(14) [nuna ishkay bestya-ta   ranti-shqa-n] alli bestyam ka-rqo-n
     Man two   horse-ACC   buy-PERF-3   good horse   be-PAST
     "The two horses that the man bought were good horses"
     (Quechua; Grosu 2002: 153-154)

(15) [jo   laRke   khaRe   haiN],   merii teacher   sochtii
     which   boys   standing   are   my   teacher   thinking
     hai   ki   ve   lambe   haiN
     is   that they tall   are
     "Which boys are standing, my teacher thinks that those are tall."
     (Hindi; Grosu 2002: 150)

(16) John bought [what(ever) there was on the topshelf]
     (Grosu 2002: 149)

Restrictive RCs are linked to their head by an operation of set intersection; appositive RCs and their head are linked through an operation of secondary predication (§2). In maximalizing RCs the maximal amount (degree or quantity) of entities (individuals or matter) that satisfies the properties described within the RC is denoted. This is an operation of maximalization. Since the set which is designated in its entirety may even be formed by a singleton, maximalizing RCs may determine a definite ('who/what') or a universal ('whoever/whatever') interpretation. This implies two important consequences: a) maximalizing RCs are only compatible with some quantifiers and determiners; b) they do not stack. Carlson (1977) indicates universal quantifiers and definite determiners compatible with maximalization in English (α): their semantics is the only one that preserves the set to which maximalization is applied in its entirety. Conversely, maximalizing RCs are not compatible with existential and degree quantifiers or with non-definite numerals (β), since their employment would imply the extraction of a part from the set by breaking its entirety:

(α) every, free-choice any, all, the, those, the + numerals (the three), partitives (three of the).
(β) few, many, some, most, no, non-definite numerals.

These constraints seem to be effective in all languages. For instance, in (14) the only possible interpretation is that the horses are exactly the two that the man bought, i.e. the whole set singled out by the internally-headed RC, and not two horses of a broader set:

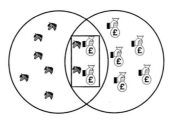

Figure 4 – Maximalizing operation (14)

This becomes clearer if (14) is compared with the equivalent restrictive prenominal one (17). In this case the RC can mean, out of contest, both "the two horses that the man bought" and "two horses that the man bought". This means that an external restrictor can be applied to the intersection between the set of horses and that of what the man bought (Figure 5), contrary to what happens in maximalization:

(17) [nuna   ranti-shqa-n] ishkay bestya   alli   bestyam ka-rqo-n
     man   buy-PERF-3 two   horse-NOM good   horse   be-
     PAST-3 "(The) two horses that the man bought were good horses."
     (Quechua; Grosu 2002: 153-154)

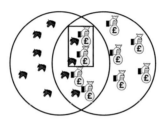

Figure 5 – Restrictive operation (17)

This does not imply a more general impossibility for external quantifiers
or determiners to occur in case of maximalizing RC. For instance, the
correlative in (15) could be realized in the following concurrent ways:

(18) [jo   laRke khaRe   haiN], merii teacher   sochtii   hai ki
     which   boys standing are   my   teacher   thinking   is that
     {ve,   dono, sab,   *do,   *kuch, *adhiktam} lambe   haiN.
     they   both all   two   few   most   tall   are
     "Which boys are standing, my teacher thinks that {those, both, all,
     *two, *few, *most} are tall." (Hindi; Grosu 2002: 150)

What the ungrammaticality of *do, *kuch and *adhiktam shows is that
once the maximalization has taken place, it is impossible to extract either a
certain number of items, e.g. two, or few items, or the majority of items
from the whole. On the other hand, definite determiners or universal
quantifiers such as ve, dono and sab, i.e. 'those', 'both (two of two)', and
'all', might occur in the matrix clause. Indeed, both the type of set
members – sortal – and their number – cardinality – are fixed through a
maximalizing operation, namely within the RC. Therefore, a possible
external determiner cannot be a real restrictor, but it can only specify the
maximalization result, making it explicit. Another consequence of the fact
that sortal and cardinality are fixed within the RC is that these features
cannot be established more than once for the same construction, and thus
stacking is impossible. This is shown, for instance, by the impossibility to
add what he likes best to the free RC in (19), compared to the possibility to
add that he likes best to the postnominal restrictive in (20), as well as, for
instance, by the ungrammaticality of the correlative in (21):

(19) John is listening to what Mary bought (*what he likes best)

(20) John is listening to the records that Mary bought (that he likes best)
(Grosu 2002: 148)

(21) Jo   laRkii   khaRii   hai (*jo   ravii kii   dost   hai),
which girl   standing   is   which Ravi Gen friend is
vo   (laRkii)   bahut   lambii hai
she girl   very   tall   is
"Which girl is standing (*who is Ravi's friend),{she, that girl} is
tall." (Hindi; Grosu 2002: 150)

These two consequences of maximalization can be considered as tests in
order to verify which types of RC have a maximalizing semantics in a
particular language.

6. Maximalizing RCs in Latin

As to Latin, it is naturally impossible to give grammaticality judgments.
However, what happens in RCs that have a maximalizing semantics from a
crosslinguistic point of view can be analysed. That is, it is possible to
apply the tests of both cooccurrence with only certain quantifiers and
determiners and the impossibility of stacking to correlatives (§6.1),
circumnominal (§6.2), free and semi-free RCs (§6.3).

6.1. Correlatives

Latin correlative clauses can be resumed in the matrix clause by an
anaphoric element, such as *is* (4), and also by *idem*:

(22) quae *hic rei publicae* vulnera *inponebat,* eadem *ille sanabat* (Cic. *fin.*
4,66)
"The former strove to heal the wounds which the latter inflicted on
the state"

In this case, it is very clear that the RC-external material does not have any
real semantic content, but rather makes the result of maximalization
explicit, by highlighting it. The same happens when the internal lexical
head occurs again in the matrix clause: the repetition of the head does not
make any contribution to the semantics, because the sortal has already

been fixed in the RC. Indeed, head reduplication is only another anaphoric strategy:

(23) quem agrum *eos vendere heredemque sequi licet, is* ager *vectigal nei siet*
      "This land they can sell and hand down will not be taxed" (CIL I², 584)

It is worth noting that in cases of head reduplication, the head has to be definite: the reduplication cannot involve a bare noun, since its usage would favor a generic interpretation of the referent, which is inconsistent with its previous introduction in the discourse, implying giveness and definiteness:

(24) *quem agrum *eos vendere heredemque sequi licet,* ager *vectigal nei siet*

When the RC-external material is different from the simple anaphora or from head reduplication, its semantics is usually one of universal quantification:

(25) *sub muro* quae pars *collis ad orientem solem spectabat,* hunc omnem locum *copiae Gallorum compleverant* (Caes. *Gall.* 7,69,5)
      "The army of the Gauls had filled all the space under the wall, comprising a part of the hill which looked to the rising sun"

(26) Quei ager *in Africa est,* [...] quae viae in eo agro *antequam Carthago capta est fuerunt,* eae omnes *publicae sunto* (CIL I², 585)
      "which field is in Africa, [...] which roads were in this field before the conquest of Carthage, let all those be public"

If there is a different semantics, resorting to a partitive construction is necessary. This preserves the integrity of the set, resuming it:

(27) quibus excusationibus *antea nimium in aliquo iudicio studium tuum defendere solebas,* earum *habere in hoc homine* nullam *potes* (Cic. *Verr.* II 5,176)
      "in the case of this man you can have none of those excuses with which you formerly used to defend your excessive zeal in any trial"

Correlatives are never resumed by quantifiers that are not consistent with maximalization, such as existential and degree quantifiers. Conversely, they can occur with externally-headed RCs:

(28) *deinde amisso centurione et* paucis militibus quos *visendis hostium copiis praemiserat trepidus remeavit* (Tac. *ann.* 15,10,2)
"Then, after losing a centurion and a few soldiers whom lie had sent on in advance to reconnoitre the enemy's forces, he returned in alarm"

(29) *dissipatis ac perterritis hostibus, ut demonstravimus,* manus *erat* nulla quae *parvam modo causam timoris adferret* (Caes. *Gall.* 6,35,3)
"The enemy having been scattered and alarmed, as we related above, there was no force which might produce even a slight occasion of fear"

Correlatives do not stack. Indeed, in cases like the following, where there are two correlatives, there is no stacking, but coordination:

(30) Quam *quisque ab opere* in partem *casu devenit* quae*que prima* signa *conspexit,* ad haec *constitit* (Caes. *Gall.* 2,21,6)
"whatever part any one came to by chance from the works, and whatever standards he saw first, at these he stood"

In the same way, there is no stacking in (26), as each RC builds a different sortal, *ager* and *viae* respectively, in two different maximalizing operations. In this case, in fact, there rather is a juxtaposition of two (new) topics.

6.2. Circumnominal RCs

The difference between the two types of internally-headed RCs, i.e. circumnominal ones and correlatives, is the fact that the former are embedding, unlike the latter (§2). Indeed, it is not very easy to distinguish them. A good example of a circumnominal RC is the following:

(31) [...] *populo ut placerent* quas *fecisset* fabulas (Ter. *Andr.* 3)
"that the plays he should compose might please the public"

In this case it is said that when the poet began to write for the theatre, he wanted the public to appreciate his plays, i.e. all of them and not only certain ones. This seems a clear instance of maximalizing semantics. The same happens in the following excerpt, in which *quae civitates* refers to all those peoples near to the places where Caesar was at war:[12]

(32) *Ipse in Carnutes, Andes, Turonos* quae*que* civitates *propinquae iis locis erant ubi bellum gesserat, legionibus in hiberna deductis, in Italiam profectus est* (Caes. *Gall.* 2,35,3)
      "He himself, having led his legions into winter quarters among the Carnutes, the Andes, and the Turones, and those states which were close to those regions in which he had waged war, set out for Italy"

Indeed, it is difficult to apply maximalization tests to circumnominal RCs, because they do not usually show links with the RC-external material. Within the *Bellum Gallicum*, for instance, only the following case can be found:

(33) *neque* eam quam *profuisse aliis* vim celeritatem*que viderant, imitari potuerunt* (Caes. *Gall.* 6,40,6)
      "and they could not imitate that vigor and speed which they had observed others to possess"

In this occurrence, the RC-external material is a cataphora; i.e., a semantically empty element, which is totally consistent with maximalization constraints.

Like correlatives, circumnominal RCs do not stack. Another hint of their maximalizing semantics is the fact that they can be introduced by so-called indefinite-relative pronouns, such as *quicumque* and *quisquis* 'whoever', whose semantic value is universal quantification. Let us consider the example below, fully equivalent to the circumnominal introduced by *qui* in (5):[13]

(34) *licere illis per se incolumibus ex hibernis discedere et*, quascumque in partes *velint, sine metu proficisci* (Caes. *Gall.* 5,41,6)
      "it is possible for them to depart from their winter-quarters safely and to proceed without fear into whatever parts they desire"

6.3. Free and Semi-free RCs

The lack of a lexical head prevents free and semi-free RCs from having a modification function, either restrictive or appositive. On the contrary, they have a referential value by themselves, since they designate entities.

This value seems to be consistent with maximalization. Indeed, in addition to cataphoric elements, whose occurrence semi-free RCs imply by definition (§2), only universal quantifiers can cooccur with this type of RC.[14]

(35) *Hac oratione ab Diviciaco habita* omnes qui *aderant magno fletu auxilium a Caesare petere coeperunt* (Caes. *Gall.* 1,32,1)
"When this speech had been delivered by Divitiacus, all who were present began with loud lamentation to entreat assistance of Caesar"

Free and semi-free RCs do not stack. They may be introduced by *quisquis* and *quicumque* (37), probably with the same semantics as they have when introduced by *qui* (36):

(36) quae *deesse operi videbantur perficiuntur* (Caes. *Gall.* 5,40,2)
"(All) the things which seemed necessary to the work are completed"

(37) quaecumque *ad proximi diei oppugnationem opus sunt noctu comparantur* (Caes. *Gall.* 5,40,6)
"whatever things are required for resisting the assault of the next day are provided during the night"

Conclusion

Even if there are neither suprasegmental nor morpho-syntactic correlates, the opposition between restrictiveness and non-restrictiveness can also be claimed for Latin. In addition to pragmatic and semantic facts, such as information structure and the degree of identification of the head noun referent, in this language the cooccurrence of cataphoric *is* with the lexical head implies restrictiveness. The distinction between restrictives and appositives only affects external-headed RCs. In the case of an internal head – i.e. correlatives and circumnominal RCs – there is no modification, either as intersection or as a secondary predication, but maximalization. In this case the whole semantic content of the relative construction is codified within the RC, while the external material is reduced to a minimum and its semantic contribution has to be traced back to a RC-internal interpretation or to an interpretation which is predictable from the RC. The same happens when there is no lexical head, namely in the case of free and semi-free RCs. Tests to identify the maximalizing semantics of RCs are: (a) their compatibility only with universal quantifiers and definite determiners, (b) the impossibility of stacking and (c) the possibility to be introduced through relative pronouns which always codify universal quantification, such as *quisquis* and *quicumque*.

Notes

[1] See e.g. Kühner and Stegmann (1914: 279; 284-285), Ernout and Thomas (1953: 333-334).

[2] According to Lehmann (1986: 664), "A relative construction is a construction consisting of a nominal [the head] and a subordinate clause [the RC] interpreted as attributively modifying the nominal. [...] The attributive relation between head and relative clause is such that the head is involved in what is stated in the clause".

[3] To refer to the pivot in the matrix clause, the term *antecedent* is often used. As Touratier (1980: 111-112) remarks, this term is misleading since an antecedent precedes by definition the element that resumes it, while what is usually called antecedent in Latin often follows the RC.

[4] The definition of *semi-free* (or *false*) RCs was made by De Vries (2002: 55). On the syntactic equivalence between semi-free and free RCs see Oniga (2007: 266-272), who proposes the structure pro_i [$_{CP}$ qui_i t_i *virtutem amat*] *deum amat* for free RCs, counter to their analysis as argumental clauses claimed by Pinkster (1990:90).

[5] For a recent discussion on the opposition of restrictive vs. non-restrictive RCs see, among others, the articles in Fuchs (1987), and de Vries (2002: 413-425), who resumes the analyses which have been proposed from a structural point of view.

[6] See Cinque (1988: 446).

[7] See Grosu and Landman (1998: 126).

[8] See e.g. Lavency (1998: 30-31) and Vester (1989: 342). According to Pinkster (1990: 81), a non-restrictive reading is natural even when RCs include a sentence adverbial which expresses the judgment of the speaker/writer. See e.g. Liv. 29, 34, 9 (*tegentibus tumulis, qui* peropportune *circa uiae flexus oppositi erant, occultus processit* 'his approach being concealed by some low hills which fortunately flanked his route').

[9] An example of degree RCs studied by Carlson (1977) and Heim (1987) is 'I took with me *the three books (that) there were__* on the table'. This RC contains a null degree expression, *d many books*, in which only *d* is bound by the relativizer. Degree RCs have a particular kind of denotation (a set of degree), and therefore cannot combine with the head noun through intersection: intersecting a set of individuals with a set of degrees is senseless.

[10] Simplex CPs are free RCs such as 'Io ho *con chi* parlare di filosofia' in Italian. The difference with regard to free RCs functioning as maximalizers is that the latter imply a phonologically null pronoun (*pro*), whereas Simplex CPs do not allow any RC-external material whatsoever, being bare clauses.

[11] On the opposition between *sortal-internal* and *sortal-external* RCs see Grosu and Landman (1998: 126): "This dichotomy takes as a criterion whether the relative construction's sortal (which is the common noun, or NP, if nominal

constructions are DPs) is *semantically* construed outside or inside the construction's CP".

[12] In this excerpt, the lack of an item such as *in eas* in the matrix clause is probably due to recoverability of the syntactic link on the basis of the circumnominal RC insertion within an enumeration by coordination (*in Carnutes, Andes, Turonos*).

[13] This also happens in the case of correlatives. An interesting example is Cic. *Verr.* II 5,145 (Quaecumque navis *ex Asia,* quae *ex Syria,* quae *Tyro,* quae *Alexandria venerat, statim certis indicibus et custodibus tenebatur* 'Every ship that came from Asia, from Syria, from Tyre, from Alexandria, was immediately seized by informers and guards that he could rely upon'): here the equivalence between the two pronouns is clear; if this really is an instance of preposed RC, instead of a circumnominal one.

[14] Indeed, there are also cases such as Cic. *Verr.* II 1,126 (multa quae *quemvis commovere possent dixit* 'he said many things which might have influenced any one') or Plaut. *Curc.* 607 (*Et* alii multi qui *nunc serviunt.* 'And so were many others, who are now in servitude'). Concerning these occurrences, firstly whether *multus* and *alii* are instances of conversion to nouns has to be questioned. However, free RCs undoubtedly require a further analysis.

References

Carlson, G. (1977) "Amount Relatives" *Language* 53: 520–542.

Cinque, G. (1988) "La frase relative", in L. Renzi (ed.) *Grande grammatica italiana di consultazione*, I, Bologna, il Mulino, 443-503.

Croft, W. (1991) *Syntactic Categories and Grammatical Relations: The Cognitive Organization of Information*, Chicago, University of Chicago Press.

Ernout, A. and F. Thomas (1953) *Syntaxe latine*, 2e éd., Paris, Klincksieck.

Fuchs, C. (ed.) (1987) *Les types de relative*, *Special number of Langages* 88.

Grosu, A. and F. Landmann (1998) "Strange relatives of the Third Kind" *Natural Language Semantics* 6: 125-170.

Grosu, A. (2002) "Strange relatives at the interface of two millennia" *Glot International* 6: 145-167.

Heim, I. (1987) "Where does the definiteness restriction apply? Evidence from the definiteness of variables", in E. Reuland and A. ter Meulen (eds) *The Linguistic Representation of (In)definiteness*, Cambridge Mass., MIT Press, 21–42.

Kühner, R. and C. Stegmann (1914) *Ausführliche Grammatik der lateinischen Sprache*, II: *Satzlehre*, 2. Auflage, Hannover, Hahn.

Lavency, M. (1998) *La proposition relative*, Louvain-la-Neuve, Peeters.

Lehmann, C. (1984) *Der Relativsatz. Typologie seiner Strukturen, Theorie seiner Funktionen, Kompendium seiner Grammatik*, Tübingen, Narr.

—. (1986) "On the typology of relative clauses" *Linguistics* 24: 663-680.

Oniga, R. (2007) *Il latino. Breve introduzione linguistica*, 2ª ed., Milano, Franco Angeli.

Partee, B. (1973) "Some transformational extensions of Montague Grammar" *Journal of Philosophical Logic* 2: 509–534.

Pinkster, H. (1990) *Latin Syntax and Semantics*, London, Routledge.

Sells, P. (1985) "Restrictive and non-restrictive modification", Stanford, Stanford University Center for the Study of Language and Information.

Touratier, C. (1980) *La relative. Essai de théorie syntaxique*, Paris, Klincksieck.

Vester, E. (1977) "On the so-called 'participium coniunctum'" *Mnemosyne* 30: 243-85.

—. (1989) "Relative clauses: a description of the Indicative-Subjunctive opposition", in G. Calboli (ed.) *Subordination and other Topics in Latin*, Amsterdam/Philadelphia, Benjamins, 327-350.

Vries, M. de (2002) *The Syntax of Relativization*, Utrecht, LOT.

DECOMPOSING SUBJECTS:
A HYPOTHESIS ON THE CONTROLLER
OF THE ABLATIVE OF THE GERUND

SILVIA PIERONI

Introduction

Various domains of Latin morphosyntax show that the notions we inherit from traditional grammatical descriptions are too coarse-grained to account for the data in detail: a model appears to be needed, capable of narrowing the focus and accounting for smaller components through subtler notions.

The notion of subject is an example. Although any definition will obviously at least partly agree with the traditional one, the need for a less monolithic idea is evident. It is a matter of fact that the distinction between a 'grammatical' and a 'logical' or 'notional' subject is found in many descriptive models, including the traditional models themselves (cf. Graffi 1988). However, if the point of view that considers morphology and semantics as the basics is abandoned, the distinction might still be refined: a different perspective, for instance, might arise if a syntactic point of view is adopted.

1. The ablative of the gerund: two types of structures

I will start from the analysis of some data concerning the ablative of the gerund.[1] The gerund is a nominal non-finite form of the verb, thus unspecific for person. Whether it is a true noun or not (which is not the point here), the gerund is a predication supplementary to the proposition where it is included.[2] Like every predicate, it has a thematic grid comprising a non-explicit subject.[3] The question is then: how can the grid be reconstructed? How can an interpretation be built?

Two types of structures can be found. The first, which is stylistically marked, is a structure where the subject of the gerund must be interpreted independently of any relationship with a nominal present in the proposition the gerund is related to. This type will be here called 'impersonal':[4]

(1)   *Fando* ego istunc hominem numquam audivi ante hunc diem (Plaut. *Epid.* 496)
       "Today is the very first time I ever heard tell of the man"[5]

(2)   Salsa autem tellus et quae perhibetur amara / (frugibus infelix ea nec mansuescit *arando*) (Verg. *georg.* 2,238-239)
       "As for salty land, the kind called bitter (unfruitful it is for crops and mellows not in ploughing ...)"

Otherwise, the subject can be interpreted in relation to a nominal (explicit or virtual) of the proposition to which it is linked. This is to say that it seeks a controller there: this type will be here called 'non-impersonal'.[6] I will focus on this second type and henceforth disregard the impersonal gerund.

When the subject of the gerund is interpreted in relation to a nominal of the proposition where the gerund is included, the question is the following: which subject for the gerund? In other words: what is the condition on the controller?

As a general rule, in non-passive structures, the subject of the gerund is the same as the subject of the proposition where the gerund is included and this happens independently of the presence of an active or deponent verbal form in the main predicate (cf. Vester 1983: 101-120; Vester 1985; Maraldi 1995):[7]

(3)   et legiones Teloboarum vi *pugnando* cepimus (Plaut. *Amph.* 414)
       "and we subdued the legions of the Teloboans by our sturdy onslaughts"

(4)   [...] *osculando* ego ulciscar potissimum. (Plaut. *Asin.* 897)
       "and that will be my favourite method of revenge - kissing him"

(5)   Quis talia *fando* / Myrmidonum Dolopumve aut duri miles Ulixi / temperet a lacrimis? (Verg. *Aen.* 2,6-8)[8]
       "What Myrmidon or Dolopian, or soldier of the stern Ulysses, could refrain from tears in telling such a tale?"

(6)   Verum ubi nulla datur dextram adfectare potestas / nec potis Ionios
      fluctus aequare *sequendo* (Verg. *Aen.* 3,670-671)
      "But when no power is given him to lay hands on us, and he cannot
      in his pursuit keep up with the Ionian rollers"

On the other hand, this is not the rule in passive structures, where, in
general, the subject of the gerund is not to be interpreted as the same of the
grammatical subject of the passive structure[9] and, in case it can be
interpreted as coreferent with a nominal of the main predication, it is
rather interpretable as its agent, usually unspecified:[10]

(7)   semper [...] alter ab altero adiutus et *communicando* et *monendo* et
      favendo (Cic. *Brut.* 3)
      "each of us was helped by the other with exchange of suggestion,
      admonition, and friendly offices"

(8)   *Amando*ne exorarier vis ted an *osculando*? (Plaut. *Asin.* 687)
      "Tease it from you [lit. passive: would you be moved] by loving you,
      or by kissing you, which?"

(9)   *exorando*, haud *adversando* sumendam operam censeo (Plaut. *Stich.*
      70)
      "But it seems to me that we should rely on appeal rather than
      opposition"

Thus evidence would seem to invite consideration of a notion which
combines grammatical subjects of non-passive structures (be they active or
deponent) and logical subjects of passive structures, in order to avoid a
disjunctive definition of the elements capable of control.

2. A comparison with reflexive structures

This condition on the controllers of the ablative gerund is reminiscent of
the condition on controllers in reflexive structures (reflexive pronouns
need an antecedent, i.e. they seek a controller: in other words, they may be
considered as predicates seeking their subject).

   The reflexive is often controlled by the grammatical subject of the
structure (this happens independently of the presence of an active or
deponent verbal form):

(10) per eos ne causam diceret se eripuit (Caes. *Gall.* 1,4,2)
      "[Orgetorix] through their means escaped from taking his trial"

(11) se ad eam rem profitetur adiutorem (Caes. *Gall.* 5,38,4)
      "[Ambiorix] offered his own assistance to that end"

But not always. For instance, this is not the case in passive structures. In (12) an impersonal passive structure shows a reflexive controlled by the implicit agent of the predicate *petitur*, in (13) the 'long-distance' reflexive which appears in the complement clause is controlled by the agentive complement *a Caesare* of the main predication:

(12) quod sibi petitur, certe alteri non exigitur (Cic. *Q. Rosc.* 52)
      "for what is claimed for oneself is certainly not demanded for another"

(13) multa a Caesare in eam sententiam dicta sunt […] neque se iudicare Galliam potius esse Ariovisti quam populi Romani (Caes. *Gall.* 1,45,1)
      "Caesar spoke at length [lit. passive: 'many statements were made by Caesar'] for the purpose of showing why ... nor did he admit that Gaul belonged to Ariovistus rather than to the Roman people"

The crucial element thus appears to be the diathetic opposition, which joins, as controllers, grammatical subjects of non-passive structures (be the verbal form active or deponent) and logical subjects of passive clauses. In fact, controllers may also be found under the form of other grammatical relations (I dealt with this variation in Pieroni 2007):

(14) neque eam unquam sui paenitet (Cic. *Tusc.* 5,54)
      "and [wisdom] is never self-repentant"

(15) an aliis licet, et recte licet, in meo metu sibi nihil timere […] (Cic. *dom.* 8)
      "Are others permitted, and rightly permitted, to find no cause for personal apprehension in what brings fear to me ..."

(16) aratoris interest ita se frumenta habere [...] (Cic. *Verr.* II 3,147)
      "it is to the advantage of the farmer to have crops so heavy ..."

In the literature on the antecedents of reflexives, the notion of 'logical subject' has been traditionally invoked (cf. Juret 1933: 103 ff.),[11] a notion which in fact resorts, though implicitly, to the idea of a semantic hierarchy of roles (in the absence of any Agent, a different semantic role may be implied). From a perspective which focuses long-distance reflexives in indirect speech, the notion of 'Speaker' has also been persuasively claimed to be relevant (a refined account in Fruyt 1987; see also Fruyt 2002).

As for the coreference of the subject of the gerund, Vester (1983: 108) established a rule, which was summarized in Vester (1985: 232) as follows:

> with [+co (*i.e.* control, SP)] states of affairs the Agent of the gerund is coreferential with the Agent of the main predication. [...] with [-co] states of affairs the Agent of the gerund is corefential with the Subject of the main predication.

However, in order to account for the variety of the semantic roles involved, she finally argued that a 'hierarchy of coreferentiality' should be invoked:

> the rule about coreferentiality of the Subject of the gerund has to be modified into a rule which states that the Subject of the gerund is coreferential with the referent of the argument in the main predication, with that semantic function which is highest in the Semantic Function Hierarchy. (Vester 1983: 115)

3. More than one subject

A syntactic counterpart to these definitions (thus, not in opposition, but neither as a mere translation of them) could however be looked for. Tools which are subtle enough to grasp the ratio of the phenomena described have been developed in the literature and are ready, as long as one accepts that notions such as 'subject' (as well as 'object' and 'predicate') are not to be referred *tout court* to propositions, thus being the same in all types of propositions. Rather, they can be decomposed, factorizing the relationships they keep with other grammatical relations (both syntagmatically and paradigmatically). A multi-stratal formalism can represent this network of relations: 'subject' may therefore be defined only in relation to a specific syntactic stratum. This idea was developed within the framework of Relational Grammar and appears to be one of the most fruitful, yet still undervalued, of the linguistic thought of the last century (see, in particular, Perlmutter 1982).

From the point of view adopted here, formalized representations are instruments to visualize relationships, without implications of generative rules.[12] As an example, representing passives as bistratal structures (thus stating that the initial stratum is transitive and the final intransitive) is a way to relate them to the corresponding active transitive structures and this relationship may in fact be claimed on the basis of the sameness of the semantic roles, given a certain predicative structure (the final 1 is an initial 2, i.e. semantically equivalent to the object of the corresponding transitive structure; the initial 1 loses its relation thus being a final chômeur, i.e. the agentive complement is semantically equivalent to the subject of the corresponding active transitive clause).

(17) magnumque ex iis numerum occidit (Caes. *Gall.* 5,51,4)
      "He slew a great number of them"

1	2	P
[III pers sing]	magnum numerum	occidit

(18) non numquam etiam latro a viatore occiditur (Cic. *Mil.* 55)
      "sometimes it is even the highwayman who is slain by the traveler"

2	1	P
1	Chô	P
latro	a viatore	occiditur

Moreover, this representation tries to account for specific morphosyntactic properties which are shared, on the one hand, by the objects of transitive structures and the subjects of the corresponding passives; on the other, for properties which are shared by all final subjects (of both actives and passives) despite the fact that they don't share the same semantic role. From a slightly different angle, we could also say that bistratal structures (and multistratal structures in general, of course) split the properties of subjects, distinguishing those which belong to the initial and those which belong to the final subject, whereas these properties conflate in the subject of a monoclausal structure, exactly for the fact that it is both the initial and the final one.

As a matter of fact, diathetic oppositions describe a more complex articulation (in Latin and not only in Latin):[13] non-passive structures may be active or not. According to a proposal first suggested by La Fauci (1988), the Latin medial domain includes, besides passive structures, unaccusative structures.[14] Unaccusative structures would thus lie behind the medial type in (19) (which is in fact opposed to the active type (20) and to its passive counterpart (21)), as well as behind the *media tantum* type (i.e. the type where a deponent verb appears, as in (22)):

(19) alii aliam in partem perterriti ferebantur (Caes. *Gall.* 2,24,3)
 "they began to rush terror-stricken in all directions"

(20) qui decimae legionis aquilam ferebat (Caes. *Gall.* 4,25,3)
 "the eagle-bearer [lit. 'the one who bore the eagle'] of the Tenth Legion"

(21) feruntur omnino condiciones ab illo (Cic. *fam.* 16,12,3)
 "These, broadly speaking, are the terms Caesar offers" [lit. passive: "these are the terms offered by him"]

(22) [...] quem di diligunt / adulescens moritur (Plaut. *Bacch.* 816-817)
 "He whom the gods love dies young"

Medial structures are therefore defined as a whole by a common feature; at the same time, differences among the subtypes are singled out. On the one hand, the common feature (which defines the medial domain as a whole) is the fact that, both in passive and unaccusative structures, final subjects bear the object relation in a preceding stratum. On the other hand, passive and unaccusative structures differ in that the former, but not the latter, have a subject different from the final one in strata preceding the final one. Here follow the diagrams:

(23) = (19) alii aliam in partem ferebantur (Caes. *Gall.* 2,24,3)

2	P
1	P
alii	ferebantur

(24) = (22) quem di diligunt adulescens moritur (Plaut. *Bacch.* 817)

2	P
1	P
[III pers sing]	moritur

(25) = (21) feruntur omnino condiciones ab illo

P	2	1
P	1	Chô
feruntur	condiciones	ab illo

From this point of view, verbal morphosyntax, which is the same in passive and unaccusative structures, is a manifestation of the common feature. As is well-known, the morphological aspect is also the same in perfective periphrases:

(26) [...] ut haec est fabrc facta ab nobis. (Plaut. *Cas.* 861)
"[There never was a playwright who invented a cleverer plot] than this masterpiece of ours (lit.: so as this one has been cleverly devised by us)"

2	P		1
1	P		Chô
1	Chô	P	Chô
haec	facta	est	a nobis

(27) [...] Tanton in re perdita, / quam in re salva Lesbonicus factus est frugalior? (Plaut. *Trin.* 609-610)
"So Lesbonicus ruined has turned much thriftier than Lesbonicus rich, eh?"

2			P
2	P		Chô
1	P		Chô
1	Chô	P	Chô
Lesbonicus	factus	est	frugalior

Morphology, however, is not the only piece of evidence which supports La Fauci's hypothesis: other phenomena go in the same direction, e.g. the possibility of absolute ablatives with past participles, which is in fact inscribed within this medial domain.[15] As a matter of fact, in absolute ablatives, past participles of medial non-passive verbs can be found (e.g. *hoc mortuo*, Caes. *Gall.* 6,3,9), as well as participles of transitive verbs (e.g. *duce hostium occiso*, Liv. 1,10,5): in the latter case, the subject of the participle may only be interpreted as the initial object of the predication manifested by the participle (i.e. the *dux* is the one who is killed, not the killer). It is worth emphasizing that the fact itself that absolute ablatives with past participles of intransitive active verbs are not attested (e.g. *pervento duce*), which is usually ascribed in didactic grammars to the morphological reason that verbs such as *pervenio* do not have the past participle (but cf. *Quoniam ad hunc locum perventum est*, Caes. *Gall.* 6,11) demand a consistent explanation from a syntactic point of view.[16] From the articulation of the medial domain in passive and non-passive (i.e. unaccusative), a description therefore follows for the occurrence of absolute ablatives with the past participle:

(28) Corollary: generalization on the absolute ablative with past participle
      The participle is accompanied by its initial direct object[17].

4. A condition on the controller

A relevant notion for the condition on the controller of the gerund thus emerges: the stratigraphic notion of 'first subject' precisely combines the final subjects of non-passive structures and the initial subjects of passive structures. If the gerund looks for its subject in the proposition where it is included, its controller is the first subject of the structure. This means that it is the final (i.e. the grammatical) subject only as long as no other subjects appear in preceding strata. The diagrams below reproduce the structures relative to the main predications of (3), (4) and (7):

(29)   2   P   P   2   ❶

            2   P   ❶   ❶   P   P   1   Chô

        legiones cepimus   [1pl]   ego   ulciscar adiutus alter ab altero

The generalization recalls the one that holds for the reflexive (as shown in Pieroni 2007), though in the case of the Latin gerund it must be once again emphasized that the search for the first subject is not always the case, since gerunds may be impersonal. To sum up, Latin reflexives select the first subject of the structure; as in the negative of a film, when gerunds, which are not bound to take a subject, do take one, they cannot but select a first subject.[18]

(30) Condition on the controller of the ablative gerund
      If any, the controller of the ablative gerund is the first subject of the predication where the gerund is included.

5. As a conclusion: gerunds and diathesis

Now consider the following examples:

(31) *Expectando* exedor miser atque exenteror (Plaut. *Epid.* 320)
"Oh, I'm devoured, disembowelled, with this damnable waiting"

(32) adulescentulus / saepe eadem et graviter *audiendo* victus est (Ter. *Haut.* 113-114)
"the lad by having this perpetually and painfully dinned into him was overcome"

(33) hominis autem mens *discendo* alitur et *cogitando* (Cic. *off.* 1,105)
"but man's mind is nurtured by study and meditation"

(34) si nimis atrociter *imperando* sociis in tantum adductus periculum videretur (Cic. *Verr.* II 2,70)
"did it appear that the reason of his incurring a danger so grave was the brutality of his orders to our allies"

(35) vulnus esse eius modi quod mihi nec dissimulandum nec pertimescendum videretur, ne aut *ignorando* stultissimi aut *metuendo* ignavissimi iudicaremur (Cic. *Att.* 1,16,9)
"the wound is such that it cannot be disguised, yet it must not be feared, lest by our fear we prove ourselves abject cowards, or by ignoring it, very fools"

In these examples, the controller of the ablative gerund is the subject of *exedor, alitur, adductus, victus est, iudicaremur*. If we adopt a traditional and morphological point of view, cases (31)-(35) could certainly be considered as passives. As such, they could raise a problem: why is the controller the grammatical subject, whereas in cases such as (7), (8) and (9) it is the logical subject? This is exactly the question raised by Vester (see § 3, above): according to her hypothesis based on states of affairs, she maintains that precisely from these occurrences we may infer that the verbal forms (namely, *victus est* ad *adductus* in examples (32) and (34)) refer

> to [-co (i.e. control, SP)] states of affairs, probably even to states, considering the perfect forms. (Vester 1985: 233)

Basically, she claims that examples such as (32) and (34) are agentless passive constructions.

The idea of morphologically passive structures which anyway differ from 'true' passives is not new: "deponentialen Passiven" is the term found in Kühner and Stegmann, "médio-passifs", i.e. "verbes ... dont le passifs peut prendre une valeur moyenne" is the description given by Ernout and Thomas:

> Die Deponenten unterscheiden sich von den deponentialen Passiven, wie *volvor, vertor*, und von den reflexiven Passiven, wie *obligor, relaxor*, nur dadurch, daß sie die aktive Form verloren haben und nur in der passiven (ursprünglich reflexiven) Form erscheinen.
> (Kühner and Stegmann 1955: 110)

> § 223. Médio-passifs. - Ce sont de verbes ayant un actif et dont le passif peut prendre une valeur moyenne, le plus souvent un sens **réfléchi**. Ils indique d'ordinaire:
> des soins corporels: *lavari* «se laver», *ornari* «se parer» [...];
> un déplacement dans l'espace: *colligi* «se rassembler», *ferri* «se porter (se diriger) vers» [...];
> des actions diverses: *dedi* «se rendre», *excruciari* «se tourmenter» […].
> (Ernout and Thomas 1953[2]: 202)

The traditional classification, in fact, considers the diathetic opposition between active and so-called medial-passive from a morpholexical perspective: passive, medial, medial-passive are labels to classify verbs.

From the point of view adopted here, however, cases as those in (31)-(35) are not passives at all: they are medial non-passive structures. Gerunds seek the first subject of the main predication: picking up the grammatical subject (i.e. final), they reveal the non-passive character of the structure.[19] As a matter of fact, looking at the opposition (within the medial domain) between passives and non-passives from a syntactic rather than from a categorial point of view avoids making sketchy lists of verbs which, in their passive form, do not have a truly passive meaning. As long as 'medial' and 'passive' are considered as syntactic notions, to be defined by factorizing features, the occurrence of many verbs in both types of structures will not require any further explanation. Moreover, the common feature will itself be responsible for the possible ambiguity in case the differential feature remains concealed (absence of agentive complement, no gerundial test at disposal), which is simply to say that ambiguity is an effect of the partial sameness between two structures. If this may appear obvious, it is however still unusual to pursue the consideration of syntax as the process which, as such, creates the whole and its single parts at the same time: that is, to take it as a starting viewpoint.

Notes

*The proposals suggested in this paper have been first developed within the research project PRIN 2008 "Mutamento e contatto tra varietà nella diacronia linguistica del Mediterraneo" ("Contact and change in the history of Mediterranean languages"), coordinated by Marco Mancini. Many of these ideas have been discussed with Nunzio La Fauci and Liana Tronci; it goes without saying that the way I developed them is my entire responsibility. Many thanks to Marina Benedetti, Ignazio Mauro Mirto and Alessandro Parenti for their comments and to Stefania D'Agata D'Ottavi for her help with the English of this article. - This is dedicated to Donatella Lumini Grillone, my Latin schoolteacher and a friend for many years.

[1] In the following discussion I will not consider ablative gerunds introduced by a preposition nor will I deal with the semantics of the ablative of the gerund (instrumental, temporal, expressing manner, etc.; cf. Touratier 1994: 154, in particular). The data that follow are not based on an exhaustive philological analysis: the descriptive hypothesis I will suggest is based on the scrutiny of the whole of Plautus, on samples from Cicero and Virgil and on data taken from grammars and previous studies. As is obvious, further refinements could be needed in case further types were found.

[2] In the literature of the last decades, gerunds (as well as other non-finite verb forms that express adverbial subordination) have been sometimes referred to as 'converbs', a term previously used for Mongolian and Turkish languages. Nedjalkov (1995: 97), for instance, explicitly referring to Jakobson's notion of 'dependent taxis' (cf. Jakobson 1957: 135), defines a converb, at least as a first approximation, "as a verb form which depends syntactically on another verb form, but is not its syntactic actant, i.e. does not realize its semantic valencies".

[3] For late occurrences of the ablative of the gerund with an explicit subject, cf. Maraldi (1994: 143).

[4] These types of cases are analysed by Calboli Montefusco (1971), who starts from the treatment of the gerund by Latin grammarians, thus discussing its categorial status (noun or verb, mood or *Aktionsart*), and eventually argues that the gerund might have a passive value in some (very marked) contexts. E.g. she quotes *Carpit enim viris paulatim uritque* videndo / *femina nec nemorum patitur meminisse neque herbae* (Verg. *georg.* 3,215-216) 'For the sight of the female slowly inflames and wastes his strength, nor suffer him to remember woods or pastures': according to her, *videndo* would be passive and thus *femina* would be the subject of both *urit* and *videndo*: 'when she is seen, because of the very fact of being seen' (cf. also Verg. *ecl.* 8,71). On the other hand, an 'impersonal' reading of these lines could also be given: 'the female takes all strength away and inflames through the sight'.

The possibility of a diathetic opposition between passive and active is naturally linked to the issue of the verbal or nominal status of the gerund, which is in its turn linked to other issues which are completely disregarded in this paper, in particular the historical relationship between gerund and gerundive. See, among the others, Aalto (1949), Risch (1984), Ambrosini (1991), Vester (1991), Stempel (1995), De Carvalho (2001), Drexler and Strunk (2004), Catalin (2008). It is worth emphasizing that all the solutions (priority of the gerund, priority of the gerundive, originary status of both gerund and gerundive) have their supporters.

[5] All translations are taken from the Loeb Classical Library; a literal gloss has been added whenever necessary.

[6] The notions of *PRO* and *pro*, as developed in the generative framework, could also suit the distinction between 'impersonal' and 'non-impersonal' gerunds.

[7] A couple of problematic cases are worth of attention: *quem Carthaginienses resectis palpebris inligatum in machina* vigilando *necaverunt* (Cic. *Pis.* 43) 'whose eyelids the Carthaginians cut off, whom they bound to a machine and did to death by sleeplessness'; *vovisse hunc dicam, si salvos domum / redisset umquam, ut me* ambulando *rumperet* (Ter. *Hec.* 434-435) 'I bet he made a vow that, if he ever got home safely, he'd burst my guts with running errands'. Here the subjects of the gerunds have the same referent of the direct object of the main predication (an extremely rare pattern, according to Maraldi 1994: 145), though in fact the subjects of *necare* and *rumpere* are responsible for the actions of *vigilare* and *ambulare*: the structures are pregnant because they are, so to say, 'causative'. An impersonal, 'quasi-nominal' reading seems to lie behind most translations: cf. also the translation of Terence's lines given by *Les belles lettres* edition: 'je dirais qu'il a fait voeu, si jamais il rentrait sauf à la maison, de m'éreinter en courses!'. On the other hand, an alternative tentative hypothesis could be advanced: at least for Cicero's passage, it could be argued that the gerund is not relevant at the propositional level, as a supplementary predication in relation to the main verb form; rather, it may be relevant *within* the object noun phrase (cf. footnote 9).

[8] Here is an instance of non-impersonal *fando*: the subject of *fando* is the same as the subject of *temperet*; cf. the impersonal *fando* in ex. 1.

[9] The only possible counterexample I encountered is the following: *cum* vigilando *necabatur* (Cic. *off.* 3,100) 'when he was being slowly put to death by enforced wakefulness'. Cf. the anonymous *verberando necati* quoted by Macrobius (*exc. gramm.* V 649, 12 ff.), where the agent implied by *necati* is the same as the subject of *verberando*, as expected. It is worth emphasizing that *vigilando necabatur* is the mirror image of Cicero's passage quoted in footnote 7 (in both the topic is M. Atilius Regulus' death): *quem Carthaginienses resectis palpebris inligatum in machina* vigilando *necaverunt* (Cic. *Pis.* 43). From a morphosyntactic point of view, it could be argued that, as in its active counterpart, in *vigilando necabatur* the gerund functions *within* the noun phrase (i.e. the subject noun phrase, in this case) rather than at the propositional level.

For the discussion of further cases, which are sometimes considered as passives (but they are not), cf. below, § 6.

[10] With the exception of ex. (7), the agent is always unspecified in the passive structures I collected. The point made here is that the subject of these gerunds can

nevertheless be interpreted in relation to an argument 'initialized' by the predicate which is expressed by the passive verb, namely to the logical subject of the passive structure. This makes the difference as compared with impersonal gerunds exemplified in (1)-(2).

[11] Ernout and Thomas (1953[2]) rather prefer the notion of 'real subject' (*sujet réel*).

[12] In the following diagrams, which should be read from top to bottom, numbers denote grammatical relations: 1 stands for 'subject', 2 for 'object', P for 'predicate'. Chô (= chômeur) is the relationship borne by an element which loses its grammatical relation without acquiring a new one. The upper level is therefore the first, in fact called the 'initial stratum'; the lower level the last, called the 'final stratum'. Between initial and final strata other levels may be found.

[13] "La "voix" situe le sujet par rapport au procès (É. Benveniste, *Problèmes de linguistique générale* ... p. 168 sq.). L'i.-e. ne connaissait que l'actif (procès se réalisant à partir du sujet) et le moyen (procès intérieur au sujet, ou rapporté à son activité interne). Le latin s'est constitué un passif avec le moyen et un impersonnel en *-r*. Le moyen subsiste dans le déponent (*sequor*) et dans le verbes médio-passifs (*vertor*); et certains emplois du passif ont gardé le souvenir de l'impersonnel en *-r*: *venitur* "on vient"." (Ernout and Thomas 1953[2]: 201)

[14] The 'Unaccusative Hypothesis' was first developed by Perlmutter (1978) within the framework of Relational Grammar. It is a fact that the nature of this hypothesis has been widely accepted in other syntactic descriptions, but, once seen within different frameworks, often misrepresented and sometimes distorted. In Relational Grammar, for instance, despite the fact that a verb may concisely be labelled as 'unaccusative', unaccusativity remains a primarily syntactic notion and not a lexical and semantic one.

[15] Actually, I am simplifying the presentation, disregarding the complexity of the medial non-passive domain, e.g. structures where a deponent verb occurs, but which look as transitive: *senex in culina clamat, hortatur coquos* (Plaut. *Cas.* 764) "the old man is clamouring in the kitchen, urging on the cooks". The hypothesis on this type of structures, which I will not discuss here, is the following:

1	P	2
1,2	P	Chô
1	P	Chô
senex	hortatur	coquos

For a comparative description of the medial domain in Indo-European languages, see the outlines suggested in Benedetti (2005) and La Fauci and Tronci (2009).

[16] The fact that the deponent transitive verbs are not found in absolute ablatives with past participles is accounted for by the representation proposed in footnote 15: on the one hand, the subject of these structures is not the initial object and cannot therefore enter the absolute ablative; on the other hand, the initial object is not available in that it is 'chômerized'. In this connection (neither intransitive actives nor transitive deponents in absolute ablatives with past participles), traditional grammars note that either the *participium coniunctum* or the *cum* + subjunctive

structure functionally substitute the missing absolute ablative. See Oniga (2007: 292).

[17] Which is the same as in Italian. For a detailed treatment of participial absolutes in Italian, cf. Loporcaro (2003).

[18] E.g. in *bene* salutando *consuescunt* compellando *blanditer,* / osculando*, oratione vinnula, venustula* (Plaut. *Asin.* 222-223) 'they become familiar through pleasant greetings, pretty speeches, kisses, cooey, captivating little whispers', which is considered as a problematic case by Vester (1983: 114), I would agree with Maraldi (1994: 153) that the gerunds are to be considered referentially independent of the nominals of the main predication (in my terms, impersonal). As I have already said, my claim is not that the gerund must take a subject; rather, that when it takes one, it is possible to determine which. Or, perhaps better, it is possible to determine which elements will never be selected as controllers.

[19] Thus the gerund turns out to be a good syntactic test, as suggested by Vester (1985), for determining the nature of the main clause: in Vester's proposal, however, the test aims at determining whether an Agent capable of intentional control on the predication is present or not, whereas in this paper the subject of the gerund is considered as a litmus test for diathesis.

References

Aalto, P. (1949) *Untersuchungen über das lateinische Gerundium und Gerundivum*, Helsinki, Druckerei-A.G. der Finnischen Literatur-gesellschaft.

Ambrosini, R. (1991) "Gerundio e gerundivo in latino" *Studi e saggi linguistici* 31: 1-53.

Benedetti, M. (2005) "Dispersioni formali del medio indoeuropeo", in L. Costamagna and S. Giannini (eds) *Acquisizione e mutamento di categorie linguistiche. Atti del Convegno della Società Italiana di Glottologia* (Perugia, 23 - 25 ottobre 2003), Roma, Il Calamo, 95-119.

Calboli Montefusco, L. (1971) "La diatesi passiva del gerundio latino" *Lingua e stile* 6.3: 463-478.

Catalin, A. (2008) "The Latin gerund and gerundive: active or passive meaning?" *Indogermanische Forschungen* 113: 197-206.

De Carvalho, P. (2001) "Du nom (dé)verbal en *-ndo/a-* «gerundium» vs «gerundiuum»", in C. Moussy (ed.) *De lingua Latina novae questiones.* Actes du X^{è} Colloque International de Linguistique Latine (Paris-Sèvres, 19-23 avril 1999), Louvain, Paris - Sterling, Virginia, Peeters, 307-320.

Drexler, H. and K. Strunk (1962) "Über Gerundium und Gerundivum" *Gymnasium* 69: 429-460.

Ernout, A. and F. Thomas (1953^{2}) *Syntaxe latine*, Paris, Klincksieck.

Fruyt, M. (1987) "Interprétation sémantico-référentielle du réfléchi latin",

Glotta 65: 204-221.

—. (2002) "Réfléchi indirect et énonciation en latin", in L. Sawicki and D. Shalev (eds) *Donum grammaticum. Studies in Latin and Celtic Linguistics in Honour of Hannah Rosén*, Leuven - Paris - Sterling, Virginia, Peeters, 123-132.

Graffi, G. (1988) "Structural subject and thematic subject" *Linguisticae Investigationes* 12.2: 397-414.

Jakobson, R. (1957) *Shifters, verbal categories and the Russian verb*, Harvard, Department of Slavic Languages and Literature; republished in Id. *Selected Writings*, II, The Hague - Paris, Mouton, 1971, 130-167.

Juret, A.C. (1933) *Système de la syntaxe latine*, Paris, Les Belles Lettres.

Kühner, R. and C. Stegmann (1955) *Ausführliche Grammatik der lateinischen Sprache*, II: *Satzlehre*, 1. Teil, 3. Auflage, Hannover, Hahn.

La Fauci, N. (1988) *Oggetti e soggetti nella formazione della morfosintassi romanza*, Pisa, Giardini.

La Fauci, N. and L. Tronci (2009) "Verb inflection in Ancient Greek and Sanskrit and auxiliation patterns in French and Italian", *Linguisticae Investigationes* 32.1: 55-76.

Loporcaro, M. (2003) "The Unaccusative Hypothesis and Participial Absolutes in Italian" *Italian Journal of Linguistics* 15: 199-263.

Maraldi, M. (1994) "Some remarks on the historical development of the ablative of the gerund in Latin", in G. Calboli (ed.) *Papers on Grammar*, IV, Bologna, CLUEB, 141-164.

Nedjalkov, V. (1995) "Some typological parameters of converbs", in M. Haspelmath and E. König (eds) *Converbs in Cross-Linguistic Perspective: Structure and meaning of adverbial verb forms - adverbial participles, gerunds*, Berlin - New York, Mouton de Gruyter, 97-136.

Oniga, R. (2007) *Il latino. Breve introduzione linguistica*, 2ª ed., Milano, Franco Angeli.

Perlmutter, D.M. (1978) "Impersonal passives and the Unaccusative Hypothesis", *Proceedings of the 4th Annual Meeting of the Berkeley Linguistics Society*, Berkeley, 157-189.

—. (1982) "Syntactic representation, syntactic levels and the notion of subject", in P.I. Jacobson and G.K. Pullum (eds) *The Nature of Syntactic Representation*, Dordrecht, Reidel, 283-340.

Pieroni, S. (2007) "Soggetto e riflessivo" in N. La Fauci and S. Pieroni (eds) *Morfosintassi latina*, Pisa, ETS, 29-41.

Risch, E. (1984) *Gerundivum und Gerundium. Gebrauch im klassischen und älteren Latein, Entstehung und Vorgeschichte*, Berlin - New York, W. de Gruyter.

Stempel, R. (1995) "Das lateinische Gerundium und Gerundivum in historischer und typologischer Perspektive" *Glotta* 72: 235-251.

Touratier, C. (1994) *Syntaxe latine*, Louvain-la-Neuve, Peeters.

Vester, E. (1983) *Instrument and Manner Expressions in Latin*, Assen, Van Gorcum.

—. (1985) "Agentless passive constructions", in Ch. Touratier (ed.) *Syntaxe et latin. Actes du 2ème Congrès International de Linguistique Latine*, Aix-en-Provence, Université de Provence, 227-240.

—. (1991) "Reflections on the gerund and gerundive", in R. Coleman (ed.) *New Studies in Latin Linguistics. Selected Papers from the 4th International Colloquium on Latin Linguistics* (Cambridge, April 1992), Amsterdam-Philadelphia, Benjamins, 295-309.

SUBJUNCTIVE MOODS IN SYNTAX: A GREEK-LATIN COMPARISON

KONSTANTIN G. KRASUKHIN

Introduction

The Greek and Latin systems of moods have some important common inherited features: the inflexional endings of the imperative (2nd.Sg.: *-e* in thematic verbs; 3rd.Sg. Greek -τω, Lat. *-tōd*) and some endings of the subjunctive (the subjunctive of the 1st conjugation *-ē-* corresponds to Greek *-η-/-ω-*;[1] the same ending in other conjugations expresses the future tense). But there are also essential differences.

In Greek there are two different moods – subjunctive and optative; the former means volition, while the latter means wish. In Latin, subjunctive and optative are a single category, namely subjunctive; traces of optative affixes are attested in such forms as *sīm, sit* (Old Latin *sied*). Some subjunctives are transformed into futures: *erit* 'will be' (*esed* in the Forum inscription), cf. Old Indian *asad,* Avestan *aŋhat* 's/he, it is'. The Greek future is a variant of the aorist subjunctive (*–se/o-*); these two forms are sometimes hard to distinguish in the context.

But the most important difference consists in the way they are used. The Latin subjunctive is widespread and often required in subordinate clauses. The *consecutio temporum* (sequence of tenses) governs the use of the many subjunctive forms that appear in subordinate clauses. The Greek subjunctive and optative are markers of different modalities and are limited to the above mentioned meanings. Their use in subordinate clauses is more restricted (the optative can replace previously other moods in the preterit); the *consecutio temporum et modorum* was present in the so-called iterative and indefinite-relative clauses, where (in the language of Xenophon) the mood is conditioned by the type of the sentence and the tense of the predicate in the main clause.

Let us first compare the Greek and Latin conditional sentences, and in particular the expression of different syntactic relations joined under the semantic concept of "condition".

1. Conditional clauses in Greek

The modal particle ἄν/κέν (κε in Lesbian, κα in West dialects) in Greek participates in building the subjunctive mood, which has three possible realizations: let us call them *casus futuralis*, *casus potentialis*, and *casus irrealis*. The mood of the future is expressed by the subjunctive:

(1)   αὐτὰρ Ἀχαιοὶ
        τριπλῇ τετραπλῇ τ' ἀποτείσομεν, αἴ κέ ποθι Ζεὺς
        δῶσι πόλιν Τροίην ἐυτείχεον ἐξαλαπάξαι (Il. I 127-9)
        "We, Achaeans, will pay you back three or four times as much, if
        Zeus will let us tear down Troy with its beautiful walls".

The subjunctive with κέ (ἄν) denotes a possible situation in the indefinite future; the predicate of the main sentence is also future (ἀποτείσομεν).

(2)   ἦ μὲν δὴ νῶϊ ξεινήϊα πολλὰ φαγόντε
        ἄλλων ἀνθρώπων δεῦρ' ἱκόμεθ', αἴ κέ ποθι Ζεὺς
        ἐξοπίσω περ παύσῃ ὀϊζύος (Od. IV.33-35)
        "Certainly we both arrived here after having often eaten at the
        hospitable table of other people, hoping that Zeus put an end to our
        misery"

Here the predicate of the main clause is in the aorist. The conditional clause denotes a state of affairs possible in the future. But the main clause, expressing the consequence of this circumstance, represents its possible world as a finished event.

We must underline the difference between the subjunctive mood and the future tense. Both mood and tense originate from the same source, but in *casus futuralis*, the former denotes a possible event, while the latter can denote an event that will come true:

(3)   ἀλλ ἐάν ζητῇς καλῶς, εὑρήσεις (Plato *Gorgias* 503 d)
        "if you seek good, you'll find (it)"

(4)   τὸν ἀνδρὶ ὅν ἂν ἕλησθε, πείσομαι ᾗ δύνατον μάλιστα (Xen. *Anab.* V 1, 4)
        "I'll submit to any person, whom you elect".

In both contexts the event expressed by the apodosis is treated as a necessary consequence. The apodosis can also have the predicate in the present, especially in a concessive clause:

(5) Κἂν τις ἡμέραν μίαν / χρηστὸς γένηται, δέκα πονηρὸς γίγνεται
     (Aristoph. *Eccl.* 177-8)
     "And if someone behaves well for a day, he will behave badly for ten
     days"

The difference from the previous examples is evident: the apodosis in (5)
deals with the customary aspect of the real event, while in (3) and (4) it
deals with the consequences of a possible state of affairs. Such a sequence
can also be expressed by the optative:

(6) Πρὶν ἂν ἀμφοῖν μῦθον ἀκούσῃς, /οὐκ ἂν δικάσαις (Aristoph. *Vesp.* 725-
     6)
     "Before you hear the speech of them both, you cannot judge".

Here the optative with ἂν has its classical meaning of possible event (see
below). The subjunctive with ἂν also means possibility in the future.

1.1. Casus irrealis

The indicative with ἀν/κέν refers to an event that cannot occur in reality:

(7) καί κέ μ᾽ ἄιστον ἀπ᾽ αἰθέρος ἔμβαλε πόντῳ
     εἰ μὴ Νὺξ δμήτερα θεῶν ἐσάωσε καὶ ἀνδρῶν (Il. XIV 258-9)
     "And he would have thrown me unseen from Aether to the sea, if the
     Night, winner of gods and peoples, hadn't saved me".

The protasis can also have the predicate in the optative:

(8) Οὐ μὲν γὰρ φιλότητί γ᾽ ἐκεύθανον, εἴ τις ἴδοιτο (Il. III 453)
     "[Nobody] would have hidden him out of friendship, if somebody
     had seen him".

    In other cases, the indicative can have the meaning of non-reality even
without particles:

(9) Αἴτ᾽ ὄφελες ἄγονός τ᾽ ἔμεναι, ἄγαμός τ᾽ ἀπολέσθαι (Il. III 40)
     "Oh, if you hadn't been born or had perished without getting
     married" [said Hector to Paris].

The conjunction εἴτε (αἴτε) can either mean wish, or express an alternative.
The latter meaning is attested in the following fragment by Erinna (4 BC):

(10) αἴτ᾽ ἀστοὶ τελέθοντ᾽ αἴτ᾽ ἑτεροπτόλιες (5.4)
    "Either they are citizens, or they come from other towns".

The contrast is evident again. Hector's assertion expresses the unrealizable wish. Erinna's sentence expresses two possibilities, containing the entire universe of the possible world of the assertion. This difference does not have any formal expression; it can be inferred only from the context. Thus the meaning of the conjunction εἴτε can be defined as follows: it is the marker of a conditional event, which can develop into an irrealis or alternative.

1.2. Casus potentialis

The optative with ἄν denotes potential action; i.e. the speaker evaluates the event as non-existing at the moment, but possible:

(11) ὥρα ἂν εἴη λέγειν (Xen. Memorab. III 5, 7)
    "There is probably the time to say"

But sometimes the possibility is interpreted as formal, and the meaning of the sentence with optative becomes near to non-real:

(12) Φαίη δ᾽ ἂν ἡ θανοῦσα, εἰ φωνὴν λάβοι (Soph. Electra 548)
    "The dead woman would say that, if she had a voice".

Thus one can see that conditional sentences in Greek denoting different types of reality are either defined by the presence/absence of a modal particle or not fully defined by the mood of predicate.

2. Conditional sentences in Latin

Conditional sentences in Latin have some similarities to and some differences from Greek ones. We can distinguish three types: casus realis, potentialis, irrealis. The Greek casus futuralis can correspond to some other clause types. We will now examine the first two types: casus realis and potentialis.

2.1. Casus realis

Reality is expressed by different tenses of the indicative, especially the present:

(13) a. *Non licet hominem esse saepe ita, ut vult, si res non sinit* (Ter. *Heaut.* 666)
"The human being cannot often be as he wishes, if the circumstance does not allow for it"
   b. *Illi vehementer errant, si illam meam pristinam lenitatem perpetuam sperant futuram* (Cic. *Catil.* 2,3,6)
"They strongly mistake, if they hope that my former soft-heartedness will remain for ever"

I.e., *casus realis* can characterize utterances involving permanent circumstances, also concrete events. A special type has the present in the apodosis and Future II in the protasis:

(14) *Nulla quamvis minima natio potest ab adversariis deleri, nisi propriis simultatibus se ipsa consumpserit* (Veg. *mil.* 3,10)
"No smallest nation can be destroyed by the enemies, if it does not destroy itself with its own conflicts"

In these contexts there is an opposition between the apodosis, which indicates reality, and the protasis, which has potential meaning, as is also the case in (15):

(15) *Non, hercle, is sum, qui sum, ni hanc iniuriam meque ultus fuero* (Plaut. *Men.* 472)
"By Hercules, I am not myself, if I do not take vengeance of this injury"

The negation of the possibility of the condition leads to the negation of the present state of the subject.

2.2. Casus potentialis

Possibility is expressed by the present or perfect subjunctive:

(16) *Dies deficiat, si reges imperatoresque in hostium terra transgressos… enumerare velim* (Liv. 28,41,16)
"The entire day wouldn't be sufficient to me, if I wanted to enumerate all the kings and leaders who went to the country of the enemies"

The meaning is sometimes close to the irrealis:

(17) *Non mihi si linguae centum sint oraque centum,*
      (…)
      Omnia poenarum percorrere nomina possim (Verg. *Aen.* 6,627)
      "Even if I had a hundred tongues and a hundred mouths, I could not
      enumerate all the punishments"

Example (16) deals with possibility (many kings exist; the author can
enumerate them), while (17) denotes a less possible state of affairs (the
author cannot have a hundred tongues!). Since the utterance is about
existing innumerable punishments (in the Hades), the sentence can be
considered potential.

2.2.1. Some peculiarities in the use of tense/mood

Different degrees of potentiality are expressed by different tenses/moods
in the apodosis, whereas the protasis consistently has the present
subjunctive:

(18) *Si, quotiens peccant homines, sua fulmina mittat*
      Juppiter, exiguo tempore inermis erit (Ovid. *trist.* 2,33)
      "If Jupiter throws his lightning every time people sin, he will become
      unarmored in a short time"

The meaning of this sentence is close to the prototypical potential one: the
protasis is about a possible situation, the apodosis is about its future
consequence. A typical sentence with the present in the apodosis is (19):

(19) *Neque enim divitiarum secura possessio est, nisi armorum defensione*
      servetur (Veg. *mil.* 3,3)
      "The possession of wealth is not secure, if it does not use the defense
      of weapons"

The indicative shows that the state of affairs in the apodosis must
necessarily arise, if the condition in the protasis is fulfilled. This shows
that Latin conditional sentences display essential differences from Greek.
They have no modal particles; therefore their meaning, their reference to
the reality is expressed by the mood and is less conditioned by the context.

3. *Consecutio temporum*

As is well known, the most important feature that characterizes Latin syntax is the so-called *consecutio temporum*. But, as concerns the use of moods, one can divide Latin subordinate clauses into three groups:

A. The first group includes clauses requiring subjunctive only: *ut/ne finale, consecutivum, explicativum*; *cum causale, historicum, concessivum*; clauses with indicative mood only: *quia, quoniam, quod causale, tametsi, quod concessivum; cum temporale*; relative clauses (with pronoun *qui, quae, quod,* coordinated with a word of main clause), allowing both moods. The subjunctive expresses the nuance of cause, goal etc.

(20) *Longiore mora opus est, ut solvas quaestionem, quam ut proponas* (Sen. *epist.* 48,1)
"One needs more time, to solve a problem, than [one needs] to raise it"

(21) *Ad multas lupa tendit oves, praedetur ut unam* (Ov. *ars* 3,419) "The wolf rushes to many sheep in order to seize one"

(22) *Noli verberare lapidem, ne perdas manum* (Plaut. *Curc.* 197)
"Don't hit a stone, not to harm [your] hand" (final sentences)

The sentences with objective *ut* have specific nuances. On the one hand, the verb can denote an achievement:

(23) *Cura, ut valeas* (Cic. *Att.* 5,20,9)
"Take care about your health (lit. - that you keep healthy)

(24) *Petit Oppianicus, ut sibi Sassia nubat* (Cic. *Cluent.* 9,27)
"Oppianicus asks that Sassia marry him"

(25) *Ita volo itaque postulo, ut fiat* (Ter. *Andr.* 550)
"I wish and require that it become so"

On the other hand, the predicate can have final meaning in the context; the complement clause is to be interpreted in this case as a final clause:

(26) *Nihil laboro, nisi ut salvus sis* (Cic. *fam.* 16,4,2)
"I do nothing except for you to be safe"

(27) *Operam dabo, ut te quam primum videam* (Cic. *fam*. 3,4,2)
      "I will do my best in order to see you as soon as possible"

The verb *imperare* cannot assign the accusative of direct object. Therefore
it needs *ut obiectivum* as an expression of the object:

(28) *Imperavi mihi, ut viverem. Aliquando enim et vivere fortiter facere
      est* (Sen. *epist*. 78.2)
      "I ordered myself to live. Sometimes in fact to live means to be
      strong"

Some other verbs of volition have the same construction:

(29) *Hortensius me coepit hortari, ut sententia desisterem* (Cic. *ac*.
      2,19,63)
      "Hortensius began to persuade me to change my mind"

The same conjunction can also denote consequence or result. In this case
one talks about *ut consecutivum*:

(30) [*Oratio Catuli*] *est pura sic, ut Latine loqui paene solus videatur*
      (Cic. *de orat*. 3,8,29)
      "The speech of Catulus is so pure, that he alone seems to be able to
      speak Latin"

(31) *Numquam imperator ita paci credit, ut non se praeparet bello* (Sen.
      dial. 7,26,2)
      "The governor never believes in the peace so that he wouldn't get
      ready for the war"

In all these cases there are deictic words (*sic, ita*) in the main clause. But
this type of sentences can exist also without such markers:

(32) *Flumen est Arar, quod per fines Aeduorum et Sequanorum in
      Rhodanum influit, incredibili lenitate, ita ut oculis, in utram partem
      fluat, iudicari non possit* (Caes. *Gall*. 1,12,1)
      "There is a river Arar, which flows into the Rhodan in the countries
      of the A. and S. with incredible swiftness, so that one cannot judge
      from one's eyes in which direction it flows"

(33) [*Hannibal*] *velut hereditate relictum odium paternum erga Romanos
sic conservavit, ut prius animum, quam id, deposuerit* (Nep. 23,1,3)
"Hannibal preserved his father's hatred to the Romans as an heritage,
so that he lost his soul earlier than that"

In all the consecutive sentences the embedded clauses indicate possible
states of affairs. But in reality these sentences, especially (33), can denote
fulfilled action, real events ('Hannibal lost his soul'). Naturally, in some
other cases the predicate can be treated as a modal. But one can see that
the choice of mood doesn't fully depend on the meaning of the predicate.

Here we must introduce an important term from formal logic: the
possible world. It designates (Wittgenstein 1926; Wright 1975) the state of
affairs, where the mentioned judgment is true. In the theory of moods, the
possible world means the non-real, but supposed state of affairs, that
depends on either the action, or wish, or order, or possibility expressed by
the main clause; i.e., all the above mentioned sentences with *ut* denote a
possible world. And it is notable that *ut* can also introduce clauses with an
indicative verb:

(34) *Qui, ut erat in dicendo non solum sapiens, sed etiam fortis, causa
prope perorata, ipse arripuit M' Aquilium constituitque in conspectu
omnium* (Cic. *Verr.* II 5,1,3)
"Who (M. Antonius), therefore he was not only wise, but also
powerful, when the speech was gone, caught Manlium Aquilium and
placed him in the face of peoples"

One can see that the sentence is nearly causal; i.e., the conjunction denotes
the state of affairs that existed before the main action. This circumstance is
expressed by the indicative. The proper sense of *ut* can be defined as a
comparison between two situations: *perge ut instituisti* (Cic.) 'continue,
as you began'; *possum falli ut homo* (Cic.) 'I can make mistakes as (any)
person (therefore I am a person)'. A special type of comparative sentence
is also attested:

(35) *Ut corpora nostra lente augescunt, cito extinguuntur, sic ingenia
studiaque oppresseris facilius, quam revocaveris* (Tac. *Agr.* 3,1)
"As our bodies are growing slowly, but perish swiftly, so one can
rather oppress than restore the talent and study"

The sentence with *ut* is an explanation of the entire situation. Therefore,
this conjunction can denote temporal relations between sentences: *ut*

Romam venit, praetor factus est (Liv.) 'when he came to Rome, he became praetor'. The possible world expressed in the embedded clause leads to the grammaticalization of the conjunction *ut*. And the comparison with subjunctives allows us to formulate such inference: The clauses with the indicative denote states of affairs existing earlier than the event of the main clause; the *ut*-clauses with the subjunctive express a state of affairs that occurs after the event of the main clause, and/or is conditioned by it. Its possible world is treated as a real one. *Ut* with the indicative is rare; therefore the customary mood here is the subjunctive.

B. Sentences with *cum* have different meanings expressed by different moods:

(36) *Caelo sereno interdiu obscurata lux est, quum luna sub orbem solis subisset* (Liv. 37,4,4)
       "With clear sky during the day, the light went out, because the Moon went under the sphere of the Sun" (causal sentence)

(37) *Pridie Nonas Junias, cum essem Brundisii, litteras tuas accepi* (Cic. *fam.* 3,4,3)
       "The day before the Nones of June, when I was in Brundisium, I received your letters" (temporal sentence)

The traditional explanation is as follows: clauses with *cum historicum* indicate not only the coordination of two events in time, but also their inner linkage, correlation, or interdependence: in the sentence above, Cicero's staying in Brundisium is a condition for receiving letters.

Another type of so-called *cum temporale* with indicative is well known. The traditional view is that this class of clauses means the pure coincidence in time of two independent events. Cf:

(38) *Cum haec accepta est clades, iam C. Horatius et T. Menenius consules erant* (Liv. 2,51,1)
       "When this slaughter was known, C.H. and T.M. were consuls"

(39) *Cum hae litterae allatae, forte Nabdalsa in lecto quiescebat* (Sall. *Iug.* 71,1)
       "When the letter was received, N. was resting in bed"

But the following sentences have a different meaning:

(40) *Nulla est igitur haec amicitia, cum alter verum audire non vult, alter ad mentiendum paratus est* (Cic. *Lael.* 40)
"Sure, it isn't friendship, when one does not wish to listen to the truth, and the other is ready to falsehood"

Both clauses are evidently connected; the embedded clause is an explanation of the main clause. It expresses a possible world as a repeated state of affairs, which is represented as real.

(41) *Quam diu Catonem civitas ignoravit! Respuit nec intellexit, nisi cum perdidit* (Sen. *epist.* 79,14)
"For how long the society ignored Cato! It despised him and didn't understand him, until he died"

(42) *Mihi crede, nemo me vestrum, cum hinc excessero, consequetur* (Cic. *Tusc.* 1,43,103)
"Believe me, no one of you will follow me, when I go out of here"

The correlation of two clauses is also expressed by Future I and II. The earlier event is a necessary condition of the later event; i.e. some temporal clauses with the indicative can denote causal links. The semantic difference between *cum historicum* and *cum temporale* is in such cases eliminated; only the difference in the moods of the predicates remains. There is another type of temporal sentence, so called *cum inversum*: the event of the subordinate clause occurs later than that of the main clause:

(43) *Cenabam apud Seium, cum utrique nostrum redditae sunt a te litterae* (Cic. *fam.* 9,7)
"I was dining at Seius' when the letters from you were received by both of us"

(44) *Vixdum tuam epistulam legeram, cum ad me Postumius Curtius venit* (Cic. *Att.* 9,2a.,3) '
"I had just read your letter, when P.C. came to me"

(45) *Iam nox appetebat, cum proelio excedunt Thraces, non fuga vulnerum aut mortis, sed quia satis praedae habebant* (Liv. 38,40,15)
"The night was already approaching, when the Thracians went out from the battle, not escaping from wounds and death, but because they had enough spoils"

These three sentences have different tenses. In the first, the main clause has the imperfect, while the *cum* clause has the perfect; in the second, we observe a *consecutio temporum* (the main clause has the plusquamperfect, while the *cum*-clause has the perfect); in the third, the predicate of the *cum*-clause has the historical present. This uncertainty suggests that this kind of clause is still undergoing a change and is not subject to strict grammatical rules. But in general this is the characteristic of *cum*-clauses. Temporal clauses use the indicative in Plautus; the subjunctive occurs first in Terence, and then develops in the classical period. The difference between the different types becomes formal: the mood has partially lost its special meaning and has been transformed into a clause type marker.

On the contrary, causal sentences introduced by *quia, quoniam, quod,* have the indicative; this is also the case of concessive sentences with the conjunction *tametsi*:

(46) [*Themistocles*], *quod non satis tutum se Argis videbat, Corcyram demigravit* (Nep. 2,8,3)
    "Themistocles escaped to Corcyra, because he was not sure of his safety in Argos"

(47) *Vitia nostra quia amamus, defendimus et malumus excusare illa, quam excutere* (Sen. *epist.* 123,6)
    "Because we like our vices, we defend them and prefer to excuse them, than to correct them"

(48) *Scaevola, quoniam in Tusculanum ire constituit, paulum requiescit* (Cic. *de orat.* 1,62,265)
    "Since Scaevola decided to go to Tusculanum, he had a little rest"

We can see that the causal clauses with conjunctions *quod, quia, quoniam* have no evident difference from *cum causale*. So we can conclude that the choice of mood also depends on the conjunction. Therefore the mood is grammaticalized also in this case. Relative clauses can allow both moods and denote cause, consequence, and goal.

(49) *Me caecum, qui haec ante non viderim!* (Cic. *Att.* 10,10,1)
    "I am blind, since I (lit. who) didn't see it earlier" (causal)

(50) *Cuius tu fidem in pecunia perspexeris, verere verba ei credere?* (Ter. *Phorm.* 60)
"Despite you know his integrity of money managing, do you hesitate to trust him with your words?" (concessive).

C. The third group is made of clauses requiring indicatives only. It is a large number of relative, causal, temporal, and concessive clauses with conjunctions *quia, tametsi, quod*. Their existence was an important factor in the grammaticalization of the subjunctive as a clause type marker.

4. Subordination in Greek

In Greek, most subordinate clauses allow indicative, subjunctive, and optative. The mood of the predicate depends on the meaning of the entire clause:

(51)   οἶδα γὰρ, ὥς μοι ὀδώδυσται κλυτὸς ἐννοσίγαιος (Od. V 423)
"I know, how the famous Earthquaker (Poseidon) hates me" (independent event) vs.

(52)   ἀλλ᾽ ἴθι, μή μ᾽ ἐρέτιζε, σαώτερος ὥς κε νέηαι (Il. I 32)
"But go forth, don't anger me, in order for you to return safe and sound" (prospective subjunctive with volitive nuance)

(53)   τὸν δὲ μνηστῆρες ἀγαυοὶ /οἴκαδ᾽ ἰόντα λοχῶσιν, ὅπως ἀπὸ φῦλον ὄληται / νώνυμον (Od. XIV 180-2)
"The noble suitors made him an ambush, going home; in order for his kinship to perish ingloriously" (prospective subjunctive)

4.1. Grammaticalized subjunctive

The prospective subjunctive is obligatory for some relative (final) clauses with conjunctions ἵνα, and ὄφρα:

(54)   τλῆτε, φίλοι, καὶ μείνατ᾽ ἐπὶ χρόνον, ὄφρα δαῶμεν,
ἢ ἐτεὸν Κάλχας μαντεύεται, ἦε καὶ οὐκί (Il. II 299-300)
"have patience, friends, and remain (here) some more time, in order to understand whether Kalchas prophesies truly or not".

Here one can see the volitional nuance (Brugmann 1900: 565) conditioning the use of the subjunctive ('we *must* recognize'); according to Brugmann (55) and (56) contain pure final clauses:

(55) ἐγὼ δ᾽ ἵππων ἀποβήσομαι, ὄφρα μάχωμαι (Il. V 227)
"I will come down from the chariot, in order to fight".

(56) Ἵνα δὲ σαφέστερον δηλωθῇ πᾶσα ἡ Περσῶν πολιτεία, μικρὸν ἐπάνειμι (Xen. *Cyropaed*, I 2,15)
"In order to better explain the entire society of Persians, I will repeat something briefly".

The use of the subjunctive is conditioned by its meaning. Final clauses denote the presupposed and ordered event. This state of affairs can be compared with Latin: ἵνα, ὄφρα = *ut*, ὥς, ὅπως = *cum*. There are two differences: 1. The *consecutio temporum* is not attested in Greek; the choice of tense is conditioned by aspect only (complete/incomplete event). 2. The choice of mood in predicates of ὥς, ὅπως-clauses is conditioned by their meaning; the opposition of *cum historicum/ temporale* is absent.

Important is the development of ἵνα: In classical Greek. it introduces final and consecutive sentences only, with verbs in the subjunctive. In Homer and other poets the meaning is more complicated. The conjunction could also occur with the indicative:

(57) Αἴας ... ἄγεν δυοκαίδεκα νῆας
στῆσε δ᾽ ἄγων, ἵν᾽ Ἀθηναίων ἵσταντο φάλαγγες (Il. II 557-8)
"Ajax led twelve ships and placed them where the phalanges of the Athenians lied".

The conjunction can mean not only direction, but also place:

(58) σοὶ δέ μ᾽ ἔπεμψε γέρων ἱππήλατα Πηλεύς,
...ἵνα τ᾽ ἄνδρες ἀριπρεπέες τελέθουσιν (Il. IX 438-41)
"The horse-leader Peleus sent me with you, where the best men are"

(59) Αἰθίοπας θ᾽ ἱκόμην, καὶ Σιδόνιας, καὶ Ἐρεμβούς,
καὶ Λιβύην, ἵνα τ᾽ ἄρνες ἄφαρ κεραοὶ τελέθουσι (Od. IV 84-5)
"I came to the Aithiopes, the Sidons and the Erembs, and to Libya, where rams grow their horns early".

The relative clause can be situated in first position:

(60) ἀλλ' ἵνα Μέντωρ ἧστο καὶ "Αντιφας καὶ 'Αλιθέρσης
οἵ τε οἱ ἐξ ἐξ ἀρχῆς πατρώιοι ἦσαν ἑταῖροι
ἔνθα καθέζετ' ἰών... (Od. XVII 68-70)
"He came and seat (on the place), where Mentor, Antiphas and
Alitherses were sitting, who were (his) father's friends from the
beginning".

In all these sentences the relative clause with ἵνα indicates the goal of the
action expressed by the verb of the main clause: 'came, placed, sent into'.
The same clause with the subjunctive and optative has another meaning:

(61) ἔνθ' αὖ Τυδεΐδῃ Διομήδεϊ Παλλὰς 'Αθήνη
δῶκε μένος καὶ θάρσος, ἵν' ἐκδηλὸς μετ πάντων
'Αργείοισι γένοιτο ἰδὲ κλέος ἐσθλὸν ἄροιτο (Il. V 1-3)
"Then Pallas Athena gave to Diomede, Tydeus son, valor and
courage, in order for him to become splendid among the Argives and
get true glory".

The clause receives an important nuance: the goal expressed by the
optative does not exist, but is presupposed as the potential result of the
action. This potential meaning is a condition to select the optative.
Therefore ἵνα-sentences are sometimes questions:

(62) τίπτ' αὖτ', αἰγιόχοιο Διὸς τέκος, εἰλήλουθας;
ἦ ἵνα ὕβριν ἴδῃ 'Αγαμέμνονος 'Ατρεΐδάο; (Il. I 202-3)
"Why did you, child of Zeus aegis-holder, come here? In order to see
the arrogance of Agamemnon Atreides?"

(63) τίπτε γὰρ οὐ οἱ ἔειπης ἐνὶ φρεσὶ πάντα ἰδυῖα;
ἦ ἵνα που καὶ κεῖνος ἀλώμενος ἄλγεα πάσχῃ; (Od. XIII 417-8)
"Why don't you speak, all-knowing in your soul? In order for him,
seized, to suffer tortures?"

(64) τίπτε σὺ δὴ αὖ μεμαυῖα Διὸς θύγατερ μεγάλοιο
ἦλθες ἀπ' Οὐλύμποιο, μέγας δέ σε θυμὸς ἀνῆκεν;
ἦ ἵνα δὴ Δαναοῖσι μάχης δ' ἑτεράλκεα νίκην
δῷς; (Il. VI 24-7)
"Why, daughter of great Zeus, did you come from Olympus, what a
great fury did you inspire? In order to give the full victory to the
Danai?"

Thus the origin of ἵνα allows us to formulate a hypothesis about the origins
of the subjunctive mood in some clause types. Primarily it is a conjunction
derived from a demonstrative root (cf. Lith. jìs 'he', Lat. iste 'this (near to

hearer)'). Pierre Monteil (1963: 377) shows that this conjunction can function anaphorically:

(65) ...κεῖνους δὲ κιχησόμεϑα πρὸ πυλάων
      ἐν φυλάκεσσ᾽, ἵνα γάρ σφι ἐπέφραδον ἠγερέϑεσϑαι (Il. X 127)
      "We'll meet with them before gates, among the sentinels, where I ordered them to gather".

Monteil claims that the presence of affirmative γάρ does not allow ἵνα to be interpreted as a relative marker. Therefore it can be demonstrative, with an anaphoric function. In relative sentences, it can either be the correlative word (γάμος Od. VI 27, ἄνδρας Il. XXIV 382), or the conjunction, or an adverb (τῇ Il. XX, 478).

Let us return to the subjunctive with ἄν. In one context it has partially lost its specific meaning of *casus futuralis*:

(66) Ἐπειδὰν δὲ κρύψωσι γῆ, ἀνὴρ ἠρημένος ὑπὸ τῆς πόλεως... λέγει ἐπ᾽ αὐτοῖ
      ς ἔπαινον πρέποντα (Thuc. II 34,6-7)
      "And when (they) hid (them) under the earth (= buried), the man elected by the city [...] said the proper praise".

Here the modal meaning of the subjunctive has evidently disappeared, therefore the sentence has habitual meaning. The development of modal meaning can be connected with verbs of thinking, perception, ordering. In this meaning ἵνα-sentences compete with the modal infinitive. This process led to full disappearance of the infinitive in later Greek; but this process already begins in Homer:

(67) ...ἀλλά με γαστὴρ / ὀτρύνει ἵνα πληγῇσι δαμείω (Od. XVIII 53-54)
      "but the stomach impels me, that I be oppressed by strokes".

This verb customarily governs an infinitive of goal, but it can be replaced by ἵνα-sentences in the oldest texts. Cf. Bourgiere (1955: 172-3), who gives a list of verbs and predicative adjectives with both constructions. Another conjunction introducing clauses with regular subjunctive is ὄφρα. It derives from the correlative pronoun, τόφρα. The conjunction is comparable with Tocharian *kupre* 'why' < *$k^u u$-bhro*, where the second element contains the root *bher- 'carry'. The meaning of the Greek adverb is originally temporal:

(68) ...ὁ δ' ὄφρα μὲν εἰλίποδας βοῦς
      βόσκ' ἐν Περκώτῃ, δηίων ἀπὸ νόσφιν ἐόντων·
      αὐτὰρ ἐπεὶ Δαναῶν νέες ἤλυθον ἀμφιέλισσαι,
      ἂψ εἰς ᾽Ίλιον ἦλθε (Il. XV 547-50)
      "He once pastured cows with movable foots in P. when the enemies
      were far; when the ships of the Danai came, he also came back to
      Ilion". (Chantraine 1951: 360; Monteil 1963: 309).

This function of the adverb can be defined as demonstrative or anaphoric.
In other cases this adverb/conjunction denotes the temporal correlation of
actions, either contemporaneous actions or temporal sequence:

(69) ῎Οφρ' ὁ γε ταῦτα πονεῖτο ἰδυίῃσι πραπίδεσσι
      τόφρα οἱ ἐγγύθεν ἦλθε θεὰ Θέτις ἀργυροπέζα (Il. XVIII 380-1)
      "When he was absorbed with his work, the silver-footed goddess
      Thetis came to him".

The clause introduced by ὄφρα indicates the background for the basic
event; and the imperfect (πονεῖτο) is also correlated with the aorist ἦλθε in
the same manner (Weinrich 1964; cf. Krasukhin 2007).
Another type of correlation is as follows: the main clause indicates the
process, when this ends, another process occurs expressed by the clause
with ὄφρα:

(70) ὣς μὲν Θρήικας ἄνδρας ἐπῴχετο Τυδέος υἱός,
      ὄφρα δυώδεκ' ἔπεφνεν (Il. X 488)
      "So Tydeus' son attacked the Thracians, he killed twelve men"

This temporal meaning can have developed into a conditional one:

(71) οὐ μὲν γάρ ποτέ φησι κακὸν πείσεσθαι ὀπίσσω,
      ὄφρ' ἀρετὴν παρέχωσι θεοὶ καὶ γούνατ' ὀρώρῃ (Od. XVIII 132-3)
      "One says that he will not suffer the bad, when (= if) the Gods give
      him the virtue and his knees rose"

Some final clauses with modal predicates are mentioned above. In
general, in such sentences different moods and tenses occur in Homer:
subjunctive, optative (present and aorist; with or without ἄν/ κεν), and
future (Monteil 1963: 314-15).

4.2. Peculiarities of the optative

The optative in historical tenses is the substitute of the subjunctive in primary tenses. The first examples occur in Homer's poems:

(72) βῆ δ᾽ ἴμεναι διὰ δώμαθ᾽ ἵν᾽ ἀγγείλειε τοκεῦσιν (Od. VI 50)
"She went home in order to inform her parents".

But in the epic language, the optative can occur in subordinate clauses, while the present occurs in main clauses:

(73) τὰ φρονέων, ἵνα μή τις ἀγαυῶν Οὐρανιώνων
ἄλλος ἐν ἀθανάτοισιν ἔχοι βασιλήιδα τιμήν (Hes. Theog. 461)
"Intending, that no other one from the glorious sons of Uranus could have the honor of a king among immortals".

The optative with μή expresses here the undesirable, unwanted state of affairs.

But one can also find this mood without this meaning. The embedded clause can also have a predicate in the optative, where this mood has no meaning of wish. This function of the optative tends to be grammaticalized as a marker of subordinate predicate in the preterit. In the following example it is hard to find any meaning of wish, or potentiality:

(74) ἀλλήλους τ᾽ εἴροντο, τίς εἴη καὶ πόθεν ἔλθοι (Od. XVII 368)
"They asked one another, who is who and where they came from".

The interrogative clause does not require the subjunctive when the main clause has a primary tense (present, future). The moods in clauses of *oratio obliqua*, unlike in Latin, depend on the speaker's treatment. In sentences denoting real states of affairs, the indicative is customary. Cf.:

(75) τίνι ἡ τύχη δίδωσι, λαβέτω (Athen. X p. 438 e)
"Let he take it, to whom the chance gives it!".

Other examples of optatives corresponding with indicatives in main tenses:

(76) εἶπεν δὲ ἕκαστα [...], ὡς ἔοι ἀθάνατος (Hymn in Ven. 214)
"he said every time, that he was immortal". (≈ λέγει, ὅτι ἐστί...)

(77) τελευτῶν ἔλεγε, ὅσα ἀγαϑὰ Κῦρος Πέρσας πεποιήκοι (Hdt. III 5)
"Before his death he said how many good things Cyrus made for the
Persians" (≈ λέγει, ὅσα πεποίηκε...).

This optative is especially characteristic of iterative sentences:

(78) ἤτοι ὅτ' ἀμφὶ πόλιν Τροίην φραζοίμεϑα βουλάς, / αἰεὶ πρῶτος ἔβαζε (Od.
XI 510-1)
"When we talked about the city of Troy, he always spoke first".

(79) ἐϑήρευεν ἀπὸ ἵππου, ὁπότε γυμνάσαι βούλοιτο ἑαυτόν τε καὶ τοὺς ἵππους
(Xen. Anab. I 2, 7)
"He hunted with a horse (every time), when he wished to exercise
himself and horse".

This use represents one of the greatest differences from Latin, where
iterative sentences use tenses of the indicative only. Repeated situations in
the past is interpreted as possible, but not real, not manifested.

Conclusion

One can see great differences between the Greek and Latin systems of
moods. In both languages, some moods change their functions; i.e. they
lose their own independent meaning, and are transformed into markers of
states of affairs. The subjunctive mood is partly grammaticalized in Latin:
it becomes the mood of subordination, depending on the speaker's
intention; one can characterize it as prospective, in the sense that this
mood denotes an undetermined, non-referential event in the future. In
Greek the moods retain their basic meanings, but Pre-Classical and
Classical Greek tend to grammaticalize the optative as a retrospective
mood, or marker of a possible event in the past.

A last problem arises from the above discussion: how are the relative
clause and the subjunctive mood connected? As Fedor (Theodor) Korsch
has shown (1886), the relative clause originated from an appositive and /
or anaphoric construction; the relative pronoun may originally be a
demonstrative with anaphoric function.[2] É. Benveniste (1966) claimed that
the first type of relative is the nominal sentence, containing the noun and a
relative pronoun in agreement with it: Greek Τεῦκρος, ὃς ἄριστος (Il. XIII
313) 'T. which is the best one', Old Indic víśve marúto yé sahásaḥ (RV
VII 34, 24) 'all the M. who is powerful', Avestan daeva ya apaoša 'Deva,
which is A.', Latin salvete, Athenae, quae nutrices Graeciae (Plautus,

Stich. 649) 'Regards, Athens, benefactress of Greece'. Then the noun which occupies the predicative position can be substituted by the verb, giving origin to a relative clause. The relative pronoun becomes the subject, if it is connected with a noun in the main clause. On the contrary, if the subordinate clause relates to the whole sentence (i.e. it does not have an attributive or objective, but a circumstantial function), it is introduced by a conjunction. And verbs that denote goal or purpose often need the dependent clause expressing the possible world; i.e. the non-real, but suggested, proposed, wished state of affairs. In Homeric Greek, there are paratactic sentences with the subjunctive: ἀπόστιχε, μή τι νοήσῃ Ἥρη (Il. I 522-3) 'go away, Hera must suspect nothing'. Three moods compete in Greek: infinitive, subjunctive and optative. The second won.

Greek and Latin syntax must be taught through contrastive analysis. Conjunctions with similar functions must be compared. One must highlight that the system of moods in Latin is more grammatical, and that the Greek system is more semantic. But the cases of grammaticalization of the subjunctive and optative in Greek must be considered above all.

Notes

*The research is supported by the Russian Foundation for the Humanities (project 08-04-00180a)

[1] Some scholars are reconstructing the subjunctive of I conjugation as an original optative: *ornem* < **ornā-jē-m*. But why the suffix of athematic verb (**-ieh₁-*) must be added to vocalic stem? The question is *sub iudice*.
[2] We can also check such sources for relative pronouns: interrogatives (the oblique question), demonstratives, and probably indefinites, cf. Gonda (1956).

References

Benveniste, É. (1966) *Problèmes de linguistique générale*, Paris, Galli-
    mard.

Brugmann, K. (1900) *Griechische Grammatik*, München, Beck.

Burgiere, P. (1960) *L'histoire d' infinitive grec*, Paris, Klincksieck.

Duhoux, Y. (2000) *Le verb en grec ancien*, Leuven, Peeters.

Gonda J. (1956) "The Indo-European pronoun **io-*" *Lingua* 4: 15-41.

Hofmann, J.B. and A. Szantyr (1965) *Lateinische Syntax und Stilistik*,
    München, Beck.

Korsch, K.F.Y. (1886) *Otnositel'noe predloženie: Glava iz sravnitel'nogo
    sintaxisa*, Moscow, Moscow University.

Krasukhin K. G. (2007) "Aspekty i vremena praindoevropeiskogo glagola. Čast' II: Aorist i imperfekt drevnegrečeskogo glagola" *Voprosy yazykoznaniya*, 6.

Leumann, M. (1977) *Lateinische Laut- und Formenlehre*. München, Beck.

Monteil, P. (1963) *Le phrase relative en grec ancien*, Paris, Klincksieck.

Palmer, L. (1950) *The Latin language*, Oxford-New York, Oxford University Press.

Schwyzer, E. and A. Debrunner (1950) *Griechische Grammatik*, II, München, Beck.

von Wright G.H. (1975) *Explanation and Understanding*, Oxford-New York, Oxford University Press.

Weinrich, H. (1964) *Tempus: Besprochene und erzählte Welt*. Stuttgart, Kohlhammer.

Wright, C. (1975) "On the coherence of vague predicates", *Synthese* 30: 325-65.

Wittgenstein, L. (1921) *Tractatus logico-philosophicus*, London, Routledge.

COMPARATIVE GRAMMAR AND THE GENITIVE CASE: LATIN SYNTAX AND THE SABELLIAN LANGUAGES

KARIN TIKKANEN

1. Towards a comparative historical syntax

Historical-comparative reconstruction is usually focused on the more "open" spheres of language, that is the phonological system and the morphological system, and to some extent also the vocabulary. Syntactic reconstruction, on the other hand, has either been systematically left unattended, or regarded as fruitless (cf. Lightfoot 1979, Harrison 2003, Mengden 2008, *inter alia*). The reason for this is that syntax is considered fundamentally different from for example phonology, where changes underlying later forms vis-à-vis earlier or reconstructed forms are explained through a series of systematic sound laws. Morphological and lexical modifications are attributed, to a certain degree, to the realization of these sound laws in their different contexts. There are no such laws explaining syntactic change, or such laws as there are, are typological parallels, and rarely affect the whole system but only parts thereof.[1] For these reasons, the study of syntax and syntactic change is not common within historical reconstructions of earlier language stages, although as of late more and more attention has been awarded to this field of research; e.g., Barðdal and Eythórsson (2009), Barðdal (2010).

In this paper, the question of the Proto-Italic hypothesis is ventured from the point of view of case syntax, a field hereto largely ignored. This is presented through the perspective of the genitive case, with attempts at a sketched reconstruction of the Proto-Italic system, together with some comments as to the possible changes underlying the different end results.

2. Latin and the Sabellian languages: the relationship issue

Within Latin historical linguistics, one of the more enigmatic questions concerns the relation of Latin to the Sabellian languages (e.g. Oscan, Umbrian, South-Picene, and the various Italic dialects from the central Apennines, attested in inscriptions from appr. 650 down to 50 BCE). From the perspective of comparative and historical linguistics, there are a great number of similarities between the two language groups, in the shape of phonological developments and changes within the nominal and verbal inflection, as well as in the structural organisation of the grammatical material. There are two possible explanations:

> 1. The two language groups are internally different. Similarities between the two language groups are the result of convergence within the close confines of the Italian peninsula, under the influence posed by the same neighbouring languages, that is Greek and Etruscan.[2]

> 2. The attested similarities between Latin and the Sabellian languages are the result of a closer genetic affiliation, that is a shared language stage intermediate between PIE and the later individual languages, reconstructed as Proto-Italic. Differences are later divergences in the development to the individual languages.[3]

The similarities and differences called for in this debate are cited in long lists, using data from the "regular" areas of comparative language studies; i.e. from phonology, morphology and also the vocabulary. When it comes to the question of syntax, however, almost all scholars state that these languages are more or less identical, whatever their view on the linguistic relationship. Thus Domenico Silvestri (favouring the language contact hypothesis): "As regards the case syntax ... it may be said that the Italic languages are almost completely identical to Latin" (1998: 340), and Philip Baldi (supporting the Proto-Italic theory): "Very little variation in case usage occurs between [Latin and the Sabellian languages], and though the syntactic evidence is scant, enough of it exists to recognize the general similarity to Latin" (1983: 32).

It is easy to understand the origin of this scholarly agreement. Both language groups are of IE origin, and as such continue certain structural features inherited from this source. In both Latin and the Sabellian languages there is, for example, a preponderance of phrases with the verb in final position, and both language groups display a nom./acc. case-marking pattern (as opposed to the ergative/absolutive system). Such patterns are easily recognizable, and provide simple points of parallelism between two different bodies of texts. However, such factors do not necessarily signal any form of "genetic identity" if they are at the same time featured in other IE languages, which is certainly the case. There are, indeed, a very large number of similarities between the two language groups in respect of case syntax, and to a large degree the opinion of Silvestri and Baldi can be verified. At the same time, as this paper will show, a closer analysis does reveal a number of greater or minor differences, which do have to be explained in some way. This happens to be especially common as regards the syntax of the genitive case, which is the case discussed in the following.

3. The Genitive Case in Latin and Sabellian

3.1. Adnominal genitives

The genitive case in adnominal position, i.e. within the noun phrase, marks the proximate relation of one object to another, whether in terms of strict object possession, family relation or geographical origin.[4] This is the most frequent use of the case in most IE languages, and this can consequently be posited as the approximate "base" meaning for the case (seen in a comparative perspective). Given the proximity between most IE languages in this respect, it is of little value to discuss this use of the case in Latin and Sabellian. Suffice it to state that the genitive is found with the above stated functions, in both language groups, with no obvious variation in terms of use.

3.2. Adverbal genitives

The genitive case in adverbal position, meaning within the verb phrase, marks the direct object in contrast with the accusative case and defines the verbal act as less complete or less absolute. The construction is sometimes also called "accusative genitive".[5] Partitive uses of the genitive case are found in the Eastern IE spectrum, in ancient languages such as Greek and Old Indic, and in modern Balto-Slavic languages. Example (1), from modern Lithuanian, contrasts the genitive case for partial use, as opposed to the complete act in (2), marked by the accusative case.[6]

(1)   Lith. *dúok mán dúonos*[GEN.sg] "give me (some of the) bread"

(2)   Lith. *dúok mán dúoną*[ACC.sg] "give me the (loaf of) bread"

The construction also appears in a few Umbrian phrases, as for example:

(3) Umbr. IIa.41 *struhçlas*$^{GEN.sg}$ *fiklas*$^{GEN.sg}$ *sufafia*$^{GEN.sg}$ *kumaltu*$^{IMP.sg}$
      "grind (a portion) of the *struhçla* cake, of the *fikla* cake, and of the
      sufafia"[7]

There are a few examples of such partitive object genitive constructions in
early Latin sources, though it is not certain how these should be
interpreted. Sentence (4) might be such a "true partitive", although a
solitary instance in Cato.[8]

(4) *Farinam in mortuarium indito, aquae*$^{GEN.sg}$ *paulatim addito* (Cato
      agr. 74)
      "pour meal into the bowl, add water gradually"

If the construction in (4) is apparently unique in Early Latin, it is even
more at odds with the language of later periods. In Classical Latin, the
difference between a complete and a partial act is stressed through
prefixation of the verb as the marker of a telic event, as in (5) as opposed
to (6).[9] There are no similar expressions attested in Sabellian.

(5) *Qui acetum*$^{ACC.sg}$*, quod forte secum habebat, ebibit et liberatus est*
      (Cels. 5,27,4)
      "who drank up the vinegar he happened to have with him, and was
      saved"

(6) *(mulier) multitatur, se uinum*$^{ACC.sg}$ *bibit* (Cato *orat.* frg. 221)
      "a woman is regularly sentenced to pay a fine, if she drinks wine"

In Classical Latin, undefined amounts can also be expressed through
ellipsis of the governing nominal head, in constructions using prepositions
de or *ex* with the ablative, as in (7). This is seen in particular with
superlatives (8). This type of expression is also unknown to the Sabellian
corpus.

(7) *DE*^{ADP} *PRAIDAD*$^{ABL.sg}$ *FORTVNE DEDET* (CIL XIV 2577)
      "... gave (this) to Fortuna, from the booty"

(8)   *Pantauchum misit ex fidissimis*^{ABL.pl} *amicis*^{ABL.pl} *ad ea perficienda*
(Liv. 44,23,2)
"he sent Pantauchus, one of his most trusty friends, to complete this
(agreement)"

The partitive object genitive is found in several IE languages, and may be
attributed to a shared origin, representing an archaic construction mostly
preserved in the Eastern IE language continuum.[10] If so, this type of
construction would have been continued in Sabellian (Umbrian) unaltered,
whereas in Latin it was replaced by different constructions.

3.3. Peripheral genitives

So-called peripheral genitives are positioned in the outskirts of the
sentence, i.e. outside of the verbal nucleus. In themselves these may be
adnominal genitive expressions, though they are (usually) not governed by
any particular element, but rather denote aspects which concern the whole
sentence, making them more like adverbials.

3.3.1. Peripheral genitive of concern

In several IE languages, peripheral genitive phrases can mark the sphere of
action, or the sphere to which an action belongs, often called "genitive of
concern" or "genitive of matter involved". This is frequent with verbs of
perceiving, of emotions, of ruling, of memory or forgetfulness, and within
the scope of competitions and games, and so on.[11] In both the Sabellian
languages and Latin this kind of genitive is very frequent within the
juridical language. The Oscan sentence (9) and the Latin sentence (10), for
example, show a parallelism in the use of an abstract concept
"thing/matter" (Osc. *egma-*, Lat. *res*) which may in itself indicate a shared
coinage.[12]

(9)   Osc. TB.24 *manim*^{ACC.sg} *aserum*^{INF} *eizazunc*^{GEN.pl} *egmazum*^{GEN.pl}
"to lay his hand on ... involving these matters"

(10) Lat. Bant. OMNIVM^{GEN.pl} RERVM^{GEN.pl} SIREMPS *LEX ESTO* (CIL
I2 582)
"the statute is to apply ... in all matters"

3.3.2. Temporal genitives

The genitive of time, or *genitivus temporis*, is a way of expressing the relation of an event to a particular time or period, sometimes explained as a simple development of the category genitive of matter or concern.[13] Temporal genitives do exist in several IE languages, but do not constitute a discrete PIE category, and different languages present alternative constructions. It is frequent in, for example, Greek (11), and is also found in Sabellian (Oscan).

(11) Gr. τοῦδ' αὐτοῦ^GEN.sg λυκάβαντος^GEN.sg ἐλεύσεται ἐνθάδ' Ὀδυσσεύς (Hom. Od.14,161)
  "in the course of this self-same year/month, Odysseus shall come here"

(12) Osc. TB.17 *eisuc*^ABL.sg-*en*^ADP *ziculud*^ABL.sg *zicolom*^GEN.pl XXX *nesimum*^GEN.pl *comonom*^ACC.sg *ni hipid*^PRES.SUBJ.3.sg
  "he may not hold an assembly for the next 30 days from that day"

In Latin, temporal genitive expressions are rare, though there is an old expression, Lat. *trinum nundinum*, with the original meaning "of three eight-day periods" (inclusive counting), which may be a remnant of an inherited feature.[14] Latin temporal expressions are otherwise usually marked by the accusative or ablative cases, with or without adpositions.[15]

3.3.3. Gerundive genitives

Both Latin and Sabellian have de-verbal forms signaling intention or purpose, using the morpheme *-nd-*, a formation peculiar to these languages.[16] In Umbrian, we see this combination with the genitive case in a handful of instances, for example (13), with the phrase *ocrer peihaner*, "for the purification of the mount".[17]

(13) Umbr. VIa.8 *pufe*^ADV *arsfertur*^NOM.sg *trebeit*^PRES.3.sg *ocrer*^GEN.sg *peihaner*^GDV.GEN.sg
  "where the *arsfertor* remains for the purpose of purifying the Mount"

In Latin, gerundive forms also combine with the genitive case to express intention or purpose, though in the earliest language this is only found in bound patterns governed by ablative forms, Lat. *causā* and *gratiā*. The "free" gerundive, as in (14), is only found in the latter language.[18]

(14) *(Aetoli) pacis*^{GEN.sg} *petendae*^{GEN.sg} *oratores ad consules miserunt*
      (Liv. 26,27,2)
      "the Aetolians sent orators to the consuls to seek peace"

3.3.4. Genitive with adpositions

Both language groups display phrases with the genitive in combination with adposition-like particles, although the sets of adpositions used differ in the two languages. In general, the development of adpositional uses of the genitive was quite a late process within PIE, and it is only to be expected that Latin and the Sabellian languages show disparities in this respect. Apart from the inherited particle Lat. *in*/Osc. –*en*,[19] there are, in fact, three quite contrasting sets of adpositions, one in Latin (15), one in Oscan (16) and one in Umbrian (17).

(15) Latin: *causa, gratia, tenus, ergo*

(16) Oscan: *amnud*,[20] *agine*,[21] *en, pernúm*[22]

(17) Umbrian: *ose* (?)*, paca* (?)[23]

3.3.5. Absolute genitives

Absolute constructions are also a rather late development in PIE. Latin and the Sabellian languages differ in the sense that Oscan shows the genitive case, where Latin favours the ablative.[24] Absolute genitives are frequent in, for example, Greek from the very earliest time onwards. In most other languages where this is said to be attested, e.g., Sanskrit, Avestan, Tocharian and Armenian, this represents much later stages of language development.[25] The Oscan construction appears in one phrase only, (18), which is used in several dedicational inscriptions, corresponding semantically to Lat. *meritō* "deservedly".[26] Absolute genitive constructions do exist in Latin, though these are very rare, and there is no equivalent use of the type presented by the Oscan phrase. Looking at the older Latin material, there are no more than a handful of instances in total, among others from the Twelve Tables, such as (19) (note that the genitive contrasts with an absolute ablative construction). Latin absolute genitives do appear to a greater extent later on, most probably under Greek influence.[27]

(18) Osc. *brateis*[GEN.sg] *datas*[GEN.sg]
      "because of favour given"

(19) Lat. *aeris*[GEN.sg] *confessi*[GEN.sg] *rebus*[ABL.pl]-*que iure iudicatis*[ABL.pl] *XXX*
      dies iusti sunto (Lex XII tab. 3 (Gell. 20,1,42))
      "when debt has been acknowledged, or judgement about matter has
      been pronounced in court, 30 days must be the legitimate time of
      grace"

4. Discussion and summary

Several scholars (e.g. Silvesteri and Baldi, see point 2 above) state that
Latin and Sabellian are more or less identical. As shown in the preceding,
this is not a complete description of the actual material, but rather an over-
simplification of the situation. It *is* possible to distinguish a number of
discrepancies in the syntax of the genitive case of these two languages,
representing independent developments in the separate languages (whether
one posits the closest shared origin of these languages as Proto-Italic, or as
PIE, and the case grammar of both of these stages can, at the same time, be
at least tentatively reconstructed).

There are, indeed, several matching patterns in terms of the grammar
of the genitive case – the reason why both Baldi and Silvestri say what
they do. In terms of the adnominal genitive (point 3.1), there are also
several partitive genitive constructions, as well as subjective/objective
genitives (the *amor patris* type). Genitives with adjectives is also an
attested category. All of these patterns are well-spread among IE
languages, and do not contribute much towards an understanding of the
more particular patterns or developments of Latin and the Sabellian
languages. Of the sample sentences discussed in this paper, however,
mostly all of the uses mentioned in point 3.2 and 3.3 differ, in one way or
another, from the Latin grammar. Depending on the type of difference,
these can be divided into three groups.

The first group involves constructions where Oscan and Umbrian have
preserved more archaic constructions attested also in other IE languages,
of which there are traces in the earliest Latin, but which have been
replaced, at later stages, with other constructions. This involves the
partitive object genitive (point 3.2), and temporal genitives (point 3.3.2).

The second group involves independent developments in Sabellian,
which appear later in Latin, (potentially under Greek influence), that is the
"free" gerundive genitive (point 3.3.3). The gerundive is a distinct, shared
Latin/Sabellian morpheme in *-nd-*, although the syntactic application of

this was a later, language-individual development. This variation can perhaps be connected with the existence of the partitive objective genitive in Sabellian (point 3.2), which allowed for a looser connection of the object with the verbal phrase, than what is found in Latin. The appearance of this construction in the later language is explained as by Greek influence, since in Greek such structures (although not using the same morpheme) are fairly common.

The third distinguishable group concerns syntactic aspects that do *not* show up in Latin, that is genitive with adpositions (point 3.3.4), and the absolute genitive (point 3.3.5). Genitive with adpositions is a very late category within PIE, and the sets of adpositions thus used differs greatly among the IE languages. The later Latin language shows some absolute genitives, also these explained by Greek influence.

The reasons for these differences in the case syntax of these languages can be attributed, partly, to phonological and morphological changes within the two systems. As it happens, both language groups altered the PIE system of genitive endings, though in very different ways. Replacing the inherited *o*-stem singular ending **-oiso*,[28] Latin introduced the new long **-ī* ending.[29] This ending in turn affected the *a*-stem pattern, causing the inherited *-ās* (as in *pater famlias*) to be replaced by the classical *-ae*.[30] The Sabellian languages preserved the inherited *a*-stem singular ending, and show a different form of analogical change in the singular of the other stems, in that the *o*-stems and consonant stems use the *i*-stem singular ending *-eis*.[31] The plural forms are mostly preserved, i.e. original **-om* (with or without stem vowel), though the Latin *o*-stems show the *-orum* form, influenced by *a*-stem *-ārum*, itself originally a pronominal form.[32]

Also, the locative remained a living case in Sabellian, whereas it was lost early on in Latin. In Sabellian, the locative case expresses location, in time or space, with all different kinds of nouns, just as in any language that continues the PIE case and its particular case morpheme.[33] Location in Latin is, for the most part, expressed by the ablative case, with or without adpositions.[34] This loss of the locative case was partly due to uncertain morphology, since after the remodification of the Latin *o*- and *a*-stem singular genitive forms, these two cases became homophonous (*-i, -ae*), making the functional use of the locative more ambiguous.

It is thus possible to align the differences between the two language groups in terms of the morphology and the syntax of the genitive case, in a more or less parallel way. Similar to the inflection of the genitive case, the syntax of the genitive in the Sabellian languages shows some particular characteristics that distinguishes this group from Latin. Sabellian is, on the whole, somewhat more conservative than Latin, in both these areas, preserving several archaic features that are lost in Latin, even in the earliest historical stages. And it is the split in the morphology that must be seen as the underlying factor for the discrepancies within the syntax of the two language groups. At some point, phonological changes in Latin led to the re-modification of the genitive singular of the *o*-stems, which in turn opened up for a differentiating use of the case in relation to the inherited PIE structures. The syntactic changes can most likely also be explained as the result of a certain row of changes, just as the locative case was lost in Latin as a result of the remodification of the genitive morphology.

Notes

[1] See discussion in Hettrich (1997: 221).

[2] See e.g. Devoto (1951), Jones (1950), Beeler (1952), (1966), Pisani (1954), Jeffers (1973), Silvestri (1998).

[3] This is the currently stronger view, see e.g. Meiser (1986), (1987), (1993), (1996), (1998), and Rix (1981), (1994), (1996), (2000), (2004).

[4] See e.g. Malchukov and Spencer (2009: 581).

[5] See Szantyr (1965: 52, 159f.), Serbat (1992: 287).

[6] In this text, the following superscript abbreviations are used in the annotation of the textual data: sg. = singular; pl. = plural; NOM = nominative; ACC = accusative; GEN = genitive; ABL = ablative; ADP = adposition; ADV = adverb; PRES = present; SUBJ = subjunctive; INF = infinitive; IMP = imperative; GDV = gerundive.

[7] Although several of the words are obscure, most scholars and editors agree on the case marking and the general translation of the phrase. The genitive forms probably refer to different types of bakery products used in the sacrifice, all of which are mentioned in the context of the severed flesh of the victims; for *struhçla*, cf. Lat. *struēs* as sacrificial cake in Cato *agr.* 134,2 (Untermann 2000: 704f.); the *fikla* is perhaps the general Umbrian term for "bread", cf. Lat. *fitilla* (Untermann 2000: 283); *sufafia-* is wholly unaccounted for (Untermann 2000: 711).

[8] Thus Bennett (1914: 35). For all other early attestations of what seems to be partitive object genitives there have been various suggestions for supposed corruptions in the manuscripts, see discussion in Löfstedt (1942: 141-144), and Tikkanen (in press).

[9] See discussion in Haverling (2010).

[10] Some scholars, for example Serbat (1992), posit this type of construction as the "most original" use of the genitive case, from which all other uses of the case eventually arose. (For an opposing view, of the subjective and objective genitive constructions as the original uses of case, see Kuryłowicz (1964: 183f.).) The later "basic" function of the case, possession and the possessive relations, were, in the earliest layers of PIE, conveyed not by aid of a separate case (the genitive), but through the use of adjectives, Lat. *-īus* and *-īlius* (see Szantyr 1965: 159f.), or the dative in combination with a copula, the *mihi liber est* type (see Kulneff and Eriksson 1999: 1). On the use of the possessive dative construction in Greek, see

Kulneff and Eriksson (1999: 169-172); for Latin, see Serbat (1996: 568f.), Bauer (2000: 181-184).
A genitive case morphology began, it is said, in partitive object genitive constructions. Starting from partitive object genitive expressions of the type in sentences (1), (3) and (4), a lexical expression for measure was added, a noun, originally merely appositional to the partitive expression, i.e. "give me of (the) bread, a piece". Later on this came to be more closely associated with the partitive with the result that it was considered the head of the phrase, thus "a piece of bread". One can note that is not possible to reconstruct one, single genitive singular morpheme for PIE, but it was only in the development of the individual languages, that the partitives were assigned a position within the declinations, thus Serbat (1992: 287-289); cf. Szereményi (1996: 184).

[11] See e.g. Löfsted (1942: 163), Szantyr (1965: 74).

[12] Bennett (1914: 99).

[13] Buck (1904: 196).

[14] Szantyr (1965: 85).

[15] See Szantyr (1965: 131f.).

[16] The morpheme appears in some Sabellian names, e.g. *Herens* "the whished-for one", *Perkens* "the prayed-for one", which indicates a very old age (Meiser 1993). Rix (1994: 28, note 23) suggests a derivation *-tno-*, a shared Latin/Sabellian innovation.

[17] Umbr. *ocrer* "mount": cf. Lat. *ocris*, cf. Fest. p.192 (Li) *ocrem antique ... montem confragosum uocabant* "they used to call an uneven mountain *ocris*". Umbr. *pihaner* "purify", cf. Lat. *piāre*, *pius* (Untermann 2000: 553).

[18] See Lötstedt (1942: 171f.), Serbat (1996: 311f.).

[19] < *H_1en "in", cf. Lat. *in*, Gr. ἐν, ἐνι with several parallels in other IE languages (Untermann 2000: 223-225, de Vaan 2008: 300).

[20] Perhaps from preverb *am-* "around", in the same manner as *comono* < *kom-*, *pernum* < *per-* etc. Same meaning/function as Umbr. *paca* (?) (Untermann 2000: 88).

[21] Perhaps comparable to Lat. *causā* "because of" (Vetter 1953: 153, 381).

[22] Etymology uncertain, perhaps neuter accusative singular of an adjective *perno-* (Untermann 2000: 538) Most editors see a correspondence with Lat. '*limitum tenus*', e.g. Vetter (1953: 9), Pisani (1964: 73f.).

[23] The meaning of both words remains uncertain, though they are both compared to Latin genitive phrases using *causā*, *gratiā* or *ergo* "because of", e.g. (Vetter 1953: 238, 419; Untermann 2000: 508, 812).

[24] A construction closely connected with the instrumental ablative, and the ablative of accompanying circumstances (Szantyr 1965: 137).

[25] Bauer (2000: 266, 285f.).

[26] Adams (2003: 132).

[27] See Szantyr (1965: 142).

[28] Attested once, in an Old Latin inscription *POPLIOSIO VALESIOSIO,* dated to second half of 6th century (De Simone 1980).

[29] Also found in Venetic, and perhaps also Celtic; the origin of the ending is still obscure, though this may have something to do with an old adjectival construction. See for example Szemerényi (1996: 184), Klingenschmitt (1992: 98-104).
[30] Lat. *-aī* was shortened and diphthongised to *-ae* during the 3rd century (Meiser 1998: 132).
[31] Klingenschmitt (1992: 108f.).
[32] Szemerényi (1996: 190).
[33] See Tikkanen (in press, Chapter 7).
[34] See Szantyr (1965: 145-147).

References

Adams, J. N. (2003) *Bilingualism and the Latin Language*, Cambridge, Cambridge University Press.

Baldi, P. (1983) *An Introduction to the Indo-European Languages*, Carbondale, Ill., Southern Illinois University Press.

Barðdal, J. (2010) "Construction-Based Historical-Comparative Reconstruction", to appear in G. Trousdaleand T. Hoffmann (eds) *Oxford Handbook of Construction Grammar*, Oxford, Oxford University Press.

Barðdal, J. and T. Eythórsson (2009) "Reconstructing Syntax: Construction Grammar and the Comparative Method", to appear in H.C. Boas and I.A. Sag (eds) *Sign-Based Construction Grammar*, Stanford, CSLI Publications.

Bauer, B. (2000) *Archaic Syntax in Indo-European – The Spread of Transitivity in Latin and French*, Berlin, Mouton de Gruyter.

Beeler, M. S. (1952) "The Relations of Latin to Osco-Umbrian" *Language* 28, 435-443.

Bennett, C. E. (1914) *Syntax of Early Latin. Vol. II. The Cases*, Boston, Leipsic.

Cuzzolin, P. and P. Baldi (2009) *New perspectives on historical syntax of Latin, vol. 1*, Berlin-New York, Mouton de Gruyter.

de Vaan, M. (2008) *Etymological Dictionary of Latin and the other Italic languages*, Leiden, Brill.

De Simone, C. (1980) "L'aspetto linguistico", in C.M. Stibbe, G. Colonna, C. de Simone and H.S. Versnel (eds) *Lapis Satricanus*, The Hague, Staatsuitgivering-'s, 71-94.

Devoto, G. (1951) *Gli antichi italici*, 2nd edition, Florence, Vallecchi.

Harrison, S.P. (2003) "On the Limits of the Comparative Method" in B.D. Joseph and R.D. Janda (eds) *The Handbook of Historical Linguistics*, Oxford, Blackwell, 343-388.

Haverling, G. (2010) "Chapter 4: Actionality, tense and viewpoint" in P. Cuzzolin and P. Baldi (eds) *New perspectives on historical syntax of Latin, vol.* 2, Berlin-New York, Mouton de Gruyter, 277-523.

Hettrich, H. (1997) "Syntaktische Rekonstruktion bei Delbrück und heute: Nochmals zum lateinischen und griechieschen AcI " in E. Crespo and J.L. Garciá Ramón (eds) *Berthold Delbrück y la sintaxis indoeuropea hoy. Actas del Coloquio de la Indogermanische Gesellschaft Madrid, 21-24 de septiembre de 1994*, Madrid/Wiesbaden, Reichert, 219-238.

Jeffers, R.J. (1973) "Problems in the Reconstruction of Proto-Italic" *The Journal of Indo-European Studies* 1: 330-344.

Jones, D.M. (1950) "The Relation of Latin to Osco-Umbrian" *Transactions of the Philological Society* 49: 60-87.

Klingenschmitt, G. (1992) "Die Lateinische Nominalflexion", in O. Panagl and T. Krisch (eds) *Latein und Indogermanisch. Akten des Kolloquiums der Indogermanischen Gesellschaft, Salzburg, 23. - 26. September 1986,* Innsbruck, Institut für Sprachwissenschaft, 89-135.

Kühner, R. and C. Stegmann (1955) *Ausführliche Grammatik der lateinischen Sprache. II: Satzlehre*, 1. Teil, 3. Auflage *durchgesehen von A. Thierfelder*, Leverkusen, Gottschalk.

Kuryłowicz, J. (1964) *The Inflectional Categories of Indo-European*, Heidelberg, Carl Winter.

Lightfoot, D.W. (1979) *Principles of diachronic syntax*, Cambridge, Cambridge University Press.

Löfstedt, E. (1942) *Syntactica,* 1. Teil, 2. Auflage, Lund, Gleerup.

Meiser, G. (1986) *Lautgeschichte der umbrischen Sprache*, Innsbruck, Institut für Sprachwissenschaft.

—. (1987) "Pälignisch, Latein und Südpikenisch" *Glotta* 65, 103-125.

—. (1993) "Das Gerundivum im Spiegel der italischen Onomastik" in F. Hiedermanns, H. Rix and E. Seebold (eds) *Sprachen und Schriften des antiken Mittelmeerraums. Festschrift für Jürgen Untermann zum 65. Geburtstag,* Innsbruck, Institut für Sprachwissenschaft, 255-268.

—. (1996) "Accessi alla protostoria delle lingue sabelliche", in L. del Tutto Palma (ed.) *La Tavola di Agnone nel contesto italico, Convegno di studio. Agnone, 13-15 aprile 1994,* Florence, Olschki, 187-209.

—. (1998) *Historische Laut- und Formenlehre des Lateinischen*, Innsbruck, Institut für Sprachwissenschaft.

von Mengden, F. (2008) "Reconstruction Complex Structures: A Typological Perspective", in G. Ferraresi and M. Goldbach (eds) *Principles of Syntactic Reconstruction,* Amsterdam, John Benjamins, 97-119.

Pisani, V. (1954) 'Zur Sprachgeschichte des alten Italiens.' *Rheinisches Museum für Philologie* 97: 47-68.

—. (1964) *Le lingue dell'Italia antica oltre il latino. Manuale storico della lingua Latina* Vol. IV, 2nd edition, Torino, Rosenberg&Sellier.

Rix, H. (1981) "Umbro e proto-osco-umbro", in E. Vineis (ed.) *Le lingue indoeuropee di frammentaria attestazione. Die indogermanischen Restsprachen. Atti del convegno della Società Italiana di Glottologia e della Indogermanische Gesellschaft. Udine, 22-24 settembre 1981,* Pisa, Giardini, 91-107.

—. (1994) "Latein und Sabellisch. Stammbaum oder Sprachbund?" *Incontri Linguistici* 17: 13-29.

—. (1996) "Variazioni locali in Osco", in L. del Tutto Palma (ed.) *La Tavola di Agnone nel contesto italico, Convegno di studio. Agnone, 13-15 aprile 1994,* Florence, Olschki, 243-261.

—. (2000). ""tribú", "stato", "città" e "insediamento" nelle lingue italiche" *Archivio Glottologico Italiano* 85: 196-231.

—. (2004) "Ausgliederung und Aufgliederung der italischen Sprachen" in A. Bammesberger and T. Vennemann (eds) *Languages in Prehistoric Europé,* 2nd edition, Heidelberg, Carl Winter, 147-172.

Serbat, G. (1992) "Zum Ursprung des indogermanischen Genitivs und seiner lateinischen Verwendung" in O. Panagl and T. Krisch (eds) *Latein und Indogermanisch. Akten des Kolloquiums der Indogermanischen Gesellschaft, Salzburg, 23. - 26. September 1986,* Innsbruck, Institut für Sprachwissenschaft, 285-291.

Silvestri, D. (1998) "The Italic Languages", in A. Giacalone Ramat and P. Ramat (eds) *The Indo-European Languages,* London, Taylor&Francis Ltd, 322-344.

Szantyr, A. (1965) *Lateinische Syntax und Stilistik von J. B. Hofmann. Neubearbeitet von A. Szantyr,* München, Beck.

Szemerényi, O. (1996) *Introduction to Indo-European Linguistics,* 4th edition, Oxford-New York, Oxford University Press.

Tikkanen, K. (in press) *Grammar of the Sabellian Languages. The Cases,* (preliminary title), Heidelberg, Carl Winter

Untermann, J. (2000) *Wörterbuch des Oskisch-Umbrischen,* Heidelberg, Carl Winter.

Vetter, E. (1953) *Handbuch der Italischen Dialekte*, Heidelberg, Carl Winter.

PREFIXES AND ASPECT OF LATIN VERB: A TYPOLOGICAL VIEW

VLADIMIR PANOV

Introduction

In this article, I will try to apply the tradition used in grammatical descriptions of certain modern languages to throw light on some phenomena found in Latin as well. The field of research here regards verbal aspect and actionality, grammaticalization, and the role which verbal prefixes play in aspectual semantics.

There are many points of view on the category of aspect, which often contradict one another. The differences between different concepts may often be explained by the fact that one or more languages can influence linguists in their descriptions of concrete language data or in their typological generalizations. Often grammatical phenomena characteristic only of a few languages are considered universal. Moreover, attention should be paid to the terminological chaos within this field of research, which results from a lack of mutual understanding between linguists dealing with these problems: even the term 'aspect' itself is often understood in very different ways. Therefore, a comparison between the aspectual systems of different languages becomes very complicated.

1. Actionality

Let us now define the terms. First of all, one should distinguish between two conceptual zones which are different, though they are closely related to each other in terms of semantics. The first semantic zone is the one called 'actionality', 'state of affairs' etc. (there are a lot of words used in different traditions to name the same thing). Actionality must be clearly distinguished from aspect. Actionality is a category in which semantics demonstrate *the internal structure of a situation*. The term 'actionality' was originally introduced by Vendler (1953) and applied to the English language. The main criterion he used to classify the predicates into different classes was their ability to combine with different types of adverbs of time. However, it is not only the formal criterion of compatibility which may be taken into consideration for the subdivision of predicates into these classes. Vendler's classes are clearly distinct in their semantics as well. Here are Vendler's classes of predicates with their semantic characteristics (Plungian (in print)):

1) States are the situations which do not have any temporal limits and do not require energy to support them: e.g. English verbs like *sleep, see, stand* etc.

2) Activities are the situations which do not have obvious temporal limits, yet require additional energy for their continuation: e.g. English verbs *read, write, speak* etc.

3) Accomplishments are the situations which contain a logical limit within themselves: *fall (down), burn (up), come, go* etc.

4) Achievements are the momentary situations which do not last anything from the point of view of language: e.g. *explode, loose, appear, disappear* etc.

Since Vendler's classification concerns the internal characteristic of the situation and not the lexeme of the verb, modifying the situation can influence its actionality. For example, 'activities' can be easily transformed to 'accomplishments' by adding a direct object: *to read vs. to read a book, to write vs. to write a letter*.

2. Aspect

Actionality is an internal characteristic of the situation. On the other hand, 'aspect' presents a perspective on the situation. The keyword in the field of aspect is "topic time" (Dahl 1985; Klein 1994; Smith 1991). This situation is presented as an interval of time within which the language is able either to distinguish different stages (the beginning, the middle, the end) or to consider the situation in its entirety. Moreover, there are two types of aspect: the *primary aspect* and the *secondary aspect*. Examples of primary aspectual values are:

A. The topic time is within the situation itself

- Prospective (for activities and accomplishments)
- Inceptive (for states, activities and accomplishments)
- Durative (for states) / Progressive (for activities and accomplishments)
- Completive (for accomplishments)
- Resultative (for accomplishments) / Perfect (for states and activities)

B. The situation is within the topic time

- Punctive (for achievements)
- Limitative (for states, accomplishments and activities)

The secondary aspect is the transformation of the class of actionality of the situation:

- Accomplishments, activities > statives: Habitual
- achievements > states: Multiplicative, Iterative
- accomplishments > achievements: Semelfactive
- activities > accomplishments: Transformative

These elementary actional and aspectual values as well as temporal and even modal ones can easily unite in groups under a certain grammatical category of a given language. For example, the Completive, the Punctive, the Inceptive and the Limitative form the perfective 'cluster'. The Perfective which comes together with the past tense is known as the Aorist (for example, the Past simple in English, passé simple in French or perfectum of Latin).

Languages can express aspectual values in very different ways from a formal point of view. The aspect can be more or less grammaticalized. For example, in English, French or Latin the two aspectual values of Aorist and Imperfect are clearly distinguished in the past tense by means of regular morphology – i.e. Past simple vs. Past continuous in English, *passé simple vs. imparfait* in French and *perfectum vs. imperfectum* in Latin. The Italian language, along with these two categories, regularly distinguishes two aspectual grammemes in the past: the aorist, the imperfect and the past progressive. The difference between the latter two grammemes consists first of all in their varied compatibility with different classes of actionality. The progressive is not compatible with states (*stavo amando) whereas the imperfect comes together with them quite well (*amavo*). Besides that, the progressive in Italian can also be used in the Present (*sto pensando*).

The perfective aspect of the kind regularly expressed by means of additive morphology and containing a number of regular paradigms, is usually born from the aorist in the process of grammaticalization. That is why the two aspectual grammemes (the Perfective and the Imperfective) are usually distinguished only at the level of the Past tense. Typical examples of such binary systems in the Past are presented by Latin (*perfectum* vs. *imperfectum*), ancient Greek (aorist vs. imperfect), Old Church Slavonic, modern Bulgarian, all the Romance languages. In the terminology of Dahl (1985), this kind of Perfective aspect is called 'anterior-based perfective'.

3. Prefixation

Another way of expressing aspectual values is the addition of different sorts of adverbial elements to the verb. Talmy, who was the first to describe this phenomenon, has called such elements 'satellites' (Talmy: 1985). In the terminology of Dahl, these are called 'bounders'. These originally adverbial particles modify the spatial characteristics of situation. In many languages the 'bounders' may have the form of prefixes, though not necessarily, for example, in most of the Germanic languages the adverbial particles can easily be separated from the verbal stem. Added to motion verbs, the prefixes change the spatial structure of situation, for example:

(1) Lat. In-greditur ad regem Archistratem, socerum suum (Hist. *Apoll.* 51)[1]

(2) a. Germ. Ich bin aus dem Haus her-aus-gegangen
     b. Rus. Ja vy-šel iz doma
     c. Lith. Aš iš-ėjau iš namų
     "I came out from the house"

In many cases adding a 'satellite' changes the actionality of situation too. This concerns motion verbs in the first place. Thus, if a prefix is added to a verb which presupposes a situation of non-directional motion, the motion verb acquires an internal limit. Therefore, the verbs of activity change their class to accomplishment. Moreover, in many cases, depending on the context, the new verb of accomplishment can be interpreted as a verb of achievement, that is, as a moment in which the internal limit of the situation is achieved. For example:

(3)   Lat. Ac-cedens ad navem Apollonii coepit stare et mirari (Hist. *Apoll.* 39)

(4)   a. Ted. Der Zug ist an-gekommen
      b. Rus. Pojezd pri-jechal
      c. Lit. Traukinys at-važiavo
          "The train arrived"

Unlike the Romance languages, in all the languages from which our examples are taken the verbal stem expresses the meaning of *manner* of motion and not of the *path*; that is, the manner and not the path is lexicalized, while the path is expressed through prefixes. In other words, we are dealing with the *satellite-framed* languages and not with *verb-framed* languages, in the framework of Talmy's theory.

Prefixes or particles which bear the same function can be combined not only with motion verbs. In these cases their primary meanings are reinterpreted in different ways according to the meaning of the verbal stem itself. Not all the prefixes are able to acquire abstract meanings and the number of such prefixes varies from language to language.

(5)   a. Rus. Ja vy-pil čaj
      b. Lit. Aš iš-gėriau arbatą
      c. Ted. Ich habe den Tee aus-getrunken
          "I drank the tee up to the end"

(6)   Lat. Factum est illud, ut ego illic vini hirneam e-biberim meri (Plaut. *Amph.* 432)

In all these examples a prefix with the special meaning OUT combines with the verbal stem DRINK. The combination of the two elements means 'to drink up to the very end'. It is notable that the same model is used within different languages. This fact will be discussed more in detail later. What is now of interest to us is the fact that in some languages this way of expressing aspectual values is highly grammaticalized. This is true first and foremost for the East and West Slavic languages. Each verb of these languages belongs to one of the two aspectual classes – the perfective or the imperfective. Almost every imperfective verb has a 'partner' perfective verb whose lexical meaning is the same and only the aspect grammeme is different. The aspectual opposition in these languages is expressed in the following formal ways:

1) Prefixation: adding a prefix to an imperfective verbal stem the new verb becomes perfective

2) Suffixation: the same verbal stem can produce two verbs of different aspectual values by adding different suffixes: Rus. *spuskat' - spustit'* to let down, lower

3) Deperfectivizing through the regular suffix -*va*- (the multiplicative suffix originally): Rus. *na-lit'* (Pfv) - *na-li-vat'* (Impfv) to pour.

The semantics of the two elements of aspectual opposition is quite complex and metaphorized as the opposition is strongly grammaticalized. The system works in the following way: the two aspectual values are distinguished in the Past, in the Future, in the Imperative mood and in the Infinitive. The perfective form of the Present is always interpreted as the perfective Future while the imperfective Future is expressed analytically through a special form of copula and the imperfective Infinitive. The Present tense, therefore, requires the imperfective aspect only. The grammatical aspect is the only way to express aspectual values in the given languages due to the lack of regular morphological means which are present in other languages as the opposition between the perfective and imperfective Past in English, Romance languages etc.

In Dahl (1985), the type of Perfective built from the Imperfective through prefixes is called 'bounder-based' perfective. This is the most widespread way of forming a perfective in the languages I have just discussed. In addition to the East and West Slavic languages where aspectual opposition of this kind is grammaticalized, many other languages present similar tendencies. In Europe, the creation of perfective verbs through adding 'bounders' to verbs is evidenced in East Europe first and foremost. Strongly grammaticalized (yet, less than in East and West Slavic) bounder-based aspect is present in Baltic languages (more in Lithuanian and less in Latvian), in Hungarian, in Yiddish (strongly influenced by the surrounding Slavic languages), in Romanian dialects of this region which usually borrow the prefixes form Slavic languages, in Istro-Romanian which, being a Romance language originally, has borrowed its prefixes from the Croatian dialects. A highly grammaticalized aspectual opposition of this kind is present in Georgian. Whether this is a regional feature, is the subject of much discussion. In Western Europe, similar tendencies exist in all Germanic languages including English and German, but aspectual opposition of this kind is much less grammaticalized (for example, *drink up vs. drink* in English and *austrinken vs. trinken* in

German). Outside Eurasia, the grammatical category of bounder-based aspect is present in the Margi language of the Chad group where the 'bounders' have the form of special suffixes rather than prefixes.

So, there are two types of Perfective. Due to their different origins (grammaticalization sources), they present some notable semantic and structural differences on the synchronic level.

Anterior-based Perfective	Bounder-based perfective
1. Morphologically regular	1. Morphologically irregular, different verbs combine with different prefixes, the choice of prefix is not always clear
2. Expresses a situation limited in time and can combine with all the classes of actionality including states and activities	2. Besides time limits, signifies that the situation reaches its limit, that is, the final point of the situation is considered. Combines with accomplishments and gets non-standard interpretations with other classes of the actionality
3. Usually combines only with the Present	4. Can combine with all or almost all temporal and mood forms

Both types of aspect can easily coexist in the same language and combine according to complex rules. This is the case in, for example, South Slavic languages, especially Bulgarian, also Georgian and partly Lithuanian. In such cases perfective aspect is normally compatible only with the Aorist in the Past and imperfective only with the Imperfect. In the opposite cases (i.e, Aorist+Imperfective or Imperfect+Perfective) verbs acquire a limitative meaning or a multiplicative meaning, respectively.

4. Latin

Latin presents a rich system of prefixes which is partially inherited from Proto-Indo-European and partially new. As is the case in all languages with such systems, the primary function of the prefixes is spatial. The prefixes combine with motion verbs in the first instance. While the verbal stem signifies the *manner* of motion, the prefix adds the *path* to the situation.

(7)   Deinde utrique curia e-grediuntur (Sall. *Iug.* 15)

(8)   Igitur Calpurnius initio paratis commeatibus acriter Numidiam in-gressus est (Sall. *Iug.* 28)

(9) Postquam, sicuti voluerat, con-gressi, dicit se missum a consule venisse quaesitum ab eo, pacem an bellum agitaturus foret (Sall. *Iug.* 109)

(10) Equites Mauri atque Gaetuli, non acie neque ullo more proeli sed catervatim, uti quosque fors conglobaverat, in nostros in-currunt (Sall. *Iug.* 97)

All the examples above denote situations where the very logic implies the end of action. Moreover, the most probable interpretation of all these examples is simply the end of a process, so, the change of actionality class is to be observed. Thus, the verb *gradior* is an Activity and its prefixal derivative *ingredior* is an Accomplishment. However, *ingredior* is quite likely to be interpreted as an Achievement in many contexts; i.e., as the moment when the action is already finished. It is also important to note that the prefixed motion verbs are rarely found in the present tense. The present forms of prefixed verbs evidenced above are used exclusively in 'praesens historicum' exactly as it is in our example. On the contrary, non-prefixed verbs are used in contexts of the Progressive. A brilliant example from Plautus reveals quite clearly the aspectual opposition between the verbs without prefixes in the progressive present and the ones without prefixes in other forms, where a perfective prefixed verb would more likely be used in other languages:

(11) Chrys. *Rogas? Con-gredere.* Nic. *Gradior* (Plaut. *Bacch.* 980)

This example can be compared with Russian (12a) or Lithuanian (12b):

(12) a. Podo-jdi s'uda! - idu!
      b. At-eik čia - einu!
          Come here! I am coming!

In all the languages where the prefix-based aspect exists in any form, grammaticalized or not, the neutral way to use a verb in the imperative is to use the perfective aspect, that is, a prefixed verb, while the non-prefixed member of an aspectual couple has specific connotations, as e.g., rudeness or a claim to act immediately. This is true even for languages which do not have a well-developed bounder-based aspect but distinguish the aspect in the Imperative by regular morphological means, such as Modern Greek, where the neutral way to use the Imperative is still the perfective form, or the 'Aorist' stem in terms of traditional Greek grammar. However, it seems that Latin presents the same tendency.

Some of Latin motion verbs express the idea of the end of process within their original semantics, even without adding prefixes, for example the verb *venire* 'come', which denotes motion towards the deictic center. Moreover, the manner of motion is not specified, as in modern Romance languages. Yet, the Latin verb *venire* can be easily used with prefixes although the spatial structure of situation is not changed. The most frequent prefixes added to *venire* are *ad-* and *per-*. Let us see some examples:

(13) **Per-venit** innocens tamen Apollonius prior ad patriam suam et introivit domum (Hist. *Apoll.* 6)

(14) **Per-veniunt** felici cursu (Hist. *Apoll.* 48)

(15) Interpositis autem diebus atque mensibus, cum haberet puella mense iam sexto ventriculum deformatum, **ad-venit** eius sponsus rex Apollonius (Hist. *Apoll.* 24)

(16) Igitur qui Tharsiam rapuerunt, **ad-venerunt** in civitatem Mytilenam (Hist. *Apoll.* 33)

Neither prefixe change the spatial structure, but underline exclusively the integrity of action. Moreover, the prefix *ad-* underlines the ultimate stage of motion: therefore, it would be reasonable to interpret the situation as an achievement. Only the ultimate point, the end of the situation, is taken into consideration. All the examples concern the Past, including (15) which is the Historical Present.

So the prefixes used with motion verbs show a clear tendency to change the actionality of situation and its aspectual characteristics, and to make forms which look quite similar to the *bounder-based perfective*.

5. Prefixes in exclusively aspectual function

However, as in other languages, Latin prefixes can be added to verbs which do not denote motion. In this usage they acquire more abstract and metaphorical meanings; yet, these meanings are developed from spatial ones. Clearly aspectual usages can often be found in such cases as well. As in other languages, which possess a similar type of preverbal Perfective, the choice of prefixes is always complex and often not very clear. This phenomenon, however, can be partially explained by the so-called 'Vey & Schooneveld effect' (Schooneveld 1951; Vey 1952).

The phenomenon was observed independently by two linguists and has to do first and foremost with the Slavic languages. When verbs make aspectual couples with an imperfective and a perfective member, the perfective member of the couple is often created from the imperfective member by adding an 'empty' prefix, which brings no new meaning to the original verb besides the aspectual, perfectivizing meaning. Different prefixes are used with different words and it is hardly predictable which prefix is to be used with a given verb. The hypothesis is that the choice of an 'empty' prefix is dictated by the pseudo-spatial semantic component of verb: in other words, each verb is conceptualized as an action having spatial characteristics. If the spatial component of the meaning of the verbal stem and the one of the prefix coincide, the prefix can be used to form the perfective verb. The classical Russian example, often used to illustrate the phenomenon of aspectual couples, is a good illustration of the Vey & Schooneveld effect as well:

(17)   *Ja pišu pis'mo* (Impfv) - *ja na-pišu (na-pisal) pis'mo* (Pfv).
       "I am writing a letter - I will write a letter up to the very end"

The spatial semantic of *na-* is 'contact with a horizontal surface'. The verb *write* is conceptualized as an action with the same spatial characteristics - writing is an action which usually takes place on a certain surface which is horizontal. Another example of this type is the English couple *sit* and *sit down*. The process of sitting down can be directed only towards the ground, a chair etc, that is DOWN, though, the verb 'sit' is not a typical motion verb because it cannot imply all the spatial characteristics of motion – the initial point, the final point and the path.

It should be added that the number of spatial values which the prefixes of each language possess is always limited; so, for making aspectual couples, the language has to choose from a limited group of values. That is why the semantic of the prefix seems fuzzy in many cases.

Latin verbs can behave in quite a similar way. The verb *advenire* is a verb with a clear perfective meaning because the prefix *ad-* signifies 'approaching to deictical center' which coincides with the lexical meaning of the verb itself. The same effect can be found in the verb *pervenire*, where the action is conceptualized as a straight line with a beginning and an end. In this case, one should notice that the prefix *per-* introduces no new lexical meaning but tends to reinforce the spatial meaning already contained within the verbal stem. Almost every verb can be presented as a spatial metaphor of time (according to the well- known cognitive metaphor TIME IS SPACE) (Lakoff 1980); this is why the prefix *per-*, which has the spatial meaning 'through something, from the beginning to the end of the path', is the prefix most often used in Latin for making perfective verbs. Let's consider some Latin examples that can, in my view, illustrate this effect:

(18) Is habuit unam filiam, virginem speciosissimam, in qua nihil rerum natura **ex-erraverat** (Hist. *Apoll.* 1)

In this example the prefix *ex-* brings no additional meaning to the verb *errare*. The only possible interpretation is that it is a perfective verb. The verb *exerrare* bears the universal meaning of the Punctive.

(19) Post haec induit tragicum: et nihilominus admirabiliter **com-placuit** ita, ut omnes amici regis et hoc se numquam audisse testarentur nec vidisse (Hist. *Apoll.* 16)

The prefix *con-* used here is a typical case of the preverbal Perfective. The value of the prefix is 'association, consistency' while the verb *placere* implies situation with two actants. So the two values coincide partially making a verb with perfective semantics.

(20) Accepta igitur mansione Apollonius bene acceptus requievit, agens deo gratias, qui ei non **de-negavit** regem consolatorem (Hist. *Apoll.* 17)

The verb *negare* is obviously understood as a spatial motion away from object. The prefix *de-* has the same value:

(21) Is Adherbalem et Hiempsalem ex sese genuit Iugurthamque filium Mastanabalis fratris, quem Masinissa, quod ortus ex concubina erat, privatum **de-reliquerat**, eodem cultu quo liberos suos domi habuit (Sall. *Iug.* 5)

The idea of motion away, separation is present here as well as in (22):

(22) Quae ubi tardius procedunt neque lenitur animus ferox, statuit quovis modo inceptum **per-ficere** (Sall. *Iug.* 11)

The verb *perficere* is a verb quite frequently used in Latin texts and means 'do up to the very end, complete'. As mentioned, time is conceptualized as a line which has an end. The meaning of the prefix is 'integrity'. Another example of a perfective with *con-* is given in (23):

(23) Interim haud longe a mari prope Cirtam oppidum utriusque exercitus **con-sedit** (Sall. *Iug.* 21)

The prefix *con-* is one of the most grammaticalized among the Latin prefixes. In this case a spatial metaphor is not very evident. Yet, a prefix with a similar meaning is a typical means to make perfective verbs in other languages. For example, the Russian prefix *s-* 'together' is used in many perfective verbs such as *pet'* - *s-pet'* 'sing - sing up to the end' or 'stop singing'. In this Latin example the prefix underlines the initial point of a static situation, therefore, the universal aspectual category which can be implied to this situation is the Inceptive.

Conclusion

The Latin language presents a developed system of aspect that is based on prefixation. The perfective members of the oppositions are made from imperfective ones by adding prefixes; so, it is the 'bounder-based perfective' which coexists in Latin with the 'anterior-based perfective' expressed by means of regular paradigms. The use of prefixed and non-prefixed verbs with different grammatical categories is not formally restricted, but presents such tendencies as for example the use of prefixed verbs in the Past and not in the Present. However, the time reference is almost never the present, even if the present tense is used. Although the mechanism of perfectivizing by means of prefixes is quite widespread in Latin, there is no mechanism of secondary deperfectivizing as in East and West Slavic languages. So, this type of aspect is not grammaticalized in Latin. The Latin system is similar to the Lithuanian, Georgian and Bulgarian. It is worth noting that the aspectual system of prefixes has almost disappeared in the modern Romance languages. The reasons for this change are not yet well explored. However, many languages endured a similar transformation in their history - for example, Old English, many Indian and Iranian languages. The only Romance language which contains a rich system of prefixes is Istro-Romanian. Here, they are also widely used in aspectual functions.

References

Bertocci D. (in press) *Tipi di preverbazione in latino: la funzionalità aspettuale.*

Dahl, Ö. (1985) *Tense and Aspect Systems*, Oxford, Blackwell.

Haverling G. (2000) *On Sco-verbs, Prefixes and Semantic Functions: A study in the development of prefixed verbs from early to late Latin*, Göteborg, Acta Universitatis Gothoburgensis.

Klein, W. (1994) *Time in language*, London, Routledge and Kegan Paul

Lakoff G. and M. Johnson (1980) *Metaphors we live by*, Chicago, University of Chicago Press.

Maysak T. (2005) Майсак Т. А. Типология грамматикализации конструкций с глаголами движения и глаголами позиции. Moscow, Языки славянской культуры.

Maslov Y. (2004) Маслов Ю.С. Избранные труды: Аспектология. Общее языкознание. Moscow: Языки славянской.

Plungian V. (in print) Введение в грамматическую семантику.

van Schooneveld, C.H. (1951) "The Aspect System of the Old Church Slavonic and Old Russian verbum finitum 'byti'", *Word* 7.2: 96-103.

Smith, C. (1991) *The Parameter of Aspect*, Dordrecht, Kluwer Academic Press.

Talmy L. (1985) "Lexicalization patterns: semantic structure in lexical forms", in T. Shopen (ed.) *Language typology and semantic description*, Vol. 3: 57-149.

Vey M. (1952) "Les preverbes 'vides' en tchéque modern" *Revue des études slaves* 29: 82-107.

Vendler, Z. (1957) "Verbs and Times" *The Philosophical Review* 66.3: 143-160, also in *Linguistics in Philosophy*, Ithaca-New York 1967, Cornell University Press, 97-146.

VERBAL PREFIXATION IN CLASSICAL LATIN AND IN ITALIAN: THE PREFIX *EX-*

ÁGNES JEKL

Introduction

Linguistic coding of spatial particles, and in particular verbal prefixation, has attracted increasing interest in recent years, as the works of Jean-Paul Brachet (2000), Anna Pompei (2010) and Sophie Van Laer (2010) reveal.

In the present paper, I analyse the functions performed by the Latin prefix *ex-* and its surviving forms in Italian – drawing on the results of my Master's thesis (defended in June 2008). In the future, this analysis will be extended to include other prefixes to try to achieve more general results and conclusions regarding the morphological and semantic relationship between prefix and verb.

For my research, I wanted to choose a prefix that was productive in Latin and that has been productive in Italian as well. For the above reason, I have chosen the Latin prefix *ex-*. Before analysing it, I would like to briefly describe the process of prefixation and its realization in the analysed languages.

1. Prefixation

Prefixation is a word formation process, with strong connections with lexicology, morphology and syntax. Word formation processes have two main types: derivation and compounding.

In Italian grammars, prefixation is traditionally considered as a derivational process (Rohlfs 1969: 347-361, Tekavčić 1980: 145, Dardano-Trifone 1999: 324-325), or placed between derivation and compounding (Fogarasi 1983: 131). Prefixation means attaching an affix to the left of a word already existing in the vocabulary. Prefixes deriving from prepositions can be found as independent words in the lexicon (e.g. *in* or *con*), which is not the case of other prefixes (e.g. *re-*). Apart from this, prefixation, unlike suffixation, does not change the category of the original word (e.g. *fare* and *rifare* are both verbs: Salvi and Vanelli 2004: 332, 336).

In Latin, prefixation is defined differently and its function is also different. Latin prefixed verbs are usually considered as compound verbs in grammars (Hofmann and Szantyr 1965: 287-304), or more recently, derived verbs (Oniga 2007: 136-139). A possible explanation for the traditional classification could be that the meaning of prefixes was more transparent in Classical Latin as they were strongly related to prepositions. Prefixed verbs were therefore interpreted as 'preposition + verb' – in the case of prefixes deriving from prepositions.

As prefixation in Latin can be considered as compounding, we can presume that most Latin prefixed verbs were transparent,[1] in the sense that speakers could recognize the two components and in many cases also their meanings. In Italian, on the contrary, we can consider transparent only those prefixed verbs in which the Latin basic verb is still an independent verb in Italian, and where the prefix has a very clear and exact meaning.

It is also important to investigate the syntactic features of prefixation in the two languages. In Italian, we can only observe that "prefixed verbs sometimes do not select the same complements as their basic verbs: e.g. *correre* and *ridere* are intransitive verbs, while *percorrere* and *deridere* are transitive ones" (in: Salvi and Vanelli 2004: 336). In Latin, the case is more complex, as Latin prefixes – because of their close relationship with prepositions – can affect the argument structure of the predicate in which they are embedded. Consequently, Latin prefixed verbs can have two different syntactic behaviours:

I) The prefix affects the argument structure of the predicate.

(1)   *Cervus nemorosis excitatus latibulis* (Phaedr. 2,8,1)

In example (1) the NP *nemorosis latibulis* does not require a preposition, as the noun and the adjective are in the ablative case as required by the prefix – the same as would be required by the missing preposition. In this case the prefix assigns its own case – in other words, it preserves all its syntactic features. The morphological structure can be described as in (2):

(2)   [[Pre]#Verb]

Here the prefixed verb has the structure of a compound word, in which the boundary sign (#) between the two elements indicates the conservation of all syntactic features.

II) The prefix does not affect the argument structure of the predicate.

(3)   ... *ex oppido / legiones educunt* (Plaut. *Amph.* 217-218)

In example (3) the preposition is needed before the NP *oppido*, as the prefix does not affect the NP. In this example the prefix does not assign its own case – so it loses its syntactic features. This morphological structure can be described as in (4):

(4)   [[Pre]+Verb]

Here the prefixed verb has the structure of a derived word, in which the boundary sign (+) between the two elements indicates the loss of the syntactic role of the prefix.

In the first case the prefix preserved its syntactic role, while in the second case the prefix has assumed a mere morphological role. It is important to note that in Italian only the second type of construction is allowed, which is the most frequent type in Latin as well (Van Laer (2010: 364-403).

2. The Latin preposition *ex*

In order to analyse the functions of the Latin prefix *ex-*, we need to study the functions and the meanings of the original Latin preposition first. The Latin preposition *ex* originally means: 'out of something', and it always indicates the direction opposite to the preposition *in* (Hofmann and Szantyr 1965: 264-265). In other words, the main function of the preposition *ex* is separation (5), to which other secondary functions were associated, which denote origin and partitivity (6)-(7).[2]

(5)   Separation: *Athenas fugere ex hac domu* (Plaut. *Mil.* 126)

(6)   Origin: *ex eodem ortum loco* (Ter. *Eun.* 241)

(7)   Partitivity: *ex copia piscaria / ... quid emam* (Plaut. *Cas.* 498-499)

The Latin preposition *ex* has not survived in Italian, and its various functions are replaced by two Italian prepositions: *di* and *da*.

3. The Latin prefix *ex-*

The Latin prefix *ex-*[3] has the same meaning as the preposition *ex* (i.e. 'out of something'), which fuses in verbs like *ēdūcō* ('to lead or bring out'). Apart from this primary function (i.e. that of separation), the prefix *ex-* also has secondary functions, which are connected to the primary function in a more or less clear way (Dér 1975; Brachet 2000). In the following part, I will classify such secondary functions following the *Dictionnaire étymologique de la langue latine* by Ernout and Meillet (1967: 204).

The first secondary function reveals an upward movement; this meaning is present in verbs, like *extollō* ('to lift up'). The second associated function denotes deprivation, which can be seen in verbs like *ērādīcō* ('to root out'). In case of inchoative verbs *ex-* indicates a metaphorical passage from one position to another (i.e. the change of position being the third secondary function), as in verbs such as *excandēscō* ('to catch fire'). This function is rather complex and can be found among the functions of the Latin prefixes *ad-* and *in-* as well (Ernout and Meillet 1967: 8, 204, 312). In the course of my analysis, I will call it 'the function of the prefix *ad-* ', because in Italian it is associated mainly with that prefix (see e.g. the verb *addormentarsi* 'to fall asleep'). The fourth secondary function is the finalizing function, which appears in verbs such as *efficiō* ('to work out', from *faciō*), and its separative sense is not transparent. Moreover, this last function results in a weakening of the meaning of the prefix, as in verbs such as *ēdoceō* ('to instruct thoroughly'), in which the prefix has a mere aspectual function. As a result of this weakening, verbs like *ēvītō* ('to avoid') were created, in which the function of the prefix is no longer visible, and both the basic and the prefixed verb have more or less the same meaning (Ernout and Meillet 1967: 204). In this case, I will use the term *reinforcing function*. We can summarize the functions of the prefix *ex-* in the following table (8):

(8)   *Primary function*   →   *Secondary function*
                                   Upward movement (*extollō*)
                                   Depriving function (*ērādīcō*)
      Separative function   Change of position (*excandēscō*)
          (*ēdūcō*)   Finalizing function (*efficiō*)
                                   Reinforcing function (*ēvītō*)

4. The Italian forms of the Latin prefix *ex-*

The Latin prefix *ex-* was preserved in three different forms in Italian, namely *e-*, *es-*[4] and *s-*. The *e-* and *es-* forms can be found mainly in later loan verbs, while the *s-* form can be found mainly in verbs derived directly from Latin. Among these three prefixes only the third is productive, i.e. the *s-* form, which is used mainly for forming new prefixed words. This *s-* form became an independent prefix in Italian, which along with the other functions inherited from Latin *ex-* also assumed a new pejorative function (e.g. in the verb *sragionare*, 'to reason falsely').[5]

I will summarize each function of the *s-* prefix on the bases of the classification of the *Dizionario etimologico della lingua italiana* of Cortelazzo and Zolli (1988: 1115) as in (9):

(9)   The *s-* prefix:
   a.   gives an opposite meaning to the words to which it is added (*sfiorire*, *sgonfiare*)
   b.   has a depriving-pejorative meaning (*sragionare*)
   c.   indicates separation, distance (*sconfinare*)
   d.   has a diminishing or derogative value (*sfamare*, *spolverare*)
   e.   has various values or a function denoting origin (*sbracciarsi*, *sbiancarsi*)
   f.   has an intensive value (*strascinare*).

5. The analysis

To provide a detailed analysis of *ex-* prefixed verbs, I have divided the verbs into four groups, the first three of which are Italian verbs coming from Latin *ex-* prefixed verbs, and the fourth contains Italian verbs with the Italian *s-* prefix.

The verbs are grouped according to their etymology. *Group 1* consists of Italian verbs, which directly derive from Classical Latin, i.e. those that belonged to the Italian vocabulary already when Italian was being born, and underwent the phonological, morphological and semantic changes as the language was developing. *Group 2* consists of Italian verbs deriving from Late Latin and Vulgar Latin but still show direct descendance. *Group 3* contains later loan verbs from Latin, which come both from Classical Latin and Late Latin. These three groups contain all the verbs with the above characteristics, while *Group 4* containing the Italian *s-* prefixed verbs is only a selection of such verbs (due to their huge quantity). All the groups (and the etymology of the verbs) were compiled on the basis of the

Dizionario etimologico della lingua italina of Cortelazzo and Zolli (1984: 369-409; 1988: 1115-1304); for great part of *Group 4*, I also used the *Lessico di frequenza della lingua italiana contemporanea* of Bortolini, Tagliavini and Zampolli (1972: 577-659). I have not listed verbs with a prefix fused phonetically with the first consonant of the root verb (e.g. Lat. *exsolvere* - It. *sciogliere*), as in such cases the prefix can be no more recognized.

In order to facilitate the investigation of verbs, my analysis will be based on two criteria: 1) morphological and 2) semantic (considering the connection between prefix and verb). When a prefix can be formally recognised, we can talk about a morphologically transparent verb - e.g. in case of Italian *sterminare* ('to destroy'), in which the prefix can be recognised compared to the root verb *terminare* ('to end'), but its function remains unclear. When the function of the prefix can also be recognised, we can talk of a semantically transparent verb (i.e., considering the semantic connection between prefix and verb) as in the in case of the Italian verb *spiantare* ('to uproot'), in which the prefix can be recognised both in form and function (deprivation). Sometimes the function of the prefix cannot be recognised because of the verb, as it does not have the same meaning as the original verb or other prefixed verbs, as in the case of the Italian verb *sporgere* ('to hand over'), in which the semantic connection between prefix and verb remains obscure as *porgere* ('to offer') in Italian no longer means 'to extend ahead, onwards'. When a prefix cannot be recognised on the morphological level either, one can talk of an obscure verb in both senses, as. in the case of the Italian verb *spedire* ('to send', from Lat. *expedīre*, 'to free the feet').[6]

Group 1

The first group consists of the following twenty verbs:[7]

emettere, eseguire, scalzare, scavare, schiamazzare, schiudere, scorrere, scusare, spandere, spedire, spendere, spianare, spiantare, spiegare, sporgere, spurgare, stendere, stentare, sterminare, storcere

Twelve verbs (out of twenty) are transparent both on the morphological and the semantic level; e.g., *scalzare*, which derives from the Latin verb *excalceāre* (in which *ex-* has a depriving function). Both in Latin and in Italian this verb means 'to take the shoes off'. The prefix can be clearly recognised on the bases of the verb *calzare* ('to put one's shoes on'). This example helps us to identify the depriving function of the prefix. The transparent verbs of Group 1 preserve three functions of the Latin prefix: the separative function e.g. *emettere* ('to give out'), the depriving function e.g. *spiantare* ('to uproot') and the reinforcing function e.g. *spurgare* ('to purge').[8]

Six verbs (out of twenty) are morphologically transparent, but they are obscure from the semantic point of view, as in the case of the verb *scorrere* ('to flow'), in which the prefix is morphologically recognisable compared to the original verb *correre* ('to run'), but its function remains obscure.

Two verbs (out of twenty) are obscure from the morphological point of view and therefore also semantically (*eseguire*, 'to execute' and *spedire*, 'to send').

We can thus state that more than half of the verbs of Group 1 are recognisable from the semantic point of view (i.e. the function of the prefix can be recognised).

Group 2

The second group consists of 45 verbs.

ergere, scadere, scaldare, scapolare, scappare, scarmigliare, scarseggiare, scartare, scattare, schiacciare, schiattare, scoiare, scomunicare, sconfiggere, scorciare, scorgere, scorticare, scottare, scuotere, sdraiare, sdrucciolare, sdrucire, sgomentare, sgominare, smaniare, smuovere, sparare, spassare, spaventare, spegnere, sperimentare, spingere, spremere, sprezzare, squadrare, squarciare, squartare, stonare, stracciare, strusciare, stufare, svagare, svaporare, svegliare, svellere

Before drawing any conclusions, we need to point out that the etymologies of the verbs of this category are rather uncertain; so we need to handle the findings with due caution.

Eleven verbs (out of 45) are transparent both on the morphological and the semantic level;[9] e.g., the verb *scomunicare*, which derives from Late Latin *excommunicāre*. The meaning of the Latin verb 'to excommunicate' lives on in Italian. In the verb *scomunicare* the prefix can be recognised compared to the words *comunicare* and *comunione* and its separative function can be also recognised. The transparent verbs of the second group preserve three functions of the Latin prefix: the separative function e.g. *spremere* ('to crush'), the depriving function e.g. *scuoiare* ('to skin') and perhaps the finalizing function as well as in the verb *svegliare* ('to wake up').[10]

29 verbs (out of 45) are morphologically transparent, but are obscure from the point of view of their semantic connection, as in the case of the verb *scadere* ('to expire'), the form of the prefix can be recognised on the bases of the verbs *cadere* ('to fall') and *accadere* ('to happen'), but its function remains obscure.

There are eleven morphologically (and consequently also semantically) obscure verbs (out of 45), e.g., the verb *scattare* ('to swing open').

Besides, this group also contains seven verbs, which present a phenomenon characteristic of Vulgar Latin: the double prefixes, as in the case of the Italian verb *scorgere* ('to discern', from spoken Latin *excorrigere*, in which we can find the prefixes: *ex- + con-*).

To summarize, we can say that this group presents a rather low number of morphologically and semantically transparent verbs: 11 verbs (out of 45). With more than half of the verbs, the prefix can only be recognised formally. However, we have a rather high number of verbs (11), which are morphologically (and consequently also semantically) obscure.

Group 3

The third group contains 107 verbs (of which 98 are loan words from Classical Latin and 9 verbs are loan words from Late Latin).

Verbs deriving from Classical Latin:

eccedere, eccellere, eccepire, eccitare, editare, educare, effeminare, effigiare, effluire, effondere, elaborare, elargire, eleggere, elevare, elidere, eliminare, elogiare, elucubrare, eludere, emaciare, emanare, emancipare, emendare, emergere, emigrare, emulsionare, enucleare, enumerare, enunciare, erigere, erodere, erogare, erompere, erudire, eruttare, esacerbare, esagerare, esagitare, esalare, esaminare, esanimare, esasperare, esaudire, esaurire, esautorare, esclamare, escludere, escogitare, escrescere, escutere, esecrare, esentare , esercire, esercitare, esibire, esigere, esilarare, esiliare, esimere, esistere, esonerare, esordire, esortare, espandere, espellere, esperire, espettorare, espiare, espirare, espletare, esplicare, esplodere, esplorare, esporre, esportare, esprimere, espugnare, espungere, espurgare, essiccare, estendere, estenuare, esternare, estinguere, estirpare, estorcere, estrarre, estrudere, esulare, esulcerare, esultare, evadere, evincere, evirare, evitare, evocare, evolvere, scarnificare

Verbs deriving from Late Latin:

emozionare, esaltare, escoriare, esorbitare, esorcizzare, espropriare, esumare, evacuare, evaporare

Due to the large number of loan words in this group, I will not analyse all the verbs but only deal with a few selected verbs. In my sample, I have tried to provide examples for each function of Latin prefix *ex-*, which I succeeded in only partially, as the function denoting upward movement cannot be recognised in any of the verbs of this category; and I could only find one example with the function 'change of position' (out of 107 verbs). The examples are shown in (10):

(10) a. Separative function: *escludere* ('to exclude', from Lat. *exclūdere*)
   b. Upwards movement: -
   c. Depriving function: *esonerare* ('to exempt', loan word from Lat. *exonerāre*)
   d. Change of position: *effeminare* ('to emasculate', loan word from Lat. *effēmināre*)
   e. Finalizing function: *elaborare* ('to elaborate', loan word from Lat. *ēlabōrāre*)
   f. Reinforcing function: with the *e-* version of the prefix: *elargire* ('to make a generous gift', loan word from the Lat. *ēlargīrī*); with the *es-* version of the prefix: *esagitare* ('to stir violently', loan word from Lat. *exagitāre*).

There are also morphologically transparent but semantically obscure verbs; e.g., *eludere* ('to elude', loan word from the Latin verb *ēlūdere*), in which the prefix is recognisable on the bases of the verbs *alludere* ('to allude') and *illudere* ('to delude'), but its function remains obscure as the meaning of the original verb is also obscure.

There are also morphologically (and consequently semantically) obscure verbs. We can generally say that if the first sound of the original word is a vowel, it is hard to recognise the *es-* form of the prefix (e.g., *esagerare*). The same phenomenon can be observed in case of the *e-*version of the prefix, where the original verb does not survive in Italian (e.g., the verb *eliminare*). Such verbs are no longer considered as prefixed verbs.

To summarize, we can say that a huge number of verbs of this category preserve four functions of the Latin prefix (the separative, depriving, finalizing and reinforcing function), while no examples were found for one function (upward movement) and there was one single example for the function of change of position.

Group 4

The fourth group contains 65 verbs which were chosen because they were considered to be the most frequent ones based on the *Lessico di frequenza della lingua italiana contemporanea* of Bortolini, Tagliavini and Zampolli (1972: 577-659).

sbagliare, sbalordire, sbandare, sbarcare, sbattere, sbrigare, sbucare, scacciare, scambiare, scampare, scaricare, scartare, scatenare, scavalcare, scocciare, scommettere, scomparire, sconcertare, scongiurare, scontare, scontrare, sconvolgere, scoprire, scoraggiare, scordare, scostare, scovare, sfamare, sfasciare, sfilare, sfiorare, sfogare, sfogliare, sfondare, sforzare, sfrattare, sfruttare, sfuggire, sfumare, sgobbare, sgomberare, sgridare, slanciare, sloggiare, smentire, smettere, smontare, spalancare, spalare, sparire, spartire, spezzare, spiacere, spiccare, spostare, spuntare, staccare, stanare, stirare, stroncare, svanire, svenire, sventolare, sviluppare, svolgere

This selection is only a sample of the Italian *s-* prefixed verbs, which are widely used in contemporary Italian.

Using the classification previously established for the functions that the Italian *s-* prefix can assume, the verbs of this category can be divided as in (11):

(11) a. the prefix denotes the opposite meaning of the verb to which it is added, e.g., *caricare* ('to charge') *scaricare* ('to discharge').

    b. the prefix has a depriving-pejorative function, e. g., *scontrare* ('to clash').

    c. the prefix has a separative function (indicating distance), e.g., *sbarcare* ('to disembark') or *spostare* ('to displace').

    d. the prefix has a depriving or extracting function, e.g., *scatenare* ('to unchain') or *scoraggiare* ('to discourage').

    e. the prefix has various functions or finalizing function, e.g., *sforzare* ('to force').[11]

    f. the prefix has a reinforcing function (with an intensifying value), e.g., *scambiare* ('to exchange').

As in the previous groups, there are verbs morphologically transparent but semantically obscure e.g. *svanire* ('to vanish').

To summarise we can say that in most *s-* prefixed verbs (as even this small sample shows), the prefix has the function of the *opposite meaning*.

Conclusion

The Latin *ex-* prefix remained productive only in its *s-* form in the course of the development of Italian from Latin. After comparing the function of the Latin *ex-* prefix and those of Italian *s-*, we can see that four functions remained the same (the *separative*, *depriving*, *finalizing* and *reinforcing* functions). Two functions of the Latin prefix have disappeared (the function denoting upward movement and the one expressing change of position). The reason why these functions have disappeared are different. The *upward movement* function disappeared because in Latin it could be attached only to verbs which already implied the meaning of upward movement. The *change of position* function disappeared probably because this function could be found in other prefixes (especially in the Italian prefix *a-*), therefore it ceased to be a function of the Italian *s*-prefix.

The new functions of the prefix (the negative and the pejorative function) might be explained by the special development of the separative sense or by the possible influence of other prefixes, especially of the prefix *dis-* (with which the *ex-* prefix had one thing in common: the separative spatial function).

We have to note that the most productive function of the analysed prefix in contemporary Italian is the *negative* function (which turns the meaning of the verb into the opposite sense), while the *separative* function becomes secondary. Finally, we can note that the Latin *ex-* prefix, which used to be extremely productive in Latin with a great number of *ex-*prefixed verbs, has been preserved only in a rather small number of Italian verbs. Despite this, the prefix remained recognisable in a certain number of verbs deriving from Latin and remained productive in Italian, in its *s*-version, becoming one of its most productive prefixes.

Notes

[1] Except for verbs in which the prefix cannot be recognized because of phonetic changes.

[2] *Thesaurus Linguae Latinae* (1931-1953: col. 1082-1131).

[3] As far as the phonetic history is considered, the etymological *ex-* form is only preserved before vowels and voiceless stops, assimilated in the form of *-f*, while it

became *e* in front of voiced stops, liquids and nasals (Ernout and Meillet 1967: 203; Leumann 1977: 204).

[4] And its assimilation with the first consonant of the original verb, as in *ecc-* e.g. in *eccedere* (an Italian phenomenon) or *eff-* e.g. in *effeminare* (a phenomenon described already in Latin grammars).

[5] "A prefix that initially corresponded to the Lat. *ex-* with the double idea of 'going out of a place or a situation' and of 'being deprived of'; but later on it assumed an independent development with an essentially negative and intensive meaning." (cf. Cortelazzo and Zolli (1988: 1115)).

[6] All the examples in this paragraph were taken from Group 1; i.e., they are verbs that derive from Classical Latin directly.

[7] In Cortelazzo and Zolli (1984: 369-409) there are four other verbs (*eccepire*, *eleggere*, *espletare* and *estrarre*), which were listed among this kind of words. However, because of their meanings and the contexts in which they occur (especially in case of the verbs *eccepire* and *espletare* - with the latter also because of its form), I moved them to the third list, among the later loan words. Therefore, I relied on Zingarelli (1973), who enlists these verbs among later loan words.

[8] Sometimes, the recognised function of the prefix does not coincide with the original function of the prefix as in the case of *schiamazzare*, which derives from the Latin verb *exclamāre* with the Italian suffix *-(i)zzare*. In the Italian verb, the prefix has a finalizing function: the Latin verb used to mean 'send/give a shout/scream', while in the Italian verb (due to the suffix) it means 'emit a hoarse sound typical of hens'. This semantic change explains also the change of function of the prefix, which assumes a pejorative function (one of the new functions of the Italian *s-* prefix). In other words, we face a reinterpretation of the function of the prefix. However, the reinterpretation is greatly influenced by the meaning of the suffix.

[9] We have some rather uncertain words in this category, because the semantic connection between the prefix and the verb is not always evident.

[10] We can also note in the second group, that the later function of the prefix does not always coincide with the orginal function of the Latin prefix; e.g., the Italian verb *scottare*, deriving from the Spoken Latin **excoctāre*. In the Latin verb, the prefix had the function of the Latin prefix *ad-*, because *excoctāre* probably meant 'set on fire' (like the Classical Latin verb *excoquere*). As far as the function of the prefix in the Italian verb *scottare* is concerned, it assumed a pejorative function (a new function of the Italian *s-* prefix compared to the functions of the Latin prefix); i.e., we have a reinterpretation of the prefix. (An exception to this is the case in which *scottare* means 'cook it very quickly', because in this case the prefix is not reinterpreted.)

[11] In Cortelazzo and Zolli, (1988: 1115), the *finalizing* function is not part of this group, but there are verbs in this category, in which the *finalizing* function can be recognised, e.g. *sfumare*, so I added this function to the fifth group.

References

Brachet, J.-P. (2000) *Recherches sur les préverbes dē et ex- du latin*, Bruxelles, Latomus.

Dardano, M. and P. Trifone (1999) *Grammatica italiana*, Bologna, Zanichelli.

Dér, K. (1975) "Semantic changes m1 (loc.) - m2 (abstract) of the preverb *ex-*" *Annales Universitatis Budapestinensis* 3: 81-95.

Fogarasi, M. (1983) *Grammatica italiana del Novecento*, Roma, Bulzoni.

García-Hernández, B. (1980) *Semantica estructural y lexematica del verbo*, Tarragona, Reus.

Hofmann, J.B. and A. Szantyr (1965) *Lateinische Syntax und Stilistik*, München, Beck.

Jekl, Á. (2008) *La prefissazione dei verbi nel latino classico e nell'italiano. Il prefisso* ex- (Master's thesis), Budapest, Eötvös Loránd University.

Leumann, M. (1977) *Lateinische Laut- und Formenlehre*, München, Beck.

Meyer-Lübke, W. (1972) *Grammatik der Romanischen Sprachen. II. Romanische Formenlehre*, Hildesheim, Olms (= 1894).

Oniga, R. (2005) "Composition et préverbation en latin: problèmes de typologie", in Moussy, C. (éd.) *La composition et la préverbation en latin*, Paris, Presses de l'Université de Paris - Sorbonne, 211-227.

—. (2007) *Il latino. Breve introduzione linguistica*, 2ᵃ ed., Milano, Franco Angeli.

Pompei, A. (2010) "De l'expression de l'espace à l'expression du temps (et de aspect) en latin: le cas des préverbes et des "verbes avec particule"" *De Lingua Latina* 3: 1-20.

Rohlfs, G. (1969) *Grammatica storica della lingua italiana e dei suoi dialetti. III. Sintassi e formazione delle parole*, It. trans. of Temistocle Franceschi and Maria Caciagli Fancelli, Torino, Einaudi, (orig. ed. *Historische Grammatik der italienischen Sprache und ihrer Mundarten. III. Syntax und Wortbildung*, Bern, Francke, 1954).

Salvi, G. and L. Vanelli (2004) *Nuova grammatica italiana*, Bologna, il Mulino.

Tekavčić, P. (1972) *Grammatica storica dell'italiano. Il lessico*, Bologna, il Mulino.

Van Laer, S. (2010) *La préverbation en latin: étude des préverbes ad-, in-, ob-, et per- dans la poésie républicaine et augustéenne*, Bruxelles, Latomus.

Dictionaries

Bortolini, U., Tagliavini, C. and A. Zampolli (1972) *Lessico di frequenza della lingua italiana contemporanea*, Milano, Garzanti.

Cortelazzo, M. and P. Zolli (1984; 1988) *Dizionario etimologico della lingua italiana*, Bologna, Zanichelli, vol. 2, vol. 5.

Ernout, A. and A. Meillet (1967) *Dictionnaire étymologique de la langue latine*, 4ᵉ éd., 2ᵉ tir., Paris, Klincksieck.

Thesaurus Linguae Latinae (1900-) Lipsiae, Teubner, vol. 5.

Zingarelli, N. (1973) *Vocabolario della lingua italiana*, Bologna, Zanichelli.

THE ALLEGED GREEK INFLUENCE ON LATIN COMPOUNDING

BENEDICTE NIELSEN WHITEHEAD

Introduction

It is a well documented fact about Latin that this was an Indo-European language in which the capacity of forming nominal compounds was quite restricted, especially as compared to Greek. The Romans knew this and commented on it on numerous occasions; see, for instance, the references in Cooper (1895: 298), Fruyt (2002: 259) and Lindner (1996: 161-211). As noted by these authors, some lamented this, but it was also considered a characteristic of good Latin that was to be respected by writers and orators.

It is also clear, however, that Latin possessed a variety of compound word-formation patterns that were indigenous to the language; many were productive and absolutely licit, even in high style. It is therefore relevant to investigate what factors were in fact favourable towards nominal composition. Given how strongly Greek influenced Latin literature, it has often been hypothesized that an important impact came from Greek.

This question is highly topical when working on compounds like *poscinummius* 'DEMAND-MONEY → money-demanding' and *verticordia* 'TURN-HEART → turner of hearts', i.e. agent-nouns composed of a verbal first member followed by a second member typically representing the object of the verb in question. In want of a better term, I shall call the type *pickpocket*, after a well-known English representative. The type is rare in Old and Classical Latin, but relatively prolific in Ancient Greek (thus, e.g. τερψίμβροτος 'DELIGHT-MORTALS → delighting mortals'), and a very persistent hypothesis claims that the Latin type owes its existence to Greek influence. There is no real evidence to support this claim. On the contrary, Plautus (*Mil.* 9) translates Greek Τρωξάρτης 'nibble-bread' with a verb-second form: *Artotrogus* 'bread-nibbler'; likewise, Caelius Aurelianus (*acut.* 3,15) suggests rendering Greek φεύγυδρος 'shun-water; hydrophobic' with *aquifuga* 'water-shunner', while Cicero (*div.* 2,64,133) seems to render Greek φερέοικος 'carry-house' with *domiporta* 'house-carrying'.[1] One of the few relatively reliable Latin examples, *verticordia*, is thought to translate a Greek simplex, ἀποστροφία, literally 'away-turneress'; i.e., 'she who turns away'. This leaves the odd Greek calque like *philograecus* 'graecophile' as the only clear vestige of a direct influence.

We do know that some Roman authorities, in fact, frowned upon the imitation of Greek compounds (see Cooper (1895: 298)), which lends little credibility to the hypothesis put forward by Pisani (1934: 124): that the difficult Latin *flexanimus*, presumably 'bend-mind', would be a poetic improvement on a more pedestrian **flectanimus* 'bent-mind', displaying a past passive participle as its first member. In an attempt to refine the formation, the participle would have been replaced by the perfect stem, by analogy with Greek compounds of the τερψίμβροτος type, which are formed on the sigmatic aorist.[2] There is, however, little clear evidence that the imitation of Greek morphology was ever exploited as a means of elevating the style, and certainly not with a derivational principle that was so foreign to Latin. Precisely how *flexanimus* came to mean 'mind-soothing', therefore, remains an enigma, at least to the present author.

Bader (1962: 397f.) argues very firmly and with copious examples that when rendering Greek compounds with Latin ones, Latin translators adapt them to the Latin system, as opposed to merely imitating them, and Oniga (1988: 157-8) notes about the pair Τρωξάρτης —*Artotrogus* that equally, "pur mantenendo tutte le caratteristiche del grecismo [...] il composto usato da Plauto si uniforma all'ordine usuale per i composti latini". Inevitably, translators sometimes calqued Greek compounds; however, as noted by Bader (1962: 397f.), they were also frequently rendered by simplicia or syntagms.

Although there is only scanty evidence for any sizeable, Greek influence on Latin composition in general, and on Latin *pickpocket* compounds in particular, Bader (1962: 398f.) concedes that these compounds may in fact all be due to Greek influence. Bork (1990: 55) likewise contends that these compounds "nicht nur, wie andere Bildungstypen [...], dem Einfluß des Griechischen eine wesentliche Förderung, sondern ihre Entstehung verdanken"; Rainer (2004: 1704) concurs. Noting the lack of parallel formations, Bork (1990: 255), who is supported by Lindner (2005: 382-4), concedes that "nicht so sehr einzelne Wörter übertragen wurden als daß vielmehr das Lateinische das Bildungs*prinzip* übernahm." An influence of such indirect nature is of course very hard to verify, which, considering the bulky counterevidence, may explain why the hypothesis of a Greek impact is so tenacious. The in my view quite plausible alternative: that the word-formation pattern arose independently in Latin, has to my knowledge only been explored by Gather (2001: 206).

One way of assessing the validity of the hypothesis of a Greek influence in Latin compounding in general is to study the statistical frequency of compounds. Cooper (1895: 300) notes that "in the main [...] statistics show a preponderance of compounds in authors of inferior Latinity", but does not present any data, just like Coulter (1916: 164-5), who suggests that the proliferation of compounds reflects Greek influence. More recently, Panagl likewise equates Greek influence to frequency of compounds:

> Während [...] in epigrafischen Texten (Grabinschriften, Elogien, laudationes), in Prosaschriften wie Catos 'de agricultura' und in der Sakralpoesie (Salierlied, Lied der fratres arvales), aber auch in anderen Werken mit stark innerlateinischem Bezug (Cato, origines; Ennius, annales), auffallend wenige Komposita begegnen, tritt dieser Wortbildungstypus in griechisch beeinflußter Dichtung deutlich stärker hervor: Ich denke dabei vor allem an die Tragödien von Naevius, Ennius, Accius und Pacuvius, so wie an die aus Griechischen Vorlagen übersetzten, besser kontaminierten Beispiele der Komödie (Palliata), von der wir hier nur die bekanntesten Vertreter Plautus und Terentz nennen wollen, daneben aber auch an das Genus des Lehrgedichts, beginnend mit den Hedup[h]agetica des Ennius.
>
> Panagl (1986: 575)

Like Cooper and Coulter, Panagl does not support his claim with figures. However, Oniga (1988) reviews the frequency of compounds in 44 Latin texts and thus provides a good tool for assessing the distribution of compounds on literary genres. Oniga makes two observations about the correlation between style and density of compounds that are relevant for our topic.

1. The frequency of nominal compounds in three textual genres

An immediate indication of the need for certain qualifications to the above-mentioned view can be obtained by observing table 1, which combine two tables from Oniga (1988: 245-6), one showing the number of different types of compounds in each text, the other the number of tokens. The 44 texts of the survey are organized according to the relative frequency or density of compounds, displayed in percentages in the right-most column:[3]

Table 1

	Author *work*	Genre	Types	Tokens	Words	Density
2	Laevius	HiPo	17	17	200	8.50
3	Laberius	LoPo	13	13	155	8.38
4	Accius *Carmina*	HiPo	5	5	201	2.50
5	Naevius *Poen.*	HiPo	5	6	320	1.88
6	Naevius, *trag.*	HiPo	6	7	415	1.69
7	Trag. Inc.	HiPo	21	24	1,566	1.53
8	Cato *Orat. fragm.*	OrPr	25	40	2,720	1.47
9	Publilius *Mimi*	LoPo	2	2	140	1.42
10	Cicero *Orationes*	OrPr	159	6,010	430,560	1.39
11	Publilius *Sententiae*[4]	HiPo	14	47	3,754	1.25
12	Cicero *Poetica*	HiPo	49	63	5,446	1.16
13	Varro, *Sat. men.*	LoPo	59	64	5,817	1.10
14	Novius	LoPo	8	8	740	1.08
15	Ennius *Scaenica*	HiPo	24	28	2,665	1.05
16	Ennius *Annales*	HiPo	26	31	3,066	1.01
17	Cato *Origines*	HisPr	12	18	1,836	0.98
18	Livius Andronicus, *trag.*	HiPo	5	5	415	0.96
19	Pacuvius	HiPo	20	22	2,456	0.90
20	Catullus	HiPo	71	98	11,470	0.85
21	Sallust	HisPr	70	333	40,980	0.81
22	Lucretius	HiPo	112	381	48,197	0.79
23	Accius, *trag.*	HiPo	34	42	5,390	0.78
24	Cato *De agri cultura*	AgrPr	48	117	15,590	0.75
25	Lucilius	LoPo	48	50	7,534	0.66
26	Sisenna	HisPr	7	7	1,170	0.59
27	Virgil *Aeneid*	HiPo	130	392	67,292	0.58
28	Com. Inc.	LoPo	4	4	735	0.54
29	Varro, prose	VarPr	227	424	79,398	0.53
30	Plautus	LoPo	278	860	165,669	0.52
31	Virgil *Ecl.*	HiPo	10	27	5,471	0.49
32	Turpilius	LoPo	5	6	1,272	0.47
33	Caesar *De bello Gallico*	HisPr	45	236	51,520	0.46
34	Cornelius Nepos	HisPr	63	126	28,875	0.44
35	Virgil *Georgica*	HiPo	41	63	14,222	0.44
36	Terence	LoPo	52	182	48,402	0.38
37	Afranius	LoPo	7	7	2,494	0.28
38	Titinius	LoPo	3	3	1,092	0.27
39	Pomponius	LoPo	4	4	1552	0.25
40	Naevius, *com.*	LoPo	2	2	816	0.24
41	Caecilius	LoPo	3	3	1611	0.18
42	Ennius *Satires*	LoPo	1	1	612	0.16
43	Livius Andronicus, *com.*	LoPo	1	1	816	0.12
44	Quadrigarius	HisPr	1	1	900	0.11
45	Livius Andronicus *Odusia*	HiPo	0	0	260	0.00
	Total			962	9,780	1,065,812	0.92

Some of these text were included in Panagl's brief overview referred to above. First, Ennius' *Annales*, Cato's *Origines* and *De agri cultura*, said to display 'auffallend wenige Komposita', are placed as number 15, 16 and 23. Furthermore, the texts said to display a strong Greek influence and thus more compounds are quite evenly distributed, occupying places number 5 (Naevius' tragedies), 15 (Ennius *Annales*), 22 (Accius), 18 (Pacuvius), 29 (Plautus) and 35 (Terence).

Numbers can be deceptive, but it is clear that these figures do not corroborate Panagl's claims. They do confirm an observation made by Coulter (1916: 161-4): that Plautus, Cicero, Lucretius, Catullus and Vergil display different figures according to the stylistic register, a point thus narrowed down by Oniga (1988: 247): 'La vera differenza tra prosa e poesia sta dunque non nella quantità, ma nella qualità di composti usati, e soprattutto nel numero di forme diverse usate.' That is, a high density of compounds marks a high artistic level, rather than poetry as such; an important dividing line therefore separates high and low register in general, but not poetry and prose.

Oniga does not go into much detail, but it is worth our while to illustrate his point more clearly. I have therefore tagged the texts of table 1 for literary genre: "LoPo" low-register poetry; "HiPo" high-register poetry; "HisPr" historical prose; "AgrPr" agricultural prose; "VarPr" Varro/various prose; "OrPr" oratorical prose. The distribution of the 44 texts by genre is as follows: 18 texts represent high-register poetry, 16 low-register poetry, and 10 represent prose.

If we divide the table into two halves, we see that among the 22 items displaying the highest frequency of compounds, the majority, fourteen, are classified as high-register poetry, four are classified as prose, and four as low-register poetry. Conversely, among items 23-44, displaying the lowest density, the majority, twelve, are classified as low-register poetry, six are classified as prose and four as high-register poetry.

That low-register poetry, such as comedy and satire, displays generally low densities, whereas high-register poetry, such as tragedy, elegy, pastoral etc. has higher ones, is sometimes discernible within the same author: we find Ennius' tragedies in places 14 and 15, but his satires in place 41; Naevius' tragedies occupy places 3 and 4, his comedies 39.

These observations help us to understand the wide variation in density within prose. Whereas more sober-minded authors like Caesar (no. 33) and Cornelius Nepos (no. 34) use very few compounds, Cicero's speeches (no. 10) and the fragments of Cato the Elder (no. 8), both oratory, are the prose texts richest in compounds. Next come Cato's *Origines*, historical prose interspersed with speeches, which rank higher (as no. 17) than his strictly prosaic *De agri cultura* (no. 24).

So much for the differences between high and low register: Oniga's survey also reveals similarities between the genres, regardless of register, namely in the proportion between types and tokens.

2. Types versus tokens

This related discovery concerns the variety and creativity of compounds within the individual genres. Plautus, who is renowned for coining words such as *sescentoplagus* 'a man of six hundred blows' and *turpilucricupidus*, literally 'dishonest-gain-desiring', surprisingly uses very few compounds overall. Oniga (1988: 247) concludes that poets, as well as the more elevated prose authors, created many more new compounds, but since they strove for variation, would avoid reusing them. By contrast, prose writers, who strove for clarity and precision, tended to stick to the more established vocabulary and to employ the same, relatively few, terms many times. The more artistic genres would therefore display more types, but fewer tokens, than the more prosaic ones. This well agrees with what is immediately observable in other IE languages, including Greek.

Oniga (1988: 247) illustrates his conclusion by adducing statistical data from Cicero. His view can be further confirmed by comparing those texts in his survey that are of approximately the same length. This limits the number of generalizations that we can base on the survey, but the results are in fact very clear.

Thus, a comparison of Caesar's *De bello Gallico* with the poetry of Virgil confirms that as predicted, Caesar tends to repeat the individual compounds more often than Virgil. *De bello Gallico* is 23% shorter than the *Aeneid*; yet its compounds occur on average (5.2÷3=) 1.7 times as often as those attested in the *Aeneid*:

Author *work*	Genre	Total wds	Types	Tokens	Density	Aver.
Caesar *Bell. Gall.*	HisPr	51520	45	236	0.46	5.2
Virgil *Aeneid*	HiPo	67292	130	392	0.58	3.0

Caesar was probably among the more extreme followers of this practice. However, a similar result emerges from a comparison of Cato the Elder's *De agri cultura* with Virgil's *Georgica*: Cato employs each compound (2.4 ÷1.5=) 1.6 times as often as Virgil:

Cato *Agri cult.*	AgrPr	15590	48	117	0.75	2.4
Virgil *Georgica*	HiPo	14222	41	63	0.44	1.5

In his speeches, Cato employs each compound on average (1.6÷1.12=) 1.3 times as often as Ennius in his *Scaenica*. This difference is smaller than the one between *De agri cultura* and the *Georgica*, perhaps because Cato's speeches are at a more elevated level than *De agri cultura*:

Cato *Orat. Fragm.*	OrPr	2720	25	40	1.47	1.6
Ennius *Scaenica*	HiPo	2665	24	28	1.05	1.2

In the above-mentioned examples, we were able to compare poetry of high register to prose, mainly of the more objective register. A comparison of the two poetic genres to each other reveals strikingly similar figures when it comes to the average number of times each compound is used:

Trag. Inc.	HiPo	1566	21	24	1.34	1.1
Caecilius, *com.*	LoPo	1611	3	3	0.18	1.0
Pacuvius	HiPo	2456	20	22	0.81	1.1
Afranius	LoPo	2494	7	7	0.28	1.0
Lucretius	HiPo	48197	112	381	0.23	3.4
Terence, *com.*	LoPo	48402	52	182	0.10	3.5

Low-register poetry thus displays as much variation as high-register poetry, which may partly explain why the name of a low-register poet like Plautus is so often brought up in discussions of Latin compounding.

Finally, the following samples of high-register poetry display very similar figures:

Accius, *trag.*	HiPo	5390	34	42	0.78	1.24
Cicero *Carmina*	HiPo	5446	49	63	1.16	1.30

Although based on a small sample of Latin literature, the comparisons I have made above thus confirm Oniga's claims about the distribution and employment of compounds in Latin literature: the more artistic the register, the less each word is reused.

3. The alleged Greek influence

The low density of compounds in low-register poetry and certain types of prose probably reflects popular speech. Whether the higher density in elevated registers reflects more than a universal tendency towards variation, namely a significant Greek impact on artistic style, has to my knowledge not been properly explored, but it is possible to argue that Greek influence must, surprisingly, have been a minor factor.

First, the extent of any Greek influence on the vocabulary can be estimated via the distribution of loanwords. Oniga's survey includes 962 different compounds altogether, of which 79 are classified as 'grecisms';, e.g., *paedagogus*, *calliblepharus* and *monogrammus*. This amounts to (79÷9.62=) 8.2% of the total of 962 compounds. According to Wharton (1890:1), the density of Greek loanwords in Latin in general is somewhat higher, namely appr. 13.30%. In other words, if we can trust Wharton's figures, nominal compounds were borrowed less often than other morphological types.

The distribution of the Greek loanwords according to genre reveals a point that was already made by Cooper (1895: 316): that popular speech was more directly influenced by Greek than the elevated registers. Thus, the majority of loanwords, 65%, occur in low-register poetry; 22% occur in prose and only 13% in high-register poetry (Oniga (1988: 309)). These figures reflect that mastery of Greek was not necessarily a characteristic of high class, since many slaves were Greeks. They probably also reflect that elevated Latin writers avoided lexical borrowings for stylistic purposes.

Now, it is crucial that the high frequency of Greek compounds in lower registers is coupled with the lowest frequency of compounds overall. This must indicate that, although most prone to borrow entire lexemes from Greek, popular speech was resistant to following the Greek model in creating novel compounds.

Conclusion

The conclusion of the present article is that a higher frequency of compounds characterizes high registers as such and cannot be assumed to be a significant, direct reflex of Greek influence on Latin nominal composition.

Notes

[1] See Oniga (1988: 157 fn. 33).
[2] See Horrocks and Stavrou (2002) for the development of this word-formation pattern.
[3] The right-most column differs from that of Oniga (1988:245-6) in that I give the density in percentages, Oniga in proportions.
[4] Publilius's mimes, from which the *sententia* were extracted, were of the lower poetic genre; the *sententia* themselves, on the other hand, were mainly moral

maxims and have therefore been tagged as high-register poetry. Seneca (*epist.* 8, par.8) observes that Publilius' verses were indeed worthy of tragic actors.

References

Bader, F. (1962) *La formation des composés nominaux du latin*, Paris, Les Belles Lettres.

Bork, H.D. (1990), *Die lateinisch-romanischen Zusammensetzungen Nomen + Verb und der Ursprung der romanischen Verb-Ergänzung-Komposita* Bonn, Romanistischer Verlag.

Cooper, F.T. (1895), *Word Formation in the Roman Sermo Plebeius. An historical study of the development of vocabulary in vulgar and late Latin, with special reference to the Romance languages*, PhD diss., Columbia College, New York.

Coulter, C.C. (1916) "Compound adjectives in early Latin poetry" *Transactions and Proceedings of the American Philological Association* 47: 153-172.

Fruyt, M. (2002) "Constraints and productivity in Latin nominal compounding", in T. Meissner and J. Clackson (eds) *Nominal composition in Indo-European, Transactions of the Philological Society* 100.3: 259-287.

Gather, A. (2001) *Romanische Verb-Nomen Komposita. Wortbildung Zwischen Lexikon, Morphologie und Syntax*, Tübingen, Narr.

Horrocks, G. and M. Stavrou (2000) "Lexeme-based separationist morphology: evidence from the history of Greek deverbal abstracts", in G. Booij and J. van Marle (eds) *Yearbook of Morphology*, Dordrecht-Boston-London, Kluwer, 19-42.

Lindner, T. (1996) *Lateinische Komposita. Ein Glossar vornehmlich zum Wortschatz der Dichtersprache*, Innsbruck, Innsbrucker Beiträge zur Sprachwissenschaft.

—. (2005) "Nominalkomposition im Vulgärlatein und Frühromanischen - sowie ein Plädoyer für die Imperativthese", in G. Schweiger (ed.) *Indogermanica. Festschrift für Gert Klingenschmitt. Indische, iranische und indogermanische Studien dem verehrten Jubilar dargestellt zu seinem fünfundsechzigsten Geburtstag*, Taimering, Schweiger VWT-Verlag, 377-387.

Oniga, R. (1988) *I composti nominali latini. Una morfologia generativa*, Bologna, Pàtron.

Panagl, O. (1986) "Griechische Komposita in der lateinischen Übersetzungsliteratur", in A. Etter (ed.) *o-o-pe-ro-si. Festschrift für*

Ernst Risch zum 75. Geburtstag, Berlin/New York, Walter de Gruyter: 574-582.

Pisani, V. (1934) "Presunti composti 'bahuvrihi' in latino" *Studi italiani di filologia classica* 11: 121-25.

Rainer, F. (2004) "From Latin to French", in G. Booij, C. Lehmann, J. Mugdan and S. Skopetas (eds) *Morphology: an international handbook on inflection and word-formation* 17.2 Berlin-New York, Mouton de Gruyter: 1698-1712.

Wharton, E.R. (1890), "Loan-Words in Latin", *Transactions of the Philological Society* 21(1): 172-197.

SECTION II.

SEMANTICS AND PRAGMATICS

METAPHOR AND THE TEACHING
OF IDIOMS IN LATIN

WILLIAM MICHAEL SHORT

Introduction

In teaching the Latin language and Latin literature, instructors inevitably confront one of the most challenging aspects of foreign language pedagogy: idioms.[1] Frequently, students are asked to learn words whose idiomatic figurative meanings are wildly divergent from and seemingly wholly unrelated to their ordinary literal uses. For instance, the word *locus* is used conventionally in Latin to mean "a location, a place"[2] as well as "an idea, an argument, a topic of discourse".[3] But what accounts for this idiomatic usage? How is one to understand the relationship between the word's literal physical sense and its idiomatic mental or intellectual sense?[4] Is this relationship merely arbitrary, or is there some semantic principle that motivates the word's specific figurative interpretation? Furthermore, can clarification of this question help students actually learn this idiom and others? Similarly, in reading literary texts, students often encounter expressions whose meanings, literally interpreted, are not immediately intelligible. For example, reading in Quintilian that "it is not even possible to 'fall into the thought' (*ne in cogitationem quidem cadere potuit*) that someone could be convicted twice of the same charge" (*decl.* 310,3), how are students to understand this metaphorical image? While it may be possible to intuit the gist of this phrase, can students be taught to reasonably predict the particular meanings and connotations of such expressions?

In this paper, I argue that the idiomatic meanings of *locus* and many other expressions in Latin, far from being a matter of arbitrary linguistic convention (and therefore unfathomable), are instead highly motivated semantically. The motivation for these meanings, I suggest, is a widely distributed metaphorical "theme" in which mental activity is regularly understood in terms of spatial motion.[5] What's more, I propose that by familiarizing students with the metaphors underlying such expressions,

Latin teachers can facilitate students' memorization of vocabulary and impart invaluable skills to aid students' understanding of Latin literature. Beginning from the hypothesis advanced by cognitive linguists that taking into account a language's metaphors contributes to comprehending – and so teaching and learning – idioms, I go on to show how Latin's vocabulary of mental activity is systematically structured through metaphors of movement in physical space, in such a way that concepts of spatial motion are inextricably part of how meaning is created in this domain. Generalizing from this, I outline a series of classroom interventions that put into practice the notion that "metaphorical competence", or an awareness of the underlying metaphorical organization of idiomatic meaning, impacts students' ability to learn linguistic data and interpret literary texts.

1. Idiom comprehension and the teaching of idioms

Idiomatic meaning has traditionally been viewed as a matter of pure linguistic convention.[6] An idiomatic expression is seen as a linguistic label, agreed upon by a community, for a special pragmatic or metaphorical meaning that cannot be derived from the literal sense of the phrasing. In this view, idioms are "frozen" expressions whose meanings are either totally arbitrary or vestiges of "dead" metaphors. For example, the meaning of the English idiom "kick the bucket" – namely, "to die" – cannot be reconstructed from the literal sense of the words "kick", "the", and "bucket", nor from their syntactic arrangement. Similarly, the meaning of "shoot the breeze" has nothing to do with shooting or with breezes as such. Because in this view the meaning of idioms is arbitrary and established by convention, they must be learned simply by rote.[7] Moreover, learning one idiom will likely be of little value in understanding any other. As knowledge of idioms bears on comprehension in only a mechanical way, it is also ancillary to the interpretation of imaginative works of literature.

A very different view has emerged in cognitive linguistics, where idioms are treated as products of the conceptual system and idiomatic meaning as motivated primarily by metaphor.[8] Cognitive linguists claim that metaphor is not merely a linguistic and literary device, but a basic mechanism of human thought.[9] They propose that the clustering of metaphorical linguistic expressions around many concepts reflects inherently metaphorical understandings that speakers of a language possess of those concepts. Speakers of a language talk about abstract domains metaphorically because they actually conceive of them metaphorically in terms of other experiences. In this view, metaphors are regular projections or mappings of knowledge that occur as a way of mentally representing concepts not directly grounded in physical experience. Cognitive linguists argue, moreover, that it is this systematic nature of metaphorical mappings that allows people to think and reason (and therefore also to speak) meaningfully about experiences that may be difficult to comprehend in and of themselves.

Idiomatic expressions, in this view, are seen not as isolated semantic units, but as reflecting coherent systems of metaphorical conceptualization. Though it is not the case of all idioms, many idiomatic usages can be seen to be part of broad patterns of metaphorical meaning identifiable throughout a language's lexical and phrasal inventory.[10] Idiomatic meaning can therefore be treated not as semantically anomalous, but as representing one pole of a spectrum of metaphorically defined meaning that runs from the more conventionalized to the more innovative.[11] Because in this view idiomatic meaning is taken to be motivated, if not determined, by larger structures of metaphor, idioms gain a degree of semantic transparency: even when they elaborate upon conventional metaphors in idiosyncratic or unexpected ways, if they can be fit to known metaphorical patterns, they become reasonable and open to interpretation by inference. Language learners thus have the possibility of making sense of idioms when their meanings can be seen to conform to established metaphorical mappings, linking the words in the idioms to their figurative meanings.[12]

2. Idioms of mental activity in Latin

In the case of Latin, the systematic nature of metaphor in shaping linguistic expression has hardly been explored. Certainly compared with the hundreds of metaphors known in English, the metaphorical underpinnings of Latin's vocabulary remain relatively uncharted. However, research suggests that the semantic domains of Latin are no less metaphorically structured.[13] An example of systematic metaphorical structuring is provided by expressions of time in Latin, which reveal that sense in this domain is organized by two metaphors only, operating in complementary distribution – time being expressed either as a moving object, when speaking about temporal processes in which the speaker's role is viewed as somehow passive, or as movement along a path, when the subject is viewed as more actively involved.[14] The semantic organization of Latin's vocabulary of auditory perception is largely given by metaphor as well: "eating", "devouring", and "tasting" are conventionalized metaphorical ways of speaking about attentiveness, eagerness, and affectivity *vis-à-vis* hearing.[15]

These are somewhat circumscribed metaphorical systems, however. While Latin's metaphors for time are systematic, they are also imagistically minimal; similarly, while Latin's metaphors for hearing utilize imagistically complex alimentary concepts, they characterize only certain special cases of auditory perception. On the other hand, ways of speaking about "thinking" in Latin represent a semantic domain that is not only regularly organized by metaphor *nearly as a whole*, but also highly structured conceptually by metaphor.[16] As an overall system, Latin's vocabulary of mental activity is given by metaphors of spatial motion that are centrally organized by a mapping in which mental constructs of all sorts ("thoughts" in a very general sense) are conceptualized in terms of "locations". However, over Latin's vocabulary of mental activity the conceptualization of a "thought" in metaphorical terms of "place" is largely covert, functioning as an implicit mapping; the conceptual structure of movement in space actually articulates Latin's vocabulary of mind through specialized submappings, which preserve in the domain of mental activity important distinctions of physical experience. Through these submappings, logically interrelated spatial concepts are utilized to define correspondingly logically interrelated mental concepts. Thus:

Metaphorical mappings in 'THOUGHTS ARE LOCATIONS'

SPATIAL MOTION	⇒ MENTAL ACTIVITY
[a location in space	→ a thought]
movement toward (a location)	→ 'acquiring' a thought
position in (a location)	→ 'having' a thought
movement from (a location)	→ 'relinquishing' a thought

But how are these mappings reflected in Latin's vocabulary of mental activity, and how do they provide a structure that in fact constitutes the semantics of that vocabulary? Consider the bold-faced phrases in the following expressions:

(1) *qui **consilium iniere**, quo nos victu et vita prohibeant / is diem dicam, irrogabo multam* (Plaut. *Capt.* 493-4)
     "To those who formulated a plan to prohibit us from vital nourishment, I will name the day and stipulate a fine"

(2) *ni **occupo** aliquod mihi **consilium**, hi domum me ad se auferent*
     (Plaut. *Men.* 847)
     "Unless I come up with some plan, they'll carry me off home"

(3) *ipse quoque huic **sententiae accedo*** (Iust. *Dig.* 36,2,12,6)
     "I agree with this opinion, too"

(4) ***veniamus ad** bonorum malorumque **notionem*** (Cic. *ac.* 2,128)
     "Let us consider the idea of Good and Evil"

(5) *ne **in cogitationem** quidem **cadit** ut fuerit tempus aliquod nullum cum
     tempus esset* (Cic. *nat. deor.* 1,21)
     "It is not even possible to conceive of a time when time did not exist"

(6) ***ire in cogitationem** iubet et dispicere quid ex hac tranquillitate
     sapientiae debeam* (Sen. *epist.* 26,3)
     "It [sc. old age] tells me to consider and examine how far I owe this
     serenity to philosophy"

As these expressions demonstrate, mental operations that involve
'acquiring' a thought in mind – in other words, that involve thoughts either
entirely new to the thinker, or to which the thinker newly turns his or her
conscious awareness – are expressed metaphorically in terms of movement
toward a location in space. Thus, Latin speakers talk about formulating
plans, agreeing with opinions, considering ideas, conceiving notions, and
so on, as "entering", "occupying", "coming to", "returning to", "moving
to", and even "falling" or "slipping into" a location. This metaphor
constitutes the normal way for Latin speakers to talk about such
experiences, moreover. Consider, for example, how Latin expresses the
concept of "paying attention to" – that is, 'acquiring' something as the
focus of mental attention: *animum advertere* (literally, "turn the mind
toward"), *mentem intendere* ("direct the mind toward"), or *cogitationem
conferre ad* ("cause thought to go toward"), mental attention being
construed as directionality of thought toward a location.

   At the same time, as the following examples show, words denoting
position in a location ("being" or "standing in") deliver concepts that
involve 'having' an idea in mind – that is, mental activity occurring over
thoughts as part of the belief system or within conscious awareness:

(7) *eum defixum **in cogitatione esse** sensisset* (Cic. *de orat.* 3,17)
     "He realized that he was deep in contemplation"

(8) *nec mihi **in cogitatione** tum lex fuit* (Quint. *decl.* 270,25)
     "Nor was the law in my thought at the time"

(9) *coniectores a me consilium petunt: / quod eis respondi, ea omnes*
     stant sententia (Plaut. *Curc.* 249-50)
     "Clairvoyants get their advice from *me*: and whatever I tell them,
     they all abide by"

(10) *quamquam **in** falsa **fuerit opinione**, demonstrandum erit neminem*
     tantae esse stultitiae, qui tali in re possit veritatem ignorare (Cic.
     inv. 2,27)
     "It must be shown that, even though he [sc. the defendant] was
     mistaken in that opinion, no one can be so foolish as to be ignorant of
     the truth in such an affair…"

(11) *adhuc **in** hac **sum sententia**, nihil ut faciamus nisi quod maxime*
     Caesar velle videatur (Cic. *fam.* 4,4,5)
     "I still am of the opinion that we should do nothing but what Caesar
     seems most to want"

(12) *qua **in sententia** et Vergilium **fuisse** video* (Plin. *nat.* 18,35)
     "I see that Virgil, too, held this opinion"

Again, this metaphor systematically structures the Latin vocabulary.
This explains why "standing (in a place) with (*constare*)" conveys the
concept of agreement: if "standing in" an opinion means to hold an
opinion, then "standing in" an opinion "with (*con*)" someone else means to
hold the same opinion as that person. It also likely accounts for the
meaning of *ex mea* (*tua, nostra, sua*) *sententia* in the sense of "according
to my (your, our, his) opinion": if the belief that someone holds is, in
metaphorical terms, a location in which he or she "is" or "stands," then
what comes "out of" (*ex*) that place can be seen as being in agreement with
– because originating from – that opinion (cf., e.g., Plaut. *Men.* 1151, *haec*
evenerunt nostra ex sententia).
     Finally, various expressions denoting movement away from a location
convey the concept of 'relinquishing' an idea from mind – that is, giving
up some idea that is under current consideration or abandoning some
closely held belief:

(13) *necessario* **sententia desistunt** *legatosque ad Caesarem mittunt* (Caes. *Gall.* 6,4,2)
"Of necessity they abandon this idea and send legates to Caesar"

(14) *perterriti Galli, ne ab equitatu Romanorum viae praeoccuparentur,* **consilio destiterunt** (Caes. *Gall.* 7,26,5)
"Fearing that the passes were already occupied by the Roman cavalry, the Gauls gave up this design"

(15) *aiunt ipsum sapientem... si ita rectius sit...* **de sententia decedere** *aliquando* (Cic. *Mur.* 63)
"They say the wise man sometimes changes his mind when it is better to do so"

(16) *ille vir... qui de civitate* **decedere** *quam* **de sententia** *maluit* (Cic. *Balb.* 11)
"That man… who preferred to abandon his city than his belief"

And again the metaphor is systematic. That is why, for example, *digressio / digressus* and *egressio / egressus* are used in the sense of a departure from the idea that forms the main subject of some discourse – a digression being viewed metaphorically as temporary movement away from a certain thought-location. The same image also explains Seneca's formulation of the complaint he puts in the mouth of Tiresias: "What can I say, roaming as I am amidst the turmoil of my dazed mind (*inter tumultus mentis attonitae vagus*)?" (*Oed.* 328-329). Combining these metaphors, Tiresias' mental confusion can be expressed by a special case of spatial motion that involves the image of freely moving from place to place in no particular order and with no particular rationale: namely, "roaming".[17]

As may be seen, the semantic structure of Latin's vocabulary of mental activity is not haphazard. Quite the contrary. Different aspects of mental experience are conveyed metaphorically by different spatial concepts in a consistent and coherent fashion. Just as "moving into" a location consistently delivers the concept of 'acquiring' an idea, "being in" a location consistently delivers that of 'having' an idea in mind, and "moving away from" consistently delivers that of 'relinquishing' an idea. Moreover, the organization of these metaphors preserves the inherent logic of spatial experience. The metaphors, that is, fit together to form a coherent system, each metaphor delivering a single concept of mental activity that is logically related to the others. In the spatial domain, MOVEMENT TOWARD, POSITION IN, and MOVEMENT FROM are logically related concepts in the sense that they convey different but systematically differentiated images of physical motion or static position relative to some location. Metaphorically, these concepts characterize correspondingly logically related concepts of mental activity.

It is crucial to recognize that the system of mappings of spatial concepts onto Latin speakers' understanding of mental activity actually constitute the semantics of that domain. In other words, it is the concepts of MOVEMENT TOWARD, POSITION IN, and MOVEMENT FROM *per se* – concepts that have literal interpretations in the domain of spatial experience – that provide and differentiate the concepts of Latin's vocabulary of mind. In a sense, then, to speak in Latin about "going into a thought" to convey the meaning of acquiring a thought in mind is not to speak figuratively: As the spatial metaphors themselves constitute Latin speakers' conceptualization of (this portion of) the mental domain, this way of speaking is in effect literal, insofar as the concepts of 'acquiring' a thought in mind and so forth are defined *exclusively* in these terms. If it is confusing to refer to these conceptualizations in terms of physical manipulation, this is because scholars have not yet developed a language-independent system for defining mental processes (as has been done for other semantic domains, such as color or kin terms). Because understandings of the mind are necessarily figurative, one is thus compelled to use the potentially very different images of one's own language to describe Latin's system of spatial conceptual metaphors.

3. Implications for classroom practice

It is now possible to answer the question whether there is some semantic principle underlying the relationship of the figurative meaning of *locus* ("an idea, thought") to its literal meaning ("a location"). It should be clear that the idiomatic interpretation of this word is motivated by the metaphoric patterns of thought that structure Latin's ways of speaking about mental activity overall. Indeed, given that the overall organization of this vocabulary is defined by systematically related concepts of spatial motion, the idiomatic extension of *locus* to include this mental or intellectual sense appears not only *not* arbitrary and unfathomable but completely reasonable and in fact logical according to the terms of the metaphor. If, as a part of Latin speakers' ordinary understanding of mental activity, thoughts of all kinds are imagined metaphorically as locations, it is entirely in keeping with this understanding that a word whose central meaning is "a location" should also develop the sense of "an idea". The idiomatic meaning of *locus* simply makes manifest the normally implicit central mapping of the 'LOCATIONS' metaphor as a whole.

Beyond simply explaining why certain words or phrases have the meanings they do, however, recognizing the metaphorical organization of meaning in Latin's semantic system has important implications for the pedagogy of Latin. Studies have demonstrated that students' acquaintance with how idioms and other figurative expressions reflect patterns of metaphor in the wider language – what Danesi (1993) calls "metaphorical competence" – is crucial to the development of linguistic and literary understanding because it enables language learners to begin to make the kinds of semantic inferences that native speakers take for granted.[18] As this research shows, in learning idioms knowledge of metaphors facilitates students' memorization because it provides a motivated explanation for why these expressions mean what they mean, even when their literal wording does not make good sense. Similarly, in interpreting works of literature, students' knowledge of metaphor provides a basis for making predictions about the meaning of other figurative expressions,[19] including in texts that are highly contextualized culturally and highly stylized rhetorically.[20]

This suggests Latin teachers must design and implement classroom interventions providing the "metaphorical competence" students need to comprehend (and thus effectively learn) idioms, as well as to interpret sophisticated works of literature.[21] With beginners, where the goal is to aid learning vocabulary, the strategy will involve providing a clear understanding of the metaphorical basis of idioms, rather than asking students to internalize rote textual correspondences. One method of developing students' awareness of this kind of semantic motivation is to compile a list of idiomatic expressions covering a defined semantic domain and representing the range of expression in that domain, the students' task then being to arrange this list into groups of related expressions, using their literal interpretation (and a dictionary) as a guide. (A preliminary exercise might ask students themselves to seek out such expressions in a limited corpus, based on syntactic structure: e.g., with a verb in the source domain and prepositional phrase with noun in the target domain).

Presented with a randomized list of the examples given above, for instance, students will recognize that idioms involving the literal concept of MOVEMENT TOWARD logically form one grouping, whereas idioms involving POSITION IN a location form another grouping, and those involving MOVEMENT FROM a third. Recognition of these groupings is facilitated by pointing out that while the specific verbs used within each grouping differ, the groupings fall together naturally because each utilizes a single spatial image. This can be demonstrated also by the distribution of prepositions among the groupings: *in* | *ad* + accusative, *in* + ablative, or *de* | *ab* + ablative. In this way, students identify the underlying metaphorical organization of the domain according to concepts, in this case, of spatial motion – and come to understand, moreover, that the groups "make sense" as a system, in that each is organized by an image logically related to the others. An illustration of how the underlying spatial metaphors relate, as in Figure 1, clarifies this point.[22]

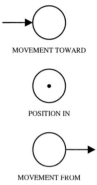

MOVEMENT TOWARD

POSITION IN

MOVEMENT FROM

Figure 1

Once the groupings have been established, students are asked to define the general meaning that each image conveys *vis-à-vis* the target domain. The teacher attempts to elicit the set of mappings that constitute the metaphors, in the form of propositions. This can be challenging, because while the figurative meaning of some expressions may be transparent due to similarities between the metaphorical systems of English and Latin, English's "preferential conceptualization"[23] of certain domains in terms different from Latin's obliges students to reason according to inferential models very dissimilar to their own. Due to English's strong preference for metaphors of physical manipulation in conceptualizing mental activity,[24] for example, any explicit statement of the mappings (e.g. "movement towards corresponds metaphorically to 'acquiring' a thought in the mind") will require explication of those metaphors. However, by inviting students to draw inferences from their knowledge of the experiential source, they will recognize the figurative meaning of each image in the target domain – e.g. "movement toward" corresponds metaphorically to thinking "new" thoughts, just as moving to a location implies being in a new place, and so on.[25]

With more advanced students, the goal is to demonstrate how knowledge of metaphor contributes to literary understanding – specifically, how inferences about the meaning of creative figurative language can be made from metaphorical structure. Accordingly, the strategy must be to encourage students to consider not only how metaphor motivates meaning, but also how the lexical make-up of an idiomatic expression can convey nuances of connotation. Asking students to create new expressions on the model of Latin's idioms, for example, allows them to explore how elaborations on the central mappings produce new meanings. Students then compare their invented expressions with examples attested in Latin literature in a discussion of how elaborations of the mappings entail subtle distinctions in meaning, always constrained by the logic of spatial motion. Similarly, cloze procedure activities, in which students are asked to "fill in the blanks" with words best matching their understanding of a sentence, teach reasoning about metaphorical meaning on the basis of contextual clues.[26]

Thus, in the case of Latin's idioms of mental activity, if "coming into" means "adopting an opinion" (*venire in opinionem*), students can be asked what additional (metaphorically defined) connotations might be expressed by "rushing into an opinion" (*ruere in sententiam*)[27] or "slipping toward an opinion" (*labi ad opinionem*).[28] If they have understood the mappings, students will reason from spatial experience to infer that these expressions respectively imply something about the haste and intentionality with which an idea is adopted. In a further exercise, reading enough of the adjoining text to understand the overall meaning of sentences such as (17), (18), and (19), students should be able to supply for the missing verbs alternative expressions with appropriate metaphorical sense.

(17) (**perducebam**) *illam ad me suadela mea* (Plaut. *Cist.* 566)
       "I won her over to my opinion by persuasion"

(18) *quoscumque adit ex civitate*, *ad suam sententiam* (**perducit**) (Caes. *Gall.* 7,4,3)
       "He (sc. Vercingetorix) won over to his sentiments such of his fellow-citizens as he has access to"

(19) *missa per legatos pecunia* (**traxit**) *in sententiam suam senatum* (Flor. *epit. 1,36*)
       "With money sent through his legates, he won over the senate to his opinion"

To do so, students must reason again in metaphorical terms, inferring from spatial experience that if "going into" is "adopting an opinion" (*ire in sententiam*), then the required sense of "persuading someone to adopt an opinion" can be expressed metaphorically by "leading" someone to that opinion or even "dragging" them there, which suggests still less willingness on the part of the recipient. Given a sentence such as (20), students should likewise be able to supply a spatial verb with literal meaning similar to the missing *depellere*, in order to yield the required metaphorical meaning of "dissuade" – on the logic that just as persuasion by force is "dragging" someone toward a thought-location, dissuasion by force (cf. *contumelia, vis, periculum*) can be expressed by "forcing someone to move away from" or "pushing away from":

(20)   *de suscepta causa propositaque sententia nulla contumelia, nulla vis,*
       nullum periculum posset (***depellere***) (Cic. *Lig.* 26)
       "No insult, no violence, no threat of danger could dislodge him from
       the cause he had undertaken and from his stated opinion"

At a higher level still, students analyze how the metaphorical meanings of idiomatic expressions interact with the thematic interests of the passages (and indeed works) in which they appear. For instance, students might read the letter of Seneca the Younger in which he advises Lucilius on how to conduct his daily philosophical practice:

(21)   *probatos itaque semper lege, et si quando ad alios deverti libuerit, ad*
       priores redi. aliquid cotidie adversus paupertatem, aliquid adversus
       mortem auxili compara, nec minus adversus ceteras pestes; et cum
       multa percurreris, unum excerpe quod illo die concoquas (Sen. *epist.*
       2,4)
       "Always read standard authors; and when you crave a change, fall
       back upon those whom you read before. Each day acquire something
       that will fortify you against poverty, against death, indeed against
       other misfortunes as well; and after you have run through many
       ideas, select one to be thoroughly cooked up that day"

Leaving aside Seneca's mixing of metaphors, students can be asked to consider not only what sorts of meaning are expressed by the image of "running through" many ideas (*cum multa percurreris*), but also why Seneca might have been particularly motivated to choose this image (He could have said simply *cum multa legeris…* or used a different metaphor, such as *deliberare*, *scrutari*, or even *ruminari*, more fitting with *concoquas*!) In the spatial domain, "running through" is a special case of MOVEMENT TOWARD characterized by purposeful, rapid motion through multiple different locations. Reasoning metaphorically, students understand that Seneca is advocating a habit of study that involves briefly surveying many different ideas before selecting one for serious reflection. This metaphor nicely encapsulates Seneca's more general argument against discursiveness (cf. 2,2 *illud autem vide, ne ista lectio auctorum multorum et omnis generis voluminum habeat aliquid vagum et instabile… nusquam est qui ubique est*) and, furthermore, fits the imagery of the "literal" *exemplum* he provides of the traveller who in journeying far and wide in fact calls no place home (2,2 *vitam in peregrinatione exigentibus hoc evenit, ut multa hospitia habeant, nullas amicitias*).[29]

Conclusion

Cognitive linguists have shown that many idioms whose meanings are opaque on the traditional account can instead be seen as motivated semantically by a language's pervasive metaphorical "themes". In this view, comprehending idiomatic language, as a subset of conventional figurative expression, becomes a matter of making metaphorically based inferences. This has clear implications for teaching and learning idioms. First, it suggests that if idioms can be connected to patterns of metaphorical meaning, the meanings of those idioms will be reasonable and inferable, and therefore easier to learn. As Irujo (1993, 217) proposes, "Teaching students strategies for dealing with figurative language will help them to take advantage of the semantic transparency of some idioms. If they can figure out the meaning of an idiom by themselves, they will have a link from the idiomatic meaning to the literal words, which will help them learn the idiom". Second, it suggests that by making clear the metaphorical structuring of a language's conventional vocabulary, teachers can help students to make informed predictions about the meaning of idiomatic and imaginative literary expression.

I have demonstrated that much of Latin's lexicon of mental activity is given metaphorically in terms of movement in physical space, and in such a way that the conceptual topology of the spatial domain is preserved wholesale in the mental domain. Given this structuring, I suggested specific strategies for enabling Latin students to benefit from an awareness of metaphorical patterns in the language. In introductory courses, rather than asking students to memorize figurative interpretations of idioms as rote correspondences for some arbitrary literal wording, teachers can design activities to illustrate how idiomatic meaning is constructed throughout Latin's lexical and phrasal vocabulary in rational and coherent ways – learning presumably being aided by understanding! Similarly, teachers can help advanced students develop the skill to infer subtleties of meaning by considering the metaphorical character of language within context. By training them to reason metaphorically in terms appropriate to Roman culture itself, and to make contextually based predictions of the sort Halliday and Hasan (1985) describe, this approach has the advantage both of empowering students as readers – and not simply decoders – of Latin literature and of lending itself to empirical validation.

Notes

[1] See Gairns and Redman (1986); Alexander (1987); Carter and McCarthy (1988).

[2] E.g. Verg. *Aen.* 1,530-1, *est locus, Hesperiam Grai cognomine dicunt.*

[3] E.g. Cic. *div.* 2,2,1, *cumque fundamentum esset philosophiae positum in finibus bonorum et malorum, perpurgatus est is locus a nobis quinque libris.*

[4] Despite disagreement over what constitutes "literality" (see Gibbs 1994: 24-79), the first sense of *locus* can be taken to be "literal" and primary on the basis of the physical concreteness of the *denotatum*, its greater frequency of occurrence relative to other senses, and its earlier attestation in the language. The second sense can be taken to be "idiomatic" and secondary on the basis of the metaphysical abstractness of the *denotatum*, its apparently arbitrary deviation from the primary concrete sense, and its relatively later appearance in the language. On the related issue of the idiomaticity of lexical items, see Katz and Postal (1963: 275-6).

[5] Cole (1991: 88-9) explains the polysemy of Greek τόπος by "a natural metonymy", linking the concept of "idea, argument" to that of "place" through "the spot [on a papyrus roll] containing a given model piece". But this simply begs the question.

[6] See Gibbs et al. (1993) and Gibbs (1994) for a review of traditional theories of idiomaticity; but also Dobrovol'skij and Piirainen (2005: 29-54) for a corrective discussion of past views.

[7] Cf. Bobrow and Bell (1973); Lewis (1997); see also Cacciari and Tabossi (1993).

[8] Geeraerts (1989); Gibbs and Nayak (1989), Lakoff (1987), Langacker (1987).

[9] Lakoff and Johnson (1980); Lakoff (1987); Johnson (1987); and Kövecses (2002 and 2006).

[10] E.g. Cacciari and Tabossi (1988); Gibbs and O'Brian (1990); Gibbs (1992); Gibbs et al. (1997).

[11] Gibbs (1994: 265-318).

[12] See Boers and Lindstromberg (2008: 33-8) and Irujo (1996).

[13] Cf. Adams (1980) on the Latin sexual vocabulary and García-Jurado (2000) on metaphorical language in Plautus.

[14] Bettini (1991: 121-33).

[15] Short (2009).

[16] "The verb *noscere* and its relatives represent perhaps the extent of Latin's literal vocabulary of mind."

[17] Cf. the literal and metaphorical senses of *errare* (and similar expressions in Greek: e.g. ἀλάομαι, ἀλύω, πλανάω).

[18] Studies by cognitive linguists have demonstrated that students of English perform significantly better on memory tasks when they are made to see the kinds of motivating links that metaphors provide between an idiom's literal sense and its figurative meaning; see Kövecses and Szabó (1996).

[19] Readers use conceptual metaphors in drawing inferences about poetic metaphors: see Gibbs and Nascimento (1996).

[20] Literary texts tend to exhibit a degree of metaphorical density that can be problematic for even advanced students: see Steen (1994).

[21] The basic rationale for and progression of the activities described below matches the three-part process of idiom teaching and learning designed by Boers, Eyckmans and Stengers (2006) and (2007) for their experiments.

[22] Boers, Demecheleer and Eyckmans (2004) suggest that associating idiomatic meaning with imagery can have positive mnemonic effects.

[23] Kövecses (2004: 82-6).

[24] Jäkel (1995: 225-6).

[25] Comparisons with English also help develop intercultural insight: cf. Skopinskaja 2003.

[26] On the use of cloze procedure for teaching text interpretation, see Weston (1996) and Rossiter (1991).

[27] Cf. Ps. Quint. *decl.* 12,6,5, *ut arma bello, ut aqua incendio inclamari publice solent, ita uno quodam consensu non aetatibus exspectatis, non honoribus, pariter rettulimus, probavimus, decrevimus, pedibus manibus ruimus in sententiam necessitatis.*

[28] Cf. Cic. *ac.* 2,138, *vos autem mihi verenti ne labar ad opinionem et aliquid adsciscam et conprobem incognitum, quod minime vultis, quid consilii datis?*

[29] Spatial metaphor also provides the overall organization of the work: Henderson (2006: 123-46) shows how Seneca structures his *Moral Epistles* spatially by using different locations to represent different stages of philosophical development.

References

Adams, J. (1982) *The Latin Sexual Vocabulary*, Baltimore, Johns Hopkins University Press.

Alexander, R. (1987) "Problems in Understanding and Teaching Idiomaticity in English" *Anglistik und Englischunterricht* 32: 105-22.

Bettini, M. (1991) *Anthropology and Roman Culture*, Baltimore, Johns Hopkins University Press.

Bobrow, S. and S. Bell (1973) "On Catching on to Idiomatic Expressions" *Memory&Cognition* 1: 343-346.

Boers, F. and S. Lindstromberg (2008) *Cognitive Linguistic Approaches to Teaching Vocabulary and Phraseology*, Berlin, Mouton de Gruyter.

Boers, F. J. Eyckmans and H. Stengers (2006) "Motivating Multiword Units: Rationale, Mnemonic Benefits, and Cognitive Style Variables", in S. Foster-Cohen, M. Krajnovic and J. Djigunovic (eds) *EUROSLA Yearbook* 6, Amsterdam, John Benjamins, 169-90.

—. (2007) "Presenting Figurative Idioms With a Touch of Etymology: More Than Mere Mnemonics?" *Language Teaching Research* 11.1: 43-62.

Cacciari, C. and P. Tabossi (1988) "The Comprehension of Idioms" *Journal of Memory and Language* 27.6: 668-83.

Cacciari, C. and P. Tabossi (1993) *Idioms: Processing, Structure, and Interpretation*, Hillsdale, NJ, L. Erlbaum.

Carter, R. and M. McCarthy (1988) *Vocabulary and Language Teaching*, London, Longman.

Cole, T. (1991) *The Origins of Rhetoric in Ancient Greece*, Baltimore, Johns Hopkins University Press.

Danesi, M. (1993) "Metaphorical Competence in Second Language Acquisition and Second Language Teaching", in J. Alatis (ed.) *Georgetown University Round Table on Language and Linguistics*, Washington, DC, Georgetown University Press, 489-500.

Dobrovol'skij, D. and E. Piirainen (2005) *Figurative Language: Cross-Cultural and Cross-Linguistic Perspectives*, Oxford, Elsevier.

Gairns, R. and S. Redman (1986) *Working With Words,* Cambridge, Cambridge University Press.

García-Jurado, F. (2000) "Las metáforas de la vida cotidiana en latín" *Proceedings of the Congreso internacional de semántica* 2, Universidad de La Laguna, Madrid, Ediciones Clásicas, 1571-84.

Geeraerts, D. (1989) "Introduction: Prospects and Problems of Prototype Theory" *Linguistics* 27.4: 587-612.

Gibbs, R. (1992) "What Do Idioms Really Mean?" *Journal of Memory and Language* 31.4: 485-506.

—. (1993) *The Poetics of Mind: Figurative Thought, Language, and Understanding,* Cambridge, Cambridge University Press.

Gibbs, R. and J. O'Brian (1990) "Idioms and Mental Imagery" *Cognition* 36: 35-68.

Gibbs, R. and N. Nayak (1989) "Psycholinguistic Studies on the Syntactic Behavior of Idioms" *Cognitive Psychology* 21: 100-38.

Gibbs, R. et al. (1993) "Literal Meaning and Figurative Language" *Discourse Processes* 16: 387-403.

—. et al. (1997) "Metaphor in Idiom Comprehension" *Journal of Memory and Language* 37: 141-54.

Gibbs, R. and S. Nascimento (1996) "How We Talk When We Talk About Love: Metaphorical Concepts and Understanding Love Poetry", in R. Kreuz and M. MacNealy (eds) *Empirical Approaches to Literature and Aesthetics*, Norwood, NJ, Ablex, 291-307.

Halliday, M. and R. Hasan (1985) *Language, Context, and Text: Aspects of Language in a Social-Semiotic Perspective*, Oxford, Oxford University Press.

Henderson, J. (2006) "Journey of a Lifetime", in K. Volk and G. Williams (eds) *Seeing Seneca Whole,* Leiden, Brill, 123-46.

Irujo, S. (1996) "A Piece of Cake: Learning and Teaching Idioms" *ELT Journal* 40.3: 236-42.

Jäkel, O. (1995) "The Metaphorical Concept of Mind: 'Mental Activity is Manipulation'", in J. Taylor and R. MacLaury (eds) *Language and the Cognitive Construal of the World*, Berlin, Mouton de Gruyter, 197-229.

Johnson, M. (1987) *The Body in Mind,* Chicago, University of Chicago Press.

Katz, J. and P. Postal (1963) "Semantic Interpretation of Idioms and Sentences Containing Them", *Quarterly Progress Report* 70, Cambridge, Ma. MIT Research Laboratory of Electronics, 275-282.

Kövecses, Z. (2002) *Metaphor*, Oxford-New York, Oxford University Press.

—. (2004) *Metaphor in Culture: Universality and Variation*, Cambridge, Cambridge University Press.

—. (2006) *Language, Mind and Culture*, Oxford-New York, Oxford University Press.

Kövecses, Z. and P. Szabó (1993) "Idioms: A View from Cognitive Semantics" *Applied Linguistics* 17.3: 326-55.

Lakoff, G. (1987) *Women, Fire and Dangerous Things: What Categories Reveal about the Mind*, Chicago, University of Chicago Press.

—. (1993) "The Contemporary Theory of Metaphor", in A. Ortony (ed.) *Metaphor and Thought*, Cambridge, Cambridge University Press, 202-51.

Lakoff, G. and M. Johnson (1980) *Metaphors We Live By*, Chicago, University of Chicago Press.

Langacker, R. (1987) *Foundations of Cognitive Grammar*, Stanford, Stanford University Press.

Lewis, M. (1997) *Implementing the Lexical Approach: Putting Theory Into Practice*, Hove, Language Teaching Publications.

Rossiter, P. (1991) "At Cloze Quarters: The Use of Gapfill in Teaching Poetry" *Essays and Studies in British and American Literature* 37: 73-96.

Short, W. (2009) "Eating Your Words: 'Oral' Metaphors of Auditory Perception in Roman Culture" *I quaderni del ramo d'oro* 2: 111-23.

Skopinskaja, L. (2003) "The Role of Cultural in Foreign Language Teaching Materials", in I. Lázár (ed.) *Incorporating Intercultural Communicative Competence in Language Teaching*, Strasburg, European Centre for Modern Languages, 39-68.

Steen, G. (1994) *Understanding Metaphor in Literature: An Empirical Approach*, London, Longman.

Weston, A. (1996) "Picking Holes: Cloze Procedures in Prose", in R. Carter and J. McRae (eds) *Language, Literature and the Learner: Creative Classroom Practice*, London, Longman, 115-37.

AMATORY FIGURES OF SPEECH IN LATIN LYRIC POETRY

IOANA-RUCSANDRA DASCALU

1. Defining figures of speech

This contribution examines, from the bulk of the Latin lexicon, a limited vocabulary common to a specialized class of speakers, i.e. the amatory vocabulary of the Latin lyric poets: Catullus, Tibullus, Horace, Propertius and Ovid, according to monolingual and bilingual editions of the text and to lexicographic sources.

Figures of speech play a very important role in this study, as the texts of lyric poets abound in metaphors, synesthesies, hyperboles, and metonymies.

I am pleading for a larger interpretation of Latin texts, that supposes excellent knowledge of the Latin language, an excellent insight into the Roman civilization and the capacity to describe the characters of a certain literary period. It is important to raise awareness about the definitions of the figures of speech and the rhetorical devices in evolution from Antiquity until today. To this end, I used definitions of the figures of speech of Greek and Roman antiquity, passing through structuralism and exploiting the theories of cognitivist authors' (such as Haser, Geeraerts).

A characteristic feature for the figures of speech in question is the transfer of signification, from a proper sense to a figurative one. Metaphor is a mechanism of thought, whereby some experiences or phenomena are verbalized by others, with which they possess common features (Blank 2001:73).

Synesthesia refers to metaphoric exchange between two different sensory domains. Hyperbole is the exaggeration of qualities or of an event, which receives enormous proportions, mythological or catastrophic. Metonymy represents a figure of speech situated at the same level as metaphor that replaces an entity by another entity (a part for the whole, the effect for the cause). The mental mechanisms are imaginative in the production of metaphors (Blank 2001:73) and logical in the creation of metonymies (Blank 2001:79). Metaphor is the figure of speech that establishes an equivalence of the two notions between which we observe a transfer of semantic features (DSL 2001:307); it constitutes a theme of rhetorics, historical semantics, textual linguistics and literary theory. In a conceptual and linguistic way, it represents a creative psychic process, whereby an object is seen as something else, taking its qualities and properties (Blank 2001:74-75).

2. Metaphor in Latin lyric poetry

In ancient Greek philosophy, metaphor was defined as a figure of speech or of logic (Lausberg 1960: 285-291; Hofmann and Szantyr 2002: 154-158; 315-319):

> Arist. *Rhet.* 3,4,1406b 20: Metaphor represents a kind of comparison; it is a little different, as, when we say that Achilles threw himself as a lion, that is a comparison; but when *the lion* rushed, that is a metaphor; because the two are courageous, we compared Achilles to a lion.

> Quint. *Inst.* 8,6,8: Metaphor represents a shorter comparison; it differs by the fact that the latter compares the objects that we want to express, while the former substitutes them.

Metaphor consists in the fact that words are used out of their normal signification, in order to express a similar concept. The contribution science brings nowadays is the idea that figures of speech are not placed in language, but in the intellect (Geeraerts 2006:185). They are a typical feature of the daily universe, of the perception whereby we perceive the world and a stable treasure of human thought. Therefore, the social and bodily experiences that human beings experiences are reflected in speech. Metaphors depend on culture, they are historical phenomena reflecting events and trends of the age (Blank 2001:76). In the lyrical poets' works, the origins of the figures of speech, based on experience, involve elements from the natural world such as light, fire, from the domestic environment, such as the closed door and from the human body, such as torture, pleasure, pain.

In structural linguistics, metaphor is classified in the category of metasememes, a figure of speech that substitutes one meaning for another, according to a feature common to both terms. Structuralism considers metaphor as a problem of language. In recent linguistics, metaphors are analysed from the cognitive point of view, as a part of our conceptual system, of thought as reflected in action. Metaphor was defined as a method to describe and know the world (Haser 2005:76). The essence of metaphor means understanding a phenomenon in the terms of another phenomenon (Haser 2005:15), an experience after another experience. Among metaphors dedicated to love, I have found many examples about light (natural, light of the eye interpreted as man's ability to see, flame, heat, burning, spark).

As organs of perception, eyes are the reference for sentimental intensity: in the verses written by Catullus, friendship is more important than eyes, which is a fine poetic exaggeration (Catull. 14,1-2).

A superior intensity of light is contained by the flame, that burns and shines; this combustion can be translated by the adjective *flagrans* (formed from the root of the verb *flagrare* = to burn, to inflame) and even the verb *flagrare* itself (Catull. 67,25; 68,73; Hor. *carm.* 1,25,13-15; Prop. 1,13, 23); the construction *flagrans amor* designates deep and ardent love.

The metaphor of love as an inner ardour is also found in the noun *ardor*, having a literal sense 'heat' and a figurative sense 'torture, suffering, heavy sadness' (Catull. 2,8). In the same lexical family of the verb *ardere* there are hyperboles, in which the forces of nature and of war coincide with the feelings of the characters (Prop. 3,13,21).

The verb *ardere* refers to the same Latin word *medulla*, more predictable in this context. Another part of the body which is presented as a source of feelings is *pectus*; in Catull. 61,176-178 we read:

(1) *Illi non minus ac tibi*
     Pectore uritur intimo
     Flamma, sed penite magis
     "Deep inside his chest,
     Even deeper
     He is burning for your flame"

From the semantic sphere of fire is chosen the term *flamma*, that is consumed deep inside the chest: *intimo pectore*, *penite magis*. The verb of combustion *urere* is used in the passive and medio-passive: in Catull. 72, 5-6, we read:

(2) *Nunc te cognoui; quare etsi inpensius uror,*
     Multo mi tamen es uilior et leuior
     "Now I do know you! Therefore if I burn harder out of love,
     Ah, once fallen in my eyes, you cannot have any price"

The action is intensified by grammatical means in order to express aspect, as, for example, the preverb *per-* (*urere-perurere*): *intestina perurere* (the intestines burn out as a sign of consumption and total destruction). In Horace (*epod.* 11,4), the verb *urere* is followed by the preposition *in*: *in pueris aut in puellis urere*, that is to say to have strong feelings towards someone else.

The human soul is very often expressed with a metaphor in Latin poetry; it is imagined in concrete, material terms; the verb *torquere* means 'to twist', referring to thoughts and feelings (Tib. 1,4,81), (Hor. *carm.* 1,2,37). The verb *tumere* (to swell) refers to the feeling of love in a positive manner.

3. The *paraclausithyron* as a poetic episode

A motif used in the Latin lyric poetry, built from metaphor, is the *paraclausithyron*, which represents the song performed by a rejected lover in front of the door of the beloved woman, after being denied entrance in the house; this poem is pronounced in a sad and melancholic mood, whereas the prayer meant to gain the benevolence of the *puella* receives dramatic accents. This domestic element, the door of the house plays an important anthropologic, literary and symbolic role in Greek and Latin civilization. Mainly, this is a sign of obstinacy and refusal, to which the lover reacts with bacchic serenades, created under the influence of alcohol, with the state of wakefulness at night in front of the door of the beloved woman, with offerings of flowers on the threshold in order to honour the house. Often people shed tears at the ceremonies for having waited so much in wind and rain, for having desperately tried to overcome cruelty.

A special type of *paraclausithyron*, a satiric or critical one (Copley 1956:47) was cultivated by Catullus, who develops motifs of marital infidelity such as adultery in his poems. Catullus' poem 67 proposes the personification of an object of the domestic environment, the door of the house, which is interrogated and establishes a dialogue with the poet's voice. In their discussion, we read the story of that thing, the masters it possessed, who cherished it by calling it *iucunda* and who treated it with positive feelings.

The role of the door (*ianua*) was presented as the role of an autonomous personality, not of a speaking object, with human duties and feelings, such as pride and resentment. It is the guardian of the house, its protector, with all the secrets it witnesses (Copley 1956:49). Another poem of Catullus dedicated to things of the environment is number 17, in which the action is placed on a bridge, symbolic of the "path" of life and of human destiny.

Catullus' poem 32 is built like a *paraclausithyron*, in which the voice of the poet ardently praises Ipsitila not to reject him and to open the door of her house in the afternoon. The entrance is designated by the phrase *tabella liminis; limen* means threshold and, by semantic extension, it represents *the door*. The threshold constitutes an element often seen in love stories; e.g. in Tib. 2,6,11-14 the poet's aspirations, who thinks and plans magnificent things (*magna loquor*), and encounters the indifference of the closed doors (*clausae fores*). Swearing he will never visit these places again, the man is obliged to come there, to those thresholds (*limina*).

In the third ode, Horace describes his vocation of lover through a martial metaphor: *militaui*, in which the tools of opening ways are *funalia* (torches*), uectes* (sticks), *arcus* (arches); they must break the closed doors, out of ambition and pride (Henderson 1973). The final prayer is addressed to Venus, who must punish Chloe with cruelty, because she refused him once (*semel arrogantem*), closing all the doors to her person.

In *Ars amandi*, Ovid outlines a code for the lovers' behaviour in amatory relationships. In the next verses (2,520-530), the episode is structured as a *paraclausithyron*, in which the man goes to the house of the beloved woman, which he finds closed and locked. He is asked to whisper gentle words in front of the closed door at night and to put roses on the door posts (*postibus*). In *Amores* 1,6 Ovid creates a song in front of the closed doors, whereby he implores the janitor to open the doors and to help him crawl inside.

In conclusion, Latin lyric poetry presents metaphors of love that are negatively connotated; they are disphorically presented as pain, torture, absence, sweetness in sadness and melancholy. Love is characterized by crying, lamentations, regret; these are exterior symptoms of anxiety and interior pain.

(3)   *Non ego tum potero solacia ferre roganti,*
        Cum mihi nulla mei sit medicina mali (Prop. 1,5,27-28)
      "I won't bring consolation to him who asks for it,
      As I have no cure for my illness"

The noun *medicina (ars)* is a member of the lexical family of the verb *mederi* (to cure an illness) (DELL 1939:599). Love imagined as a disease that conquers the entire body is a metaphor found in Latin comedy. To the pathology of this feeling is added its physiology, with the exterior signs it marks on the human complexion.

From the root *lax* is formed the verb *delicere* (to cheat by seduction) and also the plural noun *deliciae*, signifying "pleasure", "favourite object". The passion for a pet reflects instability and the aspiration for unconditioned love:

(4) *Passer mortuus est meae puellae,*
     Passer, deliciae meae puellae (Catull. 3,4-5)
     "The sparrow of my beloved died,
     The sparrow, the pleasure of my beloved"

4. Other figures of speech: synesthesia, metonymy, hyperbole

In the class of synesthesia, which represents events and phenomena of the world, I encountered the sweetness of feelings that suggest pleasures and melancholy, joy and sadness.

The Latin adjective *dulcis* is used in a physical and moral sense (DELL 1939: 287). In the amatory vocabulary, it defines comfort, stability, preference, satisfaction. Referring to the human voice, it connotes admiration and respect for an inaccessible person.

(5) *Omnia tecum una perierunt gaudia nostra,*
     Quae tuos in uita dulcis alebat amor (Catull. 68A, 95-96)
     "With you passed away all our joys,
     That your sweet love was nourishing in life"

Another metaphor is to be found in the thermic sphere of ardour and of heat. From the Latin verb *arere* derived the noun *ardor*, that lost its sense of aridity, receiving the sense of ardent heat, ardour in the physical and moral sense, brilliance. In the following verses, *ardour* refers to sadness and deep sorrow felt by the woman:

(6) *Et acris solet incitare morsus,*
     Cum desiderio meo nitenti
     Carum, nescioquid libet iocari
     Ut solaciolum sui doloris,
     Credo ut iam grauis aquiescat ardor (Catull. 2,5-8)
     "You bite sharply
     When my beloved wants
     To play with something that is precious to her
     As a relief of her pain,
     I think, in order to put off her fire"

The paroxistic feeling is expressed by the verb *perire* and its compound, *deperire*. This is infinite love, until death, that is to say the impossibility to give up love:

(7)   *Quae nunc, si mihi uera nuntiantur,*
        Illum deperit impotente amore (Catull. 35,11-12)
        "If what they say is mere truth,
        She is dying out of love for him with an endless feeling"

In the same romantic sphere of destruction we find the metaphors about the love of the beloved person or of the feeling itself (Lyne 1998). *To lose* refers to objects of the physical environment; by extension, we come to loss of feelings or of persons:

(8)   *Nam citius paterer caput hoc discedere collo,*
        Quam possem nuptae perdere amore faces (Prop. 2.7-8)
        "I would prefer to have my head cut apart from the body
        Than to lose my love for the flames of the wedding"

These verses express the steadfastness of feelings between two lovers who refuse to separate themselves; the loss of one's head is hyperbolically suggested. Weddings of obligation are compared to funerals, attracting interior death at the personal level, by lack of attraction or of pleasure.

Synesthesies mean translating some senses or sensations into other senses; thus, the adjective *dulcis* that belongs to the sensorial domain of taste, by semantic transfer refers to the love stories that young people live:

(9)   *...nec dulces amores*
        Sperne puer... (Hor. *carm.* 1,9,15-16)
        "...My child, do not despise
        The sweet love stories..."

(10)   *...Desine, dulcium*
        Mater saeua Cupidinum (Hor. *carm.* 4,1,4-5)
        "...Stop,
        Cruel mother of sweet Cupids..."

In Latin poetry, writers often combine taste and colours (the taste of milk and the colour of milk); for example, the young ladies' skin is described by the adjective *lacteolus* (as white as milk):

(11) *Num te lacteolae tenent puellae?* (Catull. 55.17)
      "Don't milky girls let you?"

Metonymy is a figure of speech similar to metaphor, receiving a variety of
functions such as the part for the whole, the whole for the part, the
recipient for the content, the tool for the action, the features for the object.
Most often, names of gods replace or represent the actions or the effects
they dominate. The common noun *Bacchus* is interpreted as "drink" and
"feast".

(12) *Neu quisquam multo percussum tempora Baccho*
         Excitet, infelix dum requiescat amor (Tib. 1,2,3-4)
      "I don't want anyone to trouble me, when, Troubled by Bacchus, my
      temple throbs and my love is laid to rest"

The name of the goddess Venus stands for "charm", "attraction": in Hor.
sat. 1,4,113, by the construction *Venerem concedere*, we understand the
legitimate and official relationship of love; Venus is the one who protects
marriage and feelings.

      Another case of metonymic replacement is the part for the whole: the
name *corpus* designates the person, the human. In Hor. *epod.* 5,13 the
expression *impube corpus* represents the young man who would have
tamed even the Thracians with his appearance. In Catull. 66,32 we read
about the lovers who cannot separate from the body of their beloved.
Corpus carum must be translated as beloved partner, analyzing this feeling
on its bodily, physical side.

      In the plural, the noun *amores* expresses love stories, the events and
their idylls. Rarely, the noun can be translated as *beloved person* (Pierrugues
1826:42) *amores pro amica: frequentissimum in colloquiis eroticis.*

      Hyperbole is a figure of speech that exaggerates the importance of the
qualities of an event or an action. It has the role of depicting a sentimental
reality in catastrophic or cataclysmic terms, such as devastating fires or
death, as death because of pain and suffering. We therefore propose as
hyperbolic elements the supernatural forces of nature, mythologic
characters, geographic regions full of history and archaeology, which
participate in the torture of the beloved: the Mount Etna and the Maliac
Gulf. The elements of global nature, the earth and the sea, are invoked at
the same time as the legendary hero Hercules, who is burning with
Nessus' blood like Mount Etna. The destructive fire burns the human body
to the bones; this autocombustion is caused by inner torture, by an endless

desire. The erotic feeling is threatened by death, which overwhelms it; thus, frequently, some characters can die out of love.

(13) *Cum tantum arderem quantum Trinacria rupes*
      Lymphaque in Oetaeis Malia Thermopylis,
      Maesta neque adsiduo tabescere lumina fletu
        Cessarent tristique imbre madere genae (Catull. 68,53-56)
      "I burned like the Etna volcano
      And the Maliae waters of the Oeteic Thermopile,
      My sad eyes didn't dry for having cried so long,
      And the cheeks got wet because of the sad rain"

Also in Horace's poetry, the earth, waters and untamed mythological forces like Venus and Hercules make up the hyperbolic description of man's soul invaded by feelings.

Conclusion

This paper intends to suggest an integrated method combining stylistic and literary analysis. I consider the study of the figures of speech, through rhetoric, linguistic and literary tools, a priority of the first order in all programmes of classics.

References

Blank, A. (2001) *Einführung in die lexikalische Semantik für Romanisten*, Tübingen, Max Niemeyer Verlag.
Copley, F.O. (1956) *Exclusus Amator. A Study in Latin Love Poetry*, Oxford, The American Philological Association&Blackwell.
DELL (1939): Ernout, A. and A. Meillet, *Dictionnaire étymologique de la langue latine*, 2ᵉ éd., Paris, Klincksieck.
DSL (2001): Bidu-Vrănceanu, A., Călăraşu, C., Ionescu-Ruxăndoiu, L., Mancaş, M. and G. Pană Dindelegan *Dicţionar de ştiinţe ale limbii*, Bucureşti, Editura Nemira.
Geeraerts, D. (2006) *Cognitive Linguistics: Basic Readings,* Berlin, Mouton de Gruyter, 2006.
Haser, V. (2005) *Metaphor, Metonymy and Experientialist Philosophy (Challenging Cognitive Semantics)*, Berlin, Mouton de Gruyter.
Henderson, W.J. (1973), "The paraklausithyron motif in Horace's Odes", *Acta Classica* 16: 51-67.

Hofmann, J.B. and A. Szantyr (2002), *Stilistica latina*, It. ed. a cura di A. Traina, aggiornamenti di R. Oniga, Bologna Pàtron (orig. ed. *Lateinische Syntax und Stilistik*, München, Beck 1965).

Lausberg, H. (1960) *Handbuch der literarischen Rhetorik (eine Grundlegung der Literaturwissenschaft)*, Vol. I, München, Hueber.

Lyne, R. (1998) "Love and Death: Laodamia and Protesilaus in Catullus, Propertius, and others", *Classical Quarterly* 48: 200-212.

Pierrugues, P. (1826) *Glossarium Eroticum linguae Latinae siue Theogoniae, legum et morum nuptialium apud Romanos explanatio noua ex interpretatione propria et impropria et differentiis in significatu fere duorum millium sermonum, ad intelligentiam poetarum et ethologorum tam antiquae quam integrae infimaeque latinitatis, auctore P.P.* Parisiis, Apud Aug.-Fr. Et Pr. Dondey-Dupré, Bibliopolas.

LINGUISTIC SEMANTICS AND THE REPRESENTATION OF WORD MEANING IN LATIN DICTIONARIES

DAVID B. WHARTON

Introduction

Acquiring accurate and detailed knowledge of word meanings is one of the most difficult tasks that face second language learners, especially when words have more than one meaning.[1] Thus those of us who study ancient languages need particularly good dictionaries, since we do not experience the full range of words and their various meanings as they usually occurred to ancient speakers in everyday life. We especially need them for words that do not occur with great frequency in authors that we usually read; for such words, dictionaries are our most important source of information about their range of meanings and uses. With this in mind, I want to explore here the semantics of a single Latin word - *horror* as a case study in the usefulness of current practices in Latin lexicography, with a particular focus on the way they handle problems of polysemy.[2] I choose the word *horror* because the problems that arise in its description are fairly typical but also quite interesting. I will focus here on its treatment in the *Oxford Latin Dictionary* (*OLD*) because the *OLD* is the most up-to-date and generally well-received[3] Latin-English dictionary in the English-speaking world, and because its article on *horror* follows the *OLD*'s standard principles and practices.[4]

We should stipulate at the beginning, however, that we can't achieve a completely accurate description of the meanings of any word, even in the best of circumstances. On this, semanticists and lexicographers agree:

> ... the sense of most lexemes ... would seem to be somewhat fuzzy at the edges. (Lyons 1995: 82)

> Not only are meanings notoriously vague, they are also (diachronically) changeable and (synchronically) flexible .... It follows that ascertaining, or

fixing, the meaning of any lexical item is virtually impossible. (Adamska-Salaciak 2006: 48)

... it may be even be impossible, in principle, to state precisely how many different meanings a word has, let alone characterize the meanings in a way which accounts for their contribution to the meaning of a complex expression .... Perhaps we need to abandon the idea of words having a fixed number of determinate meanings ... (Taylor 2003: 651)

Probably the most disadvantaged researchers . . . in the field of linguistic semantics are those who study "dead" languages. Often virtually the only direct evidence available to them is a corpus of written utterances, of somewhat fortuitous make-up, and now probably fixed for eternity. (Cruse 1989: 8-9)

Thus every attempt at lexical description is at best an approximate description of things that have an essentially protean nature. We can also agree that traditional historical lexicography does many things very well, and I echo the statement of a critic of an earlier generation of dictionaries, who said that he hoped that nothing he wrote might "seem inconsistent with the highest respect, admiration, and honor for the labourers, whether living or dead, in this field of ... lexicography". (Trench 1860: 4)

1. Historical lexicography and traditional sense divisions

The *OLD* stands squarely in the tradition of historical lexicography that was developed in the 19th century, most notably by the editors of the *Oxford English Dictionary* (*OED*). Historical lexicography rose partly in reaction to an earlier, prescriptivist tradition that sought to dictate usage and to "fix" the language. Samuel Johnson's dictionary of English is one of the great examples of that earlier tradition, as are the French dictionaries produced then (and now) by the Académie française. But the *OED* sought instead to be a complete inventory of the language that captured all forms and uses, however ancient and obscure, following the suggestion of Trench (1860: 5). The contemporary zeitgeist is well captured by a quotation from the 1880 *New York Times*:

The modern spirit of philological inquiry concerns itself less with what a language is than with what it was. It treats a word as archaeology treats an Etruscan mirror or a piece of antique Peruvian pottery, suppressing all such idle emotions as admiration for external beauty or curiosity as to use or meaning until the history of its growth or construction has been learned by a patient study of its older forms. (*New York Times*, April 4, 1880, 4)

The *OED* has succeeded brilliantly in elaborating the history and development of words' senses and in providing a detailed view of changes in the English lexicon from the time of our earliest written sources. Seeking to build on this success, the *OLD* explicitly followed in the *OED*'s path.[5] In addition to tracing the historical development of words' meanings, these dictionaries carefully categorize senses according to contexts in which words appear, and highlight fine-grained nuances of meaning. The *OLD* frequently offers a range of convenient translations for each of these uses.

All together, these qualities make the *OLD* very attractive to modern philologists, and its entry for *horror* exhibits them all:

horror ~ōris, *m.* [HORREO + -OR]

1 The action or quality (in hair) of rising or standing stiffly, bristling. **b** the ruffling (of the surface of water).

nullo..~ore comarum excussae laurus Luc.5.154; non ullo ~ore comarum terribilis Val.Fl.1.229; simplex...~ore decoro crinis Stat.*Silv.*2.6.43; capillos a fronte..retro agere us sit ~ore ills terribilis Quint.*Inst.*11.3.160; ardorem luminum, ~orem capillorum Ps.Quint.*decl.*3.7 **b** pontus..non ~ore tremit, non solis imagine uibrat Lucan.5.446; niger inficit ~or terga maris 5.564; occidit ~or aequoris Stat.*Silv.*5.4.5.

2 Stiffness, rigidity (arising from cold, etc.).

ualidi ferri natura et frigidus ~or Lucr.6.1011; subito ~ore artus reigere coepertunt Curt.3.5.3; miti..~ore quieuit (humus) Petron.123,l.186.

3 Roughness or uncouthness of appearance; (also transf. of literary style). **b** discordant sound.

cui rusticus ~or in armis Stat.*Theb.*11.32; nullus ~or in cultu, nulla tristitia Plin.*epist.*1.10.6; capillus ~ore implexus atque impeditus Apul.*Apol.*4; ueterem illum ~orem dicendi Quint.*inst.*8.5.34. **b.** serrae stridentis acerbum ~orem Lucr.2.411; clarescunt sonitus armorumque ingruit ~or Verg.*Aen.*2.301; nec tota classicus ~or nocte dieque gemit *Laus Pis.*141.

4 Grimness, severity (of manner).

nec frons triste rigens nimiusque in moribus ~or Stat.*Silv.*5.1.64.

5 Shivering, trembling (resulting from cold or other physical causes). **b** trembling (from fear, apprehension, etc.).

tremulus maestis orietur fletibus ~or Prop.1.5.15; (frigus) summam cutem facit pallidam, aridam, duram, nigram; ex hos ~ores tremoresque nascuntur Cels.1.9.4; nocturnum frigus..~ore corpora adfecit Curt.8.10.7; quos externa causa in ~orem agit Sen.*nat.*6.24.4; ——(*from illness*) quoniam iam sine ~ore est, spero esse ut uolumus Cic.*Att.*12.6.4; incipiunt (*sc.* quartanae) fere ab ~ore Cels.3.3.1; nonnumquam manus quoque destra torquetur, ~or calidus est 4.15.1; aliarum (febrium) cum ~ore et multa membrorum quassatione uenientum Sen.*epist*.95.17; ~ores frigidos Plin.*nat*.20.136; ~ores febrem praecedentes Larg.95. **b** mihi ~or membra misero percipit dictis tuis Pl.*Amph*.1118; frigida multa comes formidinis aura quae ciet ~orem membris et concitat artus Lucr.3.291; perculit ~or membra ducis Lucan.1.193; ecce repens superis aniumum lymphantibus ~or Thiodamanta subit Stat.*Theb*.10.160; (*poet.*) galeae..tremunt ~ore comarum 8.389.

6 Dread, horror, consternation. **b** fear of the supernatural, awe, dread.

iam ea res me ~ore adficit Pl.*Amph*.1068; di immortales, qui me ~or perfudit! Cic.*Att*.8.6.3; me tum primum aeuus circumstetit ~or Verg.*Aen*.2.559; ~or ingens spectantes circumsteti ~or Verg.*Aen*.2.559; ~or ingens spectantes perstringit Liv.1.25.4; praesentis periculi species omnium simul corda animosque !ore perstrinxerat Curt.5.9.1; in uiscera saeuus ~or iit Stat.*Theb*.5.239; iam non ira subit, sed leti nuntius ~or 9.863; ~or animum subit quotiens recordor feralem introitum Tac.*hist*.1.37; impietatis reum postulat. ~or omnium Plin.*epist*.7.33.8; (*pl.*) insanis lymphatam ~oribus urbem Stat.*Theb*.10.557; —— (*personified*) tum torua Erinys sonuit et caecus Furor ~orque Sen.*Oed*.591. **b** unde etiam nunc est mortalibus insitus ~or qui delubra deum noua toto suscitat orbi terrarum Lucr.5.1165; silere omnia haut alo qam solitudinum ~ore Plin.*nat*.5.7; hic numinis ingens ~or Val.Fl.2.433; uacuus..silentia seruat ~or Stat.*Theb*.4.424; non sine quodam sacrilegii metu et ~ore Flor.*epit*.1.33 (2.17.12); —— (*cf.*) his ibi me rebus quaedam diuina uoluptas percipit atque ~or Lucr.3.29; laetus..per artus ~or iit Stat.*Theb*. 1.494.

7 A quality or condition inspiring horror; a source or cause of horror. **b** a thing which brings terror; a person, etc. causing terror to a particular place.

diri tum plena ~oris imago Lucan.3.9; Stat.*Theb*.3.75; abiit ~orque uigorque ex oculis 10.641; medio noctis ~ore stricto mucrone prosiluit Ps.Quint.*decl*.7.3; —— quod spectare facientes in eadem harena feras quoque ~or est Plin.*nat*.28.4; at patulas saltu transmittere fossas ~or equis Stat.*Theb*.10.522. **b** ubi multifidus ruptis e nubibus ~or (*i.e. lightning*) effugit Val.Fl.4.661;patrias saeuus uenit ~or ad aures fata domus..ferens 8.134; —— Scipiadas, belli fulmen, Carthaginis ~or Lucr.3.1034; Acron..Roma, tuis quondam finibus ~or erat Prop.4.10.10; Sen.*epist*.86.5; orbis Hiberi ~or Lucr.5.343; nemoris sacer ~or Achaei, terrigna..serpens Stat.*Theb*.5.505.

The first meanings listed are those apparently closest to the word's origin as a verbal noun derived from *horreo*, whose conjectured etymological meaning is something like "to bristle," with more extended meanings placed farther down. Thus the notion of "bristling" gives rise to "ruffling", then to "stiffness", then to "roughness" / "uncouthness", and then to "grimness" as *horror's* core meaning spreads into different contexts.

The chain of intuitive family resemblances breaks off somewhat after sense 4, but the connections between the next three meanings — "shivering", "dread, horror, consternation" and "a quality or condition inspiring horror" — are obviously connected. Furthermore, the contexts in which the word appears are meticulously categorized, even to the point of distinguishing *horror* as "dread" arising through supernatural causes from that arising through natural ones. This arrangement of senses allows the dictionary's user to see related chains of meaning and provides a good sense of the contexts in which *horror* appeared.

But the *OLD*'s arrangement of senses almost certainly misleads modern users who want to understand how ancient speakers typically apprehended the word. First, it is not clear that the first senses the *OLD* lists are actually the oldest or most basic. All of the examples under meanings 1.a. and 1.b. are post-Augustan, as are most of those under 2, 3, and 4. The oldest attested meanings of *horror*, found in Plautus and Lucilius, are meanings 5 and 6. More importantly, meanings 5 and 6 are the most common meanings throughout the entire period covered by the *OLD*, accounting for almost two-thirds of all uses of *horror*. But meaning 1.a. comprises only about 5% of all uses; meaning 1.b about 3%; and meanings 2, 3, and 4 less than 1% each.[13]

2. Basic senses and sense divisions in linguistics

These facts invite the question: what constitutes a basic sense? From the point of view of native speakers, who know little or nothing about etymology, a word's basic senses are those that it means most often and that it brings *per se* into a context without need of further contextual modification.[7] A large body of psycholinguistic evidence establishes that the most frequently-used senses of words are activated more strongly in the mind and are accessed more easily during the act of comprehension than are more rarely-used ones.[8] Thus, in neutral contexts that don't favor one sense over another, listeners or readers are more likely to be aware of a word's frequently-used senses than its rarely-used ones. If our goal is to apprehend a word as an ancient speaker of Latin probably did, we should consider senses 5-6 more basic than those listed earlier, since they are used more often at all periods covered by the *OLD* than any of the others.

To give an example of this phenomenon in English, most speakers of American English, upon reading the sentence "She was looking at a plant", would become aware of *plant*'s frequent botanical meaning, and probably not "a person placed secretly in a group or organization". Most speakers, in most circumstances, would not even perceive the word as ambiguous. But a non-native speaker of English, unfamiliar with the word, and depending on a dictionary entry, would probably have a very different perception, and, lacking contextual clues, might be in doubt about the sense of "plant" unless the dictionary provided information about sense frequency. Imagine the reader's possible confusion if the least-frequent meaning appeared first in the dictionary. Thus knowledge of the frequency of different senses of ancient words is important for modern readers trying to choose between competing senses when contextual clues are not clear. But the *OLD* entry gives no clear information in this respect (although frequently-used senses do tend to have more examples listed), whereas some newer bilingual dictionaries of modern languages have begun listing the more frequent senses first in the dictionary entry to address this problem.[9]

2.1. Senses and contexts

We can also understand a basic sense to be one that functions in a wide range of contexts and that doesn't depend upon particular elements of context to elicit specific meanings. Thus the "codex" sense of the English word *book* is more basic than the sense "words to which music is set", which is elicited only in the narrow context of musical theatre. But the first four meanings provided by the *OLD* for *horror* appear to be very context-dependent. Meaning 1, "bristling or standing on end (of hair)" only appears in contexts where hair is explicitly mentioned, and it is doubtful whether *horror* can have this meaning in the absence of such a mention. The same is true of "ruffling (of the surface of water)", which never occurs without an explicit mention of a body of water; of "discordant sound", which only occurs in contexts including words denoting sounds; and of "uncouthness of appearance", which occurs only in contexts explicitly mentioning peoples' appearance. Thus, since these meanings are the result of *horror*'s interactions with very specific contexts, they are peripheral rather than central and basic senses.[10] Of course, that does not mean that they are not worthy of mention in a dictionary, but the *OLD* puts these context-dependent and rather peripheral meanings on the same level as *horror*'s more context-independent and central ones, giving us a distorted picture of the word's internal semantic relations.

2.2. Senses and semantic frames

A further problem is that even the basic senses of *horror* have important semantic features that are not easily captured by most second-language dictionaries' technique of using one-word translations or a series of second-language synonyms, such as "dread, horror, consternation".[11] Here, close attention to the contexts of *horror*'s commonest uses shows that they are often associated with the autonomic reflexes associated with fear, cold temperature, or fever, which include, in addition to shivering or shuddering, a sensation of cold (or cold sweat), rigidity of the subcutaneous muscles and skin, pallor, and piloerection (hair standing on end):[12]

(1)   mihi **frigidus** horror
membra quatit gelidusque coit formidine sanguis (Verg. *Aen.* 3,29-30)

(2)   nunc quoque **frigidus** artus,
dum loquor, horror habet (Ov. *met.* 9,290-1)

(3)   mihi **gelidus** horror ac tremor somnum excutit (Sen. *Tro.* 457)

(4)   cor pepulit horror, membra torpescunt **gelu**
pectusque tremuit. (Sen. *Med.* 926-7)

(5)   **gelidus**que sub ossa
pervasit miseris conspecti consulis horror (Sil. 5,390-1)

(6)   ecce meum timido iam **frigore** pectus
labitur et nequeo, quamvis movet ominis horror,
claudere suspensos oculorum in margine fletus (Stat. *Silv.* 3,2,51-53)

(7)   iamque propinquantum tacitus penetravit in artus
horror et occulto **riguerunt frigore** membra (Sil. 6,169-70)

(8)   Horrore vinctum trepidus astrinxit **rigor** ([Sen.] *Oct.* 826)

(9)   vixque ingressi subito horrore artus **rigere** coeperunt; **pallor** deinde
suffusus est (Curt. 3,5,3)

(10) obstipui, **gelidus**que **comas** erexerat horror (Ov. *epist.* 16,67)

(11) Iamdudum Minyas hac vates ambage ducemque
terrificat; sed enim contra Phoebeius Idmon
non **pallore** virens, non ullo horrore **comarum**
terribilis, plenus fatis Phoeboque quieto... (Val. Fl. 1,227-30)

(12) me **luridus** occupat horror (Ov. *met.* 14,198).

Of course these examples do not show that *horror* denotes these reflexes, but only that mention of *horror* probably evoked them as elements of a semantic frame[13] in which the word typically functioned for Latin speakers.

Furthermore, *horror* frequently interacts with human beings according to a pattern in which *horror* is the subject of an active verb whose direct object or complement is a person or part of the person, as in examples (1), (2), (3) and (5) above, and in (13) below:

(13) nam mihi horror **membra** misero **percipit** dictis tuis (Plaut. *Amph.* 1118)

(14) his ibi **me** rebus quaedam divina voluptas
      percipit atque horror (Lucr. 3,28-9)

(15) qui **me** horror **perfudit** (Cic. *Att.* 8,6,3)

(16) horror ingens **spectantes perstringit** (Liv. 1,25,4)

(17) horror **animum subit** quotiens recordor feralem introitum et hanc solam Galbae victoriam (Tac. *hist.* 1,37,10)

(18)   tum **perculit** horror
      membra ducis (Lucan. 1,192-3)

(19) horror **habet sensus** (Stat. *Silv.* 2,1,166)

(20)   pavor artus
      protinus atque ingens **Aeetida perculit** horror (Val. Fl. 6,480-1)

This feature of *horror*'s meaning – that it is often conceived as an external and active force that strikes, seizes, or penetrates human beings – is only weakly, if at all, captured by the *OLD*'s glosses, because the English words "dread", "consternation", "shivering" and "trembling" rarely behave this way, either syntactically or in their common metaphorical uses.

We see a similar phenomenon in one of *horror*'s more prosaic and frequent uses, namely, in the context of illness, where *horror* often arrives accompanied by fever:

(21) igitur si cui cum horrore febris accessit (Cels. 3,15,1)

(22) si quarto die cum horrore febris revertitur (Cels. 3,15,1)

(23) febres cum horrore venientes (Plin. *nat*. 23,92)

(24) febribus, quae cum horrore veniant (Plin. *nat*. 26,116)

Less frequently, *horror* arises or is incited by some other cause, and it may also become calm:

(25) frigus ... horrores in febribus excitat (Cels. 2,1,10)

(26) aquilo ... horrores excitat (Cels. 2,1,10)

(27) ex hoc horrores tremoresque nascuntur (Cels. 1,9,4)

(28) interdum sic evenit, ut horror oriatur (Cels. 3,9,1)

(29) nonnumquam horror aut febris oritur (Cels. 5,28,1b)

(30) nam fere talis horror ab his oritur, quae biliosa in stomacho resederunt. (Cels. 3,12,3)

(31) si tardius horror quiescit (Cels. 3,12,6)

Most medical treatments for *horror* aim at driving it out or keeping it away:

(32) bibat aquam calidam cum pipere: siquidem ea quoque adsumpta calorem movent, qui horrorem non admittit (Cels. 3,12,4)

(33) balineum neque ante febrem neque postea temptandum erit, nisi interdum iam horrore discusso. horror ipse per ea, quae supra scripta sunt, expugnandus (Cels. 3,15,4,3)

(34) lieni et pota et inlita prosunt. decocuntur et contra horrores febrium erputionesque pituitae aut in vino teruntur. (Plin. *nat*. 24,76)

(35) quae omnes horrores coercet (Plin. *nat*. 26,117)

(36) idem pollere e ventre exemptos lapillos adversus febrium horrores
     venientes tradunt (Plin. *nat.* 28,107)

(37) et contra algores horroresque prodest manibus pedibusque confricatis
     cum oleo (Plin. *nat.* 31,119)

Although this meaning of *horror* shares a common referent with English
"chills" (as in the set expression "chills and fever"), *horror* functions
differently from the English word, since in English people typically
"have" or "get" chills and fever, whereas for the Romans, *horror* arrived,
arose, or was admitted, and could be forced or driven out. Again, capturing
the underlying metaphorical frame of these uses with single English words
as translations is not really possible.

2.3. Semantic clusters

Thus far we have been assuming, with the *OLD*, that the meanings we
have been discussing are in fact discrete senses. But lexicographers are
increasingly abandoning the notion that word meanings can be neatly
divided in this way:

> ... linguists and lexicographers alike are approaching a more sophisticated
> understanding of polysemy. Specifically, the notion that a word can be
> neatly divided into discrete, mutually-exclusive senses is giving way to a
> model that more accurately reflects what the linguistic data is telling us: a
> model in which meanings are discovered in clusters of instances that share
> enough common features to justify being treated as a coherent "meaning
> group" .... This makes the task of sense differentiation both more
> complicated and more interesting ... (Atkins et al. 2003: 334)

For *horror,* in many cases, no clear denotational (as opposed to
logical) boundary exists between its emotional and physiological
meanings.[14] In many contexts, even when one of its dominant notions
(emotional or physiological) is more strongly foregrounded, the other is
frequently also present, as in ex. (1), (2), (10), (12), and in the following:

(38) Horrore quatior, fata quo vergant timens,
     trepidumque gemino pectus affectu labat (Sen. *Oed.* 206-7).

(39) ac membra et sensus gelidus stupefecerat horror (Sil. 9,122)

(40) ut vero Alcimeden etiamnum in murmure truncos
      ferre patris vultus et egentem sanguinis ensem
      conspexi, riguere comae atque in viscera saevus
      horror iit (Stat. *Theb.* 5,236-9)

(41) deriguere amini, manibusque horrore remissis
      arma aliena cadunt (Stat. *Theb.* 5.396-7)

Thus *horror*'s emotional and physical meanings are not antagonistic
senses in the same way that, for example, *table* (as a piece of furniture)
and *table* (as a matrix of information) are, where both senses cannot be
invoked simultaneously without producing a pun, or "zeugmatic oddness".[15]
Rather, the two meanings are best described as sense facets rather than full
senses, since they commonly appear together in a harmonious semantic
complex.[16]

   In the same way, *horror*'s third most frequent use, denoting some
cause of fear, can't always be distinguished from its meaning denoting an
emotion, since "fear", conceived as something that comes upon one from
outside, and "cause of fear", are often not distinct in actual use. In a
number of instances, *horror* appears as a disembodied entity, and the word
vaguely communicates either something that inspires an emotion, or the
emotion felt, or which could be felt, by those who encounter it:

(42) at me tum primum saevus circumstetit horror (Verg. *Aen.* 2,559)

(43) incolarum neminem interdiu cerni; silere omnia haut alio quam
      solitudinum horrore (Plin. *nat.* 5,7)

(44) subter operta quies, vacuusque silentia servat
      horror et exclusae pallet male lucis imago (Stat. *Theb.* 4,423-4)

(45) urbem in conspectu belli suprema parantis
      territat insomnem nox atra diemque minatur
      discurrunt muris; nil saeptum horrore sub illo,
      nil fidum satis, invalidaeque Amphione arces (Stat. *Theb.* 7,453-6)

(46) vix primo proferre gradum et munimina valli
      solvere, vix totas reserare audacia portas;
      stant veteres ante ora metus campique vacantis
      horror (Stat. *Theb.* 12,9-12)

(47)   hic numinis ingens
        horror et incautis decreta piacula linguis (Val. Fl. 2,432-3)

Thus the three most common meanings of *horror* are best understood as
sense facets organized in a meaning cluster rather than as three fully
distinct senses, and it may be represented graphically, as below, where the
indistinct lines represent indistinct semantic boundaries:

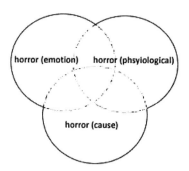

2.4. Established vs. nonce-senses

Although I have just argued that the *OLD* has distinguished senses which
are not truly distinct, I also believe that it fails to make distinctions that
could usefully be made. Specifically, it does not regularly distinguish
between well-established senses of a word and those that are creative and
temporary. Such *ad-hoc* meanings, sometimes called "nonce-senses", are
generally thought to differ from established ones because their meanings
are inferred or created on the spot by the listener or reader rather than
retrieved from the mental lexicon.[17] Since such uses tend to appear in
literary genres such as poetry or oratory in which writers often strive for
effect, I assume that it is these uses' aesthetic and cognitive effects, in
addition to their semantic content, which authors seek. And when
dictionaries obscure these effects, we lose important information about
aesthetic features such as tone and style.

    To put the problem into the context of English, consider the first three
lines of Wallace Stevens' much-anthologized poem *The Emperor of Ice-
Cream*:

(48) Call the roller of big cigars,
The muscular one, and bid him whip
in kitchen cups concupiscent curds.

Stevens' expression, "concupiscent curds", is singular and striking, and not just for its pleasing alliteration. The established meanings of the words make little sense in this context, and the reader is invited to work out what Stevens intends. We surmise that the expression refers to ice-cream, and, using our knowledge of the words' usual meanings as clues, we could decide that Stevens means that ice-cream is extravagantly, perhaps sinfully, desirable. A good deal of our pleasure in reading the line comes from an awareness that Stevens has used "curds" outside of its typical semantic field, and also from the distance he creates between the established sense of "concupiscence" ("eagerly desirous; lustful" – *OED*) and its temporary, *ad-hoc* one ("desirable"). That is, it's obvious that Stevens chose these words not only to communicate specific meanings, but also to produce aesthetic effects.[18]

Imagine yourself, then, as a 40th-century scholar of 20th-century English, trying to puzzle out the meaning of Stevens' ancient poem, poring over the entry for "concupiscent" in a 40th-century historical dictionary of English, and finding there a citation for Stevens' use. We might read there something like

1. Eagerly desirous; lustful. **1834** LAMB *Let. to Coleridge* (L.), The concupiscent clown is overdone. **1875** JOWETT *Plato* (ed. 2) III. 57 The division of the soul into the rational, irascible, and concupiscent elements.
2. Desirable. **1922** W. STEVENS *Emp. of Ice-Cream*. Bid him whip in kitchen cups concupiscent curds.[19]

Although the entry would help make sense of the semantic content of Stevens' line, it would mislead us insofar as it would encourage us to think that "desirable" was an established sense of "concupiscent" in the early 20th century. Thus it would obscure for us the invitation to aesthetic play which Stevens extended to his contemporary readers, and thereby enervate Stevens' vivacious phrase.

Unfortunately, that is what Latin dictionaries do for us when they provide convenient and ordinary English translations for creative, nonce-uses of Latin words, and promote those uses to the status of full, established senses. For example, in our entry, the *OLD* provides for *horror* a sense "discordant sound" in this passage from Lucretius:

(49) ne tu forte putes serrae stridentis acerbum
      horrorem constare elementis levibus aeque
      ac musaea mele, per chordas organici quae
      mobilibus digitis expergefacta figurant (Lucr. 2,410-13)

"Discordant sound" renders Lucretius's expression *serrae stridentis acerbum horrorem* into something easily comprehensible to English speakers ("the bitter discordant sound of the shrieking saw"), but I think it highly unlikely that *horror* ever had such an established sense. Rather, the meaning that *horror* contributes is probably the ordinary one denoting a physical reaction – a shudder or shiver – but its use is metonymic in that the whole phrase refers obliquely to a very unpleasant sound by naming the revulsive shudder or shiver that it causes.[20] Lucretius's use of *horror* in this reading is both unusual and striking, and we can approximate the metonymy in English with something like, "a shiver of squeaking fingernails on the blackboard".[21] But the *OLD*'s gloss hides Lucretius's creative and unusual metonymy from the modern English speaker.[22]

In fact, most of the senses the *OLD* proposes under headings 1-4 of the entry for *horror* look like creative, nonce uses that are derived from *horror*'s more dominant meanings, if we assume that novel expressions in general are likelier to be based upon ordinary and well-known meanings rather than ancient or rare etymological ones. For example, the uses translated under 1.b as "ruffling (of the surface of water)" appear to be personified uses of *horror* (as "shuddering") where the experiencer of *horror* is the sea rather than a human being. In particular, *niger inficit horror terga maris* (Lucan. 5,564) follows the pattern of *horror*'s typical activity described above in lines like *frigidus horror membra quatit* (Verg. *Aen.* 3,29).[23] But the gloss "ruffling" eviscerates the powerful metaphor. So also the examples cited under proposed sense 2, "stiffness, rigidity" look like nonce-uses of *horror* that narrow its meaning to a normally backgrounded semantic feature of *horror*, namely, the subcutaneous tightening of muscles that accompanies *horror*. In these instances, the writer has moved that idea out of its typical semantic frame involving people as experiencers and transferred it to inanimate substances such as iron:

(50) nec res ulla magis primoribus ex elementis
      indupedita suis arte conexa cohaeret
      quam validi ferri natura et frigidus horror (Lucr. 6,1011-13)[24]

Alternatively, Lucretius might simply be referring to iron metonymically by naming the cold shiver we feel when we come into contact with it, or the fear it can inspire when used as a weapon.

We see another probable nonce-sense in a few instances where *horror* refers to aspects of people's manner or appearance that could be thought mildly frightening or off-putting (*OLD* meaning 3.a). Here the Latin writers are probably exploiting *horror*'s established, vague sense "cause of fear", and expect their readers to derive an attenuated meaning appropriate to the context, just as we do when we say things like "I loathe cocktail parties – they're such a bore!".[25] The word "loathe" does not (yet) have a sense, "feel mild dislike toward". Neither did *horror* have a separate sense "grimness" simply because its contextually-derived meaning is easily translated into English by that word. In this case – and probably in the cases of "ruffling" and "stiffness" – the *OLD* seems to have been seduced by the urge to assign an established sense to a Latin word because English has a word that conveniently captures *horror*'s nonce-meaning.

3. A linguistically informed Latin dictionary

The principles I've used to analyze the semantics of *horror* are different in important ways from those used in historical lexicography. They may be summed up as follows:

- Use frequency data to help determine basic senses.
- Avoid proliferating unwarranted sense distinctions.
- Avoid one-word translations that mislead.
- Represent complex or fuzzy sense relations as accurately as possible.
- Represent the difference between established and nonce-senses.

A dictionary entry for *horror* based on them might look something like this:

horror ~ōris, *m.* [HORREO + -OR]
1. A powerful feeling of fear or dread, often with reflexive shuddering or shivering, that typically strikes, seizes, or penetrates the human person. Frequently accompanied by a sensation of cold, muscle rigidity, and/or piloerection (common).

    nam mihi ~or membra misero percipit dictis tuis Plaut.*Amph*.1068; mihi frigidus ~or membra quatit gelidusque coit formidine sanguis Verg.*Aen*.3.29; obstipui, gelidusque comas erexerat ~or Ov.*epist*.16.67; praesentis periculi species omium simul corda animosque ~ore perstrinxerat Curt.5.9.1.2; mihi gelidus ~or ac tremor somnum excutit Sen.*Tro*.457; gelidusque sub ossa pervasit miseris conspecti consulis ~or Sil.5.39; riguere comae atque in viscera saevus ~or iit Stat.*Theb*.5.239.

Extended uses: referring to milder feelings such as awe or reverence that may be accompanied by a shiver or thrill (rare). me ... divina voluptas percipit atque ~or Lucr.3.29; laetusque per artus ~or iit Stat.*Theb*.1.494.

With the emotional component highlighted, though a physical reaction is not necessarily excluded (common): divorsi circumspicimus, ~or percipit Pacuv.trag.224; unde etiam nunc est mortalibus insitus ~or Lucr.5.1165; cum perfusus ~ore verabundusque adstitissem Liv.1.16.6.3; ~or animum subit Tac.*hist*.1.37.10; temere adeuntibus ~or quidam et metus obiciatur Suet.*Aug*.6.1.7; tacitus subrepsit fratribus ~or Stat.*Theb*.11.476; non sine quodam sacrilegii metu et ~ore Flor.*epit*.1.33.51.

2. Referring to physical reactions alone (reflexive shuddering, shivering, etc.).

As a medical term, *horror* usually arrives or arises with illness or fever and it may be driven out or warded off by various treatments (common in technical use): Voco ... ~orem, ubi corpus totum intremit Cels.3.3.3.2; illud ... ~ores in febribus excitat 2.1.12.3; calorem ... qui ~orem non admittit 3.12.4.5; tollit praeterea ~es febrem praecedentes Larg.95.9; febribus ... quae cum ~ore veniant Plin.*nat*.26.116.5. **In reaction to cold temperature** (rare): vestimentis frigus atque ~orem exacturum putet Lucil.26.643; ...descendit in flumen. vixque ingressi subito ~ore artus rigere coeperunt Curt.3.5.2.3.

Extended uses: Metaphorically referring to the motion of water (rare): niger inficit ~or terga maris Lucan.5.564; pontus non ~ore tremit 5.446; occidit ~or aequoris Stat.*Silv*.5.4.5. **Referring to the earth shaking** (rare) totum nemus concussit ~or, terra se retro dedit Sen.*Oed*.576; ? miti ... ~ore quievit (humus) Petron.123 l.186 nisi illum ~orem soli equitum virorumque discursus et mota vehementius arma fecerunt Flor.*Epit*.1.22.58 **Referring to piloerection alone,**

sometimes **extended to hairstyles or helmet crests**: nulloque ~ore comarum excussae laurus Lucan.5.154; non ardorem luminum, ~orem capillorum, fremitum indignationis Ps.Quint.*decl*.3.7; simplexque ~ore decoro crinis Stat.*Silv*.2.6.43; cui torva genis ~ore decoro cassis *Theb*.2.716. **As a metonym for the quality of rigidity in inanimate objects** (rare, uncertain) ? validi ferri natura et frigidus ~or Lucr.6.1011; ? miti ... ~ore quievit (humus) Petron.123 l.186.

3. Something that might cause fear, dread, shuddering, etc. (common).

Scipiadas, belli fulmen, Carthaginis ~or, ossa dedit terrae Lucr.3.1034; Acron ... Roma, tuis quondam finibus ~or erat Prop.4.10.10; nemoris sacer ~or Achaei, terrigena ... serpens Stat.*Theb*.5.505; at patulas saltu transmittere fossas ~or equis 10.522; ubi multifudus ruptis e nubibus ~or effugit Val.Fl.4.661. **Sometimes with unclear distinction between a cause of fear and the emotion it inspires**: et saevus campis magis ac magis ~or crebrescit Verg.*Aen*.12.406; diri tum plena ~oris imago Lucan.3.9; quod spectare facientes in eadem harena feras quoque ~or est Plin.*Nat*.28.4.5.

Extended uses: Referring to things that might cause only mild fear or distaste, e.g. **unpolished speech** (rare) veterum illum ~orem dicendi malim quam istam novam licentiam Quint.*inst*.8.5.34.4. **Referring to a person's appearance** (rare) cui rusticus ~ore in armis Stat.*Theb*.11.32; nec frons triste rigens nimiusque in moribus ~or *Silv*.5.1.64; nullus ~or in cultu, nulla tristitia Plin.*epist*.1.10.7.1. **Referring to unpleasant sounds that may cause a revulsive shudder** (rare): serrae stridentis acerbum ~orem Lucr.2.411.

Conclusion

I believe this approach provides more accurate information about the internal semantic relations of *horror* than does the *OLD's*. It emphasizes the word's dominant, established meanings and subordinates its peripheral and unestablished ones; it orders the main meanings according to frequency; it locates senses in their typical semantic frames; it does not proliferate senses unnecessarily; it represents the vagueness and semantic fuzziness of the word; it is forthright about the fact that we sometimes don't know what the ancients meant when they used the word; and it offers few of the kinds of glosses that hide as much as they reveal. If our aim in studying ancient languages is, to the extent possible, to try to take the ancients on their own terms, then our dictionaries can help us by discouraging us from viewing the ancient lexicon through the semantic templates encoded in our own.

Notes

[1] Bensoussan and Laufer (1984); Levenston (1979); Kantor (1978).

[2] Defined as a word's having multiple, related meanings. It is standardly distinguished from homonymy, in which a word has more than one unrelated meaning, and also from vagueness, in which a word has a single, broad or general meaning.

[3] Flobert (1983); Ernout (1971); Barrow (1968).

[4] I will not consider the word's entry in the *Thesaurus Linguae Latinae* in order to focus on problems of representing word meanings in a second-language dictionary, which are not all relevant to the *TLL*'s single-language approach.

[5] "The *Oxford Latin Dictionary* is based on an entirely fresh reading of the Latin sources. It follows, generally speaking, the principles of the *Oxford English Dictionary*, and its formal layout of articles is similar". Glare (1982: v).

[6] These data are based on a comprehensive corpus search of the classical Latin authors on the Packard Humanities Institute CD-ROM 5.3 and my own semantic analysis of the search results.

[7] Cruse (1986: 79) and (2000: 200).

[8] Binder and Rayner (1998); Binder and Morris (1995); Dopkins, Morris and Rayner (1992); Duffy, Morris and Rayner (1988); Kellas et al. (1991); Paul et al. (1992); Rayner and Duffy (1986); Rayner and Frazier (1989); Sereno (1995); Sereno et al. (1992).

[9] Adamska-Sałaciak (2006: 93-96); Schofield (1997: 288-292).

[10] If they are senses at all. At best they should be considered sub-senses (see Cruse (2000: 119) and further discussion below).

[11] "There are no true 'equations' between LI and L2 items, even in such seemingly straightforward cases as concrete nouns". Peotrowski (1994: 65).

[12] "Temperature regulation and fear reaction are both controlled in the hypothalamus, as a part of the sympathetic autonomic nervous system", Ganong (1995: 214). See also Rhoads and Tanner (1995): "When the organism perceives an emergency situation, the sympathetic division [of the autonomic nervous system] can activate many effectors at once, resulting in a fight-or-flight response" (p. 118); "Frightening thoughts can trigger a fight-or-flight reaction .... The skin responds by vasoconstriction, sweating, and piloerection (raising of the body hairs), reactions otherwise associated with temperature regulation. Individuals in a state of intense fear therefore exhibit pallor, 'cold sweat' (so designated because sweating is inappropriately associated with vasoconstricted skin), and 'goosebumps' due to contraction of the pilomotor muscles" (p. 125).

[13] "Semantic frame" is here used loosely in the sense pioneered by Fillmore: "the conceptual structures and patterns of beliefs, practices, institutions, images, etc. that provide a foundation for meaningful interaction in a given speech community", Fillmore (2003: 235). See also Fillmore (1976), (1977), (1982), and the website for FrameNet: http://framenet.icsi.berkeley.edu/. One need not fully subscribe to Fillmore's lexicographical program in order to appreciate its ability to capture important semantic features that traditional dictionaries often miss.

[14] Many words have this property of denoting a plurality of existent things which are logically and ontologically distinct but semantically unified, such as the word *book*, which can denote simultaneously a physical entity and an intellectual one: "Michael's book is very well-written, but its cover art is rather ugly". Nunberg (1979) discusses many similar examples in detail.

[15] The perception of zeugmatic oddness when two senses are called into use at once is one of the traditional tests for polysemy, such as in the much-used example, "Jim and his driver's license expired on the same day". The perceptible pun on "expired" is taken as evidence for the word's polysemy, but many semanticists dispute the test's reliability: see Cruse (1986: 61-4) and Geeraerts (1993: 229-30; 237-9).

[16] Geeraerts (1993) gives the most detailed account of the weaknesses in traditional methods of sense division; see also Taylor (2002), Tuggy (1993), Cruse (2002), Dowty (2002), and Goddard (2002), and Nunberg (1979: 147-54). The term "facet" is borrowed from Cruse (2000) and (2002).

[17] Clark (1983); Cruse (2000), 201; Carston (2002).

[18] Perhaps that is part of what Stevens meant when he said that this poem "contains something of the essential gaudiness of poetry" (Stevens 1966, 263).

[19] This *OED* entry is fictitious, although it is based on the lemma for "concupiscent" found in the 1987 edition. Stevens' use of the word is not noted in the current version of the *OED*.

[20] Fingernails scraped on a blackboard or metal scraped on metal, or wood, produces this effect on many people, as can unpleasant tastes (as is intimated by Lucretius's use of *acerbus*).

[21] The fact that this metonymy may not work very well in English does not argue against Lucretius's using it in Latin. The effectiveness of such creative uses depends on the author's manipulation of the complex web of meaning connections and associations in the minds of native speakers of his language. The fact that "shiver" is less amenable to such a metonymic use in English only means that English words' connections and associations do not map very well onto those of Latin words, which is one of the main points of this article.

[22] The *OLD* cites two other passages in which *horror* apparently denotes "discordant sound", but both of them are more parsimoniously explained by attributing ordinary and frequent senses to the word. One is in the *Aeneid*:

> Diverso interea miscentur moenia luctu,
> et magis atque magis, quamquam secreta parentis
> Anchisae domus arboribusque obtecta recessit,
> clarescunt sonitus, armorumque ingruit horror.
> Excutior somno ... (Verg. *Aen.* 2,298-302)

Horror can more easily be thought to contribute its more frequent meanings here (fear; something that causes fear) than "discordant sound". In fact, *horror* may be thought to *refer* to the sound of arms in this passage - if that is what is frightening about them - but that does not mean that *horror* has a sense "discordant sound" any more than it has a sense "reptile" because Statius uses the word to refer to one (nemoris sacer horror Achaei, terrigena ... serpens (Theb. 5,505)). The *OLD* also cites the Laus Pisonis for a "sound" sense of horror in this passage:

> ... nec semper in armis
> bellica turba manet, nec tota classicus horror
> nocte dieque gemit ... (140-2)

The proposed meaning of *classicus horror* is "the discordant sound of the trumpet call". But *horror* construed in a sense "discordant sound" is unlikely as the subject of *gemit* because *gemere* typically takes a person, animal, or thing that makes a sound as its subject; nowhere else in extant Latin literature does a sound function as its own subject. Furthermore, the concept of a sound making a sound is logically incoherent. The *OLD*'s interpretation also relies on the word *classicus* being understood as "of or connected with the trumpet call" (*OLD* s.v. *classicus*), an adjectival interpretation based on a single substantival use of *classicus*, denoting one who blows a horn to summon the *comitia centuriata*. But that substantival use is attested only at Varro *ling.* 6,92, and the proposed adjectival use is attested only here in the *Laus Pisonis*. That is a slender philological thread on which to hang the formation of a word's sense. A more robust approach would attribute common meanings to both words: to *horror* its frequent meaning "cause of fear", and to *classicus* its usual denotation of a military or naval connection. Thus the phrase *horror classicus* denotes some military or naval cause of fear, that is, the fearsome navy or the marines, and the sound referred to by *gemit* may be either that of wooden ships groaning at sea or the shouting of the sailors and soldiers. This interpretation also makes *horror classicus* jibe rhetorically with its syntactic twin in the sentence, *bellica turba*, in that both refer collectively to military groups in an oblique way.

[23] The notion that the sea can shudder is not foreign to English: the phrase "shuddering sea" is found in Swinburne's "Tristram of Lyonesse", Longfellow's "Bells of Lynn", and Belloc's "The Romance of Tristan and Iseult").

[24] Also cited under this definition is a passage of poetry from Petronius where *humus* is the experiencer of *horror*:

> Fortior ominibus movit Mavortia signa
> Caesar, et insolitos gressu prior occupat ausus.
> Prima quidem glacies et cana vincta pruina
> non pugnavit humus mitique horrore quievit.
> Sed postquam turmae nimbos fregere ligatos
> et pavidus quadrupes undarum vincula rupit,
> incaluere nives. (*Sat.* 122, 183-9)

Although this passage slightly highlights an idea of stiffness of the *humus* – because it is contrasted with its later loosening (*incaluere nives*) – it is easier to understand this as another personified or transferred use of *horror* ("shudder"):

"the earth did not fight back and lay quiet with a mild shudder" – perhaps from fear of Caesar, or cold, or both.
[25] Cruse (2000: 122) uses the term "impoverishment" to describe this kind of sense modulation.

References

Adamska-Salaciak, A. (2006) *Meaning and the Bilingual Dictionary. The Case of English and Polish,* Frankfurt am Main, Peter Lang.

Atkins, S., Rundell, M. and H. Sato (2003) "The contribution of FrameNet to practical lexicography" *International Journal of Lexicography* 16.3: 334-57.

Barrow, R.H. (1968) "The *Oxford Latin Dictionary*" *Greece and Rome* 2nd Ser. 15.2: 127-9.

Bensoussan, M. and B. Laufer (1984) "Lexical guessing in context in EFL reading comprehension" *Journal of Research in Reading* 7: 15-32.

Binder, K.S. and K. Rayner (1998) "Contextual strength does not modulate the subordinate bias effect: Evidence from eye fixations and self-paced reading" *Psychonomic Bulletin&Review* 5.2: 271-276.

Binder, K.S. and R.K. Morris (1995) "Eye movements and lexical ambiguity resolution: Effects of prior encounter and discourse topic" *Journal of Experimental Psychology: Learning, Memory, and Cognition* 21: 1-11.

Carston, R. (2002) "Metaphor, ad hoc concepts and word meaning – more questions than answers" *UCL Working Papers in Lingusitics* 14: 83-105.

Clark, H. (1983) "Making sense of nonce-sense", in G. d'Arcais and R. Jarvella (eds) *The process of language understanding*, London, John Wiley and Sons, 297-331.

Cruse, D.A. (1989) *Lexical Semantics*, Cambridge, Cambridge University Press.

—. (2000) *Meaning in Language*, Oxford-New York, Oxford University Press.

—. (2002) "Aspects of the micro-structure of word meanings", in Y. Raven and C. Leacock (eds) *Polysemy. Theoretical and computational approaches.* Oxford-New York, Oxford University Press, 30-51.

Dopkins, S., Morris, R.K. and K. Rayner (1992) "Lexical ambiguity and eye fixations in reading: A test of competing models of lexical ambiguity resolution" *Journal of Memory and Language* 31: 461-477.

Dowty, D. (2002) "'The garden swarms with bees' and the fallacy of 'argument alternations'", in Y. Raven and C. Leacock (eds) *Polysemy.*

Theoretical and computational approaches, Oxford-New York, Oxford University Press, 111-128.

Duffy, S.A., Morris, R.K. and K. Rayner (1988) "Lexical ambiguity and fixation times in reading" *Journal of Memory and Language* 27: 429-446.

Ernout, A. (1971) "Deux dictionnaires latins" *Revue de philologie* 45: 298-303.

Fillmore, C.J. (1976) "Frame semantics and the nature of language", in *Annals of the New York Academy of Sciences: Conference on the origin and development of language and speech* 280: 20-32.

—. (1977) "Scenes-and-frames semantics", in A. Zampolli (ed.) *Linguistic structures processing. Fundamental studies in computer science* no. 59, Amsterdam, North Holland Publishing, 55-88.

—. (1982) "Frame semantics", in *Linguistics in the morning calm*, Seoul, South Korea, Hanshin Publishing Co., 111-137.

Fillmore, C.J., Johnson, C. and M. Petruck (2003) "Background to FrameNet" *International Journal of Lexicography* 16.3: 235-50.

Flobert, P. (1983) "Un dictionnaire latin tout neuf" *Revue de Philologie* 57: 293-5.

Flores d'Arcais, G.B. and R. Jarvella (1983) *The Process of Language Understanding*, New York, John Wiley and Sons.

Ganong, W.F. (1995) *Review of Medical Physiology*, Norwalk, Connecticut, Appleton and Lange.

Geeraerts, D. (1993) "Vagueness's puzzles, polysemy's vagaries" *Cognitive Linguistics* 4.3: 223-72.

Glare, P.G.W. (1982) *Oxford Latin Dictionary*, Oxford-New York, Oxford University Press.

Goddard, C. (2002) "Polysemy: A problem of definition", in Y. Raven and C. Leacock (eds) *Polysemy. Theoretical and computational approaches,* Oxford-New York, Oxford University Press, 129-51.

Kantor, H. (1978) *An analysis of lexical errors in the interlanguage of Hebrew learners*, Bar-Ilan University (M.A. thesis).

Kellas, G., Paul, S.T., Martin, M. and G.B. Simpson (1991) "Contextual feature activation and meaning access", in G.B. Simpson (ed.) *Understanding word and sentence*, Amsterdam, Elsevier, 47-71.

Levenston, E.A. (1979) "Second language lexical acquisition: issues and problems" *Interlanguage Studies Bulletin* 4: 147-60.

Lyons, J. (1995) *Linguistic Semantics: An Introduction*, Cambridge, Cambridge University Press.

Nunberg, G. (1979) "The non-uniqueness of semantic solutions: Polysemy" *Linguistics and Philosophy* 2: 143-84.

Paul, S.T., Kellas, G., Martin, M. and M.B. Clark (1992) "The influence of contextual features on the activation of ambiguous word meanings" *Journal of Experimental Psychology: Learning, Memory, and Cognition* 18: 703-717.

Piotrowski, T. (1994) *Problems in Bilingual Lexicography*, Wrocław, Wydawnictwo Uniwesytetu Wrocławskiego.

Raven, Y. and C. Leacock (2002) *Polysemy. Theoretical and Computational Approaches,* Oxford-New York, Oxford University Press.

Rayner, K. and S.A. Duffy (1986) "Lexical complexity and fixation times in reading: Effects of word frequency, verb complexity, and lexical ambiguity" *Memory and Cognition* 14: 191-201.

Rayner, K. and L. Frazier (1989) "Selection mechanisms in reading lexically ambiguous words" *Journal of Experimental Psychology: Learning, Memory, and Cognition* 15: 779-790.

Rhoads, R.A. and G.A. Tanner (1995) *Medical Physiology*, Little, Brown and Company.

Scholfield, P. (1997) "Vocabulary reference works in foreign language learning", in N. Schmitt and M. McCarthy (eds) *Vocabulary: Description, acquisition and pedagogy*, Cambridge, Cambridge University Press, 279-302.

Sereno, S.C. (1995) "The resolution of lexical ambiguity: Evidence from an eye movement paradigm" *Journal of Experimental Psychology: Learning, Memory, and Cognition* 21: 582-595.

Sereno, S.C., Pacht, J.M. and K. Rayner (1992), "The effect of meaning frequency on processing lexically ambiguous words: Evidence from eye fixations" *Psychological Science* 3: 296-300.

Stevens, H. (ed.) (1966) *Letters of Wallace Stevens, Selected and Edited by Holly Stevens*, New York, Knopf.

Taylor, J.R. (2003) "Polysemy's paradoxes" *Language Sciences* 25: 637-55.

Trench, R.C. (1860) *On Some Deficiences in our English Dictionaries*, London, John Parker and Son.

Tuggy, D. (1993) "Ambiguity, polysemy, and vagueness" *Cognitive Linguistics* 4.3: 273-90.

THE DISCRETE-DENSE-COMPACT CATEGORIZATION IN LATIN

SOPHIE VAN LAER

Introduction

The usual distinction between *count nouns* (Fr. *noms comptables*) and *mass nouns* (Fr. *noms massifs*) requires that extra-linguistic entities denoted by count nouns (e.g. *chair, plate, book, apple*) should be conceived as individual and countable entities, while those denoted by mass nouns (e.g. *flour, milk, butter*) are rather conceived as "an unbounded mass or aggregate of stuff or substance".[1] The two categories also differ in their syntactic properties: a count noun occurs with determiners such as Engl. *a/an, many* or with numerals, while a mass noun occurs with other determiners such as Engl. *some, much.*[2]

But in discourse this distinction is not so clear-cut, since a count noun may be used as a mass noun (Fr. *Ça, c'est de la voiture* said when looking at a beautiful car), while, conversely, a mass noun may be used as a count noun, e.g. *they served three or four (different) wines*; Fr. *ils ont servi trois ou quatre vins* (*différents*). Moreover, the use of a measure word denoting a specific quantity of substance (*glass, piece*; Fr. *verre, morceau*) builds up a count phrase from a mass noun, e.g. *a glass of milk, two pieces of sugar*; Fr. *un verre de lait, deux morceaux de sucre*. Therefore, quantification applied to a mass noun is based on an *operation of sampling*.[3]

1. The /discrete-dense-compact/ categorization: an introduction[4]

1.1. Culioli's 1983 article

In a 1983 article on the French determiner *quelque*, Culioli replaces the usual two-fold distinction between mass nouns and count nouns by a three-fold system. As shown below, he states the existence of three categories:

"On constate que la distinction *comptable* (ou *dénombrable*) / *non-comptable* (ou *indénombrable*) n'est guère satisfaisante, puisqu'on a deux désignations pour trois valeurs" (Culioli 1999: 55).

We will first summarize in French Culioli's definitions for these three categories in order to quote Culioli's own words:

(Culioli 1983 = 1999 : 55)[5]

/discret/	/compact/	/dense/
on peut dans ce cas individuer les occurrences, les désigner sous une forme ordinale	on a ici affaire à de l'insécable, à du prédicatif nominalisé, sur lequel on ne peut effectuer aucun prélèvement	catégorie composite qui possède certaines propriétés du /compact/, mais où un prélèvement est possible par l'intermédiaire d'un dénombreur.
ex. : *livre, chat, enfant*, etc.	ex. : *dureté, amertume, courage, difficulté, espoir, plaisir, tristesse*, etc.	ex : *farine, lait, sucre, viande*, etc.

The /discrete/ category seems to correspond to the usual count nouns. But within the mass noun category, Culioli establishes two categories illustrated by two kinds of nouns: those that allow a sampling operation and those that do not. According to Neveu (2005: 23), the /compact/ nouns deal with continuous entities which cannot be divided or quantified (e.g. *sadness*), while the /dense/ nouns entail continuous entities which can be divided and quantified (e.g. *milk*).

1.2. Culioli's 1991 paper

We would now like to place this three-fold system within the more general framework of Culioli's linguistic theory, as developed in his 1991 paper. We will first quote the main data, and then provide some explanations.

notion: *avoir la propriété P*
- faisceau de propriétés physico-culturelles
- première étape d'une représentation métalinguistique.
construction d'une occurrence: passage d'une représentation mentale, incorporelle à une activité permettant de référer (incarnation de la notion sous forme de langage).
occurrence: événement énonciatif qui délimite une portion d'espace/temps spécifiée par la propriété P. Elle va de pair avec la **quantifiabilisation** (ou **fragmentation**).
(Culioli 1991 = 1999: 9-11)[6]

The first concept presented here is the *notion*, which is also the first step of a meta-linguistic representation. When the *construction of an occurrence* (Fr. *construction d'une occurrence*) occurs, there is an *embodiment* (Fr. *incarnation*) of the notion by a shift from a mental and immaterial representation to an activity which is both referential and linguistic. This *occurrence* may be defined as an enunciative event which delimits a space-time section specified by property P.

According to Franckel and Paillard (1991: 166), the *construction of an occurrence* is based on two parameters which allow the *individuation* of the *notion*:

"La construction d'occurrences passe par un schème d'individuation qui met en jeu des **pondérations variables sur QNT et sur QLT.**
QNT: délimitation quantitative, associable à l'ancrage spatio-temporel de l'occurrence.
QLT: délimitation qualitative: une occurrence de la propriété *P* peut être de l'ordre du *vraiment P, pas vraiment P*, ou encore *pas du tout P*".

These parameters are fundamental, since it is their respective weights that permit the /discrete-dense-compact/ categorization.

But before we describe them in more details, we would like to introduce here another distinction, related to the referential property of natural languages. This distinction will help in improve the definition of this categorization:

Il n'existe pas de représentation sans qu'elle ne se pose relativement à un **pôle de référence**. Il correspond à deux modes d'organisation:
- **le type** : c'est par rapport à lui que s'établit la double opération d'identification/différenciation; il permet d'organiser la fragmentation de la notion en construisant une **occurrence représentative**.
- **l'attracteur** : il s'agit de construire une origine qui n'a d'autre référence possible que le prédicat lui-même.
Il y a donc une différence essentielle entre le **type**, qui correspond à une occurrence représentative, et l'**attracteur** qui renvoie à une représentation abstraite et absolue. QNT a des affinités avec le type, QLT avec l'attracteur
(Culioli 1991 = 1999: 11-13).

Using these different parameters, we can present this categorization, quoting Culioli's own words:[7]

(Culioli 1991 = 1999: 14):

Discret	Compact	Dense
QNT QLT	QLT	QNT QLT
QNT est prépondérant et le type privilégié par rapport à l'attracteur. Il s'agit d'un mode de construction d'une occurrence tel que la délimitation d'une portion d'espace-temps soit privilégiée.	C'est la construction d'un gradient qui est fondamentale. On a affaire à de l'homogène. La stabilité provient de l'attracteur. La seule singularisation possible est d'ordre qualitatif.	Correspond à un mixte, à un cas intermédiaire et instable. Ni QNT, ni QLT ne sont prépondérants. Il n'y a pas de forme type qui stabilise. L'opération de prélèvement s'effectue par une quantité non définissable indépendamment de cette opération. De ce fait, il n'y a pas de problématique d'épuisement.

The /discrete/ category is clear enough: the *notion* may be segmented, and thus allows the delimitation of a time-space section.

No segmentation is possible in the /compact/ category, due to its homogeneity, and an occurrence may be specified only by a *qualitative modulation* (Fr. *modulation qualitative*).

The /dense/ category appears to be the most difficult to define, since it is a hybrid and unstable category. In order better to define it, we will attempt to find more data in Culioli's work on French determiner *quelque*.

1.3. Culioli's theory applied to Fr. *quelque*

In the conclusions of his 1983 article, Culioli makes the following statements:

- *quelque* + N compact: On ne peut pas effectuer d'opération de qualification/quantification (c'est-à-dire, en dernier ressort, de différenciation), puisque le compact, insécable, ne permet aucune partition. *Quelque N* marque donc simplement l'existence d'une valeur non nulle.
- *quelque* + N dense: On ne peut pas, comme dans le cas du discret, travailler sur une famille d'occurrences distinctes. En effet, le dense a la propriété d'être non-dénombrable, ce qui permet seulement soit une opération sur la quotité (quantité non définie appréhendée globalement hors de toute cardinalité : *peu, beaucoup, assez,* etc.) soit, par l'intermédiaire d'un dénombreur (*paire, morceau, bout, bouteille, litre,* etc.), une opération de quantité discrète. (…)
D'une autre côté, le dense, à la différence du compact, ne permet pas d'opérer sur l'intensité (…) (à moins que l'on introduise une qualité différentielle : *quelque viande avariée*) (…) D'où l'impossibilité de *quelque N* pour N dense. (Culioli 1983 = 1999: 57-58)

Three modalities of quantification are thus postulated for nouns:

   i.   the quantification of /discrete/ entities, where plurality involves a
        set of individual entities which may be distinguished from one
        another.
  ii.   the situation of the /compact/ entities, where the *occurrence*
        coincides with the *manifestation of the property*:[8] A /compact/
        entity, since it is homogeneous, does not allow fragmentation;
        therefore qualitative modulation is the only possible process.
 iii.   the quantification of /dense/ entities, which is restricted to an
        operation of sampling.

2. The /discrete-dense-compact/ categorization
applied to Latin nouns

We have established above that Culioli's /discrete-dense-compact/
categorization is useful in order to describe the uses of Fr. *quelque*. We
will now see that it also seems to be applicable for nouns in Latin. We may
suppose the existence of the three quantification modalities in Latin.

Latin grammars usually briefly mention the grammatical notions of
plurality and quantification. Nevertheless, one of the most widely used
grammars in France, the *Précis de grammaire des lettres latines*,[9]
postulates a three-fold system which perfectly overlaps with Culioli's
analyses (even if the terminology is clearly different), as shown below:

Nom concret au pl. (choses ou personnes plus ou moins nombreuses) *multi uiri*	nom abstrait au sg. (quantité plus ou moins grande) *magna gloria*	nom concret au sg. (choses qui se mesurent) *multum auri*

Plural concrete nouns (such as *uiri*) may be considered as /discrete/ nouns,
abstract nouns (such as *gloria*) as /compact/ nouns, and singular concrete
nouns (such as *aurum*) as /dense/ nouns. The parallelism between these
two classifications seems perfect. But we need to check this in the actual
data provided by the Latin texts. We will therefore look at three main
corpuses of works from the Classical period: Cicero *In Catilinam* (I-IV)
and *Pro Milone*, and Caesar *Commentarii de Bello Gallico* (I-IV).[10]

2.1. *multi* + /discrete/ nouns

The adjective *multi* (in the plural form) is commonly used with /discrete/ nouns. Moreover, in an interesting set of occurrences, *multi* co-occurs with a qualitative meaning adjective, which is evidence for the quantitative function of *multi*:

(1) a. *ubi Oceano adpropinquauit, in plures defluit partes **multis ingentibus**que **insulis** effectis* (Caes. *Gall.* 4,10,4)
          "and on its approach to the Ocean, [the Rhine] divides into several streams, forming many large islands"
     b. *primipilo P. Sextio Baculo, fortissimo uiro, **multis grauibus**que **uulneribus** confecto* (Caes. *Gall.* 2,25,1)
          "the chief centurion, Publius Sextius Baculus, bravest of the brave, who was overcome by many grievous wounds"

The quantification may also be assumed by a numeral adjective, e.g. *duo* "two":

(2) *una aestate **duobus maximis bellis** confectis* (Caes. *Gall.* 1,54,2)
     "Two capital campaigns were thus finished in a single summer"

Nevertheless, the argument of the co-occurrence of *multi* with a qualitative meaning adjective is not enough strong to enable us to assert that the determined noun belongs to the /discrete/ category: this may be only one of the uses of the noun concerned, as shown by (3a) and (3b) with the noun *praesidium*:

(3) a. ***multis** meis **et firmis praesidiis** obsessus, ne commouere te contra rem publicam possis* (Cic. *Catil.* 1,6)
          "surrounded by many competent guards whom I have set so that you may not be able to move against the state
     b. ***Magnum** enim est in bonis **praesidium** quod mihi in perpetuum comparatum est* (Cic. *Catil.* 3,27)
          "For the defence of loyal men counts for much, and that is mine for ever"

Although in (3a) the plural *praesidiis* seems to belong to the /discrete/ category, we cannot assert that this noun, as a lexical unit, belongs to the /discrete/ category, since there exists a referential asymmetry between the singular and the plural forms of the noun. The singular *praesidium* belongs to the /compact/ category and the denoted entity is not countable. On the other hand, the plural form *praesidia* (3a) undergoes a re-categorization, since *praesidia* denotes the concrete manifestations or instantiations of the abstract meaning of the noun, *i.e.* in this passage "guards, persons assigned to protect". The plural form can be more or less stabilized in its discrete uses.

However, abstract nouns are not always used as compact nouns. In fact, they even regularly display discrete uses. The noun *causa*, when it means "case, trial" or "reason, cause", doesn't show a referential discontinuity between its singular and its plural form meanings. The singular form, just like the plural, is discrete; and the plural only denotes the plurality of the same entities:

(4) a. *quod **multis** in **causis** saepe quaesitum est* (Cic. *Mil.* 31)
          "an issue which has often been raised in many cases"
     b. *Sed iam satis multa **de causa**; **extra causam** etiam nimis fortasse multa* (Cic. *Mil.* 92)
          "But I have now said enough about the case itself; about what lies outside it perhaps too much"

(5) a. ***multis** de **causis** Caesar statuit sibi Rhenum esse transeundum* (Caes. *Gall.* 4,16,1)
          "Caesar decided for many reasons that he must cross the Rhine"
     b. *Satis est (…) docere **magnam** ei **causam**, magnam spem in Milonis morte propositam, magnas utilitates fuisse* (Cic. *Mil.* 32)
          "it is enough to demonstrate that he had a great inducement to kill Milo, and great expectations and great advantages held out to him in the even of his death"

The semantic and referential function of a particular noun (*i.e.* the way it refers to the extra-linguistic world) may also be inferred from other data, such as word-formation. (6a) and (6b) describe the same extra-linguistic event (the Gauls are weeping in order to move Caesar) with two different nouns both meaning "tears", the plural *lacrimae* and the singular *fletus*:

(6) a. *Diuiciacus **multis cum lacrimis** Caesarem complexus obsecrare coepit* (Caes. *Gall.* 1,20,1)
          "With many tears Diviciacus embraced Caesar, and began to beseech him"

b. *omnes qui aderant* **magno fletu** *auxilium a Caesare petere coeperunt* (Caes. *Gall.* 1,32,1)
"all who were present began with loud weeping to seek assistance from Caesar"

Since *lacrimae* (6a) is a discrete noun, it is determined by the quantitative adjective *multae* "many". On the other hand, *fletus* (6b) is a verbal noun, morphologically built with the Latin inherited suffix *-tus* standing behind the verbal radical *fle-*. According to Culioli's terminology, the verbal noun *fletus* would be called a *nominalised predicative* (Fr. *un prédicatif nominalisé*) and belongs to the /compact/ category, which explains the use of the adjective *magnus* "big" in (6b). We will now move on to the /compact/ nouns.

2.2. The adjective *magnus* and the /compact/ category

The adjective *magnus* "big" usually functions as a quantification lexeme within the /compact/ category. How can we explain it? According to Culioli, the /compact/ category applies to homogeneous entities and gives a key role to the *gradient* (Fr. *gradient*), since the only possible modulation is a qualitative one. In reality, the adjective *magnus* (which plays this *gradient* role and originally functions as an intensity lexeme) also involves an approximate equivalent of an indefinite large quantity: a high degree of realization for the process of "crying" in (6b), which is equivalent to "crying a lot".

This use of *magnus* is particularly noticeable with feeling nouns, expressing e.g. fear (*metus, timor*, etc.): "feeling a high degree of fear" may be the equivalent of "having great fear for...", *i.e.* *"much fear". In other words, a high degree of intensity applied to a particular feeling is similar to a "large quantity", as shown in (7a) and (7b):

(7) a. **Magno** *me* **metu** *liberabis, modo inter me atque te murus intersit* (Cic. *Catil.* 1,10)
"I shall be free from my great fear only if there is a wall between us "
     b. *cum uix se ex* **magno timore** *recreasset* (Cic. *Catil.* 3,8)
"almost before he [= Volturcius] had recovered from his abject terror "

The example (8) provides additional evidence for this equivalence between intensity and quantity in the domain of feelings:

(8) *cui (...) praesertim* **omnia** *audienti,* **magna** *metuenti,* **multa** *suspi-*
     canti, **non nulla** *credenti* (Cic. *Mil.* 61)
     "(especially seeing that the man in question [= Pompey] was one)
     who heard everything, apprehended great dangers, suspected much
     and believed not a little"

This passage of the *Pro Milone* is based on a symmetry between several
dative participles complemented by quantifiers (*omnia, multa, non nulla*).
Magna, which might seem to introduce an asymmetry, is justified by the
/compact/ nature of the verb *metuo* "fear", which uses an intensive noun
magna (issued from the lexicalization of the neuter plural form of the
adjective *magnus*) in order to express quantity.
    Even if *magnus* is usual within the /compact/ category, it is not a
specific lexical tool for this category. Its related superlative *maximus* in (9)
expresses an intensity with a purely qualitative meaning and without any
shift towards quantification:

(9) *Atque haec omnia sic agentur, Quirites, ut (...)* **bellum** *intestinum ac*
     domesticum post hominum memoriam crudelissimum et **maximum**
     me uno togato duce et imperatore sedetur (Cic. *Catil.* 2,28)
     "And all these things will be so done, citizens, that (...) a civil war,
     the most cruel and the greatest within the memory of man, will be
     suppressed by me alone, a leader and commander wearing the garb of
     peace"

2.3. The /dense/ category

Finding a lexical tool (even a non-specific one) that would be able to
express quantification within the /dense/ category is a difficult task.
According to Culioli's operation of sampling, we would expect a
quantifier to be determined by a partitive genitive case, such as *multum*
auri "a lot of gold, a large quantity of gold". But we have not encountered
such a nominal phrase in our corpus of classical texts, apart from *quam*
minimum spatii in Caesar, quoted in (10):

(10) *Huc magno cursu contenderunt, ut* **quam minimum spati** *ad se*
     colligendos armandosque Romanis daretur (Caes. *Gall.* 3,19,1)
     "Hither [= in the camp] the Gauls hastened at great speed to give the
     Romans the least possible time to assemble and to arm "

The genitive case is slightly more frequent as a determiner of a noun phrase containing the adjective *magnus* and a quantification noun, such as *magna pars* + genitive "a large part of, a large portion of". Then, the noun in the partitive genitive is treated as a dense noun and the denoted entity is perceived as a homogeneous substance, which allows sampling. Therefore, in this precise situation there occurs a neutralization of the usual difference between a plurality of discrete entities (11a) and a singular dense entity (11b), both functioning as a whole from which is extracted a particular portion:

(11) a. ***quarum [= insularum] pars magna*** *a feris barbaris nationibus incolitur* (Caes. *Gall.* 4,10,4)
"a great number of which [= islands] are inhabited by fierce barbaric tribes"

b. *ut neque uestitus praeter pellis habeant quicquam, quarum propter exiguitatem* ***magna*** *est* ***corporis pars*** *aperta* (Caes. *Gall.* 4,1,10)
" [they have regularly trained themselves] to wear nothing (...) except skins, the scantiness of which leaves a great part of the body bare "

Magna copia may also co-occur with a dense noun (such as *pabulum* "forage") as well as with a plural discrete noun (*naues* "boats"), but the conceptual difference related to their different categories seems to be still pregnant in the way they are quantified. *Nauium magna copia* (12b) is thought of as a plurality of boats, while *pabuli magna copia* (12a) is thought of as a massive substance, an aggregate:

(12) a *Nam propter frigora (...) ne* ***pabuli*** *quidem satis* ***magna copia*** *suppetebat* (Caes. *Gall.* 1,16,2)
"For reason of cold weather, there was not even a sufficient supply of forage to be had"

b. ***Nauium magnam copiam*** *ad transportandum exercitum pollicebantur* (Caes. *Gall.* 4,16,8)
"They promised a large supply of boats for the transport of his army"

The other usual noun phrases, *magnus numerus* and *magna multitudo*, usually provide an indefinite quantification for discrete entities.[11]

However, a particular construction seems to be specific for /dense/ nouns: the use of the singular *multus* denoting a sampling taken from the entity referred to by the determined noun:

(13) *uos, uos appello, fortissimi uiri, qui **multum** pro re publica **sanguinem** effudistis* (Cic. *Mil.* 101)
"to you, to you I make my suit, gallant gentlemen, who have shed your blood in torrents for the common weal"

In (13), blood is conceived as a homogeneous, continuous substance, from which a large quantity is taken.

Re-categorizations also have an important role in the use of *multus*. The nouns referring to portions of time are often used in our corpus as /discrete/ nouns: noun phrases such as *multi anni* "many years", *multi menses* "many months", *multa saecula* "many generations" or *multa horae* "many hours" are attested with quite a high frequency, and are illustrated by (14a):

(14) a. *Quos si meus consulatus (…) sustulerit, non breue nescio quod tempus, sed **multa saecula** propagarit rei publicae* (Cic. *Catil.* 2.11) "If my consulship is to destroy these men (…), not some short time, but many ages will be added to the life of the state "

But a particular period of time may also be conceived of as belonging to the /dense/ category and be apprehended as a whole for an operation of sampling:

b. ***Multo** denique **die** per exploratores Caesar cognouit et montem a suis teneri et Heluetios castra mouisse* (Caes. *Gall.* 1,22,4)
"At length, when the day was far spent, Caesar learnt from his scouts that the height was in possession of his own troops, and that the Helvetii had shifted their camp"

The lack of clear-cut properties mentioned above for the definition of the /dense/ category is confirmed by another feature: the use of a noun in the partitive genitive case depending on a quantifier (such as *multum auri* "a large quantity of gold") may also be explained by a stylistic strategy, as shown in (15):

(15) *et, cum hostes uestri* **tantum ciuium** *superfuturum putassent*
     quantum *infinitae caedi restitisset,* **tantum** *autem* **urbis, quantum**
     flamma obire non potuisset, et urbem et ciuis integros incolumisque
     seruaui. (Cic. *Catil.* 3,25)
     "And, when your enemies thought that only those citizens would
     remain who survived an indiscriminate slaughter and only as much of
     the city as the flames could not envelop, I have preserved both city
     and citizens safe and sound"

In this evocation of the crimes planned by Catilina, the use of *tantum* +
noun in the genitive plural (*ciuium*) for a plurality of discrete entities (and
even here a plurality of animate human entities) is unexpected, since this
syntactic construction is much more usual for dense entities. But in fact it
shows Cicero's strategy in reifying the Roman citizens as if they were a
shapeless and worthless inanimate aggregate from which Catilina and his
friends could easily and shamelessly deduct a (large) portion.
     In Caesar's works, the stylistic strategies often aim at hiding the
defeats and unsuccessful events undergone by his army:

(16) a. *cum* **tantum repentini periculi** *praeter opinionem accidisset ac*
         iam omnia fere superiora loca multitudine armatorum completa
         conspicerentur neque subsidio ueniri neque commeatus
         supportari interclusis itineribus possent (Caes. *Gall.* 3,3,2)
         "The danger that had arisen was as serious as it was sudden and
         unexpected, and indeed by this time almost all the higher ground
         was seen to be packed with a host of armed men, while, with the
         communications interrupted, reinforcements could not be
         attempted nor supplies brought up"
     b. *militibus autem ignotis locis, impeditis manibus,* **magno** *et* **graui**
         onere *armorum oppressis simul et de nauibus desiliendum et in*
         fluctibus consistendum et cum hostibus erat pugnandum (Caes.
         Gall. 4,24,2)
         "the troops – through they did not know the ground, had not their
         hands free, and were loaded with the great and grievous weight of
         their arms – had nevertheless at the same time to leap down from
         the vessels, to stand firm in the waves, and to fight the enemy"

Tantum in (16a) seems to be used in a qualitative way, related to intensity.[12] According to Caesar, the Romans, unfortunately for them, were submitted to a high degree of sudden danger, the so-called *repentinum periculum*, which is here treated as a formless and non-countable entity, caused by fate.

(16b) illustrates the /compact/ category. But, unlike (1a), (1b), (2) and (3a), *magnus* is here in qualitative use and its meaning is similar to that of *grauis*. Therefore the weight appears to be, undeniably, too heavy for the soldiers.

We can thus conclude that, in the area of nouns, Culioli's categorization is quite useful to explain quantification and it provides a consistent theoretical basis. /Discrete/ nouns are the only ones having their own specific lexical tool (*multi*). The use of *magnus* is usual in the /compact/ category, but *magnus* may also express intensity. Altogether, the /dense/ category is the least stable one: phrases such as *multum auri* are rare and they may be explained by stylistic strategies. The construction entailing *multus* and a quantification noun determined by a partitive genitive case is more common (even if it is a non-specific one).

3. Extension of the /discrete-dense-compact/ categorization to verbs

The extension of Culioli's classification to verbs was proposed in a 1988 paper by Franckel, Paillard and de Vogüé. But before we try to evaluate its role in Latin, we will first describe the way this theoretical framework may be applied to verbs.

3.1. Theoretical analysis

Firstly, in order to introduce the theoretical data, we will summarize two articles:

Franckel, Paillard and de Vogüé (1988: 239-243)

Discret	Compact	Dense
Solidarité complexe des deux modes de distinguabilité (qualitative + instancielle). Ancrage spatio-temporel indissociable d'un découpage notionnel [= nouvelle manifestation + autre exemplaire]. L'occurrence construite est formatée sur l'étalon. Dans le domaine verbal, l'opération de formatage va s'établir en fonction de la valeur lexicale intrinsèque du verbe, mais aussi, le cas échéant, de la détermination d'un complément d'objet.	Notion non-sécable parce que non susceptible d'une découpe notionnelle. Ne se manifeste que par un ancrage spatio-temporel. Bien plus, cette manifestation n'est possible qu'à travers la médiatisation d'une relation prédicative qui l'ancre à un support externe. C'est ce support qui fonde l'ancrage spatio-temporel de la notion.	Construction d'occurrences sans relation à un type, sans formatage. La manifestation de l'occurrence passe par un ancrage spatio-temporel mais (…) sans médiatisation par un support. La construction d'une occurrence est associée à l'opération de prélèvement Procès tels qu'on peut les gloser par "il y a (ou il y a eu) événement de ".
Sortir, tomber, traverser *Il a bu son thé* *Il a lu un livre en une heure*	*Il a été sage*	*Hier soir on a chanté, on a discuté, on a bu*

Franckel and Paillard (1991: 118-119)

Discret	Compact	Dense
Qnt ↔ Qlt	(Qnt) Qlt	Qnt (Qlt)
Lorsque s'établit un rapport entre délimitation Qnt et délimitation Qlt indépendamment de son ancrage temporel (qui ne peut qu'entériner ce rapport)	Une délimitation qualitative ne se trouve relayée par aucune délimitation Qnt. L'actualisation d'un procès compact passe par sa mise en relation à un support externe.	L'occurrence n'est délimitée que par le biais de son ancrage situationnel. Relève d'une forme de contingence
J'ai lu ce livre, tu peux le prendre	*Pierre est gentil*	*Ce matin, j'ai dormi puis j'ai marché dans le jardin*

As shown above, in the /discrete/ category, there exist both a quantitative delimitation and a qualitative one (*Qnt* ↔ *Qlt*). In other words, an individualized occurrence has a space-time location and, at the same time, it is defined by its relationship with a *type*. This occurrence appears to be formatted (Fr. *formaté*), *i.e.* it has a terminus, a final limit from which we can evaluate its conformity with the *type*. This terminus may result from the lexical meaning (*to go out, to fall*) or from the presence of an argument (*I have been reading this book*).

The same individualization of an occurrence (Fr. *découpe notionnelle*) cannot occur in the /compact/ category. The *notion* (Fr. *notion*) only receives a qualitative delimitation and it cannot be located in a space-time section, except through its relationship with another term of the predication called *support*.

Finally, in the case of the /dense/ category, there exists an external formatting (Fr. *formatage externe*[13]), *i.e.* the only delimitation for an occurrence is its space-time location.

3.2. Are there possible links with Vendler's 1967 typology?

We first present a summary of Vendler's well-known typology; our presentation is based on the interpretation developed by Martin (1988):[14]

States	Activities	Accomplishments	Achievements
[- dynamic]	[+ dynamic]	[+ dynamic]	[+ dynamic]
[- telic]	[- telic]	[+ telic]	[+ telic]
[+ durative]	[+ durative]	[+ durative]	[- durative]
to like	*running*	*running a mile*	*to reach the hilltop*
	pushing a cart	*drawing a circle*	*to spot the plane*

The first point deals with the telic or atelic feature of the process concerned. An atelic process appears as homogeneous: "any part of the process is of the same nature as the whole" (Vendler 1967: 101). This property is shared with mass nouns.[15] On the other hand, accomplishments and achievements belong to the /discrete/ category. Alternation of temporal adverbials makes this distinction clear enough:

(17) *Heluetii repentino eius aduentu commoti, cum id, quod ipsi **diebus XX** aegerrime confecerant, ut flumen transirent, illum **uno die** fecisse intellegerent* ... (Caes. *Gall.* 1.13.2)
    "[The Helvetii] alarmed at his sudden approach - for they perceived that the business of crossing the river, which they themselves had accomplished with the greatest difficulty in twenty days, had been despatched by Caesar in a single one -"

(18) *Ita **dies circiter quindecim** iter fecerunt* (Caes. *Gall.* 1,15,5)
    "The march continued for about a fortnight"

(17) denotes an accomplishment, which belongs to the /discrete/ category, while (18) refers to an activity, *i.e.* a homogeneous process. These cases we have mentioned here are adequately explained by Vendler's classification. Culioli's categorization would not add anything useful here. But the crucial point is the distinction between activities and states. The criterion commonly used for this distinction is the compatibility with the progressive form; but this is not useful for French, since the paraphrasis with Fr. *être en train de* is not a common construction.[16] The /dense/ category is characterized by a space-time location, which is relevant for an activity: its meaning, indeed, is that something is happening. Judging by this criterion, the process in (18) is a /dense/ one.

The /compact/ category only provides a space-time location through the relationship with one of the constituents of the predication, the so-called *support*. The temporal adverbial (that gives information on the duration of the process) displays the same form, but in cases such as (19) there occurs an application to a *support* which allows an instantiation:

(19) *Duces uero ii deliguntur, qui una cum Quinto Sertorio **omnes annos** fuerant summamque scientiam rei militaris habere existimabantur* (Caes. *Gall.* 3,23,5)
      "And as their leaders for the same, they selected men who had served for the whole period with Quintus Sertorius were believed to be past masters of war"

This relationship with Sertorius is felt as a distinctive feature and it became the relevant criterion for the choice.

3.3. Frequentative verbs

The frequentative suffix -*tare* and its allomorphs -*sare*, -*itare* lengthen the duration of a particular process[17] (Fr. *l'intervalle de validité du procès*). Culioli's categorization gives us a good explanation for the meaning properties of these verbs.

When the denoted process belongs to the /discrete/ category, a frequentative verb may have a conative or an iterative meaning:

(20) *et gemitum ingentem pelagi **pulsata**que **saxa** / audimus* (...) (Verg. *Aen.* 3,555-556)
      "we hear the loud moaning of the sea, the lashing of the rocks"

(21) *hunc (…) / intorto figit telo, discrimina costis / per medium qua spina dabat,* **hastam***que* **receptat** */ ossibus* **haerentem***.* (...) (Verg. *Aen.* 10,381-384)
"him [= Lagus] … he [=Pallas] pierces with hurled javelin, where the spine midway between the ribs made a parting, and pluck back the spear from its lodging in the bones"

In (21), the grammatical object in the accusative case, *hastam* "spear", denotes a particular and individual entity; the process is thus a conative (and iterative) one. This feature is confirmed by the context: this event involves a human agent (denoted by the grammatical subject), who wants to accomplish the process and has some control over it; he is trying to fulfil the process. The use of the frequentative suffix in the verb shows that the agent has great difficulty in withdrawing his spear (a conative meaning) and has to repeat the action several times (an iterative meaning) before he succeeds.
In (20), the extra-linguistic state of affairs (the continuous noise of the sea) suggests an iterative meaning for a process located within an inanimate entity (and without any human agent).
    Vendler's accomplishment verbs, which also denote /discrete/ processes, may receive a frequentative suffix. The lengthening of the valid process duration (Fr. *allongement de la durée de validité*) due to this frequentative suffix generates a kind of slow motion (such as we may see in a film) and a distortion of the process concerned. In (22), this situation occurs for an unsuccessful event and the use of the imperfect tense reinforces this interpretation:

(22) *iamque fere spatio extremo fessique sub ipsam / finem* **aduentabant***, leui cum sanguine Nisus / labitur infelix* (...) (Verg. *Aen.* 5,327-329)
"And now, with course well-nigh covered, panting they neared the very goal, when Nisus, luckless one, falls in some slippery blood "

For a /dense/ verb, the construction of an occurrence only depends on the space-time location. The frequentative suffix then refers to an unusually long process duration, which can be interpreted as a special stress set onto the process itself. In (23), Nisus is trying to justify his misfortune in a running race:

(23) *Et simul his dictis faciem* **ostentabat** *et udo / turpia membra fimo* (...)
      (Verg. *Aen.* 5,357-358)
      "And with the words he [=Nisus] displayed his face and limbs foul
      with wet filth."

   Culioli's classification is also useful in order to explain a variation in
meaning displayed by the frequentative verbs that had not been noticed
previously: the close relationship between the frequentative verb and the
extra-linguistic entity denoted by the grammatical subject, as shown in
(24):

(24) *cum duo conuersis inimica in proelia tauri / frontibus incurrunt,*
      pauidi cessere magistri, / stat pecus omne metu mutum mussantque
      iuuencae, / quis nemori **imperitet,** *quem tota armenta sequantur*
      (Verg. *Aen.* 12,716-719)
      "When two bulls charge, brow to brow, in mortal battle, back in
      terror fall the keepers, the whole herd stands mute with dread, and
      the heifers dumbly ponder who shall be lord of the forest, whom all
      the herds shall follow".

In (24), the fighting of the bulls is a crucial issue for the leadership of the
herd. The lengthening of the process duration, due to the frequentative
suffix, means a non-fragmented and continuous process, therefore a
/compact/ one. The process could be considered as a *closed whole* (Fr. *un
ensemble clos*) which is only delimitated by its *support*. The internal
formatting becomes an external one, since it is only dependent on a
predicative relationship elaborated within the utterance act. This may
explain why *impero* appears as a /discrete/ verb and the frequentative
imperito as a /compact/ one.

Conclusion

The new perspectives opened by Culioli's classification (already used for
several languages and occasionally for Latin, by S. Mellet in particular)
provide a more accurate description of Latin and allow typological
comparisons with other languages. This classification also throws light on
some specific linguistic structures in Latin, such as the quantification of
nouns and the frequentative suffix function.

Notes

* I thank M. Fruyt et P. Haffner for their assistance in the translation of this paper.
[1] Lyons (1995: 17).
[2] For similar properties in French, see Arrivé *et al.* (1986: 408).
[3] This is a translation of Fr. *opération de prélèvement*, Culioli (1999 : 40). In this article, we will attempt to translate this French linguist's terminology into English and to explain his concepts: see below §1.
[4] According to Culioli's theory. See above note 3.
[5] This article has been summarized and partially translated by Liddle (see Culioli 1995). We quote the main definitions related to this categorization: "We shall speak of the *discreteness* of what is individuatable (…) The second property is that we shall be able to order, i.e. that we shall construct an ordinal classification: 1st, 2nd, 3rd occurrence". The /compact/ is "indivisible, a nominalised predicate, on which no operation of sampling can be performed". The /dense/ "is a hybrid category possessing properties of the compact, but on which sampling can be performed by means of an enumerator". (Culioli, 1995: 145-146)
[6] Culioli's original quotation in English will help us in understanding his linguistic theory: "A notion can be defined as a complex bundle of structured physico-cultural properties and should not be equated with lexical labels or actual items (…). Notions are apprehended and established through occurrences (enunciative events) which involve: distinguishing phenomenal instances, identifying properties and assessing their distance from one another, gauging the degree and the kind of similarity, deciding whether to keep the occurrences qualitatively separate or to categorize them as equivalent relative to a type (…) It should be obvious that notions have a status of predicable entities and could be described as unfragmented solid wholes; but they are apprehended through occurrences, i.e. distinguish through separate events, broken down into units (actually localized in the physical word, or imaginary) with variable properties" (Culioli 1978 = 1990: 69-70)
[7] Culioli asserts that this analysis is not definitive: " Le grand danger serait de considérer ce qui précède comme une manière de fixer un cadre préétabli qui ne saurait souffrir de transformation " (Culioli 1991 = 1999: 15). Moreover, this analysis was reformulated afterwards by Franckel and Paillard (cf. §3.1) who preserved the three-fold system.
[8] See Paillard (in press: 5).
[9] By Gason, Thomas and Baudiffier 1965 (1st edition).
[10] We will respectively quote the translations of L. E. Lord, N. H. Watts and H. J. Edwards, from the Loeb collection.
[11] But they may also occur with a collective singular noun, as in Caes. *Gall.* 4,9; 4,34; 3,11.
[12] Although the noun *periculum* "danger" may sometimes be used in quantitative expressions (such as *ex plurimis periculis* Cic. *Catil.* 4,18), its most frequent uses are intensive ones, such as *maximis periculis* (Cic. *Catil.* 3,14) ; *in tantis periculis* (Cic. *Catil.* 1,4 ; 3,6) ; *tantis periculis* (Cic. *Catil.* 3,17) ; *tantorum periculorum* (Cic. *Catil.* 4,22) ; *magno cum periculo* (Caes. *Gall.* 1,10,2 ; 1,47,3 ; 3,1,2 ;

4,28,2) ; *magno in periculo* (Cic. *Catil.* 1,19) ; *quanto cum periculo* (Caes. *Gall.* 1,17) ; *quanto in periculo* (Caes. *Gall.* 2,26).
[13] See Paillard (in press: 5).
[14] See also Dowty (1979).
[15] See Borillo (1988).
[16] See the analysis by Franckel and Paillard (1991: 112-114 and 120-121).
[17] See S. Van Laer (2011). We quote the translation of H. Rushton Fairclough for Vergilius, *Aeneid.*

References

Arrivé, M., Gadet, F. and M. Galmiche (1986) *La grammaire d'aujourd'hui*, Paris, Flammarion.

Borillo, A. (1988) "Notions de 'massif' et 'comptable' dans la mesure temporelle", in J. David and G. Kleiber (eds) *Termes massifs et termes comptables*, Paris, Klincksieck, 215-238.

Culioli, A. (1978) "The concept of notional domain", in H. Seiler (ed.) *Language Universals*, Tübingen, Narr (also published in: *Pour une linguistique de l'énonciation* vol. 1, 1990, Gap-Paris, Ophrys, 67-81).

—. (1983) "À propos de *quelque*", in S. Fischer and J.-J. Franckel (eds) *Linguistique, énonciation. Aspects et détermination*, Paris, Éditions de l'E.H.E.S.S., 21-29. (also published in: *Pour une linguistique de l'énonciation* vol. 3, 1999, Gap-Paris, Ophrys, 49-58).

—. (1991) "Structuration d'une notion et typologie lexicale. À propos de la distinction dense, discret, compact" *BULAG* 17, Université de Franche-Comté, 7-12 (also published in: *Pour une linguistique de l'énonciation* vol. 3, 1999, Gap-Paris, Ophrys, 9-15).

—. (1995) *Cognition and Representation in Linguistic Theory*, Texts selected, edited and introduced by M. Liddle, translated with the assistance of J.T. Stonham, Amsterdam-Philadelphia, John Benjamins.

Dowty, D.R. (1979) *Word Meaning and Montague Grammar*, Dordrecht, Kluwer.

Franckel, J.-J., Paillard, D. and S. de Vogüé (1988) "Extension de la distinction *discret, dense, compact* au domaine verbal", in J. David and G. Kleiber (eds) *Termes massifs et termes comptables*, Paris, Klincksieck, 239-247.

Franckel, J.-J. and D. Paillard (1991) "Discret-Dense-Compact: Vers une typologie opératoire" *Travaux de linguistique et de philologie* 29: 103-136.

Lyons, J. (1995) *Linguistic Semantics. An Introduction*, Cambridge University Press.

Martin, R. (1988) "Temporalité et classes de verbes" *Information Grammaticale* 39: 3-8.

Neveu, F. (2005) *Lexique des notions linguistiques*, Paris, Armand Colin.

Paillard, D. (in press) "Quelque N / quelques N*", in F. Corblin and L. Kupfermann (eds) Proceedings of the Colloquium *Les indéfinis*, October 2003.

Van Laer, S. (2011) "La quantification des procès: le cas des verbes fréquentatifs", in M. Fruyt et O. Spevak (eds) *La quantification en latin*, Paris, L'Harmattan: 207-223.

Vendler, Z. (1967) "Verbs and Times" in *Linguistics in Philosophy*, Ithaca-New York, Cornell University Press, 97-146.

PRAGMALINGUISTIC OBSERVATIONS IN LATE ANCIENT VIRGILIAN COMMENTARIES

ILARIA TORZI

Introduction

Late ancient Virgilian commentators such as Servius and Ti.Cl. Donatus often include glosses which could be ascribed, using an anachronistic term, to the field of pragmalinguistics. In glossing the *Aeneid*, commentators do not merely paraphrase or draw attention to certain rhetorical processes, but underline their functional importance; they underline the message which can be inferred not from the contents of the text, but from the way in which these contents are syntagmatically organized, from the order and function of the lexical items and phrases in the text.

In this respect, the exegetes' glosses prove valuable for the analysis of the dynamics within Virgil's poem, especially when it comes to the connectives in the incipient verses of the *Aeneid*'s twelve books.

1. The connection between the first and second books

First of all, commentators emphasize Virgil's ability to closely connect different episodes in his work, his skill in 'cutting' the threads of his story only to take them up again at a later stage. The commentators' attitude must surely be understood in the light of the polemics against Virgil's detractors, who worked relentlessly to disparage his work. So, even though there is no particular connective at the beginning of the second book of the *Aeneid* (*conticuere omnes intentique ora tenebant*), Ti.Cl. Donatus does his best to prove that there exists a *continuum* between the first and the second book:[1]

> Memor poeta superiorum, quoniam dixit "fit strepitus tectis vocemque per ampla volutant atria" (1, 725) et "chitara crinitus Iopas personat" (1, 740) et "ingeminant plausu Tyrii Troesque sequuntur, nec non et vario noctem sermone trahebat infelix Dido" (1, 747), coepit secundum librum "conticuere omnes", Tyrii silicet et Troiani, qui strepebant vocibus et plausu, Iopas quoque et Dido ipsa.

And again, while analysing Dido's requests to Aeneas in the last lines of Book One (*Immo age et a prima dic, hospes, origine nobis / insidias, inquit, Danaum casusque tuorum / erroresque tuos. Nam te iam septima portat / omnibus errantem terris et fluctibus aestas*, 1, 753-756), requests which Dido makes with the aim of prolonging her relationship with Aeneas, for she now feels inevitably attracted to him, Ti.Cl. Donatus does not miss the opportunity to remark upon the articulation of the poem in the books that follow:

> *Respondetur ergo primis duabus propositionibus in secundo libro, tertiae autem in tertio. Nam in secundo insidias Danaum et suorum casus executus est, in tertio vero errores suos numeravit, licet in tertio ipso etiam casus suorum nonnullos addiderit, cum de Polydoro, de perditis luis contagione sociis et de amisso patre locutus proditur.*

Like Ti. Cl. Donatus, Servius focuses on the connections within the poem, even though he does so more succinctly: *Aen.* 2, 1, *CONTICVERE OMNES quia supra dixit fit strepitus tectis* (1, 725). Moreover, on *Aen.* 1, 748 ff. (*Nec non et vario noctem sermone trahebat/ infelix Dido longumque bibebat amorem, /multa super Priamo rogitans, super Hectore multa* etc.) Servius writes: *Nec non et vario: arte poetica utitur, ut praemittat aliquid, quo sequens liber videatur esse coniunctus: quod in omnibus servat.* Glossing *errores tuos* in 1, 755, Servius anticipates the order of events in the following two books: *et responsio hunc ordinem sequitur. Nam primo dicit Troiae ruinam, post errores suos.* Lastly, we may cite Servius Danielis' gloss to 1, 754: *et laudandum quod "insidias" tantum dixerit, non et captum Ilium; nam et ipse Aeneas "accipe nunc Danaum insidias"* (2, 65). The gloss, once again presenting an anticipation of future events, significantly recites: *Insidias: servavit ordinem respondendo ad illud quod regina interrogaverat "insidias inquit Danaum".*

These glosses can prove useful to teachers, for they demonstrate how the continuity and the articulation of a text do not rest merely upon connectives. For example, Ti. Cl. Donatus claims that *omnes* in *Aen.* 2, 1 is a collective pronoun referring to *Tyrii, Troiani, Iopas* and *Dido*, all of whom have been named in the concluding lines of Book One.[2] Continuity between the first and the second book can also be discerned in Aeneas' reply to Dido's request, which reproposes the queen's question almost *verbatim*: *insidias inquit Danaum*, she suggests in 1, 754; in 2, 65, the hero replies, *accipe nunc Danaum insidias*. Servius Danielis notes the correspondences between Dido's question and Aeneas' answer, but his gloss is less concerned with them than it is with Dido's considerate attitude: in fact, Dido does not speak of Ilium's fall, but of its enemies' unfairness. Both Ti. Cl. Donatus and Servius Danielis notice the connection between the beginning of Aeneas' speech in 2, 1 and its end in 3, 716-718 (*Sic pater Aeneas, intentis omnibus, unus / fata renarrabat divum cursusque docebat. / Conticuit tandem factoque hic fine quievit*). Servius comments: *Sane in secundi principio duo poetae sunt versus, sicut hic tres, et similis est finis initio: "conticuit" et "intentis"*. The gloss underlines Virgil's use of the same verb, though with different subjects, and the same adjective, which is referred to the audience, still rapt by Aeneas' words. Ti. Cl. Donatus lingers specifically on the latter:

> *Intentis, inquit, omnibus, hoc est adhuc intentis, ut ostenderet Aenean libenter auditum et auditores textu narrationis satiari nequisse: intenti, inquit, fuerant, cum inciperet, intenti, cum finiret. Omnibus dixit, ut ostenderet nullum illic fuisse qui non adhuc desideraret audire.*[3]

2. The beginning of the third book: *postquam*

In the *incipit* of the third book (*Postquam res Asiae Priamique evertere gentem*), a veritable temporal conjunction marks the connection with Book Two.[4] While Ti. Cl. Donatus is rather indifferent to the textual importance of *postquam*,[5] Servius is not: *POSTQUAM haec particula conectendis adiungitur rebus, ut* (3, 662) *"postquam altos tetigit fluctus": sic enim dictis sequentia copulantur*. The connective function attributed to *postquam* is made unequivocal by the presence of *conecto* and *copulo*, even though *particula* does not specifically mean "conjunction" as shown by other occurrences of the word in Servius's commentary, in Servius Danielis' glosses, and in the *Commentarium in artem Donati*. In these contexts, *particula* is used to indicate adverbial forms (either mono- or polysyllabic), enclitics, pronouns, prepositions and prefixes.[6] Furthermore, Servius' gloss makes reference to another passage (*Aen.* 3, 662): *TETIGIT FLUCTUS ET AD AEQUORA VENIT hyperbaton in sensu, ut "progressi subeunt luco fluviumque relinquunt"* (8, 125). Servius' text has been questioned as it was perhaps occasioned by the mistaken interpretation of the abbreviation for *hysteron proteron in sensu* (attested elsewhere, cf. 3, 330). *Aen.* 8, 125 contains *hypallage is sensu*, instead. The 'label' is not as important as the underlying line of reasoning. Concerning the use of *postquam*, Servius' allusion to the process of anticipation of logically posterior events is relevant, in that it validates the use of *postquam* as a connective which introduces an event preceding the event of the superordinate clause.[7]

In other parts of his commentary, Servius points to *postquam* as a possible alternative to *quoniam* (e.g. *Aen.* 9, 717), *ut* (e.g. *Aen.* 3, 53 =

Servius Danielis' glosses) or *ubi* used as a temporal connective: an example of the latter is found in Servius Danielis' gloss to *Aen.* 3, 410 or 1, 81: *et "haec ubi dicta" pro postquam, adverbium locale pro temporali.* In general, the grammatical-exegetic tradition defines *postquam* either as an adverb or as a conjunction. Priscian's *Partitiones* read as follows:[8] *Postquam quae pars orationis est? Adverbium. Quid est adverbium? Pars orationis quae adiecta verbo significationem eius explanat atque implet* (*GL* III 474, 25 ff. = p. 69, 7 ff. Pass.); and again: *Postquam igitur cuius est significationis? Temporis* (*GL* III 475, 2 = p. 69, 16 Pass.). The *Institutiones* do not number *postquam* among the conjunctions, but mention it in the section concerning the use of the locative adverbs as substitutes for time adverbs: *"Haec ubi dicta, cavum conversa cuspide in montem"* (*Aen.* 1, 81) *pro postquam* (*GL* III 85, 17-18), as Servius Danielis glosses. Donatus and his commentators, Servius and Pompeius, do not deal with *postquam* specifically, they number it neither among adverbs nor among conjunctions. Charisius, on the other hand, sees *postquam* as both a time adverb (p. 243, 7 B.) and a conjunction requiring either indicative or subjunctive mood. As for the former, Charisius refers to *Aen.* 3, 1, but claims: *Nec te moveat, si quaedam esse adverbia et coninuctiones recognoveris* (p. 292, 7-8 B.). It thus makes sense that Servius' gloss should make reference to *particula* generically, and highlight the connective function of *postquam* in more detail through the use of *conecto* and *copulo*.

As for modern scholarship, I would like to mention Zampese (2004). Even though he deals with prose texts, it is interesting to note that he lingers on the importance of temporal clauses, both because of their rhematic function, in that they give the reader new information, and because of their resumptive function: "in case the contents of the temporal structures could be considered as contextually predictable or even given, the effect as a whole is one of reaching a higher degree of cohesion or consistency of the narration with events that have already been narrated or with their consequences. The reader may or may not find confirmation of the relief he/she had attributed the previous events or of his/her hypotheses on possible development of the narration".[9] I believe the incipient verses of Book Three of the *Aeneid* are a good example of such use of temporal clauses: the second book ends with Aeneas last meeting with Creusa's ghost, and the hero's decision to flee to the mountains with his father; the third book begins with a quick summary of events in Book Two in order to proceed with the story and, at the same time, satisfy Dido's request to know the *errores* of the Trojan people. Ti. Cl. Donatus notices all of this at the end of the second book; on 2, 804 (*cessi et sublato montis genitore petivit*), he comments: *Plene respondit interrogationi Didonis quae dixit* (1, 754) *narra mihi "insidias Danaum casusque tuorum". Quod quia factum est, adgreditur alteram errores suos evidentissime relaturus.* At the beginning of Book Three, Ti. Cl. Donatus adds: *Narraturus secundum Didonis propositionem etiam errores suos inde primum sumpsit exordium unde revera convenerat, nam laborum eius caput fuit abeundi de Troia necessitas. Neque enim errare per diversa potuisset, nisi primum patriae suae finibus fuisset exclusus.*

3. *At* in the *incipit* of the fourth book

Our continued analysis brings us to the beginning of the fourth book, where we find another connective, defined by modern grammars as a conjunction introducing an adversative coordinate clause: *at regina gravi iamdudum saucia cura.*[10] Ancient commentators focus on the passage in order to highlight Virgil's ability to exalt the contrast between Dido's anxiety as she is irremediably lost to passion,[11] and Aeneas' tranquillity once he has finished recounting his *errores.* In Servius we read:

> *Iunctus quoque superioribus est: quod artis esse videtur, ut frequenter diximus; nam ex abrupto vitiosus est transitus: licet stulte quidam dicant hunc tertio non esse coniunctum - in illo enim navigium, in hoc amores exsequitur - non videntes optimam coniunctionem. Cum enim tertium sic clauserit "factoque hic fine quievit", intulit "at regina gravi iamdudum saucia cura", item paulo post "nec placidam membris dat cura quietem": nam cum Aeneam dormire dixerit, satis congrue subiunxit, ut somno amans careret.* **Alii subitum transitum factum tradunt, quia non ostendit convivium dissolutum: sed hoc subtiliter fecit, quia etiam alia convivia eam habuisse describit** (4, 80) **post ubi digressi lumenque obscura vicissim.**

The commentator's apologetic intent is obvious, as he was presumably reacting to *obtrectatores* identifiable in Servius Danielis' glosses by *quidam* and *alii.* Ti. Cl. Donatus' gloss is less pointed and more careful to underline Aeneas' ability as orator. Yet, he leaves no doubt as to the contrast between Aeneas' state of mind and Dido's, and justifies the beginning of the fourth book, using *tamen* which in my opinion paraphrases *at:*

> *Conclusis omnibus quae necessaria narratio exigebat secessit Aeneas ad requiem; conplevit enim vel quod ipse pollicitus videbatur vel quod regina desiderabat audire: Didonis tamen animus intolerabili iam dudum cura commotus accendebatur magis recordatione loquentis et secreto incendio*

torrebatur. Hoc est quod ait (1-2) *AT REGINA GRAVI IAM DUDUM SAUCIA CURA VULNUS ALIT VENIS ET CAECO CARPITUR IGNI.*

Priscian's *Partitiones* help us to better understand the late ancient interpretation of Virgil. Priscian's observations are usually very schematic and repetitive, but are very precise in this case, and careful to underline a Greek reference:

> *At quae pars orationis est? Coniunctio. Quid est coniunctio? Pars orationis adnectens ordinansque sententiam. Quot accidunt coniunctioni? Tria, potestas ordo figura. Cuius est potestas? Copulativae; est tamen etiam et adversativae, quam Graeci* ἐναντιωματικόν *vocant, sicut etiam hic. Nam Aenea quiescente regina turbatur, quod est contrarium.* (*GL* III 478, 15 ff. = p. 75, 3 ff. Pass.).[12]

In the *Institutiones, at* is only numbered among copulative conjunctions (*GL* III 93, 17 ff.), although Priscian specifies it can be used in place of *saltem, vel* or *aut. Saltem* is listed with adversative conjunctions (p. 99, 10-11), but the example the author chooses (*Aen.* 6, 405-407: *Si te nulla movet tantae pietatis imago,/ at ramum hunc (aperit ramum, qui veste latebat)/ agnoscas*) shows that *saltem* has a restrictive rather than an adversative function,[13] as he has already suggested: *haec* (= *saltem*) *etiam diminutivam significationem habent, ut Vergilius in IIII Aeneidos: Saltem si qua mihi de te suscepta fuisset/ ante fugam suboles* (327-328) (*GL* III 99, 13 ff.).[14]

Other grammarians, Charisius, Donatus and his commentators, do not appear to be interested in the potential adversative value of *at*, though Charisius attributes it the same function as *autem* (pp. 296, 21-297, 3 B.), which he does not number among conjunctions serving as adversatives (p. 290, 3 B.). It is interesting to note that among contemporary scholars C. Kroon recognizes that *at* and *autem* have similar pragmatic functions, especially when both connectives indicate a transition between two moments of a narration which are not necessarily in contrast with one another.[15]

A brief look at Servius' glosses of other occurrences of *at* predictably shows that there is no univocal meaning: in *Aen.* 7, 363; 9, 142; 10, 411, for example, *at* is considered as an alternative to *sed*, functioning as *inceptiva particula*, a conjunction indicating transition. About *Aen.* 10, 411, *SED BELLIS ACER "sed" modo inceptiva particula est, ut in Sallustio saepius, sicut "at" interdum: nam non est coniunctio ratiocinantis*, Servius nevertheless concludes that *at* may function as a conjunction indicating conclusion (*coniunctio ratiotinantis*). In *georg.* 4, 208, Servius

Danielis' glosses offer a pleonastic interpretation of *at* (*abundare*): *AT GENUS IMMORTALE M(ANET) gens manet, scilicet per successionem: ideo immortale genus. Et alibi: AT potest abundare coniunctio; est enim ordo: ergo ipsas quamvis angustus terminus aevi excipiat, genus immortale manet.*

Drawing a working conclusion as to the textual importance of *at* in the beginning of Book Four of the *Aeneid* according to the late ancient tradition, we may state that *at* is used to indicate transition, but also acquires an adversative nuance. Moreover, this specific use of *at* is no *vitiosum transitum*, since both Ovid in his *Metamorphoses* and Lucan in his *Bellum Civile* begin their fourth books with *at*, presumably as a homage to Virgil.[16]

Modern criticism is consistent with late ancient observations: Kroon (1995) studies the pragmalinguistic importance of *at* in Latin prose texts, and shows the many meanings *at* can have. Kroon is closest to our thesis when she mentions *discourse contrast* (pp. 213-214): it happens when *at* introduces a dialogic or narrative move through which the preceding topic is modified or opposed, thereby frustrating the interlocutor's or the reader's expectations (pp. 355-357). In fact, once Aeneas' narration ends in silence, the Virgilian audience expects the end of the banquet and nightly rest, but the following scene opens with Dido's inner turmoil.[17]

4. *Interea*: one of the most frequent connectors

The last connective I will deal with is *interea*. Virgil uses it often; in the incipient verses alone, it is used three times: 5, 1 *Interea medium Aeneas iam classe tenebat*; 10, 1 *Panditur interea domus omnipotentis Olympi*; 11, 1 *Oceanum interea surgens Aurora reliquit*. The latter use is formulaic, and is repeated in 4, 129. Modern studies, albeit none recent, have dealt with this topic, and, even though they are not specifically concerned with late ancient commentators, their conclusions may be compared to the commentators' glosses: *interea* "may be taken as indicating that the action it introduces is going on either (i) at the same time as events already alluded to or (ii) in the space of time between two such events or (iii) in the space of time between an event already mentioned and the narrator's own position in time".[18]

If we compare Servius' gloss of *Aen.* 5, 1 to Ti.Cl. Donatus' gloss of the same line, we find that both commentators stress the simultaneity between Aeneas' navigation and Dido's suicide, and that both remark on the fact that the narration of the former is interrupted by that of the latter only to be taken up again at the beginning of the fifth book. Servius calculates the duration of Aeneas' voyage, but as for the matter on hand, he states: *INTEREA dum fletur aut sepelitur Dido*. He then proceeds, underlining, as we have previously seen, the connection between the beginning of the fifth book and the end of the fourth: *et hoc sermone librum, ut solet, superioribus iunxit*. Ti. Cl. Donatus states instead:

> *Supra* (4, 582) *dixit Troianos navigasse, sed interposita descriptione actuum Didonis et mortis navigationis ipsorum divisa narratio est. Ad hanc igitur poeta regreditur, quia quod interposuerat constat impletam. Ergo subiungit interea medium Aeneas iam classe tenebat certus iter: interea hoc est cum illa perageret fata sua, Aeneas aliquantum provectus est; nam iam tenebat medium iter, hoc est in alto iam fuerat constitutes.*[19]

Servius' *dum* and Ti. Cl. Donatus' *cum* unequivocally point to the temporal meaning attributed to *interea*, but modern-day commentators do not appear to be convinced: Kinsey (1979) does not specifically analyse *Aen.* 5, 1, and Reinmuth (1933) after taking into consideration six different uses of *interea* in Virgil, defines the occurrence in Aen. 5, 1 as *unclassified*, claiming it is only used to draw attention to the contrast between Aeneas and Dido (p. 333). Elsewhere (p. 327) Reinmuth nonetheless interprets *interea* as an indication that the epoch of composition of Book Five follows that of Book Four. Priscian's *Partitiones* support late ancient interpretations:

> *Interea quae pars orationis est? adverbium. Quid est adverbium? Pars orationis et cetera. Quot accidunt adverbio? Tria, significatio, species, figura.* (…) *Cuius significationis est hoc adverbium? Temporalis; potest tamen esse et loci* (*GL* III 480, 21 ff. = p. 78, 9 ff. Pass.).

The *Institutiones* do not deal with adverbs as explicitly,[20] even though with reference to the prepositions (*in* and *inter*) Priscian reports the phrase *interea loci* as equivalent to ἐν τοσούτῳ that is, "in the meantime" (*ibid.* 43, 1 ff.). Of the other grammarians here mentioned, Donatus, his commentators and Charisius, only the latter specifically deals with *interea*, which he numbers among the *temporis adverbia infinita*, with *olim aliquando quondam* and many others (pp. 242, 26-243, 8 B.), opposed to the *finita* like *hodie cras* etc. (p. 243, 8-11 B.). Moreover, in Charisius we find the expression *interea loci*, exemplified using a line from Terence's *Eunuchus* (126). Charisius focuses on a prosodic feature (p. 261, 6 ff. B.), so what he says about *interea loci* is less relevant than what Donatus says in a gloss of the same passage in Terence's comedy:

TE INTEREA LOCI COGNOVI oratorie priorem amatorem facit militem quam Phaedriam; nam posterius dicit hunc cognitum per absentiam militis. Ergo cum militi Phaedria rivalis superductus sit, consequens est, ut miles queri debuerit, non Phaedria, et propterea nihil mirum, si ordine servato miles antepositus fuerit amatori postmodum cognito; et hoc, sine puellae et munerum causa, multum pro milite contra Phaedriam valet.

In the gloss, Donatus addresses ll. 124-127 (*Itast; sed sine me pervenire quo volo./ Intera miles qui me amare occeperat/ in Cariamst profectu'; te interea loci/ cognovi*), the words are pronounced by Thais who is the object of a love quarrel between Phaedria, a young Athenian, and Thraso, a soldier she has met before Phaedria. Donatus' commentary attests the temporal meaning of *interea loci*.

In his gloss to *Aen.* 10, 1, Servius uses a periphrasis with *dum* in order to claim that *interea* is expressive of simultaneity:

PANDITUR INTEREA DOMUS OMNIPOTENTIS OLYMPI secundum poeticum morem hoc dicit "factus est dies", quia poetae dicunt matutino tempore aperiri caelum, noctu vero claudi - unde est illud (1, 374) *"ante diem clauso componet vesper Olympo" - nam et paulo post descripturus est noctem, ut* (10, 215) *"iamque dies caelo concesserat", ut intellegamus alium diem esse consumptum, et nunc eum more solito noctis praetermisisse descriptionem. Quamquam "panditur caelum" etiam simpliciter possimus accipere, quovis tempore, scilicet ad numina convocanda: quod et melius est, quia ait "interea", id est dum haec geruntur: nam "interea" particula praeterita negotia coniungit futuris.*

Ti. Cl. Donatus' gloss of the same line focuses on the words Virgil uses to indicate the beginning and the end of the day, but says nothing specific about *interea*.

Modern scholars have long debated the appropriateness of the connection between Book Nine and Ten: Heinze (1996: 421), refers to ancient commentators, and claims that *Aen.* 10, 1 is a periphrasis used to indicate the dawn and to refer to Hom. *Il.* 8, 1; so both at *Aen.* 10, 1 and 11, 1, *interea* should be understood as meaning "now". Given the succession of events, to which he has already devoted some time, Heinze believes that Virgil's choice for the opening lines of the tenth book is rather unfortunate, because it is neither perspicuous nor an appropriate rendition of the Homeric precedent.[21] Reinmuth (1933: 326-327) disagrees with Heinze, and does not believe 10, 1 should be understood as the beginning of a new day: the present tense (*panditur*) merely indicates that the palace of Zeus "lies open" and not necessarily that it "is thrown open".[22] As for *interea*, Reinmuth maintains it refers to the gods' council,

which takes place while the Rutulians are attacking the Trojan camp, later
during the same day whose beginning was mentioned in *Aen.* 9, 459.
Interea thus helps establish that as far as the poem's composition is
concerned, the tenth book follows the ninth, just as the fifth follows the
fourth.
Servius' gloss to *Aen.* 11, 532 (*Velocem interea superis in sedibus
Opim*) deals with *interea* in a way that is reminiscent of the gloss of *Aen.*
10, 1. With reference to this further occurrence of *interea* Servius uses the
term *particula* again.

> *VELOCEM INTEREA licet "interea" particula negotia semper praeteritis
> futura coniungat, tamen abruptus est et vituperabilis transitus. Habet
> autem tales transitus et in superioribus libris et in sequenti praecipue, ubi
> Iuppiter appellat Iunonem.*

Servius is here uncharacteristically critical of the articulation of Virgil's
text: in fact, Virgil moves from Turnus' deployment of his troops to
Diana's narration of Camilla's story to Opis. In this way the goddess
anticipates the warrior's death. So far we have seen the commentators'
clear apologetic intent with regard to the *Aeneid*, the *Interpretationes* are
particularly relevant in this respect; but in the case of *Aen.* 11, 532, there is
no useful gloss by Ti. Cl. Donatus which can support or counter
Servius'.[23] As for modern scholars, Reinmuth (1933: 333-334) addresses
Servius' critique but does not agree with it: in fact, he gives several
examples of Virgil's use of *interea* to introduce actionless pauses in the
narrative (e.g. *Aen.* 5, 774 or 10, 164), so as to increase suspense and delay
important events, as Homer did. Late ancient commentators do not address
these passages and they are not interested in *interea*, either in *Aen.* 11, 1,
or in the identical *Aen.* 4, 129.
   Servius merely points to Virgil's recurring omission of the description
of night: *more suo praetermisit noctis descriptionem, quam transisse
indicat praesens ortus diei.*[24]
   Nonetheless, it is interesting to acknowledge the importance of ellipsis
in narratology. Its use quickens the pace of the narration and it can be
compared to the use of ellipsis in a clause or sentence as a technique to
achieve textual cohesion. Balbo (2009: 40-41) states:

> "Another strongly connecting element between sentences is ellipsis;
> namely, the absence of an element present in the previous sentence and
> easily recoverable by the hearer or the reader. Ellipsis can regard various
> elements of the clause: subject, predicate, complement, and does not imply
> omission of a term with the same case".[25]

Except for opening lines and *Aen*. 11, 532, Servius only deals with six occurrences of *interea* in Virgil (out of a total sixty-eight). His glosses are fairly schematic and can be split in two different groups: the first group focuses on the use of *interea* as connecting a new event to what has previously been narrated, and explains its use through periphrases introduced by *dum*, which indicate the simultaneity of events;[26] the second group is concerned with the use of *interea* to indicate the completion of an event and the wait for a further event. In this case, the function of *interea* is explained through the use of expressions introduced by *donec*, which underlines the quick succession of events, the definitive ending of the action described in the superordinate clause.[27] This is enough to support the claims of modern scholarship, which interprets *interea* as a connective used to express either the simultaneity of events or their quick succession.

Ti. Cl. Donatus does not always comment the same Virgilian passages featuring *interea*, glossed by Servius; in fact, his most interesting gloss concerns *Aen*. 10, 575-576 (*interea biiugis infert se Lucagus albis/ in medios fraterque Liger*), where he clearly identifies the importance of the connective in the structure of the text: *interea significat ad alia transitum, ut continuatio interrupta narrantis legentis taedium relevet removeatque ex varietate fastidium. Et alia similiter propter hanc causam inventa sunt, ut velut quandam novitatem narrationis inducant*. The temporal meaning of the adverb is less important than the *varietas* it creates in the text by drawing the reader's attention away from one event and towards another, and thereby avoiding boredom. Reinmuth (1933: 336) shows how *interea* occurs ten times in the tenth book of the *Aeneid*, and that it is used to indicate a series of simultaneous events happening in different places and therefore connected by *interea*. Again, in Book Ten, Ti. Cl. Donatus considers ll. 118-119 in order to highlight how the narrative is taken up again after a digression, and in order to indicate the simultaneity between the events introduced by the adverb and those which precede them. *Interea* is here paraphrased with a clause introduced by *cum*, as seen in the gloss to 5, 1, but also 3, 472-473 or 10, 606 and 12, 107-108. In Ti. Cl. Donatus and Servius both, *dum* is used to explain the simultaneity of the events introduced by *interea*.[28] It can be interesting to notice that modern scholars do not always agree with each other, nor do they always agree with ancient commentators. For example, Reinmuth (1933: 333) claims the occurrences of *interea* in 3, 472; 5, 1; and 12, 207 are *unclassified*. In these passages the adverb is taken to indicate a contrast: between Aeneas and Turnus in the latter case or, in the third book, between Anchises and the other Trojans who must prepare the fleet. Elsewhere (p. 328), Reinmuth claims *interea* in 3, 472 is used *to express a Transition, as a Resumptive word, 'ein lose verknüpfendes Nun'.* Kinsey (1979: 261) does not agree with Reinmuth's interpretation of 3, 472; but he agrees with Ti. Cl. Donatus in believing *interea* expresses the simultaneity of two actions: on the one hand Helenus' prediction of Aeneas' future and his order to bring gifts to the ships; on the other hand, Anchises' orders to the fleet.

Conclusion

The range of examples presented here is necessarily incomplete, but suggests, I believe, the importance of studying Virgil's exegetes both in a pedagogical perspective, so as to enhance the students' understanding of the meaning of the *Aeneid*; and in a scholarly perspective, so as to build a constructive dialogic relationship between ancient and modern linguistics.

Notes

[1] Gioseffi (2004) remarks on the unity of books 1-4, which narrate Aeneas' time in Carthage, and constitute an autonomous narrative sequence. So not only is the first book literally 'welded' to the second, but, in structural terms, it is even more deeply connected with the fourth: the harbour in Carthage, at first a safe heaven, afterwards becomes a dangerous place from which Aeneas has to flee. The banquet at the beginning of the first book serves as background to the narration in both the second and third books, as well as facilitating the transition to the fourth book, which begins with Dido's anxiety concerning the feelings she started experiencing during the banquet itself. Finally, the good omens connected to the evening's libations (1, 730-735) will be countered by the queen's curses in point of death (4, 590-629).
[2] Servius is less specific about the antecedent for *omnes*, but he states: *et bene "omnes" addidit; poterat enim simul quidam, sed non omnes, tacere.*
[3] Pinkster (1990: 243-250) stresses the importance of semantic correlation, that is, contiguity and similarity of topic, in the achievement of cohesion among several communicative units. Moreover, he numbers repetition of words belonging to the same semantic field, and the recurrence of anaphoric elements such as indefinite pronouns, among the means to achieve lexical cohesion. See Balbo (2009:38-41).
[4] For an overview of Virgil's use of coordinating and subordinating conjunctions, see Calboli (1985) and the annexed bibliography; on the use of *postquam* in Latin see Kühner and Stegmann (1912[2]: 353-359), and Hofmann and Szantyr (1965: 597 ff.).
[5] As for ll. 1-7, Ti. Cl. Donatus pays more attention to the parallel which is drawn between the four adversities of the past and the four uncertainties of the future (p. 261,17 ff.).
[6] Here are a few examples: GL IV 407, 25 (*quam* introduces the second term of the comparison); 427, 6 (adverbs such as *magis* and *maxime*); 439, 18 (enclitics); in the commentary to the *Aeneid*: adverbs (*Aen.* 1, 6 = Servius Danielis' glosses);

enclitics (*Aen.* 1, 27; 1, 116); pronouns (*Aen.* 1, 3 = Servius Danielis' glosses; 1, 181); prepositions (*Aen.* 1, 193; 2, 227); prefixes (*Aen.* 2, 330 = Servius Danielis' glosses).

[7] I have dealt with these lines and with the rhetorical processes here quoted in Torzi (2000: 185-275). On the importance of *hyperbaton* and, more generally, Latin word order see Devine and Stephens (2006: 524-610), and Oniga (2007: 94-97), even though their works are concerned with prose.

[8] Prisciani Caesarensis *Opuscola*, ed. by M. Passalacqua, vol. II, *Institutio de nomine et pronomine et verbo. Partitiones Duodecim versuum Aeneidos principalium*, Roma, Edizioni di storia e letteratura 1999, p. XXXIX. The following quotations will be taken from this text. For an in-depth analysis of Priscian's *Partitiones*, their history, and their role in the late ancient tradition see Glück (1967).

[9] Zampese (2004: 170). For a general discussion of the importance of subordinating conjunctions for the realization of grammatical cohesion see also Pinkster (1990: 257-258) and Balbo (2009: 43). Kroon (1994: 305) numbers *postquam*, and *ut*, among connectives referring to the *representational level of discourse*.

[10] About the use of *at* and, generally, adversative conjunctions in Virgil, see Guardì (1985: 440-441); about the use of *at* in Latin cf. Hofmann and Szantyr (1965:487-488).

[11] I have already dealt with the beginning of the fourth book of the *Aeneid* in Torzi (2008: 27-70); in the same article see also a detailed bibliography on Dido and her role in Virgil's text.

[12] Evidence of this is found in Dion. Tr. p. 643, 15 ed. Bek = p. 100, ed. Uhlig; and Ap. Disc. *Cons.* p. 251, 3 ed. Sch.

[13] "Restringierenden Adverb" according to Kühner and Stegmann (1912[2]: 801).

[14] Servius and Servius Danielis point to the restrictive function of *saltem* in their glosses of *Aen.* 4, 327-328.

[15] Kroon (1995: 355; 366-369).

[16] Ovid's aim is to underline "una movenza avversativa (…) lo scarto rispetto al finale disteso del libro terzo (ll. 732 ff.), conferendo a quello che si apre una tonalità oscura e minacciosa" (Ovidio, *Metamorfosi*, II, a cura di A. Barchiesi e G. Rosati, Milano, Mondadori 2007, p. 244). See also Steiner (1958: 229), and Casali (1999: 326), no. 22.

[17] Kroon (1994) already addresses the matter. About the importance of coordinating conjunctions in grammatical cohesion see Pinkster (1990: 252 ff.), and Balbo (2009: 41-43).

[18] Kinsey (1979: 259). See also Reinmuth (1933), who quotes, occasionally, Servius.

[19] In the *Interpretationes* there is no gloss of *Aen.* 4, 582 because of a lacuna; Servius refers to 4, 586-587 in order to establish the exact time of Aeneas' departure from Carthage (dawn), but his gloss is of no use to our present purpose.

[20] *Interea* is mentioned as adverb, but only with reference to the structure of the *composita* (*GL* III 65, 25 ff.).

[21] Cf. *ibid.* p. 491.

[22] Kinsey (1979: 263-264), seems to agree. The three authors here quoted rely on different bibliographical references, to which I refer readers.
[23] Macrobius (*Sat.* 5, 22, 1-10) and Priscian (*GL* III 2, 328, 7) quote the passage, but they are not useful to our present purposes.
[24] Reinmuth (1933: 328-332), and Kinsey (1979: 262 ff).
[25] See also Pinkster (1990: 251), to which Balbo refers.
[26] Cf. *Aen.* 1, 479; 6, 212; 10, 833; 11, 532. See also Reinmuth (1933: 324 and 336).
[27] Cf. *Aen.* 9, 422; 11, 22 and *georg.* 3, 40.
[28] Cf. 6, 212, in which Ti. Cl. Donatus agrees with Servius; 10,439; 12,383-386; 614.

References

Balbo, A. (2009) "Per una valorizzazione e un uso dei connettivi nella traduzione", in I. Torzi (ed.) *Il Quaderno di latino 2*, pubblicazione *on line* della rivista *Nuova secondaria* (http://www.lascuolaconvoi.it), 37-53.

Calboli, G. (1985) "Congiunzioni", in *Enciclopedia Virgiliana* I, Roma, Istituto dell'Enciclopedia Italiana fondato da G. Treccani, 873 ff.

Casali, S. (1999) "Mercurio e Ilerda: Pharsalia 4 ed Eneide 4", in P. Esposito and L. Nicastri (eds) *Interpretare Lucano. Miscellanea di studi*, Napoli, Arte tipografica (Università degli Studi di Salerno. Quaderni del Dipartimento di Scienze dell'Antichità, 22), 223-236.

Devine, A.M. and L.D. Stephens (2006) *Latin Word Order. Structured Meaning and Information*, Oxford-New York, University Press.

Gioseffi, M. (2004) "Due punti di snodo in Virgilio (Il canto di Damone - Il banchetto di Didone)", in M. Gioseffi (ed.) *Il dilettoso monte. Raccolta di saggi di Filologia e di Tradizione classica*, Milano, LED, 39-78.

Glück, M. (1967) *Priscians Partitiones und ihre Stellung in der spätantiken Schule. Mit einer Beilage: Commentarii in Prisciani Partitiones medio aevo compositi*, Hildesheim, G. Olms.

Guardì, T. (1985) "Avversative", in *Enciclopedia Virgiliana* I, Roma, Istituto dell'Enciclopedia Italiana fondato da G. Treccani, 440-442.

Heinze, R. (1996) *La tecnica epica di Virgilio*, trad. it. Bologna, il Mulino [= ed. or. 1915³].

Hofmann, J.B. and A. Szantyr (1965) *Lateinische Grammatik*, II Band, München, C.H. Beck.

Kinsey, T.E. (1979) "The Meaning of interea in Virgil's Aeneid" *Glotta* 57.3-4: 259-265.

Kroon, C. (1994) "Discourse connectives and discourse type. The case of Latin *at*", in J. Herman (ed.) *Linguistic studies on Latin*. Selected papers from the 6th international colloquium on Latin linguistics (Budapest, 23-27 March 1991), Amsterdam-Philadelphia, Benjamins, 303-317.

—. (1995) *Discourse Particles in Latin. A study of nam, enim, autem, vero and at*, Amsterdam, J.C. Gieben.

Kühner, R. and C. Stegmann (1912^2) *Ausführliche Grammatik der lateinischen Sprache*, II: *Satzlehre*, Hannover, Hahn.

Oniga, R. (2007) *Il latino. Breve introduzione linguistica*, 2^a ed., Milano, Franco Angeli.

Pinkster, H. (1990) *Latin Syntax and Semantics*, London, Routledge.

Reinmuth, O.W. (1933) "Vergil's Use of interea, a Study of the Treatment of Contemporaneous Events in Roman Epic" *The American Journal of Philology* 54.4: 323-339.

Steiner, G. (1958) "Ovid's Carmen Perpetuum" *Transactions and Proceedings of American Philological Association* 89: 218-236.

Torzi, I. (2000) *Ratio et Usus, Dibattiti antichi sulla dottrina delle figure*, Milano, Vita e Pensiero.

—. (2008) "Ipotesi Didattiche in riferimento a Verg. Aen. IV 1-30", in *Il Quaderno di latino* pubblicazione *on line* della rivista *Nuova Secondaria* (http://www.lascuolaconvoi.it), 27-60.

Zampese, L. (2004) "Dall'analisi logica alle logiche del testo", in G. Milanese (ed.) *A ciascuno il suo latino: la didattica delle lingue classiche dalla scuola di base all'università*. Atti del convegno di studi, Palazzo Bonin-Logare, Vicenza 1-2 ottobre 2001, Galatina, Congedo editore, 157-182.

SECTION III.

HISTORY AND THEORY OF TEACHING

GENERATIVE GRAMMAR AND THE DIDACTICS OF LATIN: THE USE OF EXAMPLES

BERNARD BORTOLUSSI

Introduction

By way of introduction, let me quote J.-L. Chevillard:

> Toutes les grammaires comportent des exemples. C'est là un ingrédient probablement nécessaire du discours grammairien, en tout cas dont on constate empiriquement la quasi universalité. Cependant le statut épistémologique, la forme, la fonction, le fonctionnement sémiotique, des séquences que l'on peut appeler "exemple", peuvent être différents selon les corpus que l'on observe, qu'il s'agisse de traditions différentes, ou à l'intérieur d'une même tradition, de moments historiques différents.[1]
>
> Chevillard (2007: 1)

All grammars of Latin therefore also include examples. Roughly speaking, the didactic function of grammatical examples is twofold:

- in providing a fragment of language which highlights such-and-such usage or such-and-such rule, they have a **descriptive function**;
- in putting forward a model for language production, they have a **normative function**.

Within the grammatical tradition, there has been a tendency to use examples as the literal embodiment of the relevant rules. Among recent Latin grammars M. Lavency's *VSVS* carries on this tradition. What is used as a paragraph heading is an example, not a formulation of the relevant rule:

(1)   *Romulus urbem condidit* (Lavency 1997[1:] 134 § 231)

This example means: "the subject of a finite verb-form receives the Nominative". Chevillard *et alii* (2007) refer to this feature of grammatical examples as *autonymy*: the example is a grammatical entity, not a fragment of the language.

I shall assume without any further discussion that using examples is absolutely necessary to didactics. The question I shall consider is: has this use remained unchanged since linguistics emerged, especially within the framework of a formal theory of language such as Generative Grammar?

Let us begin with a quick test: let us compare a few paradigms or contrastive series provided by sundry grammatical or linguistic descriptions:

(2) a. *et Dionysius loquitur et Trypho*   Priscian (GLK II 160)
     b. *et Apollonius scripsit et ego*
     c. *et scribit et legit Trypho*
     d. *et pugnat et uincit Aeneas*

(3) a. *Petrus appellat Paulum*   Marouzeau (1953: VIII)[2]
     b. *Petrus Paulum appellat*
     c. *Paulum appellat Petrus*
     d. *Paulum Petrus appellat*
     e. *appellat Petrus Paulum*
     f. *appellat Paulum Petrus*

(4) a. *Ioannes sororem suam uidit*   Bertocchi and Casadio (1980: 26)
     b. *Ioannes sororem eius uidit*

(5) a. *Caesarem Brutus occidit*   Devine and Stephens (2006: 3)
     b. *Brutus Caesarem occidit*
     c. *Occidit Brutus Caesarem*
     d. *Caesarem occidit Brutus*

(6) a. *Catullus amat Lesbiam*   Oniga (2007: 203)
     b. *Catullus Lesbiam amat*
     c. *amat Catullus Lesbiam*
     d. *amat Lesbiam Catullus*
     e. *Lesbiam Catullus amat*
     f. *Lesbiam amat Catullus*

From Priscian over Devine and Stephens to Oniga, examples appear to be the same or nearly the same: proper names and a verb in the present tense and active voice. Even if the last examples sound rather more Latin-like and perhaps more "classical Latin-like" than the first, they lack any attestation.

I mean to show that, in generative approaches to the Latin language, examples are used towards aims and along procedures which are quite different from what may be seen in the grammatical tradition and in grammars relying on other linguistic theories.

An "example" is one of a Latin speaker's actual "performance"; it is a fragment which reflects a competence. This virtual competence is "reconstructed" by means of investigation of a corpus; so the chosen example is inseparable from the corpus and, so to speak, summarizes it. But the example is not just an attestation: actually, it is an artefact elaborated by the linguist, who extracts it and shapes it according to some particular aim.

Only syntactic examples will be considered here, even though both phonology and morphology would provide a wealth of subject matter. I shall refer less to actual Generative Grammars of Latin – apart from R. Oniga's *Il latino* I am afraid I cannot name any other – than to some virtual Generative Grammars some of us have recourse to in our teaching.

1. Examples as evidence of competence

1.1. Competence vs. performance

Starting from Chomsky (1965: 4), Generative Grammar purports to be a theory of **competence**:

> "A grammar of a language purports to be a description of the ideal speaker-hearer's intrinsic competence".

Since there are no native speakers of Latin, are we justified in developing an aimless Generative Grammar of Latin? Several solutions have been proposed in order to circumvent this difficulty, by, e.g. R.T. Lakoff (1968: 2):

> In many cases, even nonnative speakers can judge the grammaticality of a sentence in a language they know well…therefore we do not need attestation to certify that a sentence is grammatical.

Nonnative speakers may judge grammaticality if they rely on information provided by native speakers. In the case of Latin, we may rely:

(a) On a grammatical tradition dating back to antiquity: there is no good reason for doubting the exhaustiveness and accuracy of these descriptions; therefore, traditional examples may be considered valid basic material;
(b) On attested constructions: from attested *incipit calēre* ("it is beginning to be hot") one may deduce that *incipit pluere* ("it is beginning to rain"), which is not attested, but is grammatical and acceptable.

With both methods, grammaticality is presumed to be based on a kind of judgment which is not solely intuitive but may be "reconstructed".

Since competence may be accessed neither by introspection nor by direct questioning of a speaker-hearer, it can only be accessed by indirect investigation, *i.e.* from the actual **performances**. What is traditionally called *grammatical example* is no longer perceived as representing a usage (good usage or some decadent usage), but rather as **a fragment of performance representing a certain level of competence**.

1.2. Authentic example vs made-up example

The examples provided by grammars are usually authentic examples, and have been since antiquity, excepting only the paradigms, as quoted above in the introduction. Authenticity used to fulfill two functions:

(a) vouching for the accuracy of description and analysis;
(b) supplying a model for reproducing a particular language stage.

Using made-up examples – or rather examples the grammarian creates on the basis of preliminary observation and analysis – is a stopgap solution which is unavoidable due to the fact that paradigms are not found spontaneously in common usage. However, a generative linguist may be inclined to think that those examples are even more relevant than authentic examples, for two reasons:

(a) The paradigm is an "elaborate" fragment of performance, insofar as it results from an analysis which brings together a set of data; it delineates the specific phenomenon to be described;
(b) These examples are non-literary examples, and so possibly better suited to represent standard Latin competence at a given time.

A generative linguist works with a safety net when proposing wholly made up paradigms, for he can rely on those examples that ancient grammarians invented themselves: there are **"authentic" made-up** examples at our disposal. The authenticity of such grammatical data may be questioned, however, as noted by Auroux (1998: 192): "On court […] le risque d'utiliser des exemples qui ne sont attestés que dans les grammaires, tout comme il y a des formes qui ne sont attestées que dans les dictionnaires".[3]

Then one must compare the "grammarians' examples" with literary attestations. Let us look at examples of passive forms provided by Charisius:

(7) *uerbum passiuum, ut scribo scribor, lego legor* (Char. *gramm.* p. 215,5 Barwick)

This points up the difference between grammaticality and acceptability: all later grammarians since Charisius repeat the same examples, which are wholly based on the formation rule for the passive voice and do not take into account the acceptability of the utterance (*legor* is well attested, but not *scribor*). I will not go so far as to say that Charisius is a proto-generativist, even though with *scribor* he is dealing with the mechanism of form production, *i.e.* with competence (Duso 2006). For it seems that analogy is at work here rather than consideration of competence; the same mechanism leads for instance to the invention of the form *qualisque*:

(8) *Inuenitur quisque pro quicumque, qualisque pro qualiscumque. Similiter aduerbia quoque pro quocumque, quaque pro quacumque, quandoque pro quandocumque* (Prisc. *gramm.* GLK III 138,15-17) "*Quisque* is found instead of *quicumque*, *qualisque* instead of *qualiscumque*. The same for adverbs: *quoque* instead of *quocumque*, *quaque* instead of *quacumque*, *quandoque* instead of *quandocumque*".

The few more or less exhaustive and didactically motivated descriptions that have been produced by generative linguists do not greatly differ from traditional grammars when they use authentic examples. The reason why is, as R. Oniga remarks, that:

L'obiettivo dello studio del latino non può essere il 'parlare per fare', ma il 'leggere per capire' (Oniga 2007: 15)[4]

Our point of reference is that of the person for whom the grammar is intended: what we must seek is to instill not a general Latin competence, but several competences for several synchronic stages. Ideally, we should both describe the linguistic competence of a particular writer and be able to refer it to the reconstructed competence for a particular period.

The only way to achieve this is to use homogeneous examples, *i.e.* to resort to corpora. So in this respect - at first appearance, at least - generative linguists do not differ from common custom.

2. Examples and corpus

2.1. Is resorting to a corpus justified?

We have come to a most sensitive point: are Generative Grammar and corpus grammar compatible? Corpus grammar was developed mainly in opposition to the generative model, and conversely in *Syntactic Structures* Chomsky absolutely denied probability and statistics linguistics any relevance at all.[5] Here are some of the criticisms which are usually aimed at generativist views:

(a) made-up examples do not represent (language) reality, which is much more complex than what emerges from generativist descriptions; the sophisticated hypotheses of generative linguists are only based on artificial data. E.g.:

> as a result categorical judgments are overused where not appropriate, while a lack of concern for observational adequacy has meant that successive versions have tended to treat a shrinking subset of data **increasingly removed from real usage**... generative grammar has produced many explanatory hypotheses of considerable depth, but is increasingly failing because its hypotheses are **disconnected from verifiable linguistic data** (Manning 2003: 296)

(b) judgments on such examples are binary (+/- grammatical), they ignore variations and degrees. E.g.:

> Gradations of acceptability are not accommodated in algebraic grammars: a structure is grammatical or not (Abney 1996: 14)

(c) in fields such as teaching or translation the study of actual performances is more appropriate than knowledge of an over-simplistic competence.

Such criticisms are not groundless, but appear to be unfair, especially when one considers how Chomskyan theories have changed over time:

- The aim of any Generative Grammar has always been to compete with traditional grammars as to accuracy and exhaustiveness;
- Degrees of acceptability are duly taken into account; so is the evolution of the language, with the introduction of parameters;
- What corpora supply is documentation, not examples; resorting to corpora is a possible way - perhaps the only way, in the case of a dead language - to formulate hypotheses, but example status only emerges later, once the hypothesis is constituted.

Therefore, a "reconciliation" is conceivable (cf. Harris 1988) inasmuch as an empirically based formal grammar (such as Generative Grammar) constantly switches back and forth between data and formalization. Any scrutiny of a corpus of data implies from the start not only some procedure that is independent from the corpus, but also a hypothesis about what relevant data actually are.

The "reconciliation" is even inescapable for ancient languages. Any study of Latin does use corpora and must obey the methodological criteria laid down by Habert *et alii* (1997):

- sufficient size,
- sampling,
- reference corpus,
- quantified data.

Obviously all those conditions are not always met and texts from all periods should not, strictly speaking, be used. Quantifying the data is a problem in itself, for besides quantitative analysis methods such as those used by S. Mellet or the LASLA team even simple counting may vary quite a lot because of variations in the MS. tradition.

Resorting to a corpus is not useful in the same way according to what use is made of examples; but the approaches are mainly *corpus-based* rather than *corpus-driven*, since new analyses of known facts are researched rather than new facts.

2.2. Corpus as pool

a. Pool of illustrations
Classical texts are an almost inexhaustible pool providing the canonical examples to be found in grammars and handbooks. The criteria which induce grammarians to choose a particular example do not really come under corpus methodology.

b. Pool of minimal pairs
Here Generative Grammar does not appear to break new ground compared to other approaches stemming from structuralism, such as e.g. M. Lavency's (1985: 232), who provides near-minimal pairs to highlight the contrast between indicative vs. subjunctive in temporal and relative clauses:

(9) a. *Fuit quoddam **tempus cum** in agris homines passim uagabantur* (Cic. *inv.* 1,2)
"There was a time when men wandered here and there in the fields".

b. *Fuit antea **tempus cum** Germanos Galli uirtute superarent* (Caes. *Gall.* 6,24)
"Previously there was a time when Gauls outdid Germans in valour"

(10) a. *L. Papirius **Paetus**, uir bonus amatorque noster, mihi **libros** eos, quos Ser. Claudius **reliquit, donauit*** (Cic. *Att.* 1,20,7)
"Lucius Papirius Paetus, a fine man, who loves us, has given me the books that Servius Claudius left him".

b. ***Paetus**, ut antea ad te scripsi, omnis **libros quos** frater suus reliquisset mihi donauit* (Cic. *Att.* 2,1,12)
"Paetus, as I wrote before, gave me all the books his brother had left him".

Finding strictly minimal pairs is more difficult. From generativism-inspired works we may quote Devine and Stephens (2006: 99); they give a near-minimal pair illustrating constituent order:

(11) a. *qui ciuitatem **regio dominatu** liberauit* (Cic. *Planc.* 60)
"who freed the city from a king's rule"

b. *qui ... **dominatu regio** rem publicam liberauit* (Cic. *Phil.* 1,3)
"who freed the republic from a king's rule"

We might quote (12) to illustrate the contrast between direct and indirect questions:

(12) *Quid negotist? - Quid negoti sit rogas?* (Plaut. *Aul.* 296)
"What is it about? - You're asking what it is about?"

c. Pool of paradigms
Giusti and Oniga's work (2006) on NP constituents provides N+Adj paradigms of authentic strings; they do not need to make up examples or touch them up. Here is the first series, from Cicero's corpus:

(13) *homo Romanus* (Cic. *Att.* 7,3,10)
homo consularis (Cic. *de orat.* 1,166)
homo Romanus et consularis (Cic. *de orat.* 1,231)

The second series, which illustrates patterns with possessive adjectives, lacks attestation in Cicero. This is replaced not by a made-up example, but by an example found in a different corpus. It must be presumed that what is described is not Cicero's personal competence, but the competence of some speaker whom I do not dare call ideal, but trans-paradigmatic - a competence enduring through several centuries:

(14) *homo meus* (Plaut. *Pseud.* 381)
homo Romanus (*Cic. Att.* 7,3,10)
homo meus et Romanus* (Romanus et meus*)

The fact that **homo meus et Romanus* is never attested is linked to the **ungrammaticality** of this construction. But this ungrammaticality does not follow from the lack of attestation alone – which might be due to chance, as in the case of *pluere incipit* above; it is extrapolated from a theoretical prediction and the whole paradigm of *Romanus* (classifying adjectives) and *meus* (possessive adjectives): no occurrence of any coordination between these two classes is ever attested.

This method to present and analyse data tends to be generalized: on the same question of NP constituents, Devine and Stephens (2006: 314-511) provide numerous paradigms, but these paradigms never emerge from an exhaustive investigation of the corpus, just from spot checks concerning specific lexical items.

2.3. The corpus as field for experiments

The model stemming from *Principes and Parameters* and the later *Minimalist Program* allow us to understand (a) variations inside a language and (b) diachronic changes. For linguists studying both these points, Latin is a particularly interesting field: numerous variations, which used to be excluded from Latin syntax, can henceforward be brought back into it within a structural framework, and the origin of the typological change from Latin to Romance languages can be sought in Late Latin corpora. The corpus must be an area open to investigation, and replace the obviously impossible questioning of absent speakers. Experimentation does not consist in introspection or questioning native speakers in order to evaluate examples which may have been made up to test hypotheses; it consists in sweeping across a corpus in order to verify or reject some hypothesis or other.

The simplest case consists in checking that some particular form or construction actually exists. One existing occurrence is not enough to guarantee full verification – as we saw in the case of *scribor* or *qualisque*. Several occurrences of the same form or construction must be found. Quantitative evaluation does not aim at the same conclusions as other theories. The aim is not to evaluate trends in usage, but to determine variations which can be translated into parameters evolutions.

In the case of the adnominal genitive, for instance, variations in word order can be quantitatively measured, as in Giusti and Oniga (2006) or Gianollo (2007). These figures concerning a sample may help to (a) verify hypotheses on Latin NP structure and (b) describe how this structure gradually changed from the classical period to Christian Latin.

That some examples stray from the established format is interpreted as a variation in syntactic structure, not a variation due to stylistic or other factors. For instance, if it is hypothesized that the objective genitive is postposed, then when it is preposed this will be analysed as resulting from a movement (15a), as well as the subjective genitive, when it is postposed (15b):

(15) a. [*artis*$_i$ [*descriptio* t$_i$]]
     b. [*descriptio*$_i$ [*philosophi* t$_i$]]

3. Example as made up artefact

As noted by Milner (1989: 115), any example, even an authentic one, is "une instance minimale de refutation". In other words, predictions are made on the basis of a hypothesis: a virtual example is made up, then its existence is verified.

An authentic example is not a datum; it is sought for and discovered. Therefore, a quotation is valueless by itself. Example status must be acquired and it varies according to the hypothesis which is being evaluated. For instance, example (1), which is used to show how Nominative is assigned, might equally well be used to illustrate Accusative assignation, SOV word-order, and so on.

3.1. Any example is abstract

In the true sense an example is an abstract text fragment. Its "conditions singulières d'énonciation" are not relevant[6] (Milner 1989: 109). Generally speaking, it is not "un document" (Milner 1989: 118). So it acquires metalinguistic status. It delineates some phenomenon, as we shall see below.

We may understand *abstract* in its derived meaning: an example is abstract inasmuch as the meaning of each item is as general as possible. In some cases, this meaning may even be seen as wholly irrelevant. Let us consider examples illustrating possible constituent structures for S-O-V constituents: the very words, Subject and Object, make it clear that the only relevant thing is their function, not whatever they refer to, nor even, finally, their category (NP). The role of proper nouns in (3), (5) and (6) is that of "non-instantiated variables", and so is that of indefinite pronouns (or logical variables in formal linguistics).

3.2. Any example is "refined"

On this point, I shall essentially take up Milner's (1989: 109-118) observations, which hold not only for Generative Grammar, but for any scientific study of language. Several images have been used in order to describe this process: *concrétion* (Milner 1989), *nettoyage* (Abney 1996); but all of them describe reduction as a "linguistic fact".

Refining an example allows one to isolate a certain linguistic phenomenon: that phenomenon must be illustrated, even "staged" in a contrastive series (Marandin 2001); the way to achieve this is by getting rid of scoria, *i.e.* anything which is non-relevant: context (on condition that it does not affect the phenomenon to be described), sentence elements which play no role in that phenomenon. That is why a "good" example is as simple as possible; of course it is easy to make up simple examples (cf. 1), but it is much more difficult to find authentic ones, especially in literary genres. Here is a basic case: in order to illustrate the use of the accusative case Lavency (1985: 143) gives the example in (1), which is reproduced here in (16):

(16) *Romulus urbem condidit* (Cic. *div.* 1,30)
       "Romulus founded a city"

Now, the original context of the quotation is:

(17) *Principio huius urbis parens Romulus non solum auspicato urbem condidisse, sed ipse etiam optumus augur fuisse traditur.*
"They say that at the beginning of this city not only did its (founding) father Romulus consult the auspices and found the city, but he was himself the best of augurs".

This method rests on principles that a generative linguist would not repudiate: first, eliminating those constituents which play no role in the assignation of the accusative and so may only be interpreted from the context,[7] then simplifying groups in order to reduce them to (the expression of) their kernel. These procedures imply a syntagmatic dimension in syntax; even more notably, the reduction of the so-called NcI construction *Romulus urbem condidisse traditur* to a simple clause (*Romulus urbem condidit*) rests on an analysis which is not unlike Raising.

A *fortiori* it is impossible to find complete paradigms unless they are obtained by some radical "refinement", or rather by what might be compared to mosaic or fresco restoring: missing elements are replaced by tesserae or colours produced according to the techniques of Antiquity. For instance, none of the paradigms given *supra* (2)-(5) to illustrate the linear order of major constituents is attested in the least; the only paradigm which might lay claim to being the result of refinement of authentic examples is H. Weil's (1978: 24):

(18) a. *idem ille Romulus Romam condidit*
     b. *Hanc urbem condidit Romulus*
     c. *Condidit Romam Romulus.*

(18a) may be compared with (16) and with (19):

(19) **Romulus**, *Martis filius, ultus iniurias aui* **Romam** *urbem Parilibus in Palatio* **condidit** (Vell. 1,8,4)

This example, however, shows that the refining or producing rules are not the same for paradigms as for isolated examples; for (18a) is supposed to be considered not by itself but in contrast with (18b): the complex form of the Subject *idem ille Romulus* is meant to "reveal" that initial Subject has a different informational status from postposed Subject (in 18b).

3.3. Refining techniques

Generative Grammar has introduced nothing new as far as producing examples is concerned. It just takes up (a) procedures which were used by the grammatical tradition and (b) structuralist principles, which, starting from an **analysis** of particular performances, produce minimal sentences through mere **lexical** commutation.

Such examples may be found in ancient grammarians' works, particularly when they are studying *amphibolia casuum* (case ambiguity). They quote Ennius (*ann.* 179 Vahlen[2]), then they make up simpler examples:

(20) *aio te, Aeacida, Romanos uincere posse* (Diom. *gramm.* GLK I 450)
   "I say that you, Aeacid, can defeat the Romans" or "that the Romans can defeat you"

(21) a. *certum est Antonium praecedere eloquentia Crassum* (Diom. *gramm.* GLK I 450)
   "it is an established fact that Antony outshone Crassus as an orator"or "that Crassus outshone Antony as an orator"

   b. *uidi secutorem retiarium occidisse* (Pomp. *gramm.* GLK V 295,14)
   "I saw that the *secutor* had killed the *retiarius*"or "that the *retiarius* had killed the *secutor*"

This method is explicitly adopted by R. Oniga (2007: 163); aiming at pedagogical efficiency, he suggests fiddling with two attested sentences so as to produce two new ones:

Le frasi *consuetudo | concinnat amorem* (Lucr. 4,1283) e *ueritas | odium parit* (Ter. *Andr.* 68), possono essere segmentate e ricombinate in frasi grammaticali come *consuetudo | odium parit* e *ueritas | concinnat amorem*[8]

What is new is how unacceptable and/or ungrammatical examples are used. Whatever didactic function one ascribes to them, they are made necessary by the empiricism of Chomskyan theory: since the theory is falsifiable, one may invent examples that might invalidate it and check that they are not acceptable – the kind of examples Auroux (1998) calls "anti-examples". Then the corpus question arises once more: the fact that some construction is not attested does not prove that it did not exist. However, we may make peripheral use of authentic examples quoted by ancient grammarians:

- either as ungrammatical:

(22) a. *numquid possum dicere 'qui fecit iniuriam est quis?' Per rerum naturam non potest fieri, sed in inchoandis elocutionibus ponitur.* (Pomp. *gramm.* GLK V 205,17)
"May I say 'the man who did wrong is who?' By the nature of things it is impossible: one places it (*quis*) at the beginning"

   b. *si dices 'sequor homine' pro 'sequor hominem'* (Sacerd. *gramm.* GLK VI 450)
"If one says '*sequor homine*' instead of '*sequor hominem*'"

   c. *si enim dicam 'suus seruus ministrat mihi' uel 'tibi', soloecismum facio* (Prisc. *gramm.* GLK III 167)
"For if I say "his own (*suus*) slave waits on me" or "waits on you", I am committing a solecism"

- or as less acceptable examples:

(23) a. *Imperitia lapsi 'nescio quid facis, nescio quid fecisti'; eruditius autem dicetur 'nescio quid facias, nescio quid feceris'* (Diom. *gramm.* GLK I 335)
one makes a mistake through ignorance when saying '*nescio quid facis, nescio quid fecisti*' ; if one is better educated, one will say '*nescio quid facias, nescio quid feceris*'"

   b. *Praeterea animaduertimus Quadrigarium in octauo annalium particula ista usum esse obscurissime. Verba ipsius posuimus: "Romam uenit; uix superat, quin triumphus decernatur"* (Gell. 17,13,5)
"Moreover we notice that Quadrigarius in Book VIII of his *Annals* used this particle in a most obscure way. Here are his own words: 'He arrives in Rome; he barely gets a triumph'".

The former example (23a) shows the difference between two levels of speech: using the indicative (*quid facis, quid fecisti*) is less acceptable at a speech level we might call educated. The latter example (23b) presents an idiolect: extension of the use of conjunction *quin*. So an anti-example no longer exhibits a mistake which should (from a didactic point of view) be avoided, it is a construction which is to be used in order to test a hypothesis.

3.4.The status of exceptions

I am tempted to say in a somewhat provocative manner that there are no exceptions in a Generative Grammar of Latin. All those famous examples showing exceptions to some rule and often renamed "figures" (anacoluthon and so on) may be brought together into two groups which will not have the same status in a Generative Grammar:

- "mistakes", meaning that a speaker's actual performance is affected by what Chomsky (1965: 4) calls "grammatically non relevant conditions", e.g.:

(24) *At ita studiosus est huius praeclarae existimationis,* **ut** *putetur in hisce rebus intellegens esse,* **ut** *nuper – uidete hominis amentiam: postea-quam est comperendinatus, cum iam pro damnato mortuoque esset, ludis circensibus mane apud L. Sisennam, uirum primarium, cum essent triclinia strata argentumque expositum in aedibus, cum pro dignitate L. Sisennae domus esset plena hominum honestissimorum, accessit ad argentum, contemplari unum quidque otiose et considerare coepit.* (Cic. *Verr.* 2,4,33)

This is quoted by Hofmann and Szantyr (1965: 730) as an example of anacoluthon in the following way:

(25) *Ita studiosus est huius … existimationis, ut … accessit ad argentum, contemplari … coepit*

Note how this example is refined through elimination of all "impurities". Hence things are distorted: thanks to a conjuring trick (the remaining *ut* is not the correct one) the example looks like an ordinary solecism, not a figure of speech. In fact this quotation has no example value at all, since it only exhibits a particular performance and cannot be refined: in order to describe it, one should take into account all the elements of which the utterance is composed. So even though it is possible to identify the mistake (the fact that the subordinate clause is unfinished) this utterance cannot be used even as an anti-example, for an anti-example is as refined as an example.

- other examples, which are less numerous, but do reflect competence as much as the others, insofar as they exemplify an alternative option. This type of phenomena includes various dislocated constructions:

(26) a. ***Cancer ater,*** *is olet et saniem spurcam mittit* (Cato *agr.* 157,3)
     "Black canker, this (canker) is fetid and lets out a hideous *sanies*".
   b. ***Amicos domini,*** *eos habeat sibi amicos* (Cato, *agr.* 5,3)
     "The master's friends, let him regard them as friends".
   c. ***Plerique homines,*** *quos cum nihil refert pudet, / ubi pudendum est, ibi eos deserit pudor* (Plaut. *Epid.* 166-167)
     "Most people, who have scruples when there is no cause, when they should have them, then scruples desert them"
   d. ***urbem*** *quam statuo uestra est* (Verg. *Aen.* 1,573)
     "The city I am founding, it is yours".

To quote Devine and Stephens (2006: 6), one's aim must be:

> not just to document the facts, but to understand them, to reduce the kaleïdoscopic surface complexity … to a relatively simple and coherent system of general rules.

Similarly Oniga (2007: 307) concludes that:

> molti fenomeni, alcuni dei quali in apparenza eterogenei e a volte bizzarri, hanno ottenuto proposte di spiegazione all'interno di una teoria unitaria e, tutto sommato, piuttosto semplice.[9]

The above-mentioned phenomena might well be described using parameters from two separate modules of the theory: the case theory, for instance, for nominative and accusative alternation, and the interpretative module (Logical Form) to deal with anaphora.

3.5. Is there a maximal length for examples?

Once again this depends on what examples are supposed to be there for. If it is just to point out a certain phenomenon in a language, the length of an example is irrelevant. For instance, it may be necessary to use a long example in order to highlight what type of anaphoric element is required in the informative progression: the distance between antecedent and anaphoric element may be relevant; but no symbolic expression has yet been found to describe this distance.

Let us take up example (25) once more: the dots represent a deleted sequence of non-relevant constituents, but the reader does not know how many constituents have been omitted, let alone what their nature is. And yet this information is indeed relevant, and useful for understanding the phenomenon in question.

Every time several parameters play a role in a linguistic phenomenon and cannot be taken apart, refining the example is almost impossible and therefore its prototypical value is weakened.

Now, Generative Grammars are still characterized by maximal reduction of examples, while functionalist grammars have for some time accepted rather long examples, especially in chapters about text cohesion:

(27) a. *Mittuntur ad Caesarem confestim ab Cicerone litterae … Obsessis omnibus uiis missi intercipiuntur. Noctu … turres … excitantur … Quae deesse operi uidebantur perficiuntur.* "Immediately a letter was sent to Caesar by Cicero. Because all roads were blocked the messengers were captured. During the night towers were built. Visible defects of the rampart were repaired" (Caes. *Gall.* 5,40,1-2) in Pinkster (1990: 246)

   b. *Gallia est omnis diuisa in partes tres, quarum unam incolunt Belgae, aliam Aquitani, tertiam qui ipsorum lingua Celtae, nostra Galli appellantur.* **Hi omnes** *lingua, institutis, legibus inter se differunt. Gallos ab Aquitanis Garumna flumen, a Belgis Matrona et Sequana diuidit.* **Horum omnium** *fortissimi sunt Belgae, propterea quod a cultu atque humanitate prouinciae longissime absunt, minimeque ad eos mercatores saepe commeant atque ea quae ad effeminandos animos pertinent important, proximique sunt Germanis, qui trans Rhenum incolunt, quibuscum continenter bellum gerunt.* **Qua de causa** *Heluetii quoque reliquos Gallos uirtute praecedunt, quod fere cotidianis proeliis cum Germanis contendunt, cum aut suis finibus eos prohibent aut ipsi in* **eorum** *finibus bellum gerunt. Eorum una, pars, quam Gallos obtinere dictum est, initium capit a flumine Rhodano, continetur Garumna flumine, Oceano, finibus Belgarum, attingit etiam ab Sequanis et Heluetiis flumen Rhenum, uergit ad septentriones.* (Caes. *Gall.* 1,1,1-5) from Cabrillana in Baños Baños and Cabrillana (2009: 686)

Since Generative Grammar, following Rizzi (1997), integrated functional categories for topicalized constituents into the Left Periphery, we might as well take up an example such as (27b).

4. "Analysed" examples

By "analysed examples" I mean examples which are enriched by some syntactic information, *i.e.* linked to a formal representation. In fact any "refined" example is already *ipso facto* an analysed example.

4.1. Invisible items

Since examples are supposed to illustrate linguistic phenomena, one should make invisible items (so-called "empty categories") explicit. A typical example is that of null pronouns, one category of invisible items whose relevance is claimed by generativist theories.

To describe anaphoric relations in a sentence such as:

(28) *Si in ius uocat, ito. Ni it, antestamino. Igitur eum capito* (*Lex XII Tab.* 1,1)

one may, following Oniga (2007: 193), give the example this way:

(29) *Si* pro$_i$ *in ius* pro$_j$ *uocat,* pro$_j$ *ito. Ni* pro$_j$ *it,* pro$_i$ *antestamino. Igitur* pro$_i$ *eum$_j$ capito*

This technique is, so to speak, the reverse of the above-mentioned refining process: we are introducing silent constituents that are necessary to represent and interpret the phenomenon being studied. Introducing invisible items is not enough, as shown in the previous example. Indices allow us to represent coreference relations; without these indices structures would remain ambiguous.

The same indices are used to clarify the use of reflexives; (4) might be presented as follows:

(30) a. *Ioannes$_i$ sororem suam$_i$ uidit*
      b. *Ioannes$_i$ sororem eius$_j$ uidit*

Although indices clarify the relevant phenomenon, they do not, however, explain it. With trees or parenthesizing (a less cumbersome representation) it is possible to show clearly the c-command constraint which determines reflexive use: dominant IP node *Ioannes* also dominates the branch containing *suam*:

(31) [$_{IP}$ *Ioannes$_i$* [$_{VP}$ [$_{NP}$ *sororem suam$_i$*] *uidit*]]]

In a final example, we observe the distinction between two infinitival constructions. According to Cecchetto and Oniga (2002), AcI present a null complementizer as in (32a), while control clauses do not project any CP, but present a null subject indicated as PRO in (32b), which is coreferential with the internal argument (*me*) of the main verb:

(32) a. *dicunt* [$_{CP}$ Ø [$_{C}$ *me uenire*]]

     b. *hortantur me*$_i$ [$_{IP}$ PRO$_i$ *uenire*]

4.2. Syntactic derivations

An example is no longer alone; it is worthless by itself, but it is linked to other examples in a derivational chain. Thus, an example does not represent a phenomenon in a static manner, even when it is shown within a minimal contrast; instead, it shows its dynamics.

Let us go back to the Pompeius example in (22a); it shows that the interrogative pronoun is regularly raised to frontal position; we would represent this in the following manner:

(33) a. *qui fecit iniuriam est quis?*

     b. *quis*$_i$ *est qui fecit iniuriam* t$_i$?

Introducing trace *t* and coindexation highlights the relevant dynamics.

Similarly, passive transformation, which is generally described by a simple active/passive minimal pair, might be described by way of the following sequence, where it is illustrated each partly independent phenomenon contributing to the formation of the passive with the merging of a prepositional agent:

(34) *M. Valerius … legem tulit* (Liv. 10,9,3)

     "M. Valerius proposed a law"

     a. *ita latum est* (Cic. *leg. agr.* 3,8)

        "so it was proposed"

     b. *lata lex est* (Liv. 3,31,1)

        "a law has been proposed"

     c. *a L. Pisone lata lex est* (Cic. *off.* 2,21,75)

        "a law has been proposed by L. Piso"

Each example highlights an independent operation:
(34) a. shows the loss of agentivity and intransitivation induced by passive morphology;

(34) b. shows how the object is inserted as the subject;
(34) c. illustrates how the agent can be merged as a prepositional phrase.

4.3. Diachronic changes

Example paradigms allow us to illustrate the evolution of Latin:

(35) *dico Marcum uenire* (classical Lat.)   (Lakoff 1968: 9)
      dico quod Marcus uenit (vulgar Lat.)
      digo que Marcos viene (Sp.)

Such a paradigm does not show the parametrizable changes which would
lead to an extension of completive clauses; therefore by itself it is unable
to explain anything. A more explicit paradigm (from the data and analyses
of Bodelot 2003) might do it:
a- Starting point:

(36) a.   *Scio te uenire*
      b.   With cataphora: *Illud scio te uenire / illud scio quod uenisti*

b- Extension to other verbs:

(37) *Illud intellegi quod ueneras*

c- Increased use of subjunctive:

(38) *Intellegi quod ueneras/uenisses*

    Paradigm and corpus are combined in this line of reasoning: different
paradigms taken from successive corpora are compared. The relevant
evolution is all but imperceptible at the syntactic level, but it shows up
when lexicon and frequency are taken into account.
    The parameters which play a role are many, and they cannot all be
indicated in a paradigm or an isolated example. There is a solution,
though: exhaustively enumerating the lexical items which commute with
one another in the same construction within each period of time.[10] This is a
virtual solution, of course, but it does point toward one of the two poles
grammar tends to aim at: either a description using only metalanguage or
an exhaustive description, which is possible for a language known through
a finite corpus such as Latin.

Conclusion

Summing up, Latin examples in a Generative Grammar are both similar to those used in traditional grammars and different in some respects. They are similar because:

- They may be either authentic or made-up;
- They originate from a corpus;
- Each example highlights a rule;

They are different because:

- They do not represent a standard, but a fragment of one particular speaker's performance, which in turn represents a more general linguistic competence;
- A quotation does not by itself constitute an example: one must isolate and refine it through adequate theoretical means;
- A corpus is not a pool of examples, it is a field of investigation intended for the verification of linguistic hypotheses;
- Examples provide not descriptions only, but explanations too; that is why anti-examples and " enriched " examples must be used.

The didactic use of examples is therefore different in a Generative Grammar: what it is all about, is not describing how complex the language is (a language whose workings would remain inexplicable in the end); it is starting to explain this complexity through a small number of formally defined rules which are isolated thanks to examples brought together in paradigms.

Notes

* I have to thank R. Oniga for his friendly help, A.-M. Chanet and W. Short for helping me to translate the original text.
[1] "All grammars include examples. This is presumably a necessary component of grammatical exposition; at any rate, empirical observation does show this practice to be all but universal. However, epistemological status of the strings we may call "examples", their form, their function, their semiotic behaviour, may vary according to the corpus that is observed, whether different traditions are dealt with or (within one tradition) different moments in time".
[2] Note that this paradigm is as virtual as can be, since **none** of these sequences is attested and furthermore – due to the choice of words and the meaning of *appellare* – this paradigm would have sounded most strange to any Latin speaker of the

classical age.

[3] "One runs […] the risk of using examples that are only attested in grammars, in the same way that some forms are only attested in dictionaries".

[4] "The study of Latin does not aim at 'speaking to do', but 'reading to understand'".

[5] Chomsky (1957: 17sqq). The contrast between modelisation and quantification is even stronger in Milner (1989: 24): "Nous nous séparons donc d'un point de vue largement répandu, selon lequel il n'y a de science que du quantifiable. Nous dirons plutôt: il n'y a de science que du mathématisable et il y a mathématisation dès qu'il y a littéralisation et fonctionnement aveugle". "Therefore we reject a widely held view according to which there is no science except that of quantifiable entities. We would say instead: there is no science except that of mathematizable entities, and there is mathematization whenever there is literalization and blind functioning".

[6] Except when it happens to be an example which illustrates anaphoric relations, connectors or other phenomena that fall within the province of enunciation or interphrastic relations.

[7] "Syntacticians focus on the data that they believe the fewest complications factors, and "clean up "the data to remove what they believe to be remaining complications that obscure simple, general principles of language" (Abney 1996: 11).

[8] "the sentences *consuetudo | concinnat amorem* (Lucr. 4,1283) and *ueritas | odium parit* (Ter. *And.* 68) may be segmented and recombined into grammatical sentences such as *consuetudo | odium parit* and *ueritas | concinnat amorem*".

[9] "for many phenomena, some of which look heterogeneous and sometimes quite strange at first sight, tentative explanations have been proposed in the framework of a theory which is unified and on the whole quite simple".

[10] On this point see Chevillard (2007: 6-7). For an alternative analysis of the parametric shift from Latin to Romance as concerns infinitival clauses, see Cecchetto and Oniga (2002).

References

Abney, S. (1996) "Statistical Methods and Linguistics". in J. Klavans and P. Resnik (eds) *The Balancing Act*. Cambridge (Mass.),The MIT Press, 1-26.

Auroux, S. (1998) *La raison, le langage et les normes. Sciences, modernités, philosophies*, Paris, Presses Universitaires de France.

Baños Baños, J. M. (2009) *Sintaxis del latín clásico*, Madrid, Liceus.

Baños Baños J. M. and C. Cabrillana (2009), "Orden de palabras", in J.M. Baños Baños (ed.) *Sintaxis del latín clásico*, Madrid, Liceus, 679-708.

Bertocchi, A. and C. Casadio (1980) "Conditions on anaphora: An analysis of reflexive in Latin", *Papers on Grammar* 1:1-46.

Bodelot, C. (ed.) (2003) *Grammaire fondamentale du latin. Tome X: Les propositions complétives en latin*, Bibliothèque d'Etudes Classiques 35, Louvain-Paris-Dudley, Peeters.

Cecchetto, C. and R. Oniga (2002) "Consequences of the Analysis of Latin Infinitival Clauses for the Theory of Case and Control" *Lingue e Linguaggio* 1: 151-189.

Chevillard, J.-L. *et al.* (2007) "L'exemple dans quelques traditions grammaticales (formes, fonctionnement, types) " *Langages* 166: 5-31.

Chomsky, N. (1957) *Syntactic Structures*, Berlin, Mouton de Gruyter.

—. (1965) *Aspects of the theory of syntax*, Cambridge (Mass.), MIT Press.

Chomsky, N. and H. Lasnik (1993) "Principles and Parameters Theory", in *Syntax: An International Handbook of Contemporary Research*, Berlin, Mouton de Gruyter.

Colombat, B. (1991) "L'autorité de l'exemple face au renouvellement des stratégies explicatives dans la syntaxe latine de l'accord", *La Licorne*, 19 [La constitution du document en histoire des sciences du langage], Poitiers, 135-154.

—. (2007) "La construction, la manipulation de l'exemple et ses effets sur la tradition grammaticale latine", in J.-M. Fournier (ed.) *L'exemple dans les traditions grammaticales, Langages* 166: 71-85.

Cori, M. (2008) "Des méthodes de traitement automatique aux linguistiques fondées sur les corpus", in *Construction des faits en linguistique: la place des corpus, Langages* 171: 95-110.

Cori, M. and L. David (2008) "Présentation: éléments de réflexion sur la place des corpus en linguistique", in *Construction des faits en linguistique: la place des corpus, Langages* 171: 5-11.

Devine, A.M. and L.D. Stephens (2006) *Latin Word Order. Structured Meaning and Information,* Oxford-New York, Oxford University Press.

Duso, A. (2006) "Varrone e l'analogia", in R. Oniga and L. Zennaro (eds) *Atti della Giornata di Linguistica Latina*, Venezia, Cafoscarina, 9-20.

Gianollo, C. (2007) "The Internal Syntax of the Nominal Phrase in Latin" in G. Purnelle, J. Denooz (eds) *Ordre et cohérence en latin*, Genève, Droz, 65-80.

Giusti G. and R. Oniga (2006) "La struttura del sintagma nominale latino", in R. Oniga and L. Zennaro (eds) *Atti della Giornata di Linguistica Latina*, Venezia, Cafoscarina, 71-100.

Habert, B., Nazarenko, A. and A. Salem (1997) *Les linguistiques de corpus*, Paris, Armand Colin et Masson.

Harris, Z.S. (1988), *Language and Information*, New York, Columbia University Press.

Hofmann, J.B. and A. Szantyr (1965) *Lateinische Syntax und Stilistik*, München, Beck.

Lakoff, R.T. (1968) *Abstract Syntax and Latin Complementation*, Cambridge (Mass), MIT Press.

Lavency, M. (1987), *Vsus*, Genève, Duculot.

Manning, C. (2003) "Probabilistic Syntax". in R. Bod, J. Hay and S. Jannedy (eds) *Probabilistic Linguistics*. Cambridge (Mass.), MIT Press, 289-341.

Marandin, J.M. (ed.) (2001) *Cahier Jean-Claude Milner*, Paris, Verdier.

Marouzeau, J. (1953) *L'ordre des mots en latin*. *Volume complémentaire*, Paris, Les Belles Lettres.

Milner, J.C. (1989) *Introduction à une science du langage*, Paris, Seuil.

Oniga, R. (2007) *Il latino. Breve introduzione linguistica*, 2ª ed., Milano, Franco Angeli.

Pinkster, H. (1990) *Latin Syntax and Semantics*, London, Routledge.

Weil, H. (1978) *The Order of Word in the Ancient Languages compared with that of Modern Languages*, New ed. By A. Scaglione (ed. orig. 1869) Amsterdam, Benjamins.

LINGUISTICS AND THE TEACHING OF CLASSICAL LANGUAGES

UGO CARDINALE

Introduction. The gap between teaching ancient languages and modern languages

Our tradition of language teaching in Italian high schools (Licei) has often highlighted a division between the teaching of classic and modern languages: a grammatical approach being reserved for the former and a communicative-functional approach for the latter. What have been the results of this division? A difficult dialogue between the teachers of these subjects.

On the one hand, we find the study of classics, rooted in the tradition of ancient grammarians, such as Martianus Capella, and capable of inducing reflections on various aspects of language, although this is achieved through lists of exceptions and special cases. On the other hand (in the teaching of modern languages), we find a deep understanding of the "here and now" (*hic et nunc*) of situations, progressing to inductive generalizations, free from a strong emphasis on a theoretical frame.

1. The reasons why the knowledge of classical languages enhances the learning of languages

From my position as a Principal of both a Classical and Linguistic Liceo, I have observed a surprising fact: students from the Liceo Classico, regardless of their social background and their initial talent, have always been considered to have a more efficient method of study, that would allow them an easier transfer of competence to the study of modern languages. These circumstances, which started as anecdotic, subjective observations, have since compelled me to look for a justification, not being content to simply rely on the "myth of the classics".

How could the study of a dead language, lacking such an important component to linguistic learning, as real communication with native speakers, give an advantage over the practical study of living languages, enriched as they are by communication? What was hiding behind the revival of the myth of the "classics" (already covered by the discussion with the former Minister L. Berlinguer in his essay on TreeLLLe (2008) "Latin yes Latin no"), specifically on grammatical aspects? Was it necessary to propose again as a strong contender the traditional grammatical approach, even in a world which inevitably requires the rethinking of old approaches to teaching?

If it is unthinkable to propose the study of the "aorist" for all students, what should be considered as fundamental in a syllabus of classics? Which aspects deliver better results?

2. What's behind the classical myth

It was necessary to go deeper into the "myth of Classics", without, however, bringing uncritical and biased attitudes. Was it perhaps the Classics' reflection on language, i.e. the metalinguistic dimension so punctiliously exercised by the written works of classic authors that provided a deeper and wider dimension, resulting in a better understanding of language as such? How could we think that a "dead" language could produce more cognitive transfers than a living language? It would make no sense to attribute Latin a "healing power". The opinion that Latin was by nature a supremely "logical language" does not seem an argument based on evidence.

However, many linguists, like De Mauro (in TreeLLLe 2008), who in the past had cast doubts on the usefulness of the grammatical tradition of Latin, are now rethinking their positions and expressing strong favour for the learning of classics in an attempt to limit the current "linguistic loss" of the younger generations. We therefore come, therefore, to two hypotheses:

- It may be the case that, in the past, the study of Latin as a workshop for thinking about linguistic dynamics, played a positive role, taking the place of the study of Linguistics as a proper subject (*tout court*).
- It can also be the case that translation, as a practice requiring the activation of strategies for comprehension, played a substitute role to the lack of consideration towards certain grammatical phenomena, particularly those relating to more complex fragments of the language, such as the anaphor or textual connectives, the latter being included in the vague category of conjunctions, but that nowadays are studied by textual linguistics.

Our conclusion is that the study of grammar creates language awareness and, in so doing, it seems to facilitate the study of both L1 and L2, not just classic languages, regardless of the fact that the learning must take into account their status as natural languages that are no more spoken.

3. The discovery of universal grammar beyond the grammar of various languages

Why, then, not look for a common ground for the study of all languages, beyond and above the "grammars" of the different languages, in order to explore the "grammar" specific to the human mind?

3.1. Simone's (1983) notional model

We already have a model of notional grammar (see Simone 1983) that starting from some ineluctable notions (meanings) for communication (i.e. time, space, quantity) encourages a comparative approach between languages, suggesting a common theoretical framework to the teachers of L1 and L2. This is the approach that, in a more pragmatic and functional version, has been adopted by the European Council as the basis for the syllabuses of various European languages, but (Lo Duca 2003: 157) that is not as useful for the teaching of L1 to the native speakers.

Nevertheless such an approach, whose main focus is on semantics, does not seem to get to the bottom of the question. If it is true that there are identical semantic areas in the experience of a young learner about to study a L2, this approach would not offer an appropriate competence in those languages which, though natural, cannot be easily learned primarily through use.

The study of Latin and Greek has always been based on the explicit teaching of a formal grammar, with a view to analyzing "parts of speech" and to mainly studying the language in its morphological and syntactic aspects, rather than semantically.

Renzi (1977) and Berretta (1978) underlined how at a first approach surface grammar and language forms are paramount, and how only later deep semantic considerations take place. But "surface" here does not have the negative connotation of "superficial".

To look for the forms of linguistic discourse means to work on that universal faculty of language that can be seen as a genetic trait of the human species and to work on cognitive psychology; which puts language in relation to the operational strategies of our mind.

4. An approach to grammar as a universal theory of the mind

If the theory of universal grammar, inspired by Chomsky, assumes some universal **principles** common to all languages, and some parameters learned and interiorised at an early stage of development, it is these principles that we can look at, to search for what languages have in common, beyond the apparent differences among languages.

To use such a theoretical and neo-comparative perspective when thinking about the study of languages can be helpful for a more "scientific" approach to their learning and to overcome the barrier which has traditionally divided the teaching of classical and modern languages. This, of course, without losing awareness of the different processes by which they are learnt.

The teachers of classical languages can have at their disposal neither a communicative approach, nor the discovery of neologistic mechanisms, as they work on a finite and non renewable corpus of sentences. The teachers of modern languages, instead, will find it effective to integrate their unconscious strategies with a theoretical dimension of explicit reflection. Such an approach to grammar as theory of the mind, which reminds us of a long tradition from Augustine to Pascal and the Port Royal school, as Oniga (2007) points out in his introduction, is still not well known, at least at the level of the general public. It allows us, however, to discover as many similarities rather that as differences among languages. It shows how what might appear as exceptions in one language might instead be part of the set of rules and parameters through which the universal principles of language become concrete (*we must not forget how the ancients were already convinced that there is a logos among the various manifestations of nature*).

4.1. Cardinaletti's (2008) proposal

For this point we can refer to Cardinaletti's (2008) discussion of four languages: Latin, Italian, English, German, as an example of the universal principle that "all clauses have a subject", using the "pro-drop" parameter, which is positive for Latin and Italian and negative for English and German.

We can also see how the parameter of the *order* (of words) can help us recognize common traits (beyond the variety of the definitions) in some phenomena present in a variety of languages, like that of "separable verbs", also called "verbs with a separable prefix", "verbs with particles" (particle verbs or phrasal verbs), defined in different ways in English and German, and "pre-verbs" in the Latin tradition, as Cardinaletti (2008) highlights. Only within such a theoretical framework, which is capable of explaining language as a system of virtual potentialities, grammatically possible, even though not all present in the actual "corpora" (language body) and of non-grammatical impossibilities – void of any probability even of neologism – only in this fashion can one undertake the scientific study of language, in an effort to overcome incongruities of descriptions, abuse of exceptions, etc. in seeking a satisfactory theory that goes beyond our every-day practise.

4.2. Oniga (2007): A completely renewed Latin Grammar

Such work, of a completely renewed Latin grammar, has been accomplished by Oniga (2007), with great professionalism and with the humility of one who knows that research is an endless endeavour.

To give an example, we can quote the refutation of an incongruous definition of traditional grammar, evidence of its inadequacy and in some instances of its fallibility, notwithstanding the merits of such long experience in the formalization of rules, which can only be renewed and not erased. It is the case of the theory of the **subject** as agent.

One can find, for example, an active sentence that confutes such theory: *"servus vapulat"*. Here the subject is not really acting, but suffering the action. *Vapulare*, in fact, takes a patient subject, and literally means "being caned". In Oniga's book it is shown how such a case can be better explained by distinguishing between syntactic functions (argument positions) and semantic values (thematic roles); and by using **thematic theory**, which seems to describe syntactic phenomena in a more precise way, better than the traditional logical analysis and better than Tesnière's **theory of valence**.

Thematic theory can grasp the difference between two synonymic expressions, which are different in the thematic roles expressed by the subject such as the following:

a) *Chrisis vapulat* (Petron. 132,5), focusing on the subject as 'patient'.

b) *Servus accipiet plagas* (Petron. 28,7), focusing on the subject servus as 'beneficiary'.

Even the traditional category of deponent verbs, which is limited only to the morphological aspect, could not account for the difference between active and unaccusative deponent verbs. It only described deponent verbs, as the ancients would say, as having "let/put down" the active morphological form and only having a passive form, but with an active meaning.

Let me bring up another area of classical language didactics that could take advantage from Linguistics: that is, **translation**. As Oniga (2007: 19) stresses:

> Grammatical analysis is the necessary preliminary for translation. Translation presupposes a linguistic reasoning that is not trivial, but extremely rich, which can be made explicit with the tools of grammatical analysis.

Similarly Balbo (2007: 87) affirms in his lecture on the didactics for classical languages:

> The length of the learning route for translation could be reduced if one could, from the initial two years of "liceo", reason in terms of that comparative morphology of languages proposed by A. Cardinaletti.

5. Textual linguistics contribute to translation skills

Another grammatical reflection that could offer new and better theoretical tools than those of traditional grammar to the didactic of translation is surely textual linguistics. This is more apt to discover inter-clause dynamics, on the basis of the conviction that both production and comprehension refer to the "text" and that the discourse is developing by saying "something (rheme) about something else already somehow known (theme)", in a process of thematic continuity. This theory deals mainly with the semantic correlations (theme contiguity), and syntactic correlations between communicative units (as observed in Pinkster 1990). Such correlations give a web-like image to the text.

The discovery of "knots" in the web could help students when reconstructing the structure, even though understanding the text does not simply require the ability to recognize connectives, but appears to be a more complex process that puts in play cognitive strategies of anticipation, inference, etc.

Therefore it could be useful to undertake a reconnaissance of those semantic connectives (Berretta 1978) that create cohesive relations between facts and those textual connectives that link "parts of the text as units of speech". Among the former we can find:

a) Markers of temporal "hinges" in narrative texts: suddenly (*repente*), at once *(ex abrupto)*, one day *(olim)*;
b) Elements that put two events in temporal connection: *the day after tomorrow (**postero die**), after a day, the following day, the following year (**anno sequente**)*;
c) Elements that indicate contemporaneity between two events: *at once (**uno tempore**), at the same time (**eodem tempore, simul**), at that time (**eo**);*
d) Elements that indicate anteriority: *the day before (**pristino die**), previously (**ante, antea, prius, olim**), the year before (**priore anno**);*

Among the latter we can find:

a) Elements that are useful to divide the text into parts: *first of all (**primum omnium, primario loco, princeps in agendo**), secondly (**secundo loco, deinceps, deinde, posterius**);*
b) Elements that allow us to mark the most important "hinges" in the text, that is the opening (*I would like to start with, first of all I would like to say that*), the closing (*finally, summing up, in conclusion*), or the transfer form one part to another of the text (*secondly, we said earlier that, let's now analyse three points, we'll see further on*).

Textual connectives can have the following functions:

- Additional, adding new information *(also, furthermore, in addition, beyond this)* **etiam, nec non, praeterea, ultro, atque iam amplius**
- Adversative-limitative *(anyway, even though, but, moreover)* **quoquo modo, utcumque, utique, quacumque ratione**
- Adversative **ex contrario, contra, contrarie, vero** (*on the contrary, the reverse, instead, nevertheless*)
- Concessive **licet, sane, etiamsi** (*even if*)
- Explicative, corrective, exemplificative and resumptive **exempli gratia, ut melium dicam, nam, enim, praecipue, maxime, ante omnia, praesertim, utique** (*for example, to be more precise, in fact, to be more precise, above all, that is to say*)
- Argumentative **sunt qui putant, est qui consiliat** (*let's suppose that,*

some say that, coherently with our position)
- Consecutive, as a consequence of a premise ***tunc, ergo, inde, propterea, qua re, qua de re, qua de causa*** (*then, therefore, so, for this reason*)
- Comparative ***pariter, sic, eodem modo*** (*in the same way, so, equally, in the best scenario*)
- Pragmatic, to start the communicative exchange (*well, okay, hallo*), the so called pause-fillers (*you understand, so, well, you can imagine*) ***ecce, quaeso, cedo, ergo, itaque***
- Textual deixis, concerning the structuring of the text, like ***in primis, ut supra dicimus***
- Spotting of textual cohesives like:
  Anaphoric repetitions
  Determinative pronouns in anaphoric function, referring to the already mentioned, i.e. ***is, ea, id***
  Relatives
  Deictics, for example, demonstrative pronouns, ***hic, haec, hoc***.

This reconnaissance, therefore, can be a very useful new tool for teaching, because these patterns stored in the mind (even though they are an open class, answering more to functional rather than formal criteria, as the same form can perform different functions in different texts) can offer a network of competence for the comprehension of texts, that can be reproduced in different languages, if it is true that there is a "basic universal functional communicative typology of texts" as "basic universal typology" which uses in any language *frames* (descriptive text, narrative text, argumentative text) (see Lavinio 2000).
Furthermore, there is another area of language to which the research on "universals" could prove advantageous. Universalism offers, in fact, elements of regularity, a Logos, even in areas where traditionally we had a Chaos. I am thinking of the usefulness of grammaticization even in a field such as the lexicon, usually outside the range of school grammar.

6. The recurrent mechanism of morphology

In the reconstruction of productive mechanisms to make words, generative linguistics has produced new important elements to understand the origin of words through processes of derivation (suffixation and prefixation) and composition. For example, Oniga (2007: 136) points out that:

Prefixes and suffixes are used to enrich the lexicon of a language by shaping new words. The knowledge of the semantic value of the main affixes [*in Latin, ab(s)-, ad-, am(b)-, con-, de-, dis-e(x) etc,* see page 137] is therefore an important element in grammar for learning vocabulary and the formation of new words (since the affix modifies in systematic fashion the basic meaning).

It is true, though, that the optional character of derivation calls to mind the cases of variability, of "empties" and exceptions that make it difficult to think that all languages (came to) be only "by nature".
Nevertheless, it is right to note that studies on Latin vocabulary, quoted by Oniga, have shown that prefixes and suffixes create morphological structures with rigorous non linear hierarchical organization, like traditional grammar used to think. See Oniga (2007: 149), for the example of:

    a) *In-fructu-osus*
    b) *In-cita-tor*

In the first case the basis is *fructus* to which first the suffix *–osus* and then the negative prefix *in-* is added. The opposite order (*in-fructus*) is not possible.
    In the second case to the verb *citare* one adds first the prefix *in-* (forming the prefixed *in-citare*) and then the suffix *–tor*, creating a derivate noun. In this case, too, the inversion of the order would not be possible.
    One can also see the peculiarity of the parasynthetic verbs that introduce at once a prefix and a suffix, e.g.:

From *rete*: *ir-ret-ire*
From *ager*: *per-agr-a-re*

while derivate forms with only the prefix (**irrete*) or only the suffix (**agrare)* do not exist. The same structural analysis is valid for Italian parasynthetic verbs: *arrochire, appaciare, attossicare,* (examples by Bufalino, who also uses prefixed forms like *abbruciare,* which is not parasynthetic), *abbellire* etc.
    As I said earlier, it is true that we cannot reduce the whole lexicon to logic, even though many limits to the freedom of lexical creativity are evidence of regularity. *Le regole e le scelte* is the title of Prandi's (2006) grammar, and it emphasises this element of freedom.

Polysemy and homonimy impose an awareness of the complex interplay of different linguistic and non-linguistic ingredients in the evolution of a language. Not all the complex lexicon, even of a finite corpus like the one of classical languages, can be explained just "by nature". Is there perhaps a chance factor, which can only be explained by later experience, to make sense of language the way it is? And is this nothing more than the expression of the limitations of our current theories or does it reflect the dialectic of two factors (*nómos* and *phýsis*), interpreted in various ways by theoretic research?

Much has been done to find out the regularities of language, to grasp the *nómos*, yet the impact of "lexical empties", jumping over stages of the process of derivation (for example, *calcistico*, from a non existent **calcista*) poses some doubt over the possibility of reducing lexicography to logic.

Democritus was already aware of this when he asked himself: why is it that from *phrónesis* we say *phroneîn* whilst from *dikaiosýne* we don't get a verb? But this question calls to mind that of Cratilus: do names derive from nature or from chance? This urges us never to put the word 'end' to our research.

Conclusion

The study of universal grammar, as a theory of the mind, responds to the issue of the "classical myth", which, even though conclusive, offers universal principles common to all languages, a comparative approach which highlights the common elements to various languages. Oniga's Latin grammar offers valid insights in more than a field, including the lexikon, even if its regularity is not always recurrent. The study of textual linguistics offers tools suitable to understand the mechanisms of translation, and searches the "basic universal typology" related to texts and frames.

References

Balbo, A. (2007) *Insegnare latino. Sentieri di ricerca per una didattica ragionevole,* Novara, UTET Università.
Berretta, M. (1978) (ed.) *Sviluppi della linguistica e problemi dell'insegnamento*, Torino, Giappichelli.
Cardinale, U. (2006) (ed.) *Essere e Divenire del "Classico". Atti del Convegno Internazionale (Torino-Ivrea, 21-22-23 Ottobre 2003),* Torino, UTET.

Cardinaletti, A. (2008) "Le ragioni del comparare per insegnare le lingue", in U. Cardinale (ed.) *Nuove chiavi per insegnare il classico*, Torino, UTET, pp. 267-289.

Lavinio, C. (2000) "Tipi testuali e processi cognitivi", in F. Camponovo and A. Moretti (eds) *Didattica ed educazione linguistica*, Firenze, La Nuova Italia.

Oniga, R. (2007) *Il latino. Breve introduzione linguistica*, 2ª ed., Milano, Franco Angeli.

Pinkster, H. (1990) *Latin Syntax and Semantics*, London, Routledge.

Prandi, M. (2006) *Le regole e le scelte*, Torino, UTET.

Renzi, L. (1977) "Una grammatica ragionevole per l'insegnamento", in G. Berruto (ed.) *Scienze del linguaggio ed educazione linguistica*, Torino, Stampatori Didattica, 13-56 (= in L. Renzi, *Le piccole strutture. Linguistica, poetica, letteratura*, Bologna, il Mulino 2008, 207-236).

Simone, R. (1983) "Per una grammatica nozionale", in AA.VV., *L'educazione linguistica dalla scuola di base al biennio superiore*, Milano, Bruno Mondadori, 131-147.

TreeLLLe (2008) *Latino perché? Latino per chi? Confronti internazionali per un dibattito*, Genova, Associazione TreeLLLe.

SINTASSI DEI CASI LATINA E MODERNA RIFLESSIONE LINGUISTICA: NOTE TEORICHE E DIDATTICHE

DAVIDE ASTORI

Introduzione

Questo contributo propone, sulla base di un'integrazione sinergica dell'approccio generativo-trasformazionale di matrice chomskiana, della proposta tesnièriana della 'grammatica delle reggenze' (e delle riflessioni scaturite a seguito di Tesnière 1959) e ancora della riflessione sull'Ipotesi delle Relazioni Tematiche di Ray Jackendoff (1983), un modello di rilettura degli aspetti del 'caso' nella lingua latina, in funzione anche di una ricaduta didattica. Tale modello, sperimentato, negli ultimi anni, in alcune classi (di biennio e triennio) di liceo classico, sembrerebbe coniugare positivamente lo stimolo per l'insegnante a un approfondimento del fenomeno del caso in chiave di un moderno approccio linguistico teorico con una soddisfacente possibilità di spiegare allo studente il fenomeno linguistico (in un'ottica insieme sincronica e diacronica). Il "pacchetto didattico" consiste in 10 ore spendibili in una prima fase della formazione linguistica (a cavallo fra lingue classiche, moderne e lingua materna) così declinata:

1. una prima riflessione (2 ore) sul concetto di caso superficiale ~ profondo, contestualizzato all'interno di un più generale contributo di riflessione derivante dalla moderna linguistica formale;
2. la proposta di un modello logico-funzionale della struttura profonda della frase, in cui inserire la teoria dei casi (2 ore);
3. l'analisi, anche a livello contrastivo, della gestione dei casi nel latino e nel greco, non disdegnando il parallelo con l'antico indiano (che si rivela notevole occasione di potenziamento delle competenze nelle due lingue classiche insegnate nei licei) e con le lingue moderne (4 ore);
4. un'analisi più dettagliata (2 ore) della sintassi dei casi latina.

Ripercorriamo qualche momento più significativo, riflettendo sulle strategie didattiche utilizzate per calare gli aspetti più teorici nell'attività di classe.

1. Per un inquadramento metodologico

Per un approccio alla riflessione chomskiana, accanto alla produzione diretta del noto linguista, i materiali di lavoro e di approfondimento sono talmente vasti e variegati da non necessitare in questa sede note di carattere bibliografico. Significativo è l'interesse che suscita in aula (a livello di consapevolezza linguistica) la riflessione su dislocazioni e concordanze.

Frasi possibili, quali (1), (2) e (3), rispetto a (4) e (5), non corrette, permettono una chiara percezione (a diversi gradi di approfondimento, dipendenti dalla preparazione del gruppo e dalla programmazione) dell'esistenza di un piano profondo e di uno superficiale, ulteriormente esplicitabile seguendo Chomsky 1988 (in particolare capp. iii-iv).

(1) Ho visto Maria

(2) L'ho vista

(3) Ho visto lei

(4) *Maria ho visto

(5) *Ho vistola

A conferma del grado di ricezione dei termini della questione si può estendere l'analisi ad altre lingue, anche non conosciute dallo studente. Di impatto è ad es. la problematica sottesa al romeno (6), (7), (8) e (9), che bene mostra il 'salto' fra struttura profonda e dislocamenti superficiali:

(6) Am văzut pe Ioan ("Ho visto Ioan")

(7) Am văzut pe Maria ("Ho visto Maria")

(8) L'am văzut ("L'ho visto")

(9) Am văzut-o ("L'ho vista")

2. La teoria dei casi

Contestualizzato all'interno della riflessione chomskiana, il fatto che tutte le lingue posseggano casi, e ognuna li esprima, a livello superficiale, nel suo modo specifico, è dato dunque facilmente acquisibile. Si possono proporre in classe le parole dello stesso Chomsky 1988 (pp. 87 ss. della traduzione italiana):

> Consideriamo una lingua come il latino, che possiede un sistema di casi piuttosto ricco, a differenza dell'italiano e dell'inglese, dove i casi compaiono solo nel sistema pronominale ed in questo caso solo in una forma ridotta. […] Se tutte le lingue sono essenzialmente simili nella loro natura profonda, ci si aspetta che anche l'italiano e l'inglese abbiano un sistema di casi di questo tipo generale. Dal momento che le desinenze casuali non compaiono apertamente, esse devono avere lo statuto simile a quello di categorie vuote. Devono essere presenti alla mente ma non devono essere prodotte dalla voce o udite dall'orecchio. Ci sono prove empiriche di fatto che questo sia corretto. […] Supponiamo che uno dei componenti della grammatica universale sia la *teoria del caso*, un sistema che affianca la teoria del legamento ed altri sottosistemi della facoltà del linguaggio. Un principio della teoria del caso è che le espressioni referenziali devono avere caso. La teoria generale del caso determina il modo in cui si assegna il caso, come al solito permettendo un certo grado di variabilità. […] I casi possono essere manifesti, come in generale in latino, oppure nascosti, come in generale in italiano e in inglese, ma assumiamo che siano presenti, in accordo con questi principi generali di assegnazione di caso, siano essi manifesti o nascosti.

Sottolineandone la 'funzione' e la valenza di 'relazione logica',[1] è possibile mostrare in parallelo alcuni usi dei casi nelle lingue classiche, ragionando a livello contrastivo sulle differenze formali a fronte di una logica di fondo. Più o meno esplicitata a livello didattico,[2] la riflessione intende partire dall'analisi dell'enunciato come insieme di relazioni, rappresentabile come segue:

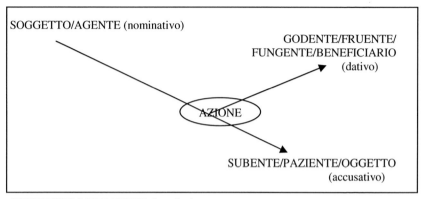

CONTESTUALIZZAZIONE (locativo)

Il modello è successivamente rileggibile, sulla scorta di Jackendoff, alla luce del fatto che ogni semantica rimanderebbe a quella spaziale:[3]

La grande intuizione di Gruber, anticipata da altri, ma da nessuno prima di lui dimostrata nei particolari, è che la semantica del movimento e della localizzazione fornisca la chiave d'interpretazione per un'ampia gamma di altri campi semantici.

Nei termini della nostra teoria l'ipotesi di Gruber potrebbe essere formulata come segue:

Ipotesi delle Relazioni Tematiche (IRT)

In ogni campo semantico di [EVENTI] e di [STATI] le principali funzioni di evento, stato, percorso e luogo sono un sottoinsieme di quelle utilizzate per l'analisi della localizzazione e del movimento nello spazio.

Eccolo schematizzato:

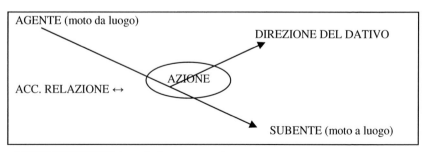

LOCALIZZAZIONE (stato in luogo - tempo)

Esplicitate e ulteriormente discusse le funzioni indicate precedentemente:

- Chi compie l'azione? = [ƒ agente]: moto da luogo
- Chi la subisce? = [ƒ subente]: moto a luogo
- Quando/dove avviene il fatto? = [ƒ contesto]: stato in luogo/tempo
- A chi giova? = [ƒ fruente]: dativo

si passerà alla presentazione dei casi nella loro "valenza spaziale", avanzando, almeno con finalità didattica, una possibile formalizzazione delle funzioni logiche principali, graficamente rendibili come nella legenda che segue:

↓ moto sul subente (oggetto diretto)
↔ relazione, attinenza, tangenza
→ moto a luogo (allativo)
> moto di allontanamento (funzione agente, che copre il soggetto come pure l'agente)
÷ direzione del vantaggio

3. Esemplificazioni

Un primo confronto fra attivo e passivo aiuta enormemente la riflessione, sottolineando da un lato il rapporto fra soggetto e oggetto diretto, e ancora la differenza fra soggetto agente e soggetto logico, dall'altro rafforzando la coscienza dell'esistenza di un piano superficiale e uno profondo, come introdotto a inizio modulo. L'espressione (10), rendibile graficamente come in (11) e ancora, con l'uso della legenda proposta, come in (12), esplicita, nell'equivalenza fra attivo e passivo (13), la medesima funzione logica soggiacente nei due sintagmi "Paulus" e "a Paulo".

(10) Paulus Marcum necat

(11) Paulus

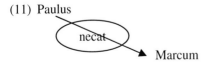

(12) Paulus [>] Marcum [↓] necat

(13) A Paulo [>] Marcus necatur

3.1. Accusativo

L'analogia d'uso dell'accusativo per esprimere più in generale la funzione logica di 'target', insieme 'obiettivo', 'meta' di un'azione (oggetto diretto) e di un movimento (allativo), non presenta difficoltà argomentative. Emblematico a riguardo è l'esempio:

(14) Romam (→) petere

Quanto allo specifico dell'accusativo di moto a luogo, la forma (15), graficamente rendibile come in (16), più conosciuta dallo studente di lingue classiche, si ritrova strutturalmente almeno in due lingue moderne - inglese (17) ed ebraico (18) - differenti per tipologia:

(15) eo domum   (16)  eo ⟶ domum

(17) I go home

(18) הביתה (אלך)

Ancora dall'ebraico (sempre nell'intento di mostrare l'unità di fondo delle lingue, anche quelle percepite come più distanti dalla propria) si possono eleggere esempi di uso dell'accusativo in funzione di moto a luogo:

(19) ירושלימה ("verso Gerusalemme")

(20) ארצה ("a terra")

(21) שמאלה - ימינה ("a sinistra - a destra")

L'accusativo di relazione (*relativus*, da *re-fero*, ancora rimanda al trasporto, al movimento), nella sua possibile traslazione spaziale di 'contatto di tangenza', troverebbe un parallelo logico (per cercare conferme in famiglie altre rispetto all'i.e.) ad es. in arabo (22), lett.: "forse che non esisti relativamente al (fatto di essere) un assistente sociale?", e (23), lett.: "quanto relativamente all'unità di stanza è nell'albergo?", esempi spiegabili forse come una forma di 'attinenza'.

(22) الست مساعدا اجتماعيا ("Non sei un assistente sociale?")

(23) كم غرفة في الفندق ("Quante stanze ci sono nell'albergo?")

La 'relazione' potrebbe considerarsi come base logica su cui poggiare le forme impersonali (24) e (25), i *verba affectuum* (26) o ancora il doppio accusativo (27) e (28):

(24) me (↔) iuvat

(25) me (↔) non solum piget stultitiae meae, sed etiam pudet (Cic. *dom.* 29)

(26) Ego nec sitio honores, nec desidero gloriam (Cic. *Q. fr.* 3,5,3)

(27) Quid nunc te [↓], asine, litteras [↔] doceo? (Cic. *Pis.* 73)

(28) me [↓] primum sententiam [↔] rogavit (Cic. *Q. fr.* 2,1,3)

3.2. Ablativo

L'ablativo nel suo valore di 'origine, allontanamento', da un lato confermato dall'etimologia (e più in generale dall'uso nelle diverse lingue i.e.), attraverso l'esempio del sanscrito (29) mostra allo studente come il celebre sallustiano (30) non sia un'eccezione, ma ricalchi la logica funzione del caso, così come nell'uso assoluto di moto da luogo (31):

(29) phalam vṛksat patati ("Il frutto cade dall'albero")

(30) nobili genere natus ("Nato da una nobile stirpe")

(31) Dionysius tyrannus Syracusis expulsus ("Il tiranno Dionisio espulso da Siracusa")

Non stupisce allora il fatto che, dove possibile, l'ablativo esprima (con o senza preposizione) l'agente da un lato, e poi la causa efficiente, e in generale la causa (con tutti quei verbi quali: *laetor, gaudeo, delector, doleo, maereor, laboro, vescor, fruor*; e aggettivi quali: *laetus, maestus, sollicitus, anxius, fessus, lassus, aeger*; che possono tutti essere di volta in volta presentati e discussi a seconda del grado richiesto di approfondimento).

Di qui è possibile mostrare come più spesso l'ablativo renda il secondo termine di paragone, proprio nella sua funzione logica di "a partire da/raggiungendo",[4] ciò che al di fuori dell'i.e. accadrebbe in una struttura come l'egiziano:[5]

(32) *nfr b3k pn r nb=f* ("questo servo è migliore del suo padrone")

Medesimo processo interpretativo varrebbe per l'ablativo di privazione, dove (33) risuonerebbe (sempre per restare con l'egiziano) con (34):

(33) curis vacuus

(34) *jnk šw(w) <m> ḥ₃w* (*Nauf.* 12-13) ("sono privo (lett.: uno svuotato) di esagerazione")

3.3. Dativo

Delle tante possibili funzioni di dativo (*dativus casus* "il caso del dare a", *dativus (in)commodi*, *dativus finalis*), che tutte rimandano a un atteso 'movimento di guadagno' [÷], un'attestazione quale (35) testimonia un uso di dativo in funzione di moto a luogo. L'analogia fra l'atto del 'dare' e la direzionalità del 'vantaggio' non stupisce:

(35) it clamor caelo (Verg. *Aen.* 5,451)

3.4. Locativo

Una "sana" distinzione fra genitivo[6] vero e proprio e locativo non solo non confonde il discente ma, anzi, gli permette di darsi ragione (anche nell'ottica del cammino formativo percorso, che spinge a intuire le diverse funzioni che i due casi esprimono e che non possono portare ad alcuna coincidenza) dell'illogicità della (comoda?) espressione di 'genitivo locativo'. Mostrando paralleli di locativo in lingue diverse, si può cogliere l'occasione per attirare l'attenzione sull'imprescindibilità, all'interno di un atto comunicativo, del contesto (tematica che la linguistica moderna ha particolarmente valorizzato, partendo dal 'sistema senso ⇔ testo' di Mel'čùk, fino alla linguistica testuale), quel quadro spazi(o-tempor)ale ponibile come base esperienziale primaria.

3.5. Sulle espressioni di tempo

Facendo nostra la felice definizione di Vladimir Panov (dall'intervento nel medesimo convegno) del tempo intendibile come "spazio con inizio e fine", non imbarazza il parallelo seguente:

stato in luogo   ~   moto per luogo

(abl. con valore locativo)   (accusativo)

tempo determinato   tempo continuato

e ancora la possibile equivalenza:

moto da luogo : moto a luogo = origine : termine (di un periodo di tempo) all'interno della quale giustificare, di conseguenza, l'uso dei casi, in linea con quanto fin qui argomentato.

4. La sintassi dei casi latina

In chiusura del modulo è possibile ridiscutere con la classe i principali aspetti della sintassi dei casi, per fissare, dopo aver valutato anche a livello contrastivo alcuni esempi, la norma d'uso nella lingua classica. Accanto a possibili esempi utilizzabili in aula, si sceglie di seguito di presentare anche qualche possibile distacco o infrazione alla norma, non usufruibile chiaramente in funzione didattica ma utile per testare la prospettiva delineata in queste pagine.

Si rifletta su una frase quale (36), dove l'alternanza di resa del destinatario può celare la doppia scelta, da un lato di reale dativo [÷], dall'altro più di sottolineatura del moto a luogo (acc. con preposizione).

(36)   ego [>] mitto litteras [↓] alicui ~ ad aliquem

Nel parallelo offerto da (37) e (38) i due diversi punti di vista emergerebbero sul piano superficiale, privilegiando il primo l'espressione di direzione ('riversare aiuto su qlc.'), il secondo quella dativa ('donare, offrire aiuto a qlc.'):

(37) iuvare aliquem   (38) succurrere alicui

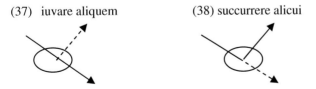

Lo stesso potrebbe essere argomentato per la doppia reggenza di *bene*:

(39) bene vos! (Plaut. *Stich.* 709)

(40) bene mihi, bene meae puellae (Plaut. *Pers.* 772)

Altra alternanza di resa sul piano superficiale è identificabile nella costruzione di *posco*, dove in (41) la meta della richiesta è sentita come 'target' e l'oggetto della richiesta come 'relazione' (lett. "io agisco una richiesta su di te in riferimento alla pace"), in (42) l'indirizzo del domandare è più concepito come a una 'fonte, origine' e l'oggetto è morfologizzato in accusativo.

(41) pacem te poscimus omnes (Verg. *Aen.* 11,362)

(42) quid a me tempus poscat (Cic. *Planc.* 79)

Altro esempio significativo è offerto da *fido*, che da un lato, in (43), privilegia la direzione del vantaggio, dall'altro, in (44), sottolinea, con un ablativo l'origine, la limitazione ("quanto a"):

(43) mihi ipse confido   (44) prudentia consilioque fidens
      (Cic. *Lael.* 17)   (Cic. *off.* 1,80)

Seguono, senza ulteriori commenti, altri possibili esempi di costruzione, da (45) a (51), e di doppia reggenza (con diversa specializzazione semantica), da (52) a (54):

(45) dono tibi librum ≠ dono te libro

(46) liber tibi donatur ≠ tu libro donaris

(47) circumdo urbi moenia ≠ circumdo urbem moenibus

(48) adspergo carni salem ≠ adspergo carnem sale

(49) induo tibi vestem ≠ induo te vestibus

(50) induor veste ≠ induor vestem

(51) intercludo tibi fugam ≠ intercludo te fugā

(52) aemulor alicui ("invidio, sono geloso") ≠ aemulor aliquem ("emulo")

(53) convenio alicui ("sono adatto a") ≠ convenio aliquem ("mi incontro con")

(54) moderor alicui rei ("freno, modero") ≠ moderor aliquem/aliquid ("regolo, governo")

Nel momento in cui l'opposizione, apparente a livello superficiale, di (55) e (56) si ricompone, nel discente, nella consapevolizzazione di uno stesso valore profondo, che nel primo caso privilegia per certi versi il vantaggio [÷], nell'altro la direzionalità [→], si è pervenuti al risultato auspicato.

(55) oboedire legibus

(56) obey the rules

Fra le possibili infrazioni (rilette in funzione descrittiva, non normativa, alla ricerca del meccanismo dell'errore, come "testimonianza - per usare le parole di Bernard Bortolussi in questa medesima sede - e frammento reale della *competence*") si può almeno citare, da quell'inesauribile bacino che è il *Satyricon*, (57) dove la funzione 'guadagno' vince su quella 'target' (almeno nell'atto di *parole*, in terminologia saussuriana, *performance*, in quella chomskiana, del parlante in questione) così illuminando la dinamica dell'errore, o ancora il "cattivo" uso della sintassi del dativo in (58) e (59), esempi, entrambi, che inferirebbero la predominanza, nello specifico, a livello profondo, della funzione di 'target' [↓] su quella di '(s)vantaggio' [÷].

(57) Saltem nobis adiutasset (62,11)

(58) Persuadeo hospitem (62,2)

(59) Aediles male eveniat (44,3)

Conclusioni

Un approccio linguistico di carattere trasversale, in quell'ottica neo-comparatista intelligentemente espressa e pervicacemente auspicata e perseguita da Renato Oniga, che allo stesso tempo potenzi le competenze nelle lingue classiche, nelle moderne come pure in quella materna, presenta indubbi vantaggi, come ha magistralmente mostrato, tra gli altri, l'intervento, nella medesima sede di Convegno, di Anna Cardinaletti sull'utilità e il guadagno derivanti dalla "comparazione linguistica nella didattica delle lingue".

Prima ancora che come eventuale modello di analisi, il percorso proposto si rende vieppiù interessante anche nell'ottica dell'attuale riforma delle scuole superiori che, se da un lato recepisce il peso sempre più significativo delle lingue straniere moderne, dall'altra consente nei Licei Classici di diminuire a loro vantaggio le ore dedicate al latino e al greco e comprime di fatto nei Licei Linguistici, in un solo biennio, lo studio del latino per lo spazio dovuto alla terza lingua straniera. Tale ciclo di lezioni – che può ben essere presentato come introduttivo alle differenti discipline linguistiche e che richiede, come sopra delineato, un numero limitatissimo di ore – fornisce competenze di base fruibili in modo trasversale, non solo all'interno del singolo ambito, con un'attenzione in più alla formazione globale del discente. Ulteriore conseguenza significativa è il fatto che l'insegnamento delle lingue classiche esce ulteriormente valorizzato in quanto strumento di riflessione privilegiato per meglio comprendere i meccanismi linguistici generali sottostanti, contribuendo a una sensibilizzazione linguistica a tutto tondo, pure all'interno delle riduzioni dei quadri-orari ministeriali.

La sempre maggiore presenza poi di stranieri nelle classi, nonché la giustamente emergente sensibilità alle difficoltà di studenti con problematiche di apprendimento (non ultima la dislessia) - entrambe categorie che vivono spesso, per ragioni evidenti, il disagio di un approccio più convenzionale all'analisi logica come tradizionalmente impartita nelle scuole a oggi - è di ulteriore stimolo a valutare l'utilità d'uso del modello proposto.

La facilità e immediatezza di comprensione da parte degli studenti depone a favore di un approccio che è "biologically correct", espressione della reale esistenza, appunto, di una 'bio-logica' talmente consustanziale e connaturata all'uomo da essere riconosciuta, quasi inconsciamente, nella sua immediatezza da parte di chiunque valuti senza pregiudizio il dato linguistico.

Summary

This paper presents a model for teaching some aspects of Case in Latin, based on a synergistic approach integrating generative grammar, Tesnière's dependency grammar, and Jackendoff's hypothesis of thematic relations. This model, recently tested with high school classes in Italian Licei Classici, has the advantage of stimulating in the instructors a renewed interest for modern Linguistics and of offering the pupils a deep insight of the phenomena which combines synchronic and diachronic perspectives.

This proposal may gain particular interest in the view of the renewed programs of Classic and Linguistic High Schools (Licei) in which Modern Languages receive an increased prominence at the expenses of Classic Languages. In a self-contained module of a limited number of hours, we can provide the pupils with basic tools of linguistic analysis that can serve all Modern and Classic Languages at the same time.

This Linguistic approach can give a new value to the teaching of Classical Languages allowing the learners to reach a deeper insight of underlying mental mechanisms of language, and could be of particular relevance in the general consideration that Italian schools are now attended by an increasing number of foreign students for whom Italian is not the first language, as well as an increasing number of students who are now certified for specific deficits such as dyslexia, which clearly make the learning of (modern and classic) languages particularly difficult if carried out with the tools of traditional grammar.

Notes

[*] Ringrazio Donatella Vignola, già insegnante di lingue classiche al Liceo "M. Gioia" di Piacenza presso cui è stato condotto l'esperimento didattico, prima ancora che per l'ospitalità nelle sue classi e la condivisione del progetto, per la lunga amicizia e le numerose altre, piacevoli e fruttuose occasioni di collaborazione.

[1] L'ottica è proprio quella di Chomsky, quando ebbe ad affermare (durante il ricevimento di una *honoris causa* il 22 novembre 2001 all'università di Calcutta, come riportato in *Frontline*, Vol. 18, n. 25, 8-21 dic. 2001) che "the first generative grammar in the modern sense was Panini's grammar", all'interno di una diffusa e condivisa valutazione di studiosi, fra cui Faddegon 1936: 19 ("con *kāraka*, Pāṇini intende le relazioni logiche o "ideational" fra un nome e un verbo, o più precisamente fra un oggetto o qualunque cosa è concepita secondo analogia fra un oggetto e un'azione o qualunque cosa è concepita secondo analogia con un'azione"), o Renou 1957, s.v. *kāraka*: "reggenza (fra un nome e un'azione verbale), reggenza casuale verbale" e ancora Renou 1960 n. 18: "Pāṇini parte dalla

funzione, non dalla categoria" (le citazioni, tradotte e riadattate, sono tratte da Al-George 1976: 27 ss. di cui si è seguita anche l'analisi dei nomi dei casi del sanscrito proposta nella successiva nota 3).

[2] L'annoso problema dell'uniformazione della terminologia, da un lato, e ancora della formalizzazione, è risolvibile (che è forma eufemistica per 'eludibile'), in aula, sacrificando minimamente la scientificità a un uso più divulgativo, insieme fruibile e adatto al grado di preparazione degli studenti.

[3] Conforto e stimolo è una, seppur rapida e sommaria, riflessione sulla terminologia utilizzata già dal Pāṇini: *apādāna* (I, 4, 24): 'ablazione, separazione' e *sampradāna* (I, 4, 32): 'donazione', movimento opposto al primo (entrambi derivanti da √ *dā* + prefissi *apā* ↔ *sampra*: 'prendere' ↔ 'dare'); *karaṇa* (I, 4, 42): 'instrumentum', "mezzo di realizzazione supremo (di un'azione)" e *adhikaraṇa* (I, 4, 45): 'locazione, referenza spazio-temporale, sostrato (dell'azione)', dove *ādhāra* vale "supporto, ricettacolo" (*adhi* 'concernente', sottolineerebbe la correlazione fra la mediazione dello strumentale e la referenza spazio-temporale); e ancora la correlazione sul piano della transitività di *karman* (I, 4, 49): 'paziente', 'ciò su cui l'agente indirizza l'attenzione sopra ogni altra cosa", e *kartṛ* (I, 4, 54-55): 'agente' (*svatantra* "indipendente", che ha la sua propria natura, identità), non escludendo a volte l'esistenza di un 'iniziatore' causale (*hetu*).
Se l'impianto della presente comunicazione è di carattere più pragmatico, *ad docendi usum*, forse, che non scientifico (nel tal caso richiederebbe una discussione approfondita, in particolare nei suoi numerosi punti più critici, e per la franchezza del dibattito ringrazio di cuore il contributo diretto donatomi da Giuliana Giusti), particolarmente stimolante risulta il modello cognitivo proposto da William M. Short, quando, inquadrandoli tra "physical experience" e "body's reality", ha argomentato il suo assunto di partenza che "thoughts are locations".

[4] La differenza, a livello superficiale, dipende dalla diversa ottica da cui si osserva: la preposizione usata in egiziano è infatti di moto a, non moto da luogo (lett.: "buono (è) questo servo se comparato a/ messo in prospettiva nei confronti (verso) del suo padrone"). Tale inversione del punto di vista si attesta in molti altri casi: per restare in ambito semitico e per limitarsi a un solo esempio, basti indicare l'aggettivo ar. قريب 'vicino' che si costruisce con la particella من (indicante il moto da luogo), e il suo opposto بعيد 'lontano' con عن (preposizione con sfumatura locativa).

[5] Gli esempi sono tratti da Grandet-Mathieu (2003), grammatica della lingua egiziana di taglio funzionale, basata su un approccio linguistico molto moderno e di struttura particolarmente interessante.

[6] In questa sede il caso genitivo (così come il vocativo, d'altronde) non è preso in esame per ragioni metodologiche che esulano dagli intenti contingenti.

Riferimenti bibliografici

Al-George, S. (1976) *Limbă şi gîndire în cultura indiană*, Bucureşti, Editura ştiinţifică şi enciclopedică.

Bortolussi, B. (questo volume) "Generative Grammar and the Didactics of Latin. The Use of Examples", 319-342.

Cardinaletti, A. (questo volume) "Linguistic Theory and the Teaching of Latin", 429-444.

Chomsky, N. (1988) *Language and Problems of Knowledge. The Managua Lectures*, Cambridge (Mass.), MIT Press [trad. it.: *Linguaggio e problemi della conoscenza*, Bologna, il Mulino 1991].

Faddegon, B. (1936) *Studies on Pāṇini's grammar*, Verhandeling der Koninklijke Akademie van Wetenschappen te Amsterdam. Afdeeling Letterkunde. Nieuwe Reeks, Deel 38, n. 1, Amsterdam.

Grandet. P. e B. Mathieu (2003) *Cours d'Egyptien Hieroglyphique*, Paris, Khéops [trad. it.: *Corso di egiziano geroglifico*, Torino, Ananke, 2007, a cura di C. Orsenigo].

Jackendoff, R. (1983) *Semantics and Cognition*, Cambridge (Mass.), MIT Press [trad. it.: *Semantica e cognizione*, Il Mulino 1989].

Panov, V. (questo volume) "Prefixes and Aspect of Latin Verb: A Typological View", 187-199.

Renou, L. (1957) *Terminologie grammaticale du sanskrit*, Paris, Champion.

—. (1960) "La théorie des temps du verbe d'après les grammairiens sanskrits" *Journal Asiatique* 248 305-337.

Short, W.M. (questo volume) "Metaphor and the Teaching of Idioms in Latin".

Tesnière, L. (1959) *Éléments de syntaxe structurale*, Paris, Klincksieck [trad. it.: *Elementi di sintassi strutturale*, a cura di G. Proverbio e A. Trocini Cerrina, Torino, Rosenberg&Sellier, 2001].

PRAGMATIC ASPECTS OF TEACHING TRANSLATION METHODS FROM LATIN TO ITALIAN

ANDREA BALBO

1. Introduction

Translating is a point of arrival, not of departure. From the didactic point of view it is an activity which encounters increasing difficulties in school. While it should be clear that the text is not merely the sum of juxtaposed sentences, but has a logical framework and determines the progressive addition of information, at school this concept enters into normal activity only with great difficulty. In this paper, I would like to introduce some elements of formal Linguistics which can improve the strategies of Latin translation at high school and in introductory courses of Latin at universities.[1]

What are the main difficulties that students encounter in translating? In general, we could say that the core problem does not consist in learning the rules or using the vocabulary: what is not easy for students, is to apply a theoretical and abstract system of rules to the texts they have to translate in their daily routine.[2] My every-day teaching experience at high school and university shows that many students have not received sufficient methodological training about the translation process; they re-write the text fitting it into the Italian word order. Such an approach can sometimes be proper, above all for students who find difficulties in text comprehension,[3] but it risks to become a negligent way of working; in fact, the essential elements are reduced to connectors, verbs and complements, in which students do not distinguish typologies and roles inside the text. These are the translation problems seen "from below", from the student's perspective. But let us now have a glance also at the top, i. e. at the advice that appears in official documents of the Ministry of Education and in some widespread textbooks and websites.

1.1. Translation according to official documents
of the Italian Ministry of Education

If we refer to the official documents (so-called *Indicazioni nazionali*) that pertain to the Latin syllabuses of the new secondary schools, the translation from Latin into Italian is mentioned several times in the normative device. We take as a reference point the most complete treatment, about the classical secondary school (Liceo classico):

"[Lo studente] pratica la traduzione non come meccanico esercizio di applicazione di regole, ma come strumento di conoscenza di un testo e di un autore che gli consente di immedesimarsi in un mondo diverso dal proprio e di sentire la sfida del tentativo di riproporlo in lingua italiana. [...] Allo scopo di esercitare nel lavoro di traduzione (nel senso sopra definito) è consigliabile presentare **testi corredati da note di contestualizzazione (informazioni relative all'autore, all'opera, al brano o al tema trattato)**, che introducano a una **comprensione non solo letterale.** Dal canto suo lo studente sarà impegnato nel riconoscere le **strutture morfosintattiche**, i **connettivi testuali**, le **parole-chiave**; nel **formulare e verificare ipotesi di traduzione** e **motivare le proprie scelte.** E' essenziale sviluppare la capacità di **comprendere il testo latino nel suo complesso** e nelle sue strutture fondamentali, **anche senza l'ausilio del vocabolario.** Sarà inoltre opportuno partire il prima possibile dalla comprensione-traduzione di brani originali della cultura latina; in tal modo lo studio, entrando quasi da subito nel vivo dei testi, abituerà progressivamente gli studenti a impadronirsi dell'*usus scribendi* degli autori latini, facilitandone l'interpretazione".

These documents underline the necessity to deal with the context of the passages, the necessity of understanding the Latin text taken as a whole, even though the aim of translating without a dictionary turns out to be not very credible owing to the current level of average knowledge of Italian students. However, the *Indicazioni nazionali* seem to pay attention to factors that definitely pertain to pragmatic rules, such as connecting particles, but they offer neither a systematic and detailed discussion of them nor deal with their connections to morphology, syntax and semantics.

Finally, from a methodological point of view, these documents offer only some interesting suggestions, but not a homogeneous methodological route.

1.2. Translation according Latin textbooks and websites

And what about Latin textbooks[4] and websites[5] for Latin? They all contain advices or "procedurals" for translation.[6] But, broadly speaking, even though it is possible to find useful advice there, I still consider them unfulfilling, because, even though these tools emphasize the importance of reading the text in depth and, from a grammatical point of view, revealing its structure in sentences and clauses, they do not pay sufficient attention to textual cohesion and to semantics; most of all, they encourage treating the text not as a coherent piece, but simply as a group of juxtaposed clauses;[7] finally, some seem to suggest that an important part of the translation process lies in a very unclear "insight" into the content.[8]

1.3. An aid from technology?

And what about text analysers? Can they really help students in translation? In 2002 the Italian publishing house Paravia offered a text analyser in CD ROM, the so-called NOMEN. With this tool I analysed the following sentence:

(1) *Dum haec ad Ilerdam geruntur, Massilienses usi L. Domiti consilio naves longas expediunt numero XVII.* (Caes. *civ.* 1,56,1)

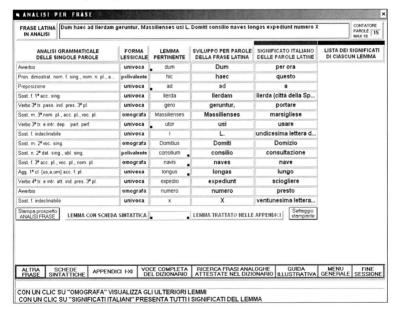

Also without a perfect knowledge of the Italian language (grammatical terms are almost universal provided by their Greek or Latin origin), a reader can easily see how uncertain and unfulfilling the results of such an analysis are:

1. Besides the objective problem of the limits of the program, which prevents it from completing the sentence with *numero XVII* because it exceeds the maximum number of insertable characters in the grid, what here is called "sentence analysis" is, actually, a morphological analysis of the individual constituents which does not take syntax into account: see for instance the translation of *geruntur* with the infinitive form.
2. So, the number of misunderstandings is high and particularly unpleasant, as in case of *L*, which is interpreted as the eleventh letter of the alphabet, and not as the abbreviation of the proper noun Lucius.
3. The suggestions for the translation remain at a very low level and do not help more than reading the dictionary.

From the analysis of all these resources (books, documents of the Ministry, websites, ICT), it is possible to draw the following observations:

1. the didactic resources for translation in Italy (and not only there) are still very repetitive;
2. the suggestions do not seem to understand and endorse the most significant advances of twentieth-century linguistics;
3. the didactic value of the automatic morphological and syntactic analysers for Latin is still definitely low.[9]

What can we deduce from this brief investigation? The scholastic tools for translation are still not suitable; the research ought to help teachers and students improve their translation methods, perhaps with the aid of modern linguistics.

2. From theory to practice

Before switching to didactic practice, I must address a question. Is it necessary and useful to address the methodological problems of translation in the context of the new reform of Italian schools that implies a drastic reduction of Latin in programs different from the Liceo classico? Why should teachers change an old-fashioned approach that has so many supporters? There could be two answers: a) the school and the university cannot remain closed to linguistic innovations, but must absorb their more useful elements; b) I am convinced that the introduction of some elements of linguistic pragmatism – such as the idea of textual cohesion – into traditional translation methods produce real performance improvements.[10]

It is necessary for students to understand the importance of cohesive mechanisms in the text and in the sentence. The text framework can be easily described as a continuous passage from known facts to new facts: every new fact undergoes an uninterrupted process of thematization and topicalization and becomes, in this way, the basis for adding new facts. It is also important to remember that some facts can be focused with the aid of emphasis and repetitions. Textual cohesion can be more or less deep in different text typologies (oral text, written text) or in different text genres (narrative, epic etc.) and the author can develop several strategies to connect the parts of the text clearly by using various elements as syntactic or semantic connectors. These elements, however, are often undervalued in the normal activity of translating from Latin to Italian.[11] In Italy, teachers put stress on clause analysis: but it is also important to deepen the connections between the sentences and the clauses, not simply listing only subjects, noun phrases, predicates and so on. It is important to grasp the idea of the network structure of a Latin text, one not too much different from that of the WWW. As there is a hierarchic structure of connected PCs with different quality levels, so in Latin texts there are syntactic and content sections that cannot be well understood and translated without paying attention to their connections with other sections and to their hierarchy.

2.1. An unpretentious proposal of some teaching tools[12]

Before I deal with the process in detail, I introduce some examples of charts that can support teaching in different ways: a) the teacher can show and explain them to the students, in order to underline the main points of the procedure; b) the students can use them during exercises or also during actual translation. Obviously, these are not prescriptive rules, but proposals which must necessarily be reworked by the teacher in his didactic mediation.

Chart 1

Topic = "What is being talking about": Spevak (2010: 6). Focus = "the salient, or most informative, element of a sentence": Spevak (2010: 7). Given-New passage = Flow of information contained in a text, which passes from well-known elements to new elements. Left periphery = Initial part of the sentence containing mostly topics and focalized elements. Semantic correlation among the sentences = Community or contiguity of the subject among sentences Syntactic correlation among the sentences = Logical connection between two adjacent clauses; they are marked by syntactic connectors as subordinating and coordinating particles. Discontinuity of constituents = Detachment of connected elements and their positioning towards the left periphery of the sentence, in order to focus the attention on a term; they are the result of the rhetorical figure of hyperbaton.[13]

Chart 2: Recapitulation of the analysis of textual cohesion

Cohesive elements	Names/ adjectives	Pronouns	Adverbs	Verbs	Connectors	Clauses/ Sentences
Repetitions, identity, semantic analogies, hyponims hyperonims						
Context relationships						
Anaphoric elements		determinative relative demonstrative indefinite	relative modal			
Constituent discontinuity						
Ellipsis						
Connectors for coordination						
Connectors for subordination						

Chart 3: Some values of connective particles

Connective	Value	Examples taken by quoted studies
At Kroon (1995)	a) indicates that the interlocutor's expectations are not satisfied	Cic. *ac.* 2,118: *Princeps Thales* [...] *ex aqua dixit constare omnia. At hoc Anaximandro non persuasit.*
	b) can mark the beginning of a new textual unity	Caes. *civ.* 3,13,1: *At Pompeius, cognitis his rebus* [...] *Dyrrachio timens diurnis eo nocturnisque itineribus contendit.*
	c) points out a contrast with the previous textual unity	Plaut. *Epid.* 262-263: Pe: *Age, dice*; Ep. *At deridebitis*; Ap.: *non edepol faciemus.*
Autem Kroon (1995)	a) has distinctive value and separates a textual segment from another previous segment	Curt. 3,1,19: (Alexander) *Amphoterum classi ad oram Hellesponti, copiis autem praefecit Hegelochum.*
	b) acts as marker of the focused element	Plaut. *Bacch.* 155: *Fiam ut ego opinor Hercules, tu autem Linus.*
	c) can show causality or hostility	Ter. *Eun.* 797-798: (Tras.) *quid tu tibi vis? ego non tangam meam?* (Crem.) *tuam autem, furcifer?*
Enim Kroon (1995) Spevak(2010)	introduces an idea of assent to the proposed assertion; never occupies the initial position in the sentence	Cic. *rep.* 2,28 *Quae cum Scipio dixisset, Verene, inquit Manilius, hoc memoriae proditum est. Tum Scipio: Falsum est enim, Manili* [...].
Iam Kroon (1998) Kroon and Risselada (2002) Bazzanella (2005)	a) has focusing function	Cic. *fam.* 13,16,1 *eius* [*sc. Crassi*] *libertum Apollo-nium iam tum equidem cum ille* [*sc. Crassus*] *viveret et magni faciebam et probabam.*
	b) is used to pass to a new subject; has a varied use since archaic age and is oriented to past, or present, or future	Liv. 9,19,9: *iam quis par Romano miles?*

Nam Kroon (1995)	a) introduces a textual unity which acts as test, justification, explanation, comment of another hierarchically more important unity	Cic. *fam.* 6,18,2 *De Hispaniis novi nihil. Magnum tamen exercitum Pompeium habere constat. nam Caesar ipse ad nos misit exemplum Paciaeci litterarum in quo erat illas XI esse legiones.*
	b) introduces a new theme in the speech;in this case it is like *autem* and to greek *dè*	Cic. *nat. deor* 1,27-28: *Crotoniates autem Alcmaeo, qui soli et lunae reliquisque sideribus animoque praeterea divinitatem dedit, non sensit sese mortalibus rebus inmortalitatem dare.*
Num, nonne, -ne, an Oniga (2007)	introduces a definite waiting for the answer (*num* and *nonne*), indetermination (*-ne*), unfavourable doubt (*an*)	Cic. *Quinct.* 44 *Non recusamus. Num quid praeterea?* (negative answer) Cic. *Sext. Rosc. Amer.* 98 *Etiamne in tam perspicuis rebus argumentatio quaerenda aut coniectura capienda est? Nonne vobis haec quae audistis cernere oculis videmini, iudices?* = compelled affirmative answer. Plaut. *Asin.* 837 (Dem.) *Credam istuc si esse te hilarum videro.* (Arg.) *An tu me tristem putas?* = doubt
Quidem Kroon (1995)	has several values: a) affirmative or assertive	Cic. *leg.* 2,24: (Marcus) *At ne longum fiat videte.* (Atticus) *Utinam quidem! Quid enim agere malumus?*
	b) adversative	Cic. *Cluent.* 133: *At in ipsum habitum animadverterunt. Nullam quidem ob turpitudinem, nullum ob totius vitae non dicam vitium sed erratum.*
	c) concessive	Cic. *Deiot.* 22: *Atque antea quidem maiores copias alere poterat; nunc exiguas vix tueri potest.*
	d) additive	Plin. *epist.* 8, 16, 1: *Confecerunt me infirmitates meorum, mortes etiam, et quidem iuvenum.*
	e) restrictive	Cic. *Lael.* 9: *Aut enim nemo, quod quidem magis credo, aut, si quisquam, ille sapiens fuit.*
	f) works as a juxtaposition element	Sen. *epist.* 99,28 *Istuc nobis licet dicere, vobis quidem non licet.*

Repente/subito Torrego (2005)	introduce a basic fact and break narration	Liv, *Ab urbe condita* 37,11,8 *Id inceptum eius Nicander a terra visus cum turbasset, repente mutato consilio naves conscendere omnis iubet*
Sane Risselada (1998b)	a) introduces a positive evaluation	Plaut. *Cas.* 740, *sapis sane.*
	b) has assertive value	Cic. *Att.* 5,10: *nihil sane.*
	c) assumes concessive value	Cic. *Verr.* 4,150: *laudent te iam sane*
Sic	a) has assertive value and can be referred to what precedes or follows	Plaut. *Cist.* 197: *haec sic res gesta est.*
	b) can have restrictive value	Verg. *Aen.* 1,253: *sic nos in sceptra reponis?*
	c) marks the situations	Cic. *Q. Rosc.* 29: *sic est volgus.*
Vero Kroon (1995)	a) shows the involvement of the speaker in the communicative act	Cic. *rep.* 1,66: *Puto enim tibi haec esse nota. Vero mihi, inquit ille, notissima.*
	b) points out the truth of an assertion;	Plaut. *Men.* 1096: *ita vero!*
	c) can show a variable level opposition	Cic. *Q.frat.* 3,1,1: *Negotia se nostra sic habent, domestica vero ut volumus.*

Chart 4: Summary of main typologies of word order in Latin

SOV	Caes. *bell.* 1,11 *Helvetii iam per angustias et fines Sequanorum suas copias traduxerant.*
SVO	Naev. *Poen.* 46 M. *Onerariae onustae stabant in flustris*
OVS	Caes. *bell.* 1,2: *Apud Helvetios longe nobilissimus fuit et ditissimus Orgetorix.*
VOS	Liv. 3,20,1: *moverat plebem oratio consulis*
OSV	Caes. *bell.* 1,53: *reliquos omnes, consecuti, equites nostri interfecerunt*
VSO	Bell. *Alex.* 70,8 *Miserat enim ei Pharnaces coronam auream*

Let us pass now to a concrete methodological proposal with the aid of a simple historiographic text, Caes. *civ.* 1,56,1.

This is the text that I propose for an Italian liceo at the end of first year or in second year.

The Massilians arm a fleet (Caes. *civ*. 1,56,1). During the civil war between Caesar and Pompeians, while Caesar is fighting in Spain near Ilerda against the Pompeian army of Afranius and Petreius, the Massilians, with Lucius Domitius' help, prepare a fleet to battle with Caesarean ships, which besiege them.

> *Dum haec ad Ilerdam geruntur, Massilienses usi L. Domiti consilio naves longas expediunt numero XVII, quarum erant XI tectae. Multa huc minora navigia addunt, ut ipsa multitudine nostra classis terreatur. Magnum numerum sagittariorum, magnum Albicorum, de quibus supra demonstratum est, inponunt, atque hos praemiis pollicitationibusque incitant. Certas sibi deposcit naves Domitius atque has colonis pastoribusque, quos secum adduxerat, complet. Sic omnibus rebus instructa classe magna fiducia ad nostras navis procedunt, quibus praeerat D. Brutus. Hae ad insulam, quae est contra Massiliam stationes obtinebant.*

These are the main steps of the translation process.

2.2. Step 1: Reading

The students read the introduction and text; the teacher explains some difficulties, *exempli gratia* giving information about *Albici* (a barbaric tribe that lived on the hills behind Marseilles).

2.3. Step 2: "Raising awareness"

The students identify some main ideas through the reading of the title and introduction. They are asked to identify the names of the characters, the relationships among them, the situations in which the characters are involved and the actions performed by them. It will be useful, at least at the initial stage, to summarize the results in a very brief, schematic way, as follows:

a) The text tells us something about the war between Caesar and Pompeius
b) Caesar is in Spain to fight against Pompeius' troops
c) The text gives information about a siege of Marseilles
d) The Massilians are hostile to Caesar
e) The Massilians prepare a fleet
f) The Massilians are helped by Lucius Domitius
g) Lucius Domitius is an enemy of Caesar.

2.4. Step 3: Lexical examination of the text

As I already tried to clarify in Balbo (2009), it is necessary that the students remember that they are not ignorant of the text and the lexicon: when they start to read, they actually know some facts and many words as a result of their cultural background. So the exercise of translation does not demand – at least at this stage – the consultation of a dictionary, but simply an act of recalling or reasoning.[14] It is also well known that the use of a dictionary can be even misleading, if the students work negligently, limiting themselves to reading the first entry or hunting for the identical or similar example, hopefully translated. Obviously, the knowledge of a minimum lexicon – to be distinguished from the basic lexicon[15] – must be the result of long work, developed with the students from the beginning of the first year, improved by continuous contact with the cultural historical context.[16] In the text under consideration, I think that a low level Italian student of Latin can understand the meaning of the following terms from the assonances with Italian, grammatical knowledge or the information acquired by the introduction:

Sentence 1	*haec ad Ilerdam Massilienses L. Domiti consilio naves longas numero quarum erant*
Sentence 2	*Multa minora navigia addunt ut ipsa multitudine nostra terreatur.*
Sentence 3	*Magnum numerum sagittariorum magnum Albicorum de quibus supra demonstratum est atque hos praemiis incitant*
Sentence 4	*Certas sibi naves Domitius atque has pastoribusque quos secum*
Sentence 5	*Sic omnibus rebus magna fiducia ad nostras naves procedunt quibus D. Brutus*
Sentence 6	*Hae ad insulam quae est contra Massiliam*

The meaning of more than 60 words of the 84 of the text can be guessed or understood; we have to set apart the numerals, usually much neglected in the teaching activity, and some verbs and assume as a matter of fact that the insufficient knowledge of some morphemes should be connected also to the poor syntactic competence of many students.

From these words the student can easily obtain following information:

Sentence 1
a) something happens at Ilerda
b) someone talks about long ships
c) Lucius Domitius has something to do with a given proposal
d) the Massilians do something

Sentence 2
a) someone talks about adding a larger number of smaller ships, so that someone is terrified (confusion of the subject and the complement of *terreatur* is possible in this phase)

Sentence 3
a) someone talks about a great number of *Albici*
b) someone incites the *Albici*
c) someone talks about rewards

Sentence 4
a) someone refers something about Domitius and ships
b) someone has someone else with himself
c) someone talks about shepherds

Sentence 5
a) someone talks about some great confidence
b) someone proceeds against our ships
c) someone talks about Decimus Brutus in relation to these ships

Sentence 6
a) someone talks about an island in front of Marseilles

The sum of the results of steps 2 and 3 is that the student is now provided with a rich amount of information even though he has not begun either the analysis or the translation of the text.

2.5. Step 4: Identification of some significant syntactic elements

According to a very traditional and usual procedure it is possible to highlight the verbs, the coordinating and subordinating connectors, and the relative pronouns:

> Dum *haec ad Ilerdam* geruntur, *Massilienses usi L. Domiti consilio naves longas* expediunt *numero XVII,* **quarum** *erant XI tectae.*
> *Multa huc minora navigia* addunt, *ut ipsa multitudine nostra classis* terreatur.
> *Magnum numerum sagittariorum, magnum Albicorum,* **de quibus** *supra* demonstratum est, inponunt, *atque hos praemiis pollicitationibusque* incitant.
> *Certas sibi* deposcit *naves Domitius atque has colonis pastoribusque,* **quos** *secum* adduxerat, complet.

Sic omnibus rebus instructa *classe magna fiducia ad nostras naves* procedunt, **quibus** praeerat *D. Brutus.*
*Hae ad insulam, **quae** est contra Massiliam stationes* obtinebant.

The text includes six sentences, of variable length, but generally quite short and characterized by a limited number of subordinate clauses. According to these considerations, the student should pay more attention to Italian expressions and less to the analysis.

2.6. Step 5: Syntactic analysis

Sentence 1	*Dum haec ad Ilerdam geruntur* = temporal clause *Massilienses naves longas expediunt numero XVII* = main clause *usi L. Domiti consilio* = dependent clause; the participle is connected to *Massilienses.* ***quarum** erant XI tectae* = relative clause
Sentence 2	*Multa huc minora navigia addunt* = main clause *ut ipsa multitudine nostra classis terreatur* = final clause (regular *consecutio temporum*)
Sentence 3	*Magnum numerum sagittariorum, magnum Albicorum inponunt* = main clause ***de quibus** supra demonstratum est* = relative clause *atque hos praemiis pollicitationi6usque incitant* = main clause (in coordination with *magnum...imponunt*)
Sentence 4	*Certas sibi deposcit naves Domitius* = main clause *atque has colonis pastoribusque complet* = main clause (in coordination with *certas ...Domitius*) ***quos** secum adduxerat* = relative clause
Sentence 5	*Sic omnibus rebus instructa classe*= prop. ablative absolute *magna fiducia ad nostras naves procedunt* = main clause ***quibus** praeerat D. Brutus* = relative clause
Sentence 6	*Hae ad insulam stationes obtinebant* = main clause ***quae** est contra Massiliam* = relative clause

Instead of these descriptions, we could also use other methods to show the syntactic connections:

(2) Multa huc minora navigia addunt

ut ipsa multitudine nostra classis terreatur

(3) *Domitius deposcit sibi certas naves*
         S   V   Term   O

(4) $\boxed{Certas}$ *sibi deposcit* $\boxed{naves}$ ***Domitius***
       AttO Term   V   O   S

(5)   *Certas sibi deposcit naves Domitius*

This analysis often concludes the examination of the text, which, according to a lot of teachers, should be translated with the aid of the vocabulary.

Nevertheless, this procedure seems to me imperfect for two reasons:
a) the relationships among clauses are not clearly explained; the result doesn't change a lot using lines or arrows; it is not in fact clear, for instance, that the connection between the participle *usi* and *Massilienses* is stronger than the link with *Dum ... geruntur*, which is, as we shall see, the element of connection to the previous context;
b) this method takes the chance on passing over significant relationships among the constituents of the text, which can help us better understand the sense of the Latin. For instance, in the second period, the explanatory sense of *ut ... terreatur* and the value of motion expressed by *huc*, which is very useful for understanding the place of action, are not clearly expressed.

So it seems necessary to increase the usual translation steps with the pragmatic elements mentioned above that can give us more useful information for a better expression of Latin into the mother tongue. Hereafter I will give some examples.

2.7. Step 6: Identification of the significant elements of textual cohesion using the above mentioned charts

Cohesive elements	Names/ Adjectives	Pronouns	Adverbs	Verbs	Connectors	Clauses/ Sentences
Repetitions identity semantic analogies, hyponims hyperonims	*nostra classis navigia multitudine Domitius Certas naves instructa classe nostras naves*		*huc*			
Context relationships		*haec*	*supra*	*demonstratum est*		*dum... geruntur*

Anaphoric elements		*quarum ipsa de quibus hos has quos quibus Hae*				
Constituent discontinuity	*Multa minora navigia Certas . naves*					
Ellipsis						*erant XI (naves) tectae quibus (navibus) incitant (Massil.)*
Connectors coordination			*sic*		*atque atque*	
Connectors subordination					*dum ut*	

2.8. Step 7: Analysis of some pragmatic elements and their evaluation

I discuss here only a selection of proposed elements.

Dum = the temporal clause reminds us that the Massilians facts occur at the same time as the Ilerdan ones and refers to the historical context.

Haec = this is the background element, from which the main element (the real Topic) *Massilienses usi L. Domiti consilio naves longas expediunt* is developed.

Usi = the participle constitutes the logic preamble on which the Massilians base their consequent action. Incidentally, it is necessary to hint at this frequent architecture of the period, that prefers subordination with the participle to coordination, as Oniga (2007: 290) correctly observes. In fact, the translation capacity can be refined by means of reflection on the various possibilities of syntactic construction of the Latin complex sentences.

Quarum erant XI tectae = the reference to the ships identifies different categories of boats.

Ut ipsa multitudine = The examination of anaphoric *ipsa*, which agrees with *multitudine*, but refers logically to *minora navigia* and *naves*, should avoid the mistake of referring *multitudo* to people and not to things and, above all, should persuade the students not to consider *nostra* an ablative, because it would be contradictory; this statement is reinforced by the opposition with *nostra classis*; finally, the teacher will show the students that the final clause *ut ... terreatur* explains the function of the Massilians' action.

De quibus supra demonstratum est = the reference is again to the previous context and can be understood turning to the introduction; *Hos* recalls the archers and the *Albici* and tightly connects their actions to the prizes.

Incitant = the ellipsis of the subject shows that here there is no reference to a new fact, but to the plural subjects responsible for the action of *addere*; therefore, it is necessary to supply in translation a form such as "the Massilians".

Sic = prepares the completion of the narration: the reader waits for a summarizing element, one that the text offers immediately, the absolute ablative *omnibus classe instructa rebus*, in which the expression *omnibus rebus* can be translated better than "with all things" because the phrase refers to the preparations.

Ad nostras naves procedunt = the reference to the Caesarian fleet should suggest that *ad* not only shows motion, but a hostile motion.

If the teacher has explained the various possibilities of word order in the Latin sentence, using for instance the model of chart 4, the students should not be too surprised at finding unusual orders in the sentence; so it would not be necessary to use the so-called "composition of the sentence" according to modern language word order.

I would underline another element: the constituent discontinuity - the result of hyperbaton - deserves special attention even in a very simple text such as this. Here are two examples:

(6)   *multa huc minora navigia addunt fines (Massilienses)*

The sentence can be rewritten as follows:

(7)   *Multa huc [~~multa~~ minora navigia] ~~huc~~ addunt (Massilienses)*

We have the detachment of the quantifier *multa* from its substantive, which is only determined by *minora*, which distinguishes it from *longae naves*. There is also the focusing of the adverb of place *huc*.

(8)   *Certas sibi deposcit naves Domitius*

(9)   *Certas sibi deposcit ~~sibi certas~~ naves Domitius*

The situation of the second expression is similar; the shifting on the left is used to point out the characteristic of the object.

2.9. Step 8: Working translation

After this work of analysis and comprehension, students can try to write a working translation with a very limited help from the dictionary. As a matter of fact, students now should be able to express the content of the text in a good draft.

2.10. Step 9: Revision and definitive composition

This is the refining work that students can achieve by reading more carefully the entries of the dictionary. This is the moment to reach a good translation in the mother tongue, even though it should to be clear that translation in high school and university is always a simulation and it is not possible to expect from students the same precision as a professional translator.

I summarize my proposals in the following table:

1. Reading of the introductory information and of the text
2. Consciousness raising
3. Lexical reflection
4. Examination of the significant syntactic elements
5. Syntactic analysis of sentences and clauses
6. Identification of the more significant pragmatic elements
7. Analysis of the pragmatic elements
8. Work translation
9. Revision and definitive translation

Conclusion

This short paper aimed only to examine some aspects of translation methods from Latin to the mother tongue. I think that three aspects should be gained from daily teaching:
a) the systematic study and application of textual linguistic elements such as the idea of cohesion of texts;

b) the role of discontinuity of constituents, which shows the educational importance of what has always been only understood as a rhetorical artifice;
c) the possibility of building a "road map" for translation procedures in the classroom.
Now the last question: who shall pick up the linguistic challenge of producing a true guide to translation on these bases, a propaedeutic to a generative grammar easy to use in school with a good set of exercises and a new model of dictionary?

Notes

* I thank a lot Renato Oniga and Giuliana Giusti for the invitation to this conference and Thomas Frazel (Tulane University) for having revised and substantially improved my English version.
[1] About this problem see Balbo (2007) and Balbo (2009).
[2] I quote only a school survey about Latin teaching in year 2002 made by Liceo "Torricelli" of Faenza: see also Balbo (2007: 24) n. 1. To the question "Where are your main difficulties in Latin language?" the 60 % of the students answered "In the enforcement of grammatic rules when we have to understand the Latin texts". For the data see http://www.liceotorricelli.it/ indaginelatino2002/indagine.html.
[3] Also Oniga (2008: 142) sometimes finds this method useful.
[4] R. Alosi and L. Caliri, *Sistema Latino*, Esercizi 1, Torino, Petrini, 2007; N. Flocchini *et alii, Maiorum lingua*, Milano, Bompiani, 2010.
[5] *Latino vivo* (http://www.latinovivo.com/studenti%20miei/Metodo/Metodo.htm), N. Marini in *Mediaclassica Loescher*:
(http://www.loescher.it/mediaclassica/latino/traduzione/propedeutica1.asp).
[6] To use the denomination adopted in N. Flocchini, *Maiorum lingua*.
[7] It is possible to find an exception in *Latino vivo* (http://www.latinovivo.com/studenti%20miei/Metodo/Metodo.htm), where we can find this statement: "Un ultimo avvertimento: quando traduci una frase, non considerarla come qualcosa a se stante di cui puoi dimenticarti, appena l'hai scritta sul tuo foglio. Niente di più sbagliato! Il discorso continua e le proposizioni spesso si chiariscono l'una con l'altra". This advice (do not think that the clause is something alone: it is connected to other clauses) is reasonable, but does not help the student much, because it does not give him a clear method to work.
[8] Even Marini's paper, which is definitely the most complete, refers also to keywords and the literary form of the text, so implicitly going in the direction traced by the *Indicazioni nazionali*
[9] This is not only an Italian feature: if the students read some pages on the websites *Collatinus* (http://www.collatinus. org/moteur/),
Perseus (http://www.perseus. tufts.edu/hopper/) and *Biblioteca Classica Selecta* (http://pot-pourri. fltr.ucl.ac.be/itinera/), they could find interesting tools but of limited usefulness.

[10] Similar approach is given by the so-called predictive analysis which teaches how to recognize some fixed structures of Latin clauses (the symmetry between *non solum ... sed etiam...*, for instance) and expect them in the translation process, while the reading: see Notarbartolo (1998)

[11] See Zampese (2004), 159.

[12] At the end of my paper, I list a selection of important bibliography. I underline that teachers can find a good starting point in Oniga (2007: 245-255). Very useful are the contributions of Kroon (1995), Rizzi (1997), Risselada (1998b) and (2005), Torrego (2005), Devine and Stephens (2006), and of the old Pinkster (1990): all of these offer rich repositories of examples and broad, scientific coverage of many topics in textual linguistics. Spevak (2010), the most recent work about Latin constituent order, is also of great help: it is rich with helpful examples and the *Appendix* offers three texts commented from a pragmatic point of view; other interesting materials in http://www.olgaspevak.nl.

[13] It would be opportune to rewrite from a didactic point of view and in an analytical way pages 525-608 of Devine and Stephens (2006), that represent the most complete scientific contribution on the subject, also with the support of Spevak (2010).

[14] Only a very effective list of questions will allow the student to understand the text deeply. Questions ought be thorough to connect tightly syntactic structure with thematic progression through the cohesive elements analysed. It is necessary to encourage students to acquire the skill of "predicting" about upcoming information, at least as a possibility. The less interested students perceive the discipline more as a kind of way to obstacles, than as an organized system that allows them to increase their culture and acquire refined tools for the comprehension of the world in which they live. For this reason the teacher who tries to guide the students along the translation process should become a kind of "midwife of knowledge", in a Socratic sense, able to raise to a conscious level the lexical and syntactic knowledge that students already have without being aware of them.

[15] The teaching of a basic lexicon on the ground of Guillaumin and Cauquil (1992) involves some methodological problems, as argued by Flocchini (2001).

[16] I refer to Balbo (2004).

References

Balbo, A. (2004) "Una proposta concreta per l'insegnamento del lessico latino" *Aufidus* 54: 243-256.

—. (2007) *Insegnare latino. Sentieri di ricerca per una didattica ragionevole*, Novara, UTET Università.

—. (2009) "Per una valorizzazione e un uso dei connettivi nella traduzione" *Il Quaderno di latino* 2 - *Nuova secondaria on line* (http://www.lascuolaconvoi.it): 37-53.

Bazzanella, C., Bosco, C., Calaresu, E., Garcea, A., Guil, P. and A. Radulescu (2005) "Dal latino *iam* agli esiti nelle lingue romanze: verso una configurazione pragmatica complessiva" *Cuadernos de Filología Italiana* 12: 49-82.

Calboli, G. (1983) "Problemi di grammatica latina" *ANRW* II, 29.1: 3-177.

Devine, A.M. and L.D. Stephens (2006) *Latin Word Order. Structured Meaning and Information*, Oxford-New York, Oxford University Press.

Flocchini, N. (2001) "Lo studio del lessico nell'insegnamento del latino. Problemi di metodo e di organizzazione didattica" *Latina Didaxis* 16: 123-145.

Guillaumin, J.Y. and G. Cauquil (1992) *Vocabulaire essentiel de latin*, Paris, Hachette Classique.

Giusti, G. and R. Oniga (2006) *La struttura del sintagma nominale latino*, in R. Oniga and L. Zennaro (eds) *Atti della Giornata di linguistica latina - 7 maggio 2004*, Venezia, Cafoscarina, 71-100.

Kroon, C. (1994) "Discourse connectives and discourse type. The case of Latin", in J. Herman (ed.) *Linguistic studies on Latin*. Selected papers from the 6th international colloquium on Latin linguistics (Budapest, 23-27 March 1991), Amsterdam, Philadelphia, 303-317.

—. (1995) *Discourse particles in Latin: a study of* "nam", "enim", "autem", "vero" *and* "at", Amsterdam, J.C. Gieben.

—. (2005) "The relationship between grammar and discourse: evidence from the Latin particle *quidem*", in G. Calboli (ed.) *Papers on grammar. 9, Latina lingua! Nemo te lacrimis decoret neque funera fletu faxit. Cur? Volitas viva per ora virum. Proceedings of the twelfth international colloquium on Latin linguistics (Bologna, 9-14 June 2003)*, Roma, Herder, 577-590.

Kroon, C. and R. Risselada (1998) "The discourse functions of "iam"", in B. García-Hernández (ed.) *Estudios de lingüística latina. Actas del IX coloquio internacional de lingüística latina. Universidad Autónoma de Madrid, 14-18 de abril de 1997*, Madrid, Ediciones Clasicas, 429-445

—. (2002) "Phasality, polarity, focality: a feature analysis of the Latin particle *iam*" *Belgian Journal of Linguistics* 16: 63-78.

Lohnstein, H. and S. Trissler (2004) *The Syntax and Semantics of Left Periphery*, Berlin, De Gruyter.

Notarbartolo D. (1998) "La didattica breve nell'insegnamento del latino" *Zetesis* 1: http://www.rivistazetesis.it/la_didattica_breve_nell.htm).

Oniga, R. (2007) *Il latino. Breve introduzione linguistica*, 2ª ed., Milano, Franco Angeli.

—. (2008) "La manualistica universitaria sulla lingua latina tra ricerca e didattica" *Latina Didaxis* 23: 119-150.

Panhuis, D.J. (1982) *The communicative perspective in the sentence. A study of Latin word order*, Amsterdam, Benjamins.

Penello, N. (2006) "Applicazioni di elementi di linguistica formale alla didattica del latino" in R. Oniga and L. Zennaro (eds) *Atti della Giornata di linguistica latina* - 7 maggio 2004, Venezia, Cafoscarina, 159-178.

Pinkster, H. (1990) *Latin Syntax and Semantics*, London, Routledge.

Risselada, R. (1998a) ""Nunc"'s use as discourse marker of "cohesive" shifts", in Ch. M. Ternes and D. Longrée (eds) "Oratio soluta" - "oratio numerosa"*: les mécanismes linguistiques de cohésion et de rupture dans la prose latine. Actes du colloque*, Luxembourg, Centre Alexandre Wiltheim, 142-159.

—. (1998b) "The discourse functions of *sane*: Latin marker of agreement in description, interaction and concession" *Journal of Pragmatics* 30: 225-244.

—. (2005) "Particles in questions", in G. Calboli (ed.) *Papers on grammar. 9, Latina lingua! Nemo te lacrimis decoret neque funera fletu faxit. Cur? Volitas viva per ora virum. Proceedings of the twelfth international colloquium on Latin linguistics (Bologna, 9-14 June 2003)*, Roma, Herder, 663-679.

Rizzi, L. (1997) "The Fine Structure of the Left Periphery", in L. Haegeman (ed.) *Elements of Grammar. Handbook in Generative Syntax*, Dordrecht, Kluwer, 281-337.

Salvi, G. (2005) "Some Firm Points on Latin Word Order: the Left Periphery", in K. É. Kiss (ed.) *Universal Grammar and the Reconstruction of Ancient Languages*, Berlin, De Gruyter, 429-456.

Spevak, O. (2010) *Constituent Order in Classical Latin Prose*, Amsterdam, J. Benjamins.

Torrego, M.E. (2005) "Grammar and pragmatics: the textual uses of *repente* and *subito*", in G. Calboli (ed.) *Papers on grammar. 9, Latina lingua! Nemo te lacrimis decoret neque funera fletu faxit. Cur? Volitas viva per ora virum. Proceedings of the twelfth international colloquium on Latin linguistics (Bologna, 9-14 June 2003)*, Roma, Herder, 763-773.

Zampese, L. (2004) "Dall'analisi logica alle logiche del testo", in G. Milanese (ed.) *A ciascuno il suo latino: la didattica delle lingue classiche dalla scuola di base all'università*. Atti del convegno di studi, Palazzo Bonin- Logare, Vicenza 1-2 ottobre 2001, Galatina, Congedo, 157-182.

WORKING MATERIALS FOR THE TEACHING OF LATIN IN THE PERSPECTIVE OF CONTEMPORARY LINGUISTICS

PIERVINCENZO DI TERLIZZI

Introduction

The following paper focuses on a teaching experience that took place during the school year 2009/2010 in the Liceo Leopardi (Pordenone, Italy). It involved a first-year class of Liceo Classico, of sixteen students. This was, therefore (and this is one of the key elements of the work), a group of students already trained in Latin grammar from the two previous years (5 hours of Latin a week, for 33 weeks of school).

An indispensable prerequisite for the project was a seminar held under the aegis of the Doctorate in Science of Antiquities (Philology and Literature), at the University of Udine in May of 2009, with Renato Oniga, which was dedicated to illuminating certain aspects of the morphological and syntactic system of the Latin language, considered in the perspective of generative grammar. Reflecting on the elegant explanation that this approach permits of various phenomena habitually confronting students, I discussed with Professor Oniga the possibility of conducting an experiment in a class of an Italian high school, to see the actual implications of the generative approach to language within the practical curriculum. I wish to express to Professor Oniga my thanks for his support and participation in this experience; of course, I also thank my students for their enthusiasm and timely feedback.

1. The place of Latin in Italian high schools

The context of the experience was a Latin course in a high school (Liceo classico), that is, the type of school in which students devote the largest portion of their time to the study of Latin and Greek. The overall approach of the course, regularly including the translation of written materials from Latin into Italian, commits students only to a specific language operation.[1] Examination at the end of the course confirms (and perhaps even strengthens) a historical fact, namely that the language skills of Italian students in the humanities are essentially identified with translation skills.

What is not well defined, on the other hand, is the place of these competences in the part of the school program that concerns the "authors", (that is essentially the history of Greek and Latin literature), which includes the knowledge of the classics in their original languages. The reference base of examinations is so very heterogeneous, and brings with it a diversity of indicators for the assessment of the skills.[2]

To these factors, specifically addressing the subject of linguistic competence and its assessment, a more general question should be added: that is, the placement of Latin in the Italian school system. While Latin retains its centrality in Liceo Classico (but with the precautions mentioned above), it is also true that in other circumstances its position, in relationship with the study of the Italian language, seems much more precarious.

1.1. Translation: limits of a merit-rating tool

It is not the place here to recall the importance of the translation in cultural education.[3] However, in evaluating its presence as an indicator of language competence in the students, there are some critical points that the practice of teaching should point out.

First, the attention of the student is often too oriented in the direction of the outcome. The various procedural steps, the single intermediate stages, are not taken into account in the evaluation, and therefore are lost.[4] During the training process, this often produces difficulties of definition and communication of critical points on which the students can take account to improve their skills and their preparation.

Second, translation is an instrument easy to manipulate. From the well-known *Tom Brown's School Days* by Thomas Huhes (Cambridge 1857), muddling through Latin tests by the art of bad copying is an old practice for generations of students, that has also been worth its own field of study, as an important element in the reception of the classical tradition.[5] Today, with the availability of personal computers (and even mobile phones) connected to the Internet, the copying process is even simpler, shareable, and maskable.[6]

Finally, looking at things from the perspective of the student, the translation remains an operation wholly directed and judged only by teachers: the results are not easy to understand and manage in terms of self-evaluation.[7]

2. The proposed method

On the basis of the evidence that I quickly pointed out above, I set my work in the high school class where the experience took place. It was a class made up of students who had already studied the entire morphology and syntax of the simple and complex sentence in the preceding two years of school (the Ginnasio). Thus, the subsequent three years of school (the Liceo), is the moment for the revision and deepening of the whole grammatical system and for reading classical authors. In essence, the space for action on language skills is broad.

Starting from this premise, I have divided my work into two segments:

a) some basic notions about the structure of simple sentences;
b) the essential features of the syntax of the period.

As our reference grammar we used Oniga (2007).[8] I chose to highlight two key issues for the structure of the simple sentence, namely the identification of the phrases and of the "thematic roles" assigned by the heads of the phrases, and another key issue for the structure of the period, namely the complementation.

2.1. Recognition of phrases

I began by presenting some examples of detection and recognition of phrases. I worked in the classroom focusing on the following steps:

a) sentence parsing, in terms of immediate constituents analysis: the subject of two class hours;
b) understanding of the formal structure of phrases, by means of the tree diagram format, a decisive step to acquire operational awareness: in four class hours;
c) presentation of the analogies and differences between the different types of phrases, that is Noun Phrase, Verb Phrase, Adjectival Phrase and Prepositional Phrase: during another two-hour lesson;
d) comprehensive review of the whole subject, for two hours;
e) a final written test, lasting an hour, testing the recognition and the analysis of phrases in a Latin text.

2.2. The theory of thematic roles

The notion of argument structure, from the theory of valency to the more refined theory of thematic structure, is a very useful tool in understanding the semantic relationships between the verb and its arguments. Here the work was divided as follows:

a) the notion of "valency", to which four hours of lessons were devoted, especially in selective reading and recognition of the verbal valency in the dictionaries used in high school and in the corpus of the Perseus Project;

b) the notion of "thematic role" , to which six hours of teaching were devoted, which had as its centre the idea that the knowledge of the various semantic roles assigned by the verb to its arguments is part of the knowledge of the native speaker. So, the Latin language appeared not too different from Italian. It must be said, incidentally, that in this context I found students particularly interested, since the "theory of the role" is useful also in the interpretation of poetic texts of the Italian tradition;

c) a two-hour lesson for revision;

d) a one-hour written test, concerning the identification, in a Latin text, of the meanings of verbs and the recognition of the major thematic roles assigned by each verb.

3. Complex sentences: the complementation

Since the very beginning of generative approaches to Latin syntax (Lakoff (1968), a crucial element in the analysis of the sentence was the system of complementation. The concept of "complementizer" is not known in Latin school grammars, but its more general meaning, instead of the traditional term of "subordinating particle", appeared very useful for students to unify the structure of the various types of subordinate clauses. The topic was presented as follows:

a) a two-hour lesson to introduce the concept of Complementizer as the functional head of a particular phrase (CP), which hosts the subordinate clause and determines its nature;

b) four hours on the structures of the various types of interrogative clauses;

c) four hours on the relative clauses;

d) two hours for the revision;

e) a written test of two hours, on the recognition of the structures of complex sentences.

3.1 Tree diagrams

The practical exercises enabled students to become gradually familiar, with the practice of drawing up schemes for the description of phrases, simple sentences and complex sentences. This practice of drawing tree diagrams became, increasingly, a custom job for students, confirming that this tool is to be regarded with favour by the general pedagogy.

4. Some provisional conclusions

The idea to select some terms and concepts of Generative Grammar, basically in the terminology of the approach outlined by Oniga in his book, reached the result to make them available to a group of Italian high school students of Latin. In its implementation, the linguistic instruments proved very useful to enhance awareness in the students, who are now able to better describe and justify their interpretive operations when approaching with a classic text.

My intention and hope for the future is to build a more comprehensive approach to teaching Latin in these terms, starting from the first exposure to this language in early higher education. This hope reflects my enthusiasm for the study of classical languages. My enthusiasm is always connected to the question: "Why is that?". That is to say: "why" is a key word for students – even for students of classical authors – and formal linguistics is a good way to try to answer this "why".

Notes

[1] About the question, see also Balbo (2007).

[2] I quote here a translation of the text of the Italian Ministry of Education, *Rules of the High Schools* issued March 15, 2010, Annex A, also taken from the *National Guidelines* of May 26, 2010, on the language skills that students must possess in a classical school at the end of the course: "Having acquired the necessary knowledge of classical languages for the understanding of Greek and Latin texts, through the study of their language structures (morphosyntactic, lexical, semantic) and the tools necessary for their stylistic and rhetorical analysis, in order to achieve a more fluent Italian in relation to its historical development" (p. 8, in the *National Guidelines* , p. 13). As you can see, the powers are aimed at a general understanding. More specific the wording of page 21 of the *National Guidelines on the Classical High School* (Liceo Classico) of 26 May 2010 on the competences of

Latin language to possess at the end of the course: "At the end of the course the student is able to read, understand and translate texts of the author of various kinds and different argument, at the same time acquired the ability to compare linguistically, with particular attention to the vocabulary and semantics, Latin and Italian and other modern languages, reaching a more mature and aware knowledge of the Italian domain, especially for the architecture of the sentence and for the mastery of abstract vocabulary. The practice of the exercise of translation is not a mechanical application of rules, but an instrument of knowledge of a text and an author, in order to identify him in a world different form our own and feel the challenge of trying to present it again in the Italian language". Here, as shown, the practice of translation is based precisely on a key contrast. Similar prescriptions are found in the text of the *Guidelines for Scientific High School* (Liceo Scientifico) (p. 21). The only difference lie in the degree ("enough") of proficiency.

[3] Just look at the text of the *National Guidelines* set out in note 2 above.

[4] Taking account of what can be called "by-the-way translation" was, at the beginning of the Nineties (when the writer of this paper began his work as a teacher), a topic of discussion in working groups around the project of a reform of Italian High schools, coordinated by Beniamino Brocca.

[5] For a very interesting, and also amusing survey of this topic, see the fine essay given by Stray (1994).

[6] A simple fact: try typing in a search engine on any text of a classic author. You will notice that the top results will stand the reference to an Italian translation of sites for the students.

[7] I underline this point, as the self-evaluation is, on a matter of fact, a key point of the *curriculum*. See, in fact, the text of the *National Guidelines* of 26 May 2010 on the "The profile of educational, cultural and vocational high school student". Among the objectives to be achieved in the methodological area, there is the following point (p. 11): "Being aware of the diversity of methods used by various disciplines and be able to assess the reliability criteria of the results they achieve". As you can see, a strong emphasis is set on the acquisition of mastery of the training process.

[8] Formerly, I found some ideas about a formal approach to the teaching of Latin in Rampioni (1998).

References

Balbo, A. (2007) *Insegnare latino. Sentieri di ricerca per una didattica ragionevole*, Torino, UTET Università.

Lakoff, R.T. (1968) *Abstract Syntax and Latin Complementation*, Cambridge (Mass.), MIT Press.

Rampioni, G. (1998) *Manuale per l'insegnamento del latino nella scuola del 2000 : dalla didattica alla didassi,* Bologna, Pàtron.

Oniga, R. (2007) *Il latino. Breve introduzione linguistica*, 2ª ed., Milano, Franco Angeli.

Stray, C. (1994) "The Smell of Latin Grammar. Contrary Imaginings in English Classrooms", *Bulletin of the John Rylands Library* 76.3: 201-222.

Sitography

http://www.indire.it/lucabas/lkmw_file/licei2010///Regolamento.pdf
Regolamento del 15.3. 2010 recante "Revisione dell'assetto ordinamentale, organizzativo e didattico dei licei ai sensi dell'articolo 64, comma 4, del decreto legge 25 giugno 2008, n. 112, convertito dalla legge 6 agosto 2008, n. 133" (*Rules of the High Schools*);

http://www.indire.it/lucabas/lkmw_file/licei2010///indicazioni_nuovo_impaginato/_Liceo%20classico.pdf
Indicazioni nazionali (National Guidelines) del 26 maggio 2010 per i Licei Classici.

TESNIÈRE'S DEPENDENCY GRAMMAR AND ITS APPLICATION IN TEACHING LATIN: A SLOVENIAN EXPERIENCE

MATJAŽ BABIČ

1. Tesnière and his scholarly work in Slovenia

In Slovenia, Lucien Tesnière is greatly respected for even more reasons than his achievements in syntax theory. He is connected to Slovenia by his academic teaching career that he began as a French lecturer at the newly founded University of Ljubljana. During his stay in Slovenia from 1920 to 1923, he achieved the following:

- He learned the Slovenian language.
- He initiated the first systematic research of the Dual number in Slovene and published the results of his research in a book that is still one of the authoritative manuals on the topic of Dual in Slovene. (Tesnière (1925-2))
- He composed the first Atlas of Slovene Dual whereby he was, at the time, the first to apply the principles of Dialect Geography on Modern Slovene. (Tesnière (1925-2))

As a by-product of his project on Slovenian Dual, he established a division of Slovene dialects in main groups; this distribution, at least in its broader outline, remains unchallenged and is still considered to be the basis of Slovene dialectology. His name still commands a great respect in our country even more than elsewhere, since Tesnière is not only considered to be brilliant, but also an extremely serious and practice-oriented linguist.

2. Latin in Slovenian educational system
from 1900 to 2010

Until 1918, Slovenia was a part of the Austro-Hungarian monarchy and its educational system was the same as everywhere else in the monarchy. It wasn't much different from the system in Germany with its "Classical Gymnasium" as the central point.

After the end of the 1st World War, Slovenia became part of the new kingdom of Yugoslavia, which was strongly dominated by Serbian influence. This influence made itself felt in the educational system no less than in other areas of government and life. Still, Classical languages remained an integral part of the curriculum, though they had to give some way to other subjects, among others modern languages in the sense that German never used to be.

Here is a diagram on the presence of Classical languages in Slovene education in the 20th century:[1]

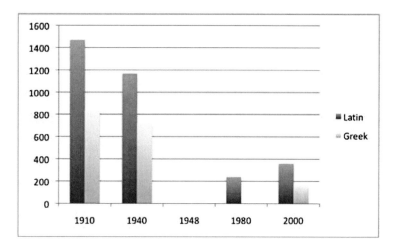

The reduction that took place shortly after the WW1 and WW2 was partly justified by a shrewd way to make a case that is often used against Classical languages, especially Latin. Latin was promoted as an element of the "formal knowledge", meaning a subject that is useful to convey basic and general elements of linguistic knowledge instead of particular skills which are to be used in everyday life. This flattering argument was first put forth even before WW1, during the general educational reform in Austria which took place in the years 1909-10.[2] What makes this argument especially dangerous is its structure, it consists of two parts, of which the first part is often passed over silently:

(1)   Latin is useful to convey general linguistic notions.

This sounds nice in itself, but, in reality, it is often short for:

(2)   a.   Latin is of no practical use,
        b.   but it is useful to convey general linguistic notions.

If one concedes the second point, one may well have conceded the first one without knowing it. Therefore, one should be careful about it for several reasons:

- This argument is a convenient way to make Latin teachers do with less hours, which can subsequently turn into a process of a gradual erosion.
- It is a welcome excuse to push Latin classes out of lower years of education, as being "too difficult for young children".
- This argument also raises expectations of the general public to an enormous height, but, so to speak, a fall from such height is almost impossible to survive.

Although the situation in Slovenia before WW2, from today's point of view, does not seem to have been extremely critical, even then the teachers of Classical Languages complained and predicted a catastrophe in the future. But these dire predictions did not come true until 1945. Following the Communist takeover in the wake of the WW2, Classical Languages were almost completely banned from our schools,[3] since they were considered to be a prominent feature of "bourgeois" education. Nevertheless, the formal reasons that were given for their ban were not unlike those that one often hears today. The ban was justified by the authorities saying:[4]

- Latin and Greek are of little practical value.
- Among the pupils, there is little interest in learning them.
- In times of a crisis, one has to economise, so "less useful" subjects have to be, at least temporarily, put aside.
- And, lastly, Latin is chiefly the language of the Church.

Particularly the last statement was, at the time, tantamount to death sentence, since the Church was widely accused to have collaborated with occupational forces during WW2.

Fortunately, this full ban on classical languages did not last long. Three years later (in 1948), Yugoslav Communist Party broke with Stalin's Soviet Union and was isolated from the Eastern Communist bloc. Looking for a way out of the isolation, the Party attempted to present themselves as more Pro-Western in order to get financial aid.

Now, in this effort to present itself as Pro-Western, Yugoslav-Communist Party discovered Classical Languages as a convenient means to distance themselves from their former Pro-Soviet educational policies.[5] Latin and, to a smaller extent, Greek, were reintroduced for some time to almost full extent of the former Classical Gymnasium. This reintroduction lasted for a decade, until, in 1959, a general educational reform shrunk Latin to 4 years of the newly formed "High School". In this reform, former Elementary School and Lower Gymnasium were combined to form a new, unified 8-year Elementary School. This reform was also the end of the traditional Classical Gymnasium.

For Classics in Slovenia, the consequences of this reform were severe: from then on, Latin was taught only in some High Schools for 4 years, 2 hours per week (which amounted to under 300 hours). This was only a fraction of former 1200 hours in the original Classical Gymnasium. From then on, Latin was present only at the very margin of Slovenian education, whereas Greek was confined to University level.

In the years of the great political and social turnaround from 1990 on, the tide turned again. Latin became an expression of the traditional European education and, partly reinforced by a certain "pendulum effect", it turned out to be a prominent sign of a "new education".

In the transition period, from the end of the 80ies into the first years of the next decade, the situation regarding Latin was in disarray, where much of the planning was left to the teachers and to school panels. After several attempts, Latin was finally given a formal status as a part of certain High School curricula, with total amount of hours of 320-360 in 4 years. This, however, brought new problems. The textbooks that were still in use were no longer suitable for High-school teaching. They were mostly translation-oriented and were still composed for the curricula of the old system. Even the teachers of the old system had long retired and young graduates were coming fresh from the university with little or no teaching experience.

3. University curriculum of Latin Grammar in Slovenia

Before 1990, the Department of Classical Studies of the University of Ljubljana (the only department of classical studies in Slovenia) had only few students. These students had no hope to ever get a regular teaching job at any school in Slovenia, so there was little incentive to change the way grammar was presented to them in university courses.

On the other hand, since Latin was taught in a sufficient level only at two High Schools, this inevitably meant that previous knowledge of Latin could not be a pre-requisite to enrol, because this would make only graduates from these two High Schools eligible to study Classics. So a Latin course for beginners was included in the Program of Studies. Greek was only taught from beginner level on, since Greek had disappeared from our High Schools in 1959.

After 1990, prospects to get a teaching post became better, but it was clear that the times had changed. The students before WW2 did their Classical Studies assuming that, when they eventually get a teaching post, they would do the teaching the way they had been taught during their own schooling and indeed, when they finally faced the pupils in the classroom, they knew almost instinctively what to do. In the 90s, it was completely different: most university graduates had to begin their teaching career without such instinctive teaching awareness. They had to give a lot more thought to teaching methods and possibilities. Since then, the students' attitude to their university classes changed radically in two aspects:

- They showed a vivid interest in the methods of language teaching.
- They perceived the classes on Latin grammar and linguistics as closely connected to their future teaching jobs.

Therefore, it was necessary to present them with a new, more adaptable approach to teach syntax. The curriculum was modernised: stylistically oriented teaching of grammar made less sense than before WW2, so it had to give way to a different approach to language which could be applied in more classroom situations.

4. Latin and Slovenian: syntactic concurrencies

Since the amount of hours of Latin in our High Schools remains so drastically reduced, the school explanation of syntax likewise has to be reduced to a bare minimum. For Slovenians, as for other native speakers of most Slavic languages, this is a relatively easy thing to do, since Slovenian:

- has approximately the same number of cases as Latin and
- likewise has no definite or indefinite article;
- does not pronominalise the sentence subject, if anaphoric;[6]
- has free word order similar to Latin.

For these reasons, at least in some cases, almost a word-to-word translation is feasible. Consider a passage like:

(3)   *quo quis ingenio minus valet, hoc se magis attollere et dilatare conatur, ut statura breves in digitos eriguntur et plura infirmi minantur.* (Quint. *inst.* 2,3,8-9) (22 words)

(4)   Slovenian translation: *kolikor kdo po naravi manj velja, toliko se bolj poskuša vzpenjati in širiti, kakor po postavi majhni stopajo na prste in šibki največ grozijo.* (24 words)

(5)   English translation (Trans. H. E. Butler, Loeb Classical Library edition): *and the less talented a man is, the more he will strive to exalt and dilate himself, just as short men tend to walk on tip-toe and weak to use threat.* (31 word)

In Slovenian, one has only to add two prepositions. All a student has to do is to replace each Latin word with its Slovenian semantic and grammatic counterpart and finally put everything in the appropriate word order. In the English translation, on the contrary, 9 words must be added.

Yet such an easy translation has its downside as well. On one hand, it makes Latin easy for the students to translate, but on the other hand it also makes it easy for a Latin teacher to skip large portions of syntax in the hope that students would intuitively understand it as they get along. One is tempted to explain Latin syntax only where it diverges from Slovenian, e. g. *accusativus cum infinitivo* and *ablativus absolutus*. Which is something teachers have to do, if they run out of time. Nevertheless, one still has to give a general overview of syntax at some point. The traditional time-consuming method being out of the question, our teachers always have to look for another theoretical model that could provide them with a convenient starting point.

5. How to present syntax?

The first solution to this problem was in accordance with the Slovenian tradition, which is to present the syntactic structure by means of sentence constituents. It works well for simple sentences with a structure of SVOA like

(6)   *Pater filio librum dedit.*

But, in Latin, one stumbles upon borderline cases sooner than one might expect. Even in the well-known example

(7)   *Antiochus epistulis bellum gerit.* (Cato *orat.* 75)

One might wonder whether *epistulis* is to be considered an adverbial or a nominal complement. It is even much worse in sentences like

(8)   *Quod si humaniter mecum questus esses, libenter tibi me et facile purgassem.* (Cic. *fam.* 7,27)

If one is to classify *mecum* as a "prepositional object", what classification should one assign to *tibi*? Therefore the first, immediate solution, by which we would have returned to traditional Sentence Constituent analysis, turned out to be inefficient, since it is less applicable in the analysis of complex propositions, as are common in the classical authors that the students are expected to read in school.

That's where Tesnière's valency theory offers help. If a student tries to translate – or even understand – a Latin sentence according to the predicational sentence model, he has to look for two sentence constituents at once, namely Subject and Predicate. Following Tesnière's notion of the sentence, one knows what to look for first, namely the verb, which, in this way, serves as a very convenient and easily identifiable starting point.[7]

6. Case syntax

On account of the above-mentioned similarities between the Slovenian and the Latin case system, one of the first simplifications that took place in our university teaching was to skip the case syntax: already in Mihevc and Gabrovec (1978), a Greek textbook, which was used at our Department in the late 70s, only brief mentions of Case Syntax are made. This way of teaching Greek proved to be very successful.

(9) Consider the well-known sentence model:

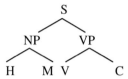

Now let's compare this to a typical presentation of Case syntax in a Latin Grammar, where diverse functions of each case are laid out, whereby the distinction between a nominal group and a sentence/verb group is treated as secondary.

(10) Levels in case syntax:

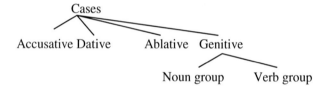

This model seems structurally unsound, since the distinction between noun group and verb group is demoted to the lowest level. This is less surprising if one takes into account the history of Case syntax and its hybrid nature. In its model, it looks as if the most important question were not: "How does one form a correct Latin Sentence?" but: "How and where does one implement a certain morphological feature?" This leads us to the familiar problem of arrangement, especially in a textbook kind of Grammar: if Case syntax is taken seriously, then phrases like (11)-(12) can not be dealt with in the same chapter, because the first one includes a genitive case, whereas the second two include prepositions:

(11) *unus multorum*

(12) *unus de tribus*

(13) *unus e captivis*

One can either explain (11)-(13) as: "the Genitive and the Preposition are nothing but different expressions/realisations of one and the same function" or to, put it in another way, one can say: "All of it is Genitive".

And yet it is clear that, from the viewpoint of the phrase structure, we are dealing with the same thing.[8] Notwithstanding this obvious problem, no modern Latin grammar managed to completely do away with Case syntax.[9]

7. Dependency Grammar as a solution

The traditional sentence model, which has been, in its foundation, adopted by Generative Grammar, is characterised by its bipartite structure. To quote one of Tesniere's examples (Tesnière 1959: 105):

(14) *Filius patrem amat*   *Filius a patre amatur.*

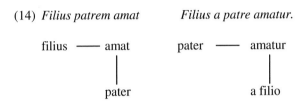

In Valency Grammar, the structure is arranged more clearly, because it starts at the top, which means at the true sentence level. The same two sentences are structured as:

(15) *Filius patrem amat*   *Filius a patre amatur*

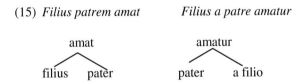

Tesnière's renown as the originator of Dependency Grammar sometimes overshadows his other theoretical approach to the sentence which is characterised by the use of the notions of "translation" and "translatif" (which nowadays could be put on a par with "conversion" and "converters/conversion markers"). The element that in examples (11)-(13), would usually be referred to as "preposition" is, according to Tesnière, a marker by which a noun is transferred to/converted to what he calls an "adjective", rather in a sense of a "complement".[10]

    This innovation seems to be put forth by Tesnière in his universalist quest for "a grammar to end all grammars" or, in other words, it was one further step towards bringing all the intraphrasal relations to one common denominator. So it is possible to see him founding a model for Universal Grammar, in which one would not be imprisoned by morphology

(Tesnière (1959), 361). This approach, that is not so far from Generative Grammar, seems to be somewhat disregarded by newer applications of his theory. C. Touratier, in his *Syntaxe Latine*, dismisses it altogether as "a bit excessive".

Touratier, 1994, 17: *Tesnière parlait alors de translation, ce qu'il définissait comme un phénomène consistant "à transférer un mot plein d'une catégorie grammaticale dans une autre catégorie grammaticale, c'est-à-dire à transformer une espèce de mot en une autre espèce de mot. (Tesnière, 1966, 364)". Cette façon de présenter les choses est un peu excessive et a l'inconvénient de lier exclusivement les fonctions syntaxiques aux classes syntaxiques de morphèmes:*

Yet, as obsolete as this concept of Tesnière might seem at first glance, it can nevertheless be considered to be of no lesser importance than the notion of "valency", for it establishes a strict hierarchy in the syntax of the sentence as well as word groups. It could be additionally justified by the great importance which Tesnière gave to a syntactic complement as an indivisible unit which is processed by our linguistic capability as such. This concept can prove itself to be of great use in teaching Classical Languages because of the small amount of time that our teachers have, due to which the teaching of syntax had to be compressed to an absolute minimum. It is badly needed in our High-school teaching of grammar and it may well prove to be of some benefit to our teaching of Latin for two reasons:

- it does not overburden the teacher nor does it confuse the students with additional linguistic terminology and
- it can replace the previous time-consuming separate presentation of syntactic features by one all-embracing approach based on the basic terminology.

Tesnière's discoveries and his verb-oriented model of syntax are easy to apply in practice and can be used as a compressed model to explain diverse Latin noun phrases. Due to these advantages, it was and is certainly welcome in Slovenia as well as in any other educational system where there are problems caused by objective constraints of the amount of teaching hours and the percentage of school population.

Notes

[1] Data from Hriberšek (2005) and Nećak Lük (2003).
[2] Cf. Hriberšek (2005), 227.
[3] With the Classical Gymnasium as a temporary exception.
[4] Cf. Hriberšek (2006), 79-81
[5] Cf. Movrin (2010), 288-291.
[6] In other words, Slovenian and Latin can be characterized as 'pro-drop languages'.
[7] Cf. Happ (1975) and, to a lesser extent, Scherer (1975).
[8] The traditional prominence of Case Syntax has an inconvenient consequence that one must first study a Latin Grammar to know where each topic is treated.
[9] Cf. among others: Bortolussi (1999) and Panhuis (2006).
[10] Tesnière himself probably would not have been entirely happy with the term "conversion", since it implies that something is being transformed, whereas what he had in mind was not that something goes through a metamorphosis, but that something gets relocated from one class to another, so only a change of category takes place.

References

Bortolussi, B. (1999/2008) *La grammaire du latin*, Paris, Hatier², Collection Bescherelle.

Happ, H. (1975) *Grundfragen einer Dependenzgrammatik des Lateinischen*, Göttingen, Vandenhoeck&Ruprecht.

Glücklich, H.J., Nickel, R. and P. Petersen (1980) *Interpretatio. Neue lateinische Textgrammatik*, Würzburg, Ploetz.

Hriberšek, M. (2005) *Klasični jeziki v slovenskem šolstvu 1848-1945*, Ljubljana, Filozofska fakulteta Univerze Ljubljane.

—. (2006) "Zaton klasičnega šolstva (1945-1958)" *Keria* 8.1: 73-101.

Mihevc-Gabrovec, E. (1978) *Grščina. Teksti in vaje za pouk grščine*; Ljubljana, Filozofska fakulteta Univerze Ljubljane.

Movrin, D. (2010) "Gratiae plenum : latinščina, grščina in Informbiro", *Keria* 12.2-3: 281-304.

Nećak Lük, A. (2003) *Language Education Policy in Slovenia*, Ljubljana, Ministry of Education, Science and Sport, Education Development Unit.

Panhuis, D. (2006) *Latin Grammar*, Ann Arbor, University of Michigan Press.

Pfister, R. (1988) *Lateinische Grammatik in Geschichte und Gegenwart*, Bamberg , Buchner.

Scherer, A. (1975) *Handbuch der lateinischen Syntax*, Heidelberg, Winter.

Stati, S. (1992) "Modèle de phrase, métataxe et traduction" *La Linguistique* 28.1: 3-14.

Swiggers, P. (1004) "Aux débuts de la syntaxe structurale: Tesnière et la construction d'une syntaxe" *Linguistica* 34.1: 209-219.

Tesnière, L. (1925) *Les formes du duel en slovène*, Paris, Champion.

—. (1925-2) *Atlas linguistique: pour servir a l'étude du duel en slovéne*, Paris, Champion.

—. (1959) *Éléments de syntaxe structurale*, Paris, Klincksieck.

Touratier, C. (1994) *Syntaxe Latine*, Louvain-la-Neuve, Peeters.

LATINO E ALBANESE: PROSPETTIVE LINGUISTICHE PER L'INSEGNAMENTO UNIVERSITARIO NELLA NUOVA EUROPA

EVALDA PACI

Introduzione

Dopo la fine della Seconda Guerra Mondiale, l'Albania subì cambiamenti politici decisivi, che segnarono la vita dell'intero paese. Di conseguenza seguì un periodo difficile, che ebbe un riflesso anche nei programmi scolastici dei diversi livelli. Negli anni '80 del secolo scorso si arrivò persino a ridurre l'insegnamento della stessa lingua albanese nei licei e nelle scuole medie superiori, per lasciare maggior spazio a materie di carattere politico, allo studio della letteratura albanese del cosiddetto *realismo socialista* o alla *letteratura straniera*, controllata rigidamente dal regime politico dell'epoca.

In Albania era esistito però in precedenza un periodo in cui il latino era una materia di studio importante ed apprezzata nei programmi scolastici delle scuole statali e dei licei privati. Parliamo degli anni 1920-1930, quando non solo vennero pubblicate diverse grammatiche latine ma videro la luce nelle migliori riviste culturali dell'epoca traduzioni pregevoli, anche se parziali, delle opere dei classici latini: ad esempio, brani dall'*Eneide* e dalle *Bucoliche* di Virgilio. Traduttori come Frano Alkaj, Henrik Lacaj, Ethem Haxhiademi avevano ricevuto un'ottima formazione nelle culture classiche in diverse università europee.[1]

La pubblicazione di molti testi di uso scolastico è testimonianza diretta della presenza e dell'importanza che si attribuiva allo studio della cultura classica nelle scuole albanesi. In questa relazione saranno perciò presentate in primo luogo le caratteristiche delle principali grammatiche scolastiche dell'epoca. Esse testimoniano la buona tradizione di studi classici esistente in Albania e nello stesso tempo dimostrano che lo studio della lingua latina era apprezzato nelle scuole albanesi.

1. Grammatiche latine e dizionari bilingui

A. La Grammatica latina dei padri gesuiti di Scutari riporta questi dati: *GRAMATIKA LATINE, TUBË LIBRASH PËR SHKOLLA GYMNAZIKE E TREGTARE BOTUE PREJ ETENVE JEZUIT,* SHKODËR, SHTYPSHKROJA E SË PAPERLYEMES, 1921. Si tratta di un manuale che si propone di descrivere molti fatti della lingua latina.[2] Caratteristica principale è la sinteticità nella descrizione dei fatti grammaticali che riguardano il latino, ma che attirano comunque l'attenzione di chi lo studia con un occhio rivolto anche alla traduzione in albanese di certi vocaboli; spesso la terminologia albanese adoperata è simile a quella corrispondente in latino.[3] Questo fatto si può riscontrare anche in altre grammatiche pubblicate più o meno nello stesso periodo. La sinteticità cui abbiamo accennato si nota anche nella trattazione introduttiva alle nozioni dell'alfabeto e della fonologia latina, dell'ortoepia e delle regole di accentazione.[4]

Particolarmente interessanti sono i "calchi" linguistici introdotti per i termini dell'ambito fonologico e dell'accentazione: *e tretëmramja* "la terzultima", *e paramramja* "la penultima", ecc. Riteniamo si tratti di formazioni originali, ricostruite sulla base di quelle italiane e quindi non più in uso nelle grammatiche successive.[5] Per il dittongo troviamo due versioni: l'albanese *dyzantore* e la greca *diftong.*[6]

Per quanto riguarda la morfologia nominale e le declinazioni latine, c'è da mettere in evidenza che la questione del genere dei sostantivi di ognuna delle cinque declinazioni si trova nelle note a piè di pagina, anche se rimane uno degli argomenti più interessanti e legati direttamente alla semantica dei nomi latini. Il confronto con la stessa categoria in lingua albanese è sempre un argomento che suscita riflessione e osservazioni interessanti sia da parte del docente che da parte degli alunni.[7]

Qui sarebbe il caso di fare delle osservazioni anche per quanto riguarda la denominazione del participio o per meglio dire l'adattamento di una serie di denominazioni che riguardano il *participio latino.* Il participio albanese non è una forma nominale-verbale e non concorda con il soggetto in genere e numero, rimane sempre invariabile e nelle grammatiche albanesi viene trattato come una forma implicita verbale. Quindi, nella grammatologia albanese non si verifica la differenza tra participio presente o participio passato. Per questo motivo le denominazioni dei relativi participi in latino sono delle formazioni originali in albanese, create apposta per definire questa forma nominale e verbale latina: *Particip qetash-*participio presente *(qi qorton): hortans-hortantis; particip i kryem-*

participio passato *(qi ka qortue): hortatus,-a, -um; particip i pertardhm-*participio futuro *(qi asht kah qorton): hortaturus, -a, -um.*[8]
    Nella breve *Praefatio* di questa grammatica vengono chiarite le abbreviazioni usate. Il glossario che precede la stesura degli argomenti grammaticali contiene una terminologia che concerne diverse discipline linguistiche: fonologia, morfologia, sintassi della proposizione e del periodo. Si deve notare che chi ha curato questa grammatica e l'apposito glossario conosce bene anche la terminologia grammaticale in uso nei testi scolastici albanesi e tende ad usarla solo quando questo è possibile. Alcune denominazioni latine sono conservate e sono simili a quelle già esistenti in italiano, altre invece sono state tradotte in albanese e a nostro parere sono veramente ben realizzate.[9]
    Per le parti del discorso si è adoperata una terminologia che mira alla conservazione delle denominazioni che contengono la radice latina: *verbi* "il verbo"; *adjektivi* "l'aggettivo"; *adverbi* "l'avverbio"; *coniunkcjon* "congiunzione"; *prepozitë* "preposizione"; *interjekcjon* "interiezione".
    Alquanto simile a quella adoperata nelle grammatiche italiane è la denominazione di certe parti del discorso, come gli aggettivi numerali *(adjektiva numrorë)*, che nelle grammatiche attuali della lingua albanese sono chiamati in altri modi.
    Ricostruite invece in albanese sulla base latina sono le denominazioni dei casi: *êmnore* "nominativo"; *dishmore* "accusativo"; *dhantore* "dativo"; *lindtore* "genitivo"; *hjektore* "ablativo". Una ricostruzione è a nostro parere anche il termine *perêmen* per il pronome, seguito anni dopo dalle denominazioni *mbiemër* per l'aggettivo, *ndajfolje* per l'avverbio.

B. *FJALUER LATIN-SHQYP*, SHKODËR, SHTYPSHKROJA E SE PAPERLYEMES, 1925.
    La collana composta dalla grammatica sopra citata (al punto A.) e da tre volumetti di esercizi comprende anche un *Dizionario bilingue latino-albanese* di circa 400 pagine. Si tratta di un'opera assai riuscita dal punto di vista lessicografico. Il *Dizionario* contiene una *Praefatio* utilissima, nella quale gli autori chiariscono aspetti tecnici e la destinazione precisa dell'opera, e va apprezzato dal punto di vista della metodologia adoperata che dimostra una preparazione accurata. [10] Le principali caratteristiche dell'opera sono le seguenti:
1. Si sottolinea la preoccupazione degli autori di stimolare una corretta lettura dei vocaboli latini da parte dello studente. È stata segnata correttamente la quantità della penultima sillaba. Ricordiamo che nel manuale, la cui pubblicazione risale a pochi anni prima (1921), si accennava alla difficoltà tecnica di poter riportare la quantità vocalica negli esempi

dati,[11] difficoltà che nel 1925 sembra più che superata, poiché specialmente le parole polisillabiche sono sempre accompagnate dall'apposito segno diacritico che chiarisce la quantità della penultima.

2. Si tende a dare una precisa etimologia dei vocaboli contenuti nel *Dizionario*, si specifica quando si tratta di parole di origine greca (la maggior parte di queste hanno conservato la radice greca anche nella parola albanese corrispondente);[12] non si pretende di dare tutti i significati che la parola può assumere in latino, ma almeno quei significati che sono stati adoperati negli eserciziari della collana; spesso si ricorre alla parola italiana e francese corrispondente;[13] questo è sottolineato già nella *Prefazione* e fa capire che gli studenti ricevevano una completa educazione linguistica e filologica nel campo della cultura romana e neolatina.[14]

3. Nel *Dizionario* si tende a dare anche spiegazioni che riguardano la formazione della parola. Viene citato spesso il tema o la parola di base, che è servita per formarne un'altra, e che spesso appartiene a una diversa categoria grammaticale.[15] Anche da questo punto di vista il *Dizionario* è ben realizzato: la formazione delle parole viene spiegata specialmente nel caso delle parole composte o di quelle formate con suffissi specifici: ad es. *carnifex* (*caro* e *facio*, p.46); *capripes* (*caper* e *pes*, p.46); *centimanus* (*centum* e *manus*, p.49).

Per quanto riguarda invece le parole formate con il suffisso diminutivo, a volte si è scelto di tradurre con un diminutivo corrispondente anche in albanese, a volte la traduzione assomiglia ad una spiegazione perifrastica: nel caso di *calcŭlus* (*deminutivi i calx, gelqere*) si trova la traduzione *guralec*; *guralec per llogari; llogari...*;[16] nel caso di *calceŏlus, i m.* (*deminutivi i calceus*) si traduce con il sintagma nominale *kepuce e vogel*, "piccola scarpa".[17]

Infine, si scorge spesso una derivazione latina delle voci albanesi messe a fronte di quelle latine: *castanĕa, ae f. - kështejë,p.47; castellum, i n.- kështjel, p.47; laurus-làr (bima e Apolit), p.184; laus, laudis f.- lavd, levdim, p.184*.[18]

La questione della traduzione delle parole latine in albanese merita una particolare attenzione, poiché essa è stata fatta in ghego, quindi in un dialetto molto importante e produttivo, ma che ai giorni d'oggi non è più alla base della lingua standard.

C. FERDINAND SCHULTZ: GRAMATIKA LATINE, PJESA I, FONOLOGJI E MORFOLOGJI, PROF.KARL GURAKUQI, EDIZIONI KRISTO LUARASI, TIRANA, 1938.

Si tratta della versione, tradotta e adattata da Karl Gurakuqi, della *Grammatica latina* che ha per autore Ferdinand Schultz.[19] L'opera è stata pubblicata nel 1938 dalla casa editrice *Kristo Luarasi* per approvazione del Ministero Albanese della Pubblica Istruzione.

Oltre alle riflessioni sul contenuto e sull'articolazione dei capitoli e degli argomenti, si deve considerare e valutare il ruolo che in questo caso indiscutibilmente assume chi intraprende questa difficile impresa di traduzione e adattamento al contesto albanese.[20]

Nella *Prefazione* il traduttore descrive la situazione dello studio e dell'insegnamento del latino nelle scuole albanesi e si presenta molto affezionato all'opera, definendola *una preziosa grammatica, il primo libro che egli ha utilizzato quando era studente al liceo, un inseparabile amico e una guida insostituibile per anni interi nello studio e nell'insegnamento del latino nelle scuole* albanesi.[21]

L'opera di Gurakuqi, terminata già nel 1926, fu pubblicata solo dodici anni più tardi, quando, per via delle riforme scolastiche nei licei albanesi, al latino venne attribuita una particolare importanza, al punto che "*ormai è una materia obbligatoria nei licei e nelle medie superiori albanesi dell'epoca*".

La strutturazione della *Grammatica* di Schultz, che risale all'Ottocento, è assai tradizionale ed è poi stata ripresa anche nelle grammatiche latine compilate più tardi da altri studiosi albanesi, di solito docenti di lingua e cultura latina nelle università albanesi.[22]

La *Grammatica* di Schultz contiene nozioni di fonologia e morfologia. La morfologia occupa la maggior parte del volume. Si inizia dalla morfologia nominale, per passare poi al trattamento degli aggettivi e altre parti del discorso. La flessione nominale e quella verbale sono ampiamente trattate. Il volume si chiude con le parti invariabili del discorso.

La terminologia adoperata è interessante dal punto di vista di chi studia la grammatica in un contesto albanese, tenendo presente la terminologia relativa adattata poi dagli autori di grammatiche contemporanee o successive sulla lingua albanese. In alcuni casi Gurakuqi ha preferito mettere tra parentesi la denominazione latina, specialmente quando la terminologia corrisponde esattamente.[23]

In particolare, per quanto riguarda la denominazione delle parti del discorso, Gurakuqi mette tra parentesi quella latina. Questo confronto mette in evidenza l'affinità o a volte la diversità rispetto al termine corrispondente in albanese:[24]

1. Emnat (*nomina*).[25] Gli esempi che Gurakuqi ha scelto sono: *Vir-burri; rosa-trendafili; virtus-burrnija*, virtyti;[26] *verbum-fjala*.[27]

2. Adjektivat (*adiectiva*): *bonus -i mirë*; *pulcher -i bukur*; *amabilis -i dashun*. Vengono classificati nella stessa classe anche i numerali.

3. Përemnat (*pronomina*): *ego-unë*; *tu-ti*; *qui-i cili etj.*[28]

4. Verbat (*verba*): *sum-unë jam*; *amo-unë due mirë*; *monere-me qortue*; *dormire- me fjetë.*[29]

D. LORENC VIEZZOLI S.J.: *KAH LATINISHTJA*, ANALIZË LOGJIKE MBAS METHUDËS "SANTINI-CAMPANINI", SHTYPSHKROJA ZOJA E PAPERLYEME, SHKODRA, 1942.

Si tratta di un manualetto di modeste dimensioni, ma molto interessante, perché tratta in modo originale molti concetti della sintassi della proposizione, con l'intento di mettere a confronto le stesse nozioni in latino e albanese. Questo fatto rende ancora più interessante l'opera di Viezzoli. Latino ed albanese sono messi a confronto sul piano sintattico. Il confronto inizia dalle nozioni primordiali degli elementi della proposizione per passare poi alle denominazioni dei complementi: il confronto è interessante poiché tutte e due le lingue hanno un consolidato sistema di casi.

Anche la terminologia adoperata da Viezzoli merita attenzione. Le denominazioni date ai complementi sono diverse da quelle usate ai giorni d'oggi nella sintassi albanese. Si può parlare di un influsso della terminologia italiana dell'epoca, che si trova ancor oggi nelle grammatiche italiane.[30]

Motivando le ragioni della pubblicazione dell'opuscolo, l'autore accenna all'importanza del confronto tra latino ed albanese: "*Menduem me u lëshue në dorë nxanësavet qi po hyjnë në Licè, këtë fashikull t'analizës logjike, ashtuqi t'u mësohet qyshë ndër orët e para përpjekja e gjuhës amtare me gjuhën e Cezarëvet.*[31]"

L'opera può essere di grande aiuto per l'educazione linguistica degli alunni che ne faranno uso: "*Vjetë të gjata mësimi na kanë mbushë menden se gjuha latinishte nuk del e vishtirë për nxanësin shqiptár, mjaft qi qyshë në fillim, posë se në themelet gramatikore, të pështetet mirë edhe mbi ato të sintaksit. Këta vyen më e arësyetue botimin e këtij fashikulli.*[32] "

L'attenzione di Viezzoli è rivolta particolarmente alla terminologia: "*Deshtem edhe, për sa i perket terminologjis, me mbajtë atë t'Aleksander Xhuvanit, terminologji qi nxanësat e kanë në vesh qyshë ndër klasët fillore. Vumë, aty-këtu, ndër kllapa edhe fjalën latine të shqiptarizueme*".[33]

E. AUGUST SCHEINDLER: "*SINTAKSI I GJUHËS LATINE*", PUNUE MBAS GJERMANISHTJET PREJ P.DONAT KURTIT O.F.M. SHKODRA, EDIZIONI FRANCESCANE, 1940.

Concludiamo questa rapida panoramica menzionando un'altra pubblicazione, che è più di una semplice traduzione della *Sintassi latina* di August Scheindler.[34] La pubblicazione, adattata in albanese dal padre

Donat Kurti O.F.M., è un vero trattato della sintassi latina, con dei cenni importantissimi che richiamano il confronto tra il latino e l'albanese. Si tratta di un lavoro più approfondito in confronto a quello di Viezzoli, che era rivolto ad un livello più elementare di apprendimento. Questo manuale di *Sintassi latina* tradotta ed elaborata da Kurti contiene una trattazione completa delle seguenti tematiche: gli elementi principali della proposizione latina; questioni di concordanza tra soggetto e predicato, terminologia apposita che concerne ognuno degli elementi, sia il soggetto che il predicato; la sintassi dei casi (specialmente in questi ultimi paragrafi e anche in quelli in cui si tratta l'uso delle preposizioni latine si accenna al confronto con l'albanese); la sintassi del periodo e questioni relative alla *consecutio temporum*.

Nel complesso, il problema principale, che appare evidente dallo studio critico delle opere qui citate, rimane la questione della terminologia: nella maggior parte dei casi è precisa e congrua, ma non è unificata e si presenta diversa da una grammatica all'altra.[35]

2. Studio ed insegnamento della lingua latina nelle scuole albanesi negli ultimi due decenni

Gli ultimi due decenni hanno comportato un periodo di trasformazioni significative per l'Albania e per il sistema dell'istruzione albanese. Questi cambiamenti hanno segnato profondamente la scuola e l'educazione e hanno fatto sentire l'esigenza di una riorganizzazione dei programmi scolastici, di una nuova integrazione del latino nello studio e nell'insegnamento della lingua e della letteratura albanese. In questo periodo sono state realizzate le pubblicazioni delle versioni complete dell'*Eneide*[36] e delle *Georgiche*[37] di Virgilio, dell'*Ars Poetica* di Orazio,[38] della *Congiura di Catilina* di Sallustio[39] e *della Guerra civile* di Cesare.[40] La maggior parte di queste traduzioni erano già terminate prima della caduta del regime politico dittatoriale, ma hanno visto la luce solo negli anni '90 del secolo scorso.

Comunque, attualmente, in Albania il latino non viene più studiato ed insegnato nei licei o scuole medie superiori. La formazione universitaria è limitata agli studenti destinati poi a insegnare il latino nelle Facoltà albanesi oppure ad occuparsi di studi specializzati in filologia dei testi biblici tradotti in albanese oppure delle traduzioni dei testi giuridici scritti in latino medievale e che riguardano direttamente l'Albania.

Il latino viene insegnato e studiato in diverse Facoltà delle università albanesi: Medicina; Storia e Filosofia (o Scienze Sociali); Giurisprudenza; Lingue Straniere.

Ultimamente, anche la *Storia della lingua latina* viene studiata a
livello di laurea specialistica, come ad esempio all'Università di Scutari ed
anche nella scuola di dottorato del *Centro di Studi di Albanologia* di
Tirana. Questo insegnamento è destinato ad un numero ristretto di
studenti, i quali si presuppone abbiano già delle buone conoscenze della
grammatica e della civiltà latina. Insegnare storia della lingua latina in un
contesto albanese comporta un'impostazione specifica da parte del
docente. Gli studenti sono laureati in storia della lingua e letteratura
albanese oppure sono orientati agli studi storici. Occorre conoscere bene la
grammatica albanese, la storia dell'albanologia e possedere delle
competenze buone per quanto riguarda l'interpretazione dei testi scritti in
albanese dal 1500 al 1700. Chi insegna questa materia deve aver presente
quali argomenti sono più interessanti ed utili allo studio.

In conclusione, le condizioni attuali dell'insegnamento universitario
del latino nel contesto albanese ci consigliano di riprendere in prospettiva
rinnovata il metodo comparativo. Come già aveva fatto la generazione di
latinisti che aveva prodotto le prime grammatiche latine in albanese, si
tratterà ancor'oggi di mettere a confronto le due lingue, facendo capire
bene sia le diversità sia le convergenze che vengono fuori da un simile
confronto. Gli argomenti dovranno essere presentati in modo naturale, ad
esempio si potrà mettere in evidenza la somiglianza fonologica con la
versione latina o greca (*cypressus, cerăsus*) oppure quella esistente in
albanese: *laurus, gaudium, aurum, piscis, rete* ecc.[41] Il progetto di un
nuovo corso di latino per le università albanesi potrà perciò avere la
seguente articolazione:

• Il sistema nominale di tutte e due le lingue (categorie grammaticali
  quali caso e genere; sostantivi neutri, maschili e femminili); specialmente
  il neutro latino e quello albanese fanno riflettere su possibili
  congruenze o diversità dovute poi anche all'evoluzione indipendente di
  ognuna delle due lingue; i casi poi sono sempre da confrontare in tutte
  e due le lingue: fanno capire in un certo modo che l'albanese in alcuni
  aspetti è una lingua conservativa rispetto ad altre lingue indoeuropee
  che non hanno conservato questa importante categoria morfosintattica
  e logica.

• Il sistema verbale (inclusi i verbi suppletivi, verbi medi o deponenti,
  per usare la terminologia delle grammatiche latine); la diatesi del verbo
  in tutte e due le lingue, specialmente quando si studia la morfologia del
  verbo e si traducono certi verbi di significato attivo in latino: *sedĕo,
  respondĕo* ecc. Anche in albanese ci sono i verbi medi, ma non sempre
  si possono confrontare con quelli deponenti latini.

- Gli elementi lessicali latini della lingua albanese, con la loro descrizione e classificazione cronologica. Il contesto storico dovrà partire dai primi contatti tra le popolazioni romane ed illiriche nell'antichità, con l'attestazione della presenza romana tramite le numerose iscrizioni latine che risalgono a diversi periodi storici.

Nei contesti in cui lo studio del latino serve a completare la formazione classica e professionale degli studenti albanesi si sente oggi forte l'esigenza di un testo o di una collana specifica destinata allo studio universitario, che contenga nozioni fondamentali di grammatica e cultura latina. Ne dovrebbe arricchire il contenuto il confronto continuo con la morfologia e la sintassi albanese o con il lessico che riguarda le denominazioni dei fiumi, delle isole, delle divinità nel mondo antico. Di modelli da seguire ce ne sono tanti, ma a nostro parere l'approccio linguistico rimane fondamentale[42]. Serviranno poi certamente delle appendici apposite secondo l'indirizzo degli studi (storia, archeologia, linguistica, letteratura straniera, giurisprudenza, medicina ecc.).

Il contatto più diretto negli ultimi due decenni con il mondo europeo rende questa esigenza fattibile e realizzabile concretamente. Legata alla stessa esigenza va considerata la compilazione e la pubblicazione di un nuovo *Dizionario della lingua latina* in albanese, che certamente richiederà un équipe specializzata. L'istituzione più adatta a compiere questo importante passo rimane pur sempre *il Centro di Studi di Albanologia* di Tirana, istituzionalizzato dal Ministero della Pubblica Istruzione come uno specializzato centro di ricerche scientifiche con una scuola di dottorato. Si apre insomma un progetto di lavoro impegnativo per il futuro.

Summary

After World War II, Albania went through some political changes which shaped the life of the entire country. As a consequence, a difficult time occurred, and it influenced the school programs, terminating the study of Latin in high schools. In Albania there was however a time, when Latin was an important and valued subject within the school programs. We are referring to the years between 1920 and 1930, when not only a number of Latin grammars appeared, but also some excellent translations of the major Latin classics.

This paper is divided into two parts. In the first we give a brief survey on a number of school texts published in Albania in the first half of last century. Those texts are the *Latin Grammar* (1921) by the Jesuit Fathers of

Shkoder, followed by three small exercise books and a Latin-Albanian bilingual Dictionary (1925) and other publications for schools very well made from the point of view of the adaptation of concepts and proper use of terms from Latin to Albanian. These texts also provide a grammatical comparison of Latin and Albanian. Such a comparison is particularly evident in the handbook by Lorenzo Viezzoli S.I. (*Kah latinishtja*, 1941) or in the *Latin Syntax* by August Scheindler, the latter translated and arranged by the Franciscan Father Donat Kurti. In this context the *Latin Grammar* by Schultz (*Phonology, Morphology* 1938) has been highly dealt with, this was translated and arranged by the professor Karl Gurakuqi. These grammars are however written in Gheg, an important dialect of the Albanian Language, which is however not the basis of the Albanian Standard. For this reason many terms which were directly translated or derived from it cannot be used any longer in the teaching of the Latin language within Albanian universities. Even though the terms used in these grammars are not always the same, they bring however some contribution also to Albanian grammatology.

In the second part, we observe that the last two decades involved a period of relevant changes for Albania and the Albanian school. These changes have made school and education aware of the need to reorganize the school programs and to complete the learning and teaching of the Albanian Language and Literature. Presently Latin is no more taught in high schools, but it is included in the Albanian university programs in Albanian Language and Literature, Medical Schools, History and Philosophy Faculties, Foreign Languages Faculties. Also the History of Latin Language has been recently introduced at the PhD level.

We conclude presenting the project of a new Latin course for Albanian universities, connected with the compilation and publication of a new Dictionary of Latin Language in Albanian. It will absolutely need a high specialized team - a part from the subject we have been hereby talking about - even in lexicographic and editorial issues. The most suitable institution to carry out such a step still remains the Albanology Studies Centre in Tirana.

Notes

[1] Le traduzioni dei brani dell'*Eneide* da parte di F. Alkaj sulla rivista "*Hylli i drites*" (1936-1938) sono più o meno contemporanee a quelle di H. Lacaj (1910-1991) sulla rivista "*Leka*" (tra il febbraio e il maggio 1937). Per ulteriori informazioni vedi Paci (2009).

[2] Ognuno dei manuali che qui verranno descritti o trattati contengono delle particolarità uniche dal punto di vista della strutturazione oppure della metodologia adoperata.

[3] Vengono chiamati *substantiva* i sostantivi, per i verbi deponenti è stata conservata la stessa denominazione ma per quelli *semideponenti* è stato usato un termine che contiene un prefissoide albanese, *gjysëdeponenta*. Su questo vedi *Gramatika latine*, op. cit., p.78.

[4] Per il resto si rimanda alle lezioni successive o alla pratica concreta dell'insegnante.

[5] Ad esempio, attualmente invece di *e tretëmbramja* (letteralmente significa proprio "la terzultima") si usa un'espressione perifrastica del tipo: *rrokja e tretë duke filluar numërimin nga fundi:* "la terza sillaba iniziando la numerazione dalla fine".

[6] Nei riguardi di *ae* e *oe* si dice semplicemente che vanno pronunciati col valore di una sola vocale; ciò significa che l'insegnante che usa la grammatica deve adoperare la *pronuncia scolastica*, non quella *scientifica*. Questo termine preciso per il dittongo *(dyzanore)* si trova anche nella *Grammatica latina* di Schultz tradotta da Karl Gurakuqi e inoltre in alcuni manuali usati anche attualmente nelle università albanesi.

[7] Io ho osservato in modo particolare l'introduzione alla morfologia nominale. Si dice pochissimo sui tre generi e si descrivono i casi denominandoli con i termini dell'epoca: *êmnorja (nominativo), lindtorja (genitivo), dhantorja (dativo), dishmorja (accusativo), thirrtorja (vocativo), hjektorja (ablativo).* Di questi alcuni sono sopravvissuti e vengono conservati anche ai giorni d'oggi: *emërore* per *il nominativo, dhanore* per *il dativo.* Gli altri sono stati poi sostituiti da altre denominazioni. Inoltre si fa un'osservazione importante sul fatto che in latino non ci sono mezzi formali che distinguono la forma determinata da quella indeterminata del sostantivo. Questa particolarità che riguarda la flessione nominale è presente in albanese già nei suoi primi documenti scritti. Significa che si tratta di un fenomeno già consolidato in quest'ultima. Ma poi in ogni grammatica latina scritta in albanese viene sempre fuori il problema della giusta traduzione delle forme casuali che un sostantivo latino assume nel corso della declinazione (lo stesso vale anche quando si tratta di spiegare la declinazione ad un *auditorium* italiano). Un sostantivo latino può essere tradotto sia con la forma determinata che con quella indeterminata, mentre se lo si trova usato in un contesto concreto si decide quale delle due forme adoperare.

[8] *Gramatika latine,* Shkodër, 1921, p.75. Da notare il fatto che si è dovuto ricorrere a delle specifiche denominazioni per quanto riguarda il participio latino. In albanese il participio è una forma implicita verbale che serve a costruire i soliti tempi composti dei modi verbali, ma non accorda con il soggetto della proposizione. Esistono diversi tipi di participi verbali, ma non si usa neanche il termine *participio passato*, visto che questa forma verbale non riflette il tempo mediante suffissi appositi.

[9] Si tratta di un piccolo glossario molto interessante dal punto di vista del confronto dei termini o denominazioni in italiano e in albanese. Il glossario contiene circa 165 termini, che includono la terminologia fonologica, morfologica, sintattica ecc.:

Ablativo, hjektore, ja, et; Accento, theksë, a, at; Accento acuto, theks' e prehtë; Accento circonflesso, theks' e persjelltë; Accento grave, theks'e randë; Accentuare, me theksue; Accentuazione, theksim, i, et; Accusativo, dishmore, ja, et; Affermativo, pohenik, e; Affermazione, pohim, i, et; Aggettivo, adjektiv, i, at; Alfabeto, alfabet, i, at; Appositivo, adpozituer, ore; Apposizione, adpozitë, a, at; Assoluto, absolute, e; Astratto, abstrakt, e; Attivo, vepruer, ore; aktiv, e; Attributivo, atributive; Attributo, atribut, i, at.

[10] Il Dizionario *latino-albanese* del 1925 viene citato anche nella *Prefazione* del *Dizionario latino-albanese* di Lacaj e Fishta (1942), riveduto e ripubblicato negli anni successivi (1966 e ultimamente 2004). Gli autori ammettono di aver consultato anche quest'ultimo per la compilazione del loro *Dizionario* oltre al Georges e al Campanini e Carboni. Il Dizionario di Fishta e Lacaj rimane pur sempre il dizionario ufficiale latino-albanese anche ai giorni d'oggi.

[11] *Gramatika latine*, Shkodër 1921, *Sasí e rrokeve*, p.170: *Giatija e nji rrokes zakonisht shenjohet tue vûe mî zantore nji vizë (‾),shkurtija, tue vû sypri nji lmaje të vogel (˘).Tue kênë qi kto shêje mungojnë në shtypshkrojën t'onë, kemi per të shenjue giatín me karakterë mâ të trashë, e shkurtín tue vû karakterët e ndrejtë në vend të kursivëve, më të cillët janë shkrue në ket libër fjalët latine.*

[12] Come nel caso di *calămus*, *i* m. (fjalë grekishte, latin. harundo), si traduce in albanese *kallam*, llulë; zumare; pupul per me shkrue. Cf. Paci (2008).

[13] *Fjaluer latin-shqyp*, Shkodër 1925, *Dý fjale me xâsa: Per kah ana e perkthimit të fjalve latine ne giuhë shqype, bahet me dijtë se nuk janë vue të tana veshtrimet qi mundet me pasë nji fjalë, por vetun njato qi ka nder libra të përdoruem nder shkollë t'ona. Ka 'I herë, per me spjegue ma mirë veshtrimin e vertetë të fjalës latine, kena shti në sherbim edhe francezishten e italishten; do vue n'oroe se fjala franceze, nder kto rasa, asht e dame prej italjanes me pikëpresë (;).*

[14] Bisogna precisare però che non in tutti i casi viene citata la parola francese o italiana che mantiene anche una composizione fonetica affine alla parola latina. Abbiamo preferito citare appunto quegli esempi in cui anche il corrispondente francese o italiano conserva la stessa radice con la parola latina: *p. 42: buxus, i f. bush, fr.buis; it.bosso; p.42: circus, i m. fr.cercle; it.circolo; p.73: conviva, ae m. (convivo), fr.convive; it.convitato; p.147: imāgo, igĭnis f. fr. image, it. immagine; p.159: inficio.. fr.infecter; it.infettare; p.184: lectīca, ae f. fr. litière, it.lettiga; p.181: lancĕa, ae f. fr. lance, it.lancia.*

[15] *Fjaluer latin-shqyp*, Shkodër 1925, *Dý fjale me xâsa, p.5: Brî fjalës latine qi rrjedhë prej ndoj tjetres latine, kena vûe, në kllapë, atê prej së cilles vjen; e në ket punë kena ndjekë vetun etimologjín mâ të pavishtirëten e mâ të sugurten. I vêhet porosí xâsit mos me pritue m'e kerkue veshtrimin o veshtrimet e fjalës së vûeme në kllapë, pse âsht punë e dobishme fort.*

[16] *Fjaluer latin-shqyp*, Shkodër 1925, p.43.

[17] *Fjaluer latin-shqyp*, Shkodër 1925, p.43. Rappresentano casi difficili di traduzione le voci composte di *circum, cis* ecc. Queste voci latine vengono tradotte con spiegazioni perifrastiche.

[18] Molto importanti i cenni aggiunti: *bima e Apolit, la pianta sacra ad Apollo.*

[19] Schultz F. *Gramatika latine, Pjesa I, Fonologji e morfologji*, prof.Karl Gurakuqi, Simbas vendimit të Komisjonit teknik, pëlqyem prej Ministris s'Arsimit me nr.96

d.28-X-1938. L'originale tedesco è: *Leteinische Sprachlehre, zunächst für Gymnasien*, Paderborn, Schöningh 1848.

[20] Il traduttore conosce molto bene le lingue classiche, insegna lingue e culture classiche nelle scuole albanesi, cerca da tempo di adattare un testo del genere alle esigenze di insegnamento e studio del latino in queste scuole. Lo stesso Gurakuqi è autore della *Grammatica albanese dell'uso moderno (con prefazione di G.Valentini)*, Palermo, 1958.

[21] Schultz F. *Gramatika latine, Pjesa I, Fonologji e morfologji*, Tirana 1938, *Parathanje (Prefazione): Në vjetin 1926, kur ishte Ministrija e Arsimit Drejtori e përgjithëshme, pata qênë ngarkue të përkthejshem nji gramatikë latine për shkollat e Shqipnis. Për të çue në vend ket urdhën epruer, i u vûna përkthimit të gramatikës së çmueshme të Ferdinand Schultz-it për nji arsye mâ tepër vehtjake: ky ká qênë shok i pandám i emi deri në ditët e sotme; ká qênë udhëheqsi i em vjetë me rradhë në mësimin e latinishtes, qi kam dhânë në shkollat shqiptare me përfundime të kënaqshme.*

[22] Certe nozioni poi sono state adottate anche nelle grammatiche albanesi (come nel caso di nomi concreti ed astratti trattati anche nella *Grammatica* di Schultz).

[23] Usa invece il termine straniero quando in albanese non esiste il concetto corrispondente (come nel caso dei *verbi deponenti*, una particolarità del sistema verbale latino, così anche il concetto del *supino*).

[24] Riguardo a questo bisogna ricordare che Gurakuqi si occupò dell'opera già negli anni '20 dello scorso secolo e questa versione tradotta in albanese della *Grammatica latina* di Schultz è più o meno contemporanea alla collana già presentata contenente il manualetto, gli eserciziari e il *Dizionario latino-albanese*, curati dai padri gesuiti di Scutari.

[25] Riguardo ai nomi lo stesso Gurakuqi mette tra parentesi anche il termine *substantiva*, proprio per specificare la distinzione tra nomi ed aggettivi.

[26] Si noti che anche in albanese esiste un legame tra *burri* e *burrnija*, così come in latino tra *vir* e *virtus*. Si tratta dello stesso modello di formazione delle parole, tramite formanti o suffissi poi speciali per ognuna delle lingue.

[27] La classificazione fatta ai nomi in questo paragrafo è categorica e riguarda anche la semantica dei sostantivi. Come si e già detto prima, alcune denominazioni qui presenti sono state conservate poi anche nelle grammatiche albanesi compilate più tardi:a.të përgjithshëm (nomina appellativa): arbor-druni, lisi.b. të përveçëm (nomina propria): Caesar- Cezari.c. përmbledhës (nomina collectiva): multitudo: shumsija.ç. abstraktë (nomina abstracta): mens-mendja.

[28] Si sottolinea (p.11) che queste tre parti del discorso sono *declinabili* (per tradurre letteralmente il termine *të lakueshme)*. Molto importante l'osservazione sulla mancanza dell'articolo in latino, che trattato in una versione di questa grammatica tradotta in albanese stimola ad un confronto con la presenza dell'articolo in quest'ultima. La questione poi in un certo modo condiziona anche la traduzione a fronte delle forme nominali relative a quelle latine.

[29] Per ultime vengono rappresentate le parti indeclinabili o invariabili del discorso: 5. Adverbat (adverbia): valde- mjaft; saepe- shpesh; ibi- aty, atje. Per queste ultime parti del discorso le denominazioni sono albanesi: 6. Parafjalët (praepositiones):

ad-kah, afër; ante-përpara; 7. Lidhëzat (coniunctiones): et-e, edhe; sed- por; si- në qoftë se; quia-pse; 8. Pasthirrmat (interiectiones): vae-vaj; ah-ah.
[30] Il complemento viene denominato *plotsor*. Il termine stesso può essere considerato un calco dalla terminologia grammaticale italiana. I complementi trattati nell'opera di Viezzoli sono: *Plotsori i çfarsís*- complemento di specificazione (p.12); *Plotsori i cakut*-complemento di limitazione (p.13); *Plotsori i thirrjes*- complemento vocativo o di vocazione (p.14); *Plotsori veprues*- complemento d'agente (p.15); *Plotsori i êmnimit*- complemento di denominazione (p.16); *Plotsori i shoqnimit*-complemento di compagnia (p.17); *Plotsori i mjetit dhe i vegles*- complemento di mezzo e strumento (p.18); *Plotsori i vendit*- complemento di luogo, con delle specificazioni ulteriori: *gjendje në vend*- stato in luogo; *levizje kah nji vend*- moto a luogo; *levizje prei nji vendi*- moto da luogo (p.19); *levizje neper nji vend*- moto per luogo; *Plotsori i kohes*- complemento di tempo (p.22); *Plotsori i shkakut*-complemento di causa (p.23); *Plotsori i menyres*- complemento di modo o di maniera (p.25).
[31] "Abbiamo pensato di mettere in mano agli alunni che cominciano il liceo questo fascicolo di analisi logica, in modo che venga insegnato loro dalle prime ore il confronto tra lingua materna e la lingua dei Cesari".
[32] "Lunghi anni di insegnamento ci hanno convinti che la lingua latina non viene difficile all'alunno albanese se già dagli inizi dello studio si ferma sia sulla grammatica che sulla sintassi. Queste sono delle valide ragioni che motivano la pubblicazione del fascicolo".
[33] "Per quanto riguarda la terminologia, abbiamo voluto tenere quella di A. Xhuvani, essendo una terminologia che gli alunni conoscevano già alle elementari. Quando è stato possibile, abbiamo messo anche la parola adattata in albanese".
[34] A. Scheindler, *Lateinesche Schulgrammatik*, Leipzig, Freytag, 1889.
[35] Questi fatti si spiegano anche con la diversa formazione che gli autori potrebbero aver avuto o anche con il fatto che non tutti erano di origine albanese. E anche quelli albanesi, quali Gurakuqi e Kurti, in diversi casi hanno scelto il termine latino non essendo ancora stato unificato quello corrispondente in lingua albanese. La tendenza comunque di rendere in lingua albanese le denominazioni grammaticali è più che chiara e testimonia la serietà nell'impresa di adattare le nozioni della grammatica latina al contesto albanese.
[36] Virgjili, *Eneida*, trad. di H. Lacaj, edizioni Toena, Tirana 1996 (=edizioni Buzuku, Prishtina 2000); Virgjili, *Eneida*, trad. di M. Dema, Shtëpia botuese enciklopedike, Tirana 1996.
[37] Virgjili, *Gjeorgjikat*, trad. di G. Shllaku, edizioni Shpresa, Prishtina 2000.
[38] Horaci, *Arti poetik*, trad. di E. Sedaj, edizioni Buzuku, Prishtina 2000.
[39] Salusti, *Komploti i Katilinës*, trad. di N. Basha, edizioni Bargjini, Tirana 2001.
[40] J.Caesar, *Mbi luftën civile*, trad. di N. Basha, edizioni Bargjini, Tirana 2007.
[41] Da ricordare anche gli elementi latini o quelli più tardi nei testi della letteratura albanese del 1500-1700, di origine latina: *vollundetja, pushtetja, qytetja, ligja, regji, regjënia, kështjel, engjëllë ecc.* Anche la terminologia liturgica contiene tracce evidenti dell'influsso latino: **meshë - missa, hostja - hostia, sakramend - sacramentum, peendohem - poenitet me, shëlbues - salvator** ecc. Questi fatti

vanno evidenziati specialmente quando si studiano i testi della letteratura albanese di questo periodo, degli autori Buzuku, Budi, Bardhi, Bogdani ecc.
[42] Si vedano in proposito Pieri (2005), Oniga (2007), Traina Bernardi Perini (2007) e Puliga (2008).

Riferimenti bibliografici

Fjaluer latin-shqyp (1925) *Tubë librash per shkollë gymnazike e tregtare botue prej etenve jezuit*, Shtypshkroja e së Paperlyemes, Shkodra.

Lacaj H. and F. Fishta (1942) *Fjaluer latin-shqip,* edizioni Luarasi, Tirana.

—. (2004) *Fjalor latinisht-shqip,* edizioni Saraçi, Tirana.

Oniga, R. (2007) *Il latino. Breve introduzione linguistica*, 2ª ed., Milano, Franco Angeli.

Paci, E. (2008) "De casuum usu dissertatio in latina et albaniensi lingua" *Classica e Christiana*, n.3, Universitatea *"Alexandru Ioan Cuza"*, Iaşi, pp.209-221.

—. (2009) "Le traduzioni dal latino all'albanese, un panorama descrittivo" in A. Brettoni (ed.) *Albanie. Traduzione - tradizione. La traduzione dalle varianti linguistiche alle varianti culturali*, Roma, Bulzoni, 87-98.

Pieri, M.P. (2005) *La didattica del latino (Perché e come studiare lingua e civiltà dei Romani)*, Roma, Carocci.

Puliga, D. (2008) *Percorsi della cultura latina (per una didattica sostenibile)*, Roma, Carocci.

Scheindler, A. (1940) *"Sintaksi i gjuhës latine"*, punue mbas gjermanishtjet prej P.Donat Kurtit O.F.M. Shkodra, edizioni Francescane.

Traina, A. and G: Bernardi Perini (2007) *Propedeutica al latino universitario*, a cura di C. Marangoni, Bologna, Pàtron[6].

Viezzoli, L. (1942) *"Kah latinishtja", analizë logjike mbas methudës "Santini- Campanini"*, Shkodra, Shtypshkroja e së Paperlyemes.

Conclusion

Linguistic Theory and the Teaching of Latin

Anna Cardinaletti

Introduction

In this chapter, I discuss the contribution that formal linguistic theory can provide to language teaching in general and to the teaching of Latin in particular.

Explicit teaching can be particularly helpful when learning a language which does no longer have native speakers. In this case, it is crucial to rely on good descriptions of the language, based on a solid and coherent linguistic theory, to replace traditional grammars used at school and at the university, which are unfortunately often incomplete, hardly systematic, not based on a coherent linguistic theory and which often contain imprecise formulations and terminology.

Based on a new approach to language and language acquisition, linguistic theory can provide new descriptive tools and a new comparative approach to language teaching.

1. A new approach to language

The linguistic research in the past 50 years has shown that language is the product of the speaker's mental grammar (for general introductions, see Jackendoff 1993 and Pinker 1994). As in its traditional usage, "grammar" refers to a set of rules. When they speak, human beings use the rules of their mental grammar. The core set of grammatical rules combine discrete units into larger units, both on the morpho-syntactic and the prosodic level:

(1) a. morpho-syntactic hierarchy:
         morpheme > word > phrase   > sentence
         book-   books   these books   [[these books] [have
         s-   [always [impressed [me]]]]][1]

     b. prosodic hierarchy
         phoneme > syllable >   foot > word >   phrase
         /i/ /m/ /p/   /im/ /prest/   ∧   /im'prest/ /im'prest mi/
         /r/ /e/ /s/ /t/   /im//'prest/

An important property of human mental grammar is that a finite set of
recursive rules produces a potentially infinite number of sentences. No
linguistic rule, but extralinguistic limitations establish when the
subordinating operation embedding one sentence into the superordinate
one, as in (2a), or a noun phrase into the superordinate one, as in (2b),
should stop:

(2) a.   [John will arrive soon]
                          [Mary thinks[that John will arrive soon]]
                 [Bob said   [that Mary thinks [that John will arrive soon]]]
        [I believe [that Bob said[that Mary thinks [that John will arrive soon]]]]

     b.   [Chomsky]
                                 [the book [by Chomsky]]
                        [the review   [of the book   [by Chomsky]]]
         [the publication   [of the review   [of the book   [by Chomsky]]]]

2. A new theoretical model: principles and parameters

The common observation that languages have different grammars acquires
a new value in the approach to language outlined in the previous section.
Language must be conceived as a system of similarities and differences.
Languages share a number of invariant properties, i.e., universal principles,
and are characterized by language-specific properties, expressed by
parameters (Chomsky 1981).
    Some instances of principles and correlated parameters are provided in
(3). The sentences in (4) and (5) exemplify the described properties:

(3) a. Principle: All sentences have a subject.
         Parameter: The subject is phonologically realized or not (the pro-
         drop parameter, Rizzi 1982).

b. Principle: The verb and its complement(s) form the verb phrase (see section 4 below).
Parameter: The verb (V) precedes or follows its complement(s) (O) inside the verb phrase.

(4) a. Ø piove.
     b. Ø pluit.
     c. It is raining
     d. Es regnet

(5) a. Ø ha **visto Gianni.**
     b. Caesar **exercitum reduxit.** (Caes. *Gall.* 3,29,3)
     c. She **saw John.**
     d. Sie hat **Hans gesehen.**

The principles-and-parameters model is a very powerful means to express language variation. Combining the two parameters, formulated in terms of the binary properties ±pro-drop and ±VO, respectively, four types of languages can be described:

(6)	Italian/Spanish	Latin	English/French/Scand. languages	German/Dutch
±pro-drop	+	+	−	−
±VO	+	−	+	−

If one more parameter is added, e.g. the V2 parameter in (7), exemplified in (8c) with data from German, eight types of languages are obtained, as in (9), and so on:[2]

(7) Principle: All sentences, including main sentences, contain the position occupied by the complementizer in subordinate clauses.
Parameter: In main sentences, the finite verb occupies or does not occupy the pre-subject position usually filled by the complementizer in subordinate clauses (±V2).

(8) a. Fino ad ora   _ Maria ha ammirato Gianni.
     b. Until now   _ Mary has admired John.
     c. Bis jetzt   hat Maria ~~hat~~ Hans bewundert.

(9)	It.	Lat.	Old It.	Old Germ.	Eng/Fr.	Japanese	Scand. languages	German/Dutch
±pro-drop	+	+	+	+	–	–	–	–
±VO	+	–	+	–	+	–	+	–
±V2	–	–	+	+	–	–	+	+

Comparative linguistic analysis aims at establishing the invariant properties of language, common to all human languages, and the language-specific properties, which characterize different types of languages.

3. A new approach to language acquisition

The principles and parameters model presented in section 2 suggests a new approach to language acquisition. While universal principles are not acquired, being part of the innate endowment of the human species, the values of parameters must be learnt, together with the linguistic units (e.g. phonemes, morphemes, and lexical items) (see Guasti 2002 for an overview of recent literature on language acquisition).

To acquire a language thus means to develop an innate potential capacity of the human mind. This potentiality is stimulated by the language input in one or more languages. People can learn the standard language and a dialect, the colloquial variety of a language (spontaneously) and its formal variety (at school), a foreign language and/or a classical language, and so on.

In the case of the acquisition of a classical language, which is no longer acquired as a native language by a speech community, the linguistic input is qualitatively and quantitatively different from the input of a language which still has native speakers. First, the input is only written, and language experience is limited to reading. This also implies that access to the linguistic input necessarily takes place later than with spoken languages. Second, the input is incomplete: in spite of the fact that the Latin corpus is quite large, not all possible sentence combinations are attested, as is always the case with language corpora.

Nonetheless, we may hypothesize that the acquiring of Latin proceeds as for other native and foreign languages: students have to learn the linguistic units and have to assign a value to the parameters that characterize this language. This process is presumably slower and more difficult than in the case of a language which is still used by a speech community. In this peculiar instance of acquisition, explicit rules play an important role in supporting language acquisition, by accompanying and presumably speeding up the implicit acquisition process that is nevertheless spontaneously activated through exposure to linguistic data.

3.1. "Possible" and "impossible" rules

Explicit rules can help in language acquisition only if they are "possible". As shown in an experiment reported by Moro (2008), a portion of Italian grammar explicitly taught to adult native speakers of German has activated the brain areas involved in speech only if it contained rules that are "possible" in natural languages. A rule formulated in terms of syntactic positions to be counted in a linear order, which is not attested in any natural language, did not have the same effects on the brain of the investigated subjects.

Another instance of impossible rule, often used in traditional grammars, is the so called "subject – verb inversion" rule to form interrogative sentences in e.g. English or German. The interrogative sentence (10b) is said to derive from (10a) by inverting the subject *your friend* and the auxiliary verb *is*:

(10) a. **Your friend is** talking to John.
   b. **Is your friend** talking to John?

Inversion is an "impossible" rule for two kinds of reasons. First, in the case of inversion, one of the two elements is moved to the right. This operation violates the universal principle according to which all movements take place toward the left (see Kayne's 1994 antisymmetric approach). Second, in inversion, two different elements are manipulated: in (10) a single element (the auxiliary *is*) and a string of words (*your friend*). This is a very clear instance of incoherent traditional rule: how can a word and a string of words be inverted? How is the string of words defined in order to avoid ungrammatical sequences (such as **your is friend talking to John?*) in which the auxiliary *is* is inverted with *friend*? The inversion rule somehow implicitly implies that the string *your friend* is a syntactic unit, which can be manipulated as a whole. But in phrase structure theoretic terms (Chomsky 1970, Jackendoff 1977), *is* and *your friend* have a different status and do not occupy the same type of positions: the former is a head and occupies a head position, the latter is a phrase and occupies a phrase position. This implies that they cannot literally "invert", i.e. exchange their positions.

The syntactic phenomenon observed in (10) can be characterized in more precise and coherent terms as follows: to form an interrogative sentence, the auxiliary verb is moved to the left across the subject to the head position immediately above the position occupied by the subject noun phrase:

(11)   [**your friend**   [**is**   [talking to John]]]
    [*is*   [**your friend**   [i̶s̶   [talking to John]]]]?

The alternate sequence of head and phrase positions observed in (11) is established by the X-bar theoretic module of grammar, according to which a head combines with a complement, the unit so formed combines with a phrase, and so on: [$_{XP}$ phrase [$_{X'}$ head [$_{YP}$ phrase [$_{Y'}$ head [$_{ZP}$ ...

As we have just seen, new grammatical descriptions based on formal linguistic theory represent a better and closer approximation to what we think is the mental grammar used by speakers than traditional grammar. Teaching 'possible' rules can especially help in the case of teaching an ancient language, whose acquisition cannot be reinforced by the linguistic exchange in a speech community.

4. New descriptive tools

The new grammatical descriptions based on linguistic theory lead to a reformulation of very basic grammatical notions such as those of subject and object. Let's analyse a simple Latin sentence as the one given in (12):

(12) locorum asperitas hominum ingenia duraverat (Curt. 7,3,6)

While traditional grammar takes the subject to be the noun *asperitas* and the object to be the noun *ingenia*, a more precise characterization, which makes use of the syntactic notion of phrase seen above, considers the whole string *locorum asperitas* to be the subject noun phrase, formed by the head noun *asperitas* and its complement *locorum*, and the whole string *hominum ingenia* to be the object of the verb *duraverat*, formed by the head noun *ingenia* and its complement *hominum*. The noun and its complement(s) (or modifiers, e.g. adjectives and relative clauses) always build a syntactic unit together, namely a noun phrase. This is shown by the fact that grammatical rules, which always apply to string of words that represent syntactic units, apply to these complex sequences.

Consider for instance the rule of pronominalization. A pronoun such as *it* can replace the string *that book* in (13b), because it is a unit, namely a noun phrase. *It* cannot replace *that book* in (14b) because the syntactic unit in (14a) also contains the complement of the head noun *book*, namely *by Chomsky*:

(13) a. I read that book.   (14) a. I read that book by Chomsky.
     b. I read **it**.   b. *I read **it** by Chomsky.
                                          c. I read it.

The hierarchical structure we arrive at is depicted in (15):

(15) I read [that book [by [Chomsky]]]

A similar reasoning applies to the pronominalization of a subject noun phrase. While the pronoun *it* is grammatical in (16b), it is not grammatical in (17b) because *that book* is not a syntactic unit by itself. The sentence is grammatical only if the whole sequence *that book by Chomsky* is pronominalized, (17c). The resulting structure is depicted in (18):

(16) a. That book is on the shelf.
     b. It is on the shelf

(17) a. That book by Chomsky is on the shelf.
     b. ***It** by Chomsky is on the shelf.
     c. **It** is on the shelf.

(18) [that book [by [Chomsky]]] is on the shelf

In traditional grammar, the string *that book* is taken to be the subject in (17a) on a par with (16a) and the object in (14a) on a par with (13a). The analysis based on phrase structure is different: the subject of the sentence in (17a) is the whole string *that book by Chomsky*, while in (14a) the same sequence of words has the function of complement of the verb. The string *by Chomsky* is a syntactic unit, namely a prepositional phrase, contained in the larger noun phrase.

Similar remarks hold for the so called verbal predicate. In traditional grammar, the verbal predicate is taken to be the verb itself, which expresses a relation between the subject and the object. It is often represented as in (19b) for a sentence like (19a) (this representation is common in the *Dependency Grammar* developed in Tesnière 1959):

(19) a. Caesar exercitum reduxit (Caes. *Gall.* 3,29,3)
　　　b.　　　　　　　reduxit
　　　　　Caesar　　　　　　exercitum

In formal linguistics, two aspects must be kept distinct which are not in previous grammatical descriptions.[3] On the one hand, the so called "valency" of the verb must be considered, namely its selectional properties, which can be represented as in (19b) for a sentence like (19a). The verb *reduxit* is a transitive verb that selects two noun phrases: *Caesar* is assigned the agent role, while *exercitum* is the patient. On the other hand, the internal structure of the sentence must be taken into consideration. Differently from what we see in (19b), the verb does not form a syntactic unit on its own, it rather builds a syntactic unit, namely the verb phrase (VP), with its complement(s), The syntactic representation of the sentence in (19a) is provided in (20), where the sentence is the projection of the Tense head and is called TP:

(20) [$_{TP}$ [$_{NP}$ Caesar] [$_{VP}$ [$_{NP}$ exercitum] reduxit]]

If an auxiliary is also present in the clause, it is external to the VP and inserted in the Tense head. This is clearly shown in English, where the auxiliary is moved by itself to the pre-subject head position to form interrogative sentences (see (11) above):

(21) [*is* [$_{TP}$ [$_{NP}$ **your friend**]　~~is~~ [$_{VP}$ talking [$_{PP}$ to John]]]]?

5. A new comparative approach to language teaching

As we have seen in section 2, language comparison aims at establishing the invariant properties of language and the parameters where language variation is found. The new comparative approach to grammar, which has led to important results in the contemporary linguistic research of the past 30 years (see Haegeman 1997 for an introductory perspective), can also be very useful in language teaching. It allows teachers and students to point out the similar aspects on which learning of a new language can rely, and to minimize the differences among languages, which always represent a problematic aspect of language learning.

　　In what follows, I discuss some cases of comparative analysis which will allow us to point out the advantages of a comparative approach to language teaching.

5.1. Aspectual verbs

Let's start with the class of prefixed verbs, where the prefix expresses aspectual information. These verbs are present, with very similar properties, in Latin and in modern languages: see Lat. *rescribo*, Ger. *zurückschreiben*, It. *riscrivere*.[4] In some languages such as English, the aspectual information is not conveyed by a bound morpheme, but by a free morpheme, cf. *write back*. It is however useful to consider prefixed verbs and particle verbs as representing one and the same phenomenon. This is also suggested by the fact that the same type of aspectual information is expressed over and over again by the two types of verbs. Cf. Eng. *go away, go on*; It. *andare via, andare avanti*, Ger. *weggehen, weitergehen*, etc. Also see verbs expressing the completive aspect, e.g. Lat. *comedo*, Eng. *eat up*, Ger. *aufessen*, etc. In Italian, the number of prefixed verbs of this type is more limited than in the other languages, but Italian dialects display similar prefixed verbs: e.g. *magnar sulfora* 'eat up' in the dialect of Treviso (see Cini ed., 2008).[5] Notice also that in the different languages, completive aspect is expressed by the same lexical elements, namely the prepositions meaning "up" and "out".

To explicitly point out these similarities has a number of advantages for the language learner. First, the load in memorizing these classes of verbs can be minimized. Second, grammatical phenomena acquire a familiarity flavour if they are shown to be present not only in the language to be learnt but also in the native language or in another familiar language. Furthermore, the same grammatical terminology can be used in the different languages. Consider the different terms used in different grammatical traditions to name complex verbs expressing aspectual information together with the lexical meaning. They are called *particle verbs* o *phrasal verbs* in English, *trennbare Verben* ("separable verbs") in the German tradition, *verbi analitici* 'analytical verbs' (Vicario 1997) or *verbi sintagmatici* 'phrasal verbs' (Simone 1997) in Italian. To this, the term *verb prefixed with a preverb* used in the Latin tradition should be added. Different names make the similarities among these verbs opaque. It would be much more useful and less frustrating for students to use one and the same grammatical term to name one and the same grammatical phenomenon.

5.2. Unstressed anaphoric pronouns

Unstressed anaphoric pronouns are found in all languages, although they *prima facie* display different properties in different languages. Consider

the Italian pronoun in (22a), which appears cliticized on the verb, and the
Latin pronoun in (22b), which does not exhibit this property and can
appear far away from the verb:

(22) a. Molto **mi** commuoveva questo discorso.
       b. Vehementer **me** haec res commovebat (Cic. *Verr.* I 20)

In spite of the superficial differences, unstressed anaphoric pronouns share
a common property: they cannot occupy the typical position of non-
pronominal objects and have to appear toward the left of the sentence.
This is also the case in e.g. English, whose pronoun (23) seems to occupy
the same position as regular objects. The special distribution of English
unstressed pronouns however clearly appears when phrasal verbs are
considered, as in (24). The data in (25) confirm the peculiar distribution of
other unstressed pronouns, such as *him* and its reduced version:

(23) a. I bought a book.
       b. I bought it.

(24) a. They turned   on   the light/*it.
       b. They turned   the light/it   on.

(25) a. They took   in   HIM/him and her.
       b. They took   in   *him/*[m].
       c. They took   him/[m]   in.

Two classes of unstressed pronouns have been identified in recent
linguistic analysis, which share a number of syntactic and semantic
properties (Cardinaletti and Starke 1999): clitic pronouns, which end up
being adjacent to a verbal form, and weak pronouns, which move to the
left to a position independent from the verb. Italian pronouns are of the
former type, Latin and English pronouns are of the latter type. While
English pronouns occur in the middle field of the clause, Latin pronouns
display a behavior typical of second position pronouns, similar to clitic
pronouns in Slavic languages (Wackernagel 1892, Salvi 2004).
Interestingly, pronouns belonging to this class were common in Old
Italian, with a behavior similar to Latin pronouns (Cardinaletti 2010), and
are residual in Modern Italian, as shown by the following example, where
the weak dative pronoun *loro* is not adjacent to a verbal form and occurs,
like English pronouns, in the middle field:

(26) Non ho consegnato mai **loro** un pacco di questo tipo
"[I] not have delivered ever to them a package of this type"

Weak pronouns are also found in German, with a distribution that recalls the second position of Latin pronouns:

(27) (ganz) ausserordentlich hat **mich** diese Sache bewegt.
..., dass **mich** diese Sache ausserordentlich bewegt hat.

If the distribution of pronouns is described in terms of their clitic or weak status (±clitic) and in terms of their position around the second position or the middle field of the clause (±2nd position), the following typology can be arrived at:

(28)	It./Span.	Latin/German	Eng./Scandin. languages / Italian *loro*	Slavic languages
±clitic	+	–	–	+
±2nd position	–	+	–	+

Once again, an approach that builds on the similarities of unstressed anaphoric pronouns, across the different languages that may be known to the students, allows a common treatment of the phenomenon. The differences can be reduced to very few superficial properties.

5.3. Restructuring verbs

In Italian, with some verbs selecting infinitival clauses, clitic pronouns can either appear on the embedded verb or climb onto the matrix verb, a phenomenon called *clitic climbing*. This possibility is found with modal and aspectual verbs, but not with ordinary control verbs such as *detestare* 'detest', with which the pronoun cannot climb:

(29) a. Posso far**lo**.   b. **Lo** posso fare.
[I] can do it   [I] it can do
Comincio a far**lo**.   **Lo** comincio a fare.
[I] begin to do it   [I] it begin to do
Detesto far**lo**.   ***Lo** detesto [fare].
[I] detest to do it.   [I] it detest to do

Modal and aspectual verbs are functional verbs on a par with auxiliaries. Their class is called *restructuring verbs* (Rizzi 1982). Like auxiliaries, they form a monoclausal structure with the lexical verb they combine with (Cinque 2006). Latin also display restructuring verbs; they belong to the same verb classes as in Italian: modal verbs (*possum*, *debeo*, *volo*), aspectual verbs (*coepi*, *incipio*, *desino*), passive *verba dicendi*, *videor*, and other verbs in the so-called "personal construction"[6]. With these verbs, unstressed pronouns can appear in second position before the main verb and the sentential adverb *videlicet*, similarly to what we see in (29b) for Italian clitic pronouns:

(30) tu **eum** videlicet non potuisti videre (Cic. *fam.*16,17,2)

Restructuring verbs do not have complements. This explains why clitic climbing is only found in the absence of the dative complement of the verb *sembrare* 'seem', as in (31), and impossible if this complement is realized, as in (32):

(31) a. Gianni sembra apprezzar**lo** molto.
        Gianni seems to appreciate it much
    b. Gianni **lo** sembra apprezzare molto.
        Gianni it seems to appreciate much

(32) a. Gianni sembra **a tutti** [apprezzar**lo** molto].
        Gianni seems to everybody to appreciate it much
    b. *Gianni **lo** sembra **a tutti** [apprezzare molto].
        Gianni it seems to everybody to appreciate much

The same happens in Latin. The quasi-auxiliary usage of passive *verba dicendi* (found in the so-called personal construction) is only possible if the dative complement of the matrix verb is absent (33). In this case, the embedded object *eos* appears in the second position of the monoclausal structure containing both the lexical verb *arcuisse* and the quasi-auxiliary *dicitur*:

(33) inde **eos** nec sua religio nec verecondia deum arcuisse dicitur (Liv. 6,33,5)

The presence of the dative complement *mihi* in (34) implies that the verb is not used as a restructuring, i.e. quasi-auxiliary verb, but as a lexical verb. In this case, only the impersonal construction is found, which means that the verb selects for an embedded infinitival clause:

(34) nuntiatur **mihi** tantam isti gratulationem esse factam ut…(Cic. *Verr.* I 21)

In traditional analyses of Latin, these data are usually presented as a list of (exceptional) properties of single verbs which combine with infinitival embedded verbs. They can be better understood if the lexical vs. functional status of the verbs is taken into account and if a comparative analysis of these verbs is adopted.

Conclusion

To sum up, linguistic theory can offer new descriptive tools to language teaching. This is particularly useful in the teaching of a language which is no longer spoken by native speakers and is learnt in an unnatural setting, only at school, only through reading.

The comparative approach inspired by contemporary linguistic theory has a number of advantages for language teaching. It allows to better identify invariant and language-specific properties, to simplify the linguistic description by using the same descriptive categories and the same terminology for more than one language, and to have a more natural perception of the phenomena encountered in the ancient language if the same phenomena are found in the native language or in another language known to the students.

The comparative approach in language teaching is now made possible by a number of grammatical descriptions of European languages including Latin, which share a common theoretical framework. For Latin see Oniga (2007), for English Haegeman and Guéron (1999), Haegeman (2006), for Italian Renzi, Salvi and Cardinaletti (eds) (1998-2001), Salvi and Vanelli (2004), for Old Italian Salvi and Renzi (eds) (2010), for Spanish Bosque and Demonte (eds) (1999), for German Cardinaletti and Giusti (1996), for French Abeille, Delaveau and Godard (eds) (in press).

Notes

[1] As we will see in section 4, this hierarchy is different from the traditional one.
[2] That the verb can occupy the position of the complementizer when this is empty is very clearly shown by the following German data (in (i) and throughout, the point of departure of a moved element is indicated with the barred character):

(i) a. Er tat so, als   ob   er nichts wüßte.
      he did so, as   if   he nothing knew
   b. Er tat so, als   *wüßte*   er nichts ~~wüßte~~.
   c. *Er tat so, als   ob *wüßte*   er nichts ~~wüßte~~.

In table (9), Japanese is taken as a –pro-drop language because its zero pronouns have different properties with respect to non-realized subjects in e.g. Italian (see Hasegawa 1985, Jaeggli and Safir 1989).

[3] See Babič (this volume) and Giusti and Oniga (this volume) for a more detailed discussion.

[4] See Panov (this volume) and Jekl (this volume) for examples and discussion.

[5] If a prefixed verb is not present in the lexicon of a language, the aspectual information is conveyed by aspectual verbs or adverbs. See the following Italian means to express the same meaning as English particle *up* in *eat up*:

(i) a. Gianni ha mangiato la torta **completamente**.
      Gianni has eaten the cake completely
   b. Gianni ha **finito** di mangiare la torta.
      Gianni has finished to eat the cake

[6] Zennaro (2006 a,b). For a possible analysis of *iubeo* as a restructuring verb see Costantini (this volume).

References

Abeille, E., Delaveau, A. and D. Godard (eds) (in press) *La Grande Grammaire du français*, Paris, Bayard.

Babič, M. (this volume) Tesnière's Dependency Grammar and its Application in Teaching Latin: A Slovenian Experience", 401-412.

Bosque, I. and V. Demonte (eds) (1999) *Gramática descriptiva de la lengua española*, I-III, Madrid, Espasa Calpe.

Cardinaletti, A. (2010) "Il pronome personale obliquo", in G. Salvi and L. Renzi (eds) *Grammatica dell'italiano antico*, Bologna, il Mulino, 414-450.

Cardinaletti, A. and G. Giusti (1996) *Problemi di sintassi tedesca*, Padova, Unipress.

Cardinaletti, A. and M. Starke (1999) "The typology of structural deficiency: A case study of the three classes of pronouns", in H. van Riemsdijk (ed.) *Clitics in the Languages of Europe*, EALT / EUROTYP 20-5, Berlin-New York, Mouton de Gruyter, 145-233.

Chomsky, N. (1970) "Remarks on nominalization", in R. Jacobs and P. Rosenbaum (eds) *Reading in English Transformational Grammar*, Waltham, Ginn, 184-221.

—. (1981) *Lectures on Government and Binding*, Foris, Dordrecht.

Cini, M. (ed.) (2008) *I verbi sintagmatici in italiano e nelle varietà dialettali. Stato dell'arte e prospettive di ricerca*, Frankfurt am Main, Peter Lang.

Cinque, G. (2006) *Restructuring and Functional Heads*, Oxford-New York, Oxford University Press.

Costantini, F. (this volume) "Iubeo and Causative Structure", 101-115.

Guasti, M.T. (2002) *Language Acquisition. The Growth of Grammar*, Cambridge, Mass., MIT Press.

Giusti, G. and R. Oniga (this volume) "Why Formal Linguistics for the Teaching of Latin", 1-20.

Haegeman, L. (ed.) (1997) *The New Comparative Syntax*, London, Longman.

Haegeman, L. and J. Guéron (1999) *English Grammar: A Generative Perspective*, Oxford, Blackwell.

Haegeman, L. (2006) *Thinking Syntactically. A Guide to Argumentation and Analysis*, Oxford, Blackwell.

Hasegawa, N. (1985) "On the so-called 'zero pronouns' in Japanese", *The Linguistic Review* 4: 289-243.

Jackendoff, R. (1977) *X-bar-Syntax: A Study of Phrase Structure*, Linguistic Inquiry Monograph 2, Cambridge, Mass, MIT Press.

—. (1993) *Patterns in the mind. Language and human nature,* Harvester Wheatsheaf, Hemel Hempstead.

Jaeggli, O. and K.J. Safir (1989) "The null subject parameter and parametric theory", in id. (eds) *The Null Subject Parameter*, Kluwer, Dordrecht, 1-44.

Jekl, Á (this volume) "Verbal Prefixation in Classical Latin and in Italian. The Prefix *ex-*", 201-214.

Kayne, R.S. (1994) *The Antisymmetry of Syntax*, Cambridge, Mass., MIT Press.

Moro, A. (2008) *The Boundaries of Babel. The Brain and the Enigma of Impossible Languages*, Cambridge, Mass, MIT Press.

Oniga, R. (2007) *Il latino. Breve introduzione linguistica*, 2ª ed., Milano, Franco Angeli.

Panov, V. (this volume) "Prefixes and Aspect of Latin Verb: A Typological View", 187-199.

Pinker, S. (1994) *The language instinct. How the mind creates language,* London, Penguin.

Renzi, L., Salvi, G. and A. Cardinaletti (eds) (1998-2001) *Grande grammatica italiana di consultazione*, I-III, Bologna, il Mulino.

Rizzi, L. (1982) *Issues in Italian Syntax*, Dordrecht, Foris.

Salvi, G. (2004) *La formazione della struttura di frase romanza. Ordine delle parole e clitici dal latino alle lingue romanze antiche*, Tübingen, Niemeyer.

Salvi, G. and L. Renzi (eds) (2010) *Grammatica dell'italiano antico*, Bologna, il Mulino.

Salvi, G. and L. Vanelli (2004) *Nuova grammatica italiana*, Bologna, il Mulino.

Simone, R. (1997) "Esistono verbi sintagmatici in italiano?", in T. De Mauro and V. Lo Cascio (eds) *Lessico e grammatica*, Roma, Bulzoni, 155-170.

Tesnière, L. (1959), *Éléments de syntaxe structurale*, Paris, Klincksieck.

Vicario, F. (1997) *I verbi analitici in friulano*, Milano, Franco Angeli.

Wackernagel, J. (1892) "Über ein Gesetz der Indogermanischen Wortstellung", *Indogermanische Forschungen* 1, 334-436.

Zennaro, L. (2006a) La sintassi di *possum* e *debeo* e la ristrutturazione, in R. Oniga and L. Zennaro (eds) *Atti della giornata di linguistica latina*, Venezia, Cafoscarina, 237-251.

—. (2006b) *La sintassi dei verbi a ristrutturazione in latino*, PhD diss., Università Ca' Foscari Venezia.

Contributors

Astori Davide
davide.astori@unipr.it
Università degli Studi di Parma
Dipartimento di Filologia Classica e Medievale
Via Massimo D'Azeglio, 85
43100 Parma
Italy

Babič Matjaž
Matjaz.Babic@ff.uni-lj.si
University of Ljubljana
Department of Classics
Aškerčeva cesta 2
1001 Ljubljana
Slovenia

Balbo Andrea
andrea.balbo@unito.it
Università degli Studi di Torino
Dipartimento di Filologia, Linguistica e Tradizione Classica "A. Rostagni"
Via S. Ottavio, 20 - 10124 Torino
Italy

Bortolussi Bernard
bortolus@u-paris10.fr
Université Paris Ouest - Nanterre La Défense
Département de Latin
200, avenue de la République
92001 Nanterre
France

Cabrillana Concepción
concepcion.cabrillana@usc.es
Universidad de Santiago de Compostela
Departamento de Latín e Grego
Campus universitario norte
Avda. Castelao, s/n
E-15782 Santiago de Compostela
Spain

Cardinale Ugo
ugocardinale@virgilio.it
C.so Vercelli, 64
10015 Ivrea
Italy

Cardinaletti Anna
cardin@unive.it
Università Ca' Foscari Venezia
Dipartimento di Studi Linguistici e Culturali Comparati
Dorsoduro 1075
30123 Venezia
Italy

Costantini Francesco
fc@unive.it
Università Ca' Foscari Venezia
Dipartimento di Studi Linguistici e Culturali Comparati
Dorsoduro 1075
30123 Venezia
Italy

Dascalu Ioana-Rucsandra
rucsicv@yahoo.com
University of Craiova
Department of Classical and Modern Languages
Str. Al. I. Cuza 13
200585 Craiova
Romania

Di Terlizzi Piervincenzo
piervincenzo.diterlizzi@gmail.com
Università degli Studi di Udine
Dipartimento di Studi Umanistici
Via Mazzini, 3
33100 Udine
Italy

Giusti Giuliana
giusti@unive.it
Università Ca' Foscari Venezia
Dipartimento di Studi Linguistici e Culturali Comparati
Dorsoduro 1075
30123 Venezia
Italy

Iovino Rossella
rossella.iovino@unive.it
Università Ca' Foscari Venezia
Dipartimento di Studi Linguistici e Culturali Comparati
Dorsoduro 1075
30123 Venezia
Italy

Jekl Ágnes
agibutty@t-online.hu
Eötvös Loránd University, Budapest
Faculty of Arts, Doctoral School of Linguistics
Múzeum krt. 4/C
1088 Budapest
Hungary

Krasukhin Konstantin G.
krasukh@mail.ru
Institute of Linguistics
B. Kislovsky per, 1/12, str.1
125009, Moscow
Russia

Oniga Renato
renato.oniga@uniud.it
Università degli Studi di Udine
Dipartimento di Studi Umanistici
Via Mazzini, 3
33100 Udine
Italy

Paci Evalda
evaldapaci@yahoo.it
Center for Albanian Studies
Sheshi "Nene Tereza"
Tirana
Albania

Panov Vladimir
panovmeister@gmail.com
Institute of Linguistics
B. Kislovsky per, 1/12, str.1
125009, Moscow
Russia

Pieroni Silvia
silvia.pieroni@ymail.com
Università per Stranieri di Siena
Dipartimento di Scienze dei Linguaggi e delle Culture
Piazza Carlo Rosselli 27/28
53100 Siena
Italy

Pompei Anna
pompei@uniroma3.it
Università degli Studi di Roma Tre
Dipartimento di Linguistica
Via Ostiense, 234
00146, Roma
Italy

Salvi Giampaolo
salvi.giampaolo@btk.elte.hu
Eötvös Loránd University, Budapest
Faculty of Arts, Department of Romance Languages and Literatures
Múzeum krt. 4/C
1088 Budapest
Hungary

Short William Michael
William.Short@utsa.edu
University of Texas at San Antonio
Department of Philosophy and Classics
One UTSA Circle
San Antonio, TX 78249
USA

Szilágyi Imre
szilagyi.imre@btk.elte.hu
Eötvös Loránd University, Budapest
Faculty of Arts, Department of Romance Languages and Literatures
Múzeum krt. 4/C
1088 Budapest
Hungary

Tikkanen Karin
karin.tikkanen@lingfil.uu.se
University of Uppsala
Department of Linguistics and Philology
P.O. Box 635, S-751 26
Uppsala
Sweden

Torzi Ilaria
latorzi@tiscali.it
Liceo Scientifico Statale "Vittorio Veneto" Milano
Università degli Studi di Bergamo
Dipartimento di Lettere, Arti e Multimedialità
Via Pignolo 123
24121 Bergamo
Italy

Van Laer Sophie
sophie.vanlaer@laposte.net
Université de Nantes
Département de Lettres Anciennes
Chemin de la Censive du Tertre
44312 Nantes Cedex
France

Wharton David B.
wharton@uncg.edu
University of North Carolina at Greensboro
Department of Classical Studies
PO Box 26170
Greensboro, NC 27402-6170
USA

Whitehead Benedicte Nielsen
dicten@hum.ku.dk
University of Copenhagen
Institut for nordiske studier og sprogvidenskab
Njalsgade 120
2300 Copenhagen S
Denmark